THE
GREATEST
LEAP

Andrew Hatcher

Matador
9 Priory Business Park
Wistow Road
Kibworth
Leicester LE8 0RX, UK
Tel: (+44) 116 279 2299
Email: books@troubador.co.uk
Web: www.troubador.co.uk/matador

ISBN 978 1784621 735

British Library Cataloguing in Publication Data.
A catalogue record for this book is available from the British Library.

Typeset in 11pt Adobe Casion Pro by Troubador Publishing Ltd, Leicester, UK
Printed and bound by CPI Group (UK) Ltd, Croydon, CR0 4YY

Matador is an imprint of Troubador Publishing Ltd

For my mum,
and in memory of my dad.

Contents

White Man's World
The 1900s

January 1901
(The Death of Queen Victoria)

to

August 1911
(The Passing of the Parliament Act)

The Legacy of the Victorians

European and British Pre-eminence in the Edwardian Period

Challenges in Africa and China: the Boer War and the Boxer Rebellion

The USA at the Turn of the Century

Germany under Kaiser Wilhelm II and Russia at War and in Revolution

The Alliance System and the Deepening Divide with Germany

The Anglo-German Naval Arms Race and the First Bosnian Crisis

The People's Budget and the Constitutional Crisis in Britain

The Legacy of the Victorians

In the early evening of 22 January 1901, Queen Victoria died of a brain haemorrhage at Osborne House, her country retreat on the Isle of Wight. The queen was related to nearly all the royal families of Europe and so, consequently, many of their number came to London to pay their last respects. After a funeral that incorporated much of the pomp and splendour that late Victorians had come to expect from large state and imperial occasions, her body was laid to rest next to that of her beloved husband, Prince Albert, in the royal mausoleum that she had built for him in the grounds of Frogmore House in Windsor.

In retrospect, this was to be one of the last great meetings of the old dynasties of Europe. The old world of the nineteenth century was crumbling away and, within a generation, most of the monarchs who followed Victoria's cortege on horseback through the streets of London and then Windsor had been forced from their thrones. After the carnage of World War One, the old dynastic empires of Europe were torn apart, and new democratic nations were to emerge from the chaos that the war had brought.

Victoria had ruled Britain and its ever-expanding empire for over six decades, and she had seen her country come to dominate the world in a way that no other nation had ever done before. Through trade, industry and military conquest, the British under Victoria had amassed an empire upon which the sun never set, and in 1901, as the old queen was laid to rest, it incorporated a quarter of the world's population. But Victoria did not only lend her name to the age of British domination over which she presided. She also personified the Old Order that was so well represented at her funeral. Her death, then, perhaps more than any other event at the turn of the century, symbolised the end of the old century and the beginning of the new.

The world that the eighty-one-year-old queen departed in 1901 was very different from the one in which she had been crowned in 1837. Perhaps the most obvious evidence of this could be found in the massive urban and industrial transformations that had altered the world so markedly over these intervening sixty-four years. This had all begun with the Industrial Revolution in the late eighteenth century that had made Britain a world leader, and this had been a major reason why Britain was able to wage such a long and expensive war against Napoleon. British domination at this earlier time was based on the cotton, coal and iron industries, and this had led to the massive growth of cities such as Liverpool, Manchester, Leeds, Sheffield, Birmingham, Glasgow and Belfast.

The products of these cities and towns, and many others like them across

Britain, were sent to markets all over the world, and this domination had increased dramatically in the first decade of the new queen's reign as a result of the great railway boom of the 1840s. This had made Britain far and away the world's greatest industrial and commercial nation, the Workshop of the World. Britain was to maintain this domination through much of the Victorian Age and continue to claim a massive share of the flourishing global market.

But as the old century drew to a close, this was beginning to change. Britain remained the dominant industrial and imperial power, but the USA, Germany and France, as well as many other emerging nations, were all beginning to offer stiff competition to this British pre-eminence. The USA was blessed with huge economic potential and unlimited land and raw materials that stretched across a continent, Germany with industrially strong regions such as the Saar and the Ruhr, and France was rich in coal and iron reserves, especially in the north. In the Far East, Japan had also put in place a dynamic programme of industrialisation that was soon used to expand its interests into China, and later across the Asian continent.

With the spread of industrialisation in the late nineteenth century, technological improvements and developments spawned a myriad of new industries. The electrical industry was still in its infancy as the new century began, as was the manufacture of cars and other vehicles driven by the internal combustion engine. The first car had been built in Germany only fifteen years before the end of the century, but its enormous impact was soon to revolutionise both transport and warfare. Among the early beneficiaries of this new boom were the huge oil companies that grew massively in the early years of the century, especially in California and Texas. Most of the oil extracted by these companies in around 1900 had been used for street lighting. With the advent of the car and the aeroplane a little later, this was all soon to change.

Huge advances had also been made in photography and cinema since the first images had been recorded in the 1830s and the first moving pictures were shown at a theatre in Paris in 1895. In 1900, photography was made accessible to the masses when Kodak brought out the Box Brownie, the world's first hand-held camera, at the cost of only $US1. Soon the centre of the new cinema industry moved across the Atlantic, finding a home in the Los Angeles suburb of Hollywood, although this was not before the first-ever narrative film, the twelve-minute-long, *The Great Train Robbery*, had been made in New York by Edison Studios in 1903.

At the same time, football, which was to become one of the most important social developments of the century, was beginning to draw huge crowds. Soon sport and television, which developed in the 1920s out of early developments in cinema, were to unite, and by the end of the century more than half of the world's population were tuning in to watch events such as the football World Cup and the Olympic Games. These events over time were to generate huge profits in revenue for an advertising industry that in 1900 was also in its infancy.

Huge strides had also been made in medicine after the Frenchman Louis Pasteur had established the link between germs and disease in the 1860s. This had led to important developments in the treatment and prevention of killer diseases, and by 1900 vaccines had been found for such diseases as rabies and diphtheria. In 1905, Pasteur's great German rival, Robert Koch, who in the 1870s had proved the link between germs and disease in humans, received the Nobel Prize for his research into a cure for tuberculosis. At the beginning of the century, this was the world's greatest killer. The world was also massively transformed by the pioneering work of Marie Curie, the only scientist ever to win Nobel Prizes in two different subjects. Curie, whose prizes were for physics and chemistry, worked predominantly at the Sorbonne where she developed, among other things, her ideas concerning radiology in the years leading up to World War One.

By 1900, many Western European countries had already adopted vaccination programmes, although it would still be forty years until an effective and widespread answer to combating infection was developed in the form of penicillin. In 1901, the Austrian pathologist, Karl Landsteiner, discovered the existence of the four different blood groups, a discovery that paved the way for further advances that included successful blood transfusions during World War One. Crucial advances had also been made in surgery where antiseptic, and then aseptic, conditions were increasingly adopted.

Just as important was progress in the fields of chemotherapy and pharmacology, with the development in 1909 of Salvarsan 606, a chemical compound that cured syphilis, being an early example. Demand for this new wonder drug was extraordinary and, within a year, 14,000 vials a day were being produced, making huge profits for the nascent pharmaceutical companies involved. Indeed, pharmaceutical companies in time were to become some of the biggest and most profitable multinational companies of the century. All these discoveries were to save millions of lives through the century.

Great leaps forward were also taking place in many other fields of science.

In 1905, the twenty-six-year-old patent clerk, Albert Einstein, published three papers in a German scientific magazine that outlined the ideas that revolutionised the scientific understanding of the universe. Einstein's Special Theory of Relativity and his famous equation, $E=MC^2$, provided the cornerstone of modern physics throughout the century as scientists and astronauts looked still further into outer space and the universe beyond. Of equal importance was the work of Sigmund Freud whose book, *The Interpretation of Dreams,* first published in German in 1899, revolutionised the sciences of psychology and psychiatry. Freud was increasingly influential as the century went on and his visit to the USA in 1909 was widely reported. In the world of art, many changes were taking place as the new century progressed, with Pablo Picasso founding the cubist movement in 1907.

Communications had also been revolutionised during the last years of the nineteenth century, with the world technologically becoming a much smaller place. The telegraph dated from the 1830s and the telephone from the 1870s, and both were important developments of the nineteenth century that made the spread of information infinitely quicker than anything that had come before. Crucial also was the work done to develop radio communication by men such as Guglielmo Marconi who successfully sent a radio signal across the English Channel in 1899. Two years later, he bettered this when he managed to communicate with the USA across the Atlantic from his radio station in West Ireland. Coming at a time of European colonial domination, these developments in communications allowed leaders in European capitals to direct colonial affairs much more closely and remain in charge of large tracts of the world for much of the century.

Another hugely important development in the first decade of the new century was the aeroplane, which the Wright brothers, mechanics and bicycle shopowners from Ohio, flew for the first time in the small Atlantic coastal town of Kitty Hawk, North Carolina, on 17 December 1903. Their interest in flying had begun in 1896, and, before their success, they made over 700 trial glider flights. This first flight was piloted by Orville Wright who flew a distance of 197 feet in twelve seconds. Later in the day, Wilbur took control of their flying machine, the *Wright Flyer,* and flew 850 feet in fifty-nine seconds. In 1909, the English Channel was crossed for the first time by Louis Blériot, the French aviator, and within five years aircraft development had advanced so quickly that aerial warfare could be waged above the trenches of World War One. The aeroplane was to become the premier war machine of the twentieth century.

European and British Pre-eminence in the Edwardian Period

The importance of the industrial, technological and communication advances of Victoria's reign were perhaps less obvious to the millions of indigenous people who in 1900 still remained under the yoke of European colonial rule. Britain remained the largest colonial power, with early victories over France in Canada and India in the eighteenth century and Napoleon's defeat at the beginning of the nineteenth giving a head start over its main rival that had been maintained throughout Victoria's long reign. In 1900, its colonies and dominions stretched across the world.

But Britain's empire was just one of many that European countries had acquired over four centuries of foreign conquest, and this process had increased after massive industrialisation in Europe in the late nineteenth century. This led to a series of rivalries between various European nations that vied with each other for new markets and new sources of raw materials increasingly available around the world. Among those countries involved in this scramble for empire were Britain, France, Germany, the Netherlands, Belgium, Spain and Portugal, with many of the rivalries that colonialism brought ultimately settled on the battlefields of World War One between 1914 and 1918.

Economic motives often lay behind the acquisition of empire during the nineteenth century. However, various other altruistic reasons, such as the benefits to a native population of Christian enlightenment and benevolent paternalism, were often given as to why European countries claimed the right to move into vast tracts of land across the world. The reality was often very different, with many of these European empires ruled with great barbarity.

The most infamous case of this kind took place in the Congo Free State, a colony that since the 1880s had been the personal property of King Leopold II, the king of the Belgians. By the turn of the century, thousands of indigenous workers were employed in the rubber plantations there that supplied the expanding European market. As the demand for rubber increased, predominantly because of the need for car tyres, the king became richer and richer. However, scandal erupted in 1903 when accusations concerning the treatment of the plantation workers were published in Europe. It was subsequently proved that systematic atrocities, such as the severing of hands as punishment for slow work, were carried out by the king's representatives, and in 1908 the king was forced to hand over the colony to the Belgian government.

Britain's huge colonial possessions and its immense domestic industrial base

л, to a great extent, created by the middle classes. They ran the factories
che warehouses, the shipping lines and the railways, the insurance
mpanies and the banks on which Britain and its empire had been built, and
they increasingly had come to take on an active role in the political life of the
nation. But the working class was also learning to organise and, especially after
1880, a trade union movement had begun to develop and grow in strength.
From its ranks, the first working-class MPs were elected in the 1890s, and it
was to be only just over twenty years before the first Labour government took
office in January 1924. The working class at the beginning of the twentieth
century looked at the various developments, innovations, inventions and
advances that were sweeping the world, and demanded their part in this new
world order under the British flag.

Through the last decades of the Victorian Age, the growing power of the
working class in Britain had forced both Liberal and Conservative governments
to work harder on its behalf. As a consequence, living conditions and
educational opportunities for the working class had slowly improved, and by
1900 a more comprehensive public health programme had been adopted.
During a similar time, the same story was being experienced in many other
parts of Europe and the USA.

Many politicians, though, were shocked to find that 40% of those
volunteering for service in the Boer War had to be turned down on health
grounds, resulting in a series of other welfare improvements through the
Edwardian period that aimed to improve the health of the nation. Free school
meals for poor children began in 1906, and a year later local authorities were
required by law to offer a school medical service. However, improvement in
the lives of the working class was not universal and the last of the Victorian
workhouses were not finally closed down until long after the end of World War
One.

Despite the advances made by the working and middle classes during the
last years of the old century, it was still the aristocracy who in 1900 owned
much of the nation's wealth and ran most of its more important institutions.
This was despite the growing importance of the House of Commons as the
central organ of government, and despite the fact that the monarch had come
to play an increasingly diminished role in the political decision-making process
of the nation over the previous century or so. So, Britain remained uniquely
class structured in its social anatomy as the Victorian Age gave way to the
Edwardian period, with the aristocracy maintaining its privileged position
within British society well into the new century. The willingness of the

aristocracy and the Establishment to recruit from the most successful upper reaches of the middle class was one important reason for this. Iron masters and bankers, shipping magnates and railway entrepreneurs were happy to be ennobled into a life that revolved around the country estate and the House of Lords. The public school system and the Oxbridge universities were also crucial in maintaining Britain's distinctive class make-up. Of these, the most successful as well as one of the most private, was Sir John Ellerman, the shipowner and investor, who was made a baronet in 1905 for services during the Boer War. Ellerman, an accountant by training and the son of an immigrant German corn merchant, was for a generation, by a considerable amount, the richest man in Britain.

One issue that remained unresolved at the beginning of the century was the role of women within British political life. Some progress concerning female suffrage had been made in the nineteenth century, with the influential liberal philosopher, John Stuart Mill, lending his support to the idea in the 1860s. The women of New Zealand had been given the vote in the 1890s, and a similar reform was also implemented in Australia in 1902. These successes abroad, together with the enfranchisement of other sections of society, resulted in various movements for women's suffrage in Britain that were diverse and represented many different political views.

However, it was the Women's Social and Political Union, set up in 1903 by Emmeline Pankhurst and her two daughters, Christabel and Sylvia, that was to become the most popular of these during the early years of the new king's reign. The WSPU was militant and sometimes violent in nature, and it played a central role in getting the issue of women's rights onto the political agenda. The campaign continued up until the outbreak of war and became increasingly extreme, with one suffragette killing herself by throwing herself in front of the king's horse at the Epsom Derby in 1913. Others were involved in a series of hunger strikes that were thwarted by the government's so-called 'Cat and Mouse' Act. This allowed the hospitalisation and force-feeding of hunger strikers until such time as they were out of physical danger when they were released. Then the process was repeated again once the hunger striker had returned to a state of critical illness, and repeated over and over until such time as the hunger striker gave up.

In reality, little in substance was achieved until after World War One in which female workers played such an important role in factories and farms at home while so many men were away fighting. As a result, some women in Britain over the age of thirty were finally given the vote in 1918 although this ct to a property qualification. In 1928, the age of voting in Britain andardised, with both men and women over the age of twenty-one ifying for the electoral register.

Many other women in many other parts of the world joined them in the aftermath of World War One and they followed the women of Finland who had been the first in Europe to be enfranchised in 1906. The USSR in 1917, Germany, Austria, Poland and Czechoslovakia in 1919, and the USA and Hungary in 1920 all extended their franchises. Indian women received full voting rights in 1949 and they were joined by the women of Pakistan in 1956. Most other decolonised countries also granted full voting rights to both male and female citizens after independence in the 1950s and 1960s. But the fight for female suffrage was often a hard and long battle, with Swiss women, for instance, only finally gaining full voting parity with their male counterparts in the early 1970s.

As the new century began, Britain was led by a prime minister who sat in the House of Lords along with many of his cabinet, his advisers and his senior colonial appointees. Lord Salisbury was a Conservative who had become prime minister for the first of his three terms in office in 1885. By 1900, he was at the end of a long political career that had started with his election to the House of Commons in 1853 just before the Crimean War. For most of his time as prime minister, he also held the position of foreign secretary, choosing to concern himself predominantly with colonial and imperial matters. This coincided with a time of huge expansion into Africa, with Britain adding Egypt and the East African colonies of Kenya and Uganda to its already huge empire.

Salisbury had continued Britain's traditional overseas policy of 'Splendid Isolation' that had, with the exception of the Crimean War in the 1850s, kept Britain out of major European conflicts since Waterloo. He ensured that Britain remained outside the series of alliances and treaties that were developing in continental Europe although his very nineteenth-century attitude to foreign policy was abandoned soon after his successor, Arthur Balfour, came to power in July 1902.

Under Balfour and his Liberal successors, Sir Henry Campbell-Bannerman and Herbert Asquith, Britain began the process of abandoning 'Splendid Isolation' and instead entered a series of agreements and pacts over the next few years, the most notable of which were with France and Russia. These were primarily entered into in order to protect Britain from what was seen as increasingly belligerent German aggression. Asquith had taken over from

Campbell-Bannerman in April 1908 when the latter had become the only prime minister ever to die while in residence at Number 10 Downing Street. This came during a period of convalescence when he was too ill to be moved, just less than three weeks after a heart attack had forced his resignation.

Challenges in Africa and China: the Boer War and the Boxer Rebellion
However, Britain's most immediate problem at the beginning of the century was not Germany. Salisbury and his colleagues were more concerned with resolving the Boer War, which had begun the previous year and in which a British victory was far from certain. The Boers were settlers, mainly of Dutch ancestry, who had arrived on the coast of southern Africa in the seventeenth century. From their original base around Table Mountain where Cape Town was built, they had spread out into the surrounding hinterland.

Britain had taken control of Cape Town in 1795 and was formally awarded the colony in the treaty that concluded the Napoleonic War in 1815. Britain originally intended to use Cape Colony as no more than a supply port on the way to far more important colonial possessions in India. But as more and more British settlers came to stay, tension rose between the two immigrant communities, with problems particularly focused on the question of slavery. This was banned throughout the British Empire, but it was a practice widely supported by the Boers.

After a series of struggles against not only the British but also the local African population, the Boers began their Great Trek in 1835. This northwards migration away from British interference was to last for much of the next decade, and it led to the formation of two Boer republics, the Orange Free State and Transvaal, on the high veldt 1,000 miles away to the north. Relations between the British and the Boers remained tense for many years, yet never erupted into full-scale war. This remained the case even when the discovery of diamonds and gold in the Boer republics led to a huge influx of British prospectors in the 1880s.

Indeed, the Boers originally welcomed this influx because of the economic prosperity that it brought. But as the British presence grew more and more widespread, the Boers became concerned about the threat that this posed to their unique way of life. At the same time, the amount of gold and diamonds discovered led to the adoption of an increasingly aggressive policy towards the Boer republics by the British government. This was encouraged not only by imperialists and businessmen in London, but also by many British colonists in southern Africa itself.

These colonists were led by Cecil Rhodes, the imperialist entrepreneur and founder of de Beers who had made a fortune out of diamonds and gold and who later gave his name to Rhodesia. Rhodes wanted to see the British Empire spread across the whole of Africa from Cairo in the north to the Cape in the south. But despite his wealth and political importance, he had been forced to resign as prime minister of the Cape Colony in 1896 when a pro-British raid into the Boer territory, led by Dr L. S. Jameson but sponsored by the government run by Rhodes, failed to foment rebellion.

But this Jameson Raid did galvanise anti-British feeling within the Orange Free State and Transvaal, which united behind the leadership of Paul Kruger. The political crisis intensified when Kruger published the contents of a telegram that he had received from the German Kaiser in the aftermath of the Jameson Raid. Wilhelm II made it clear in the telegram that he backed the Boers and criticised British claims in the area. Tension continued to intensify as the century drew to an end and war finally broke out in October 1899. This began with a series of Boer attacks on British interests in Natal and Cape Colony, and soon the towns of Ladysmith, Mafeking and Kimberley came under siege. However, by early 1900 reinforcements from Britain and India had begun arriving and a counter-attack was launched.

The twenty-six-year-old Winston Churchill arrived with these reinforcements although he had in fact just left the army, having served in the recent war in Sudan. He had been employed to go to South Africa as a war correspondent. But Churchill soon returned to active service, taking part in action around Ladysmith during which he was captured by a Boer patrol. Churchill was held captive in Pretoria for two months before escaping, with his subsequent 300-mile journey to freedom in Mozambique covered widely in the popular press. This also led to the issue of Wanted posters for Churchill, with the leader of Britain in World War Two having a price of £25 put on his head.

The British counter-attack slowly gathered pace, and the relief of Mafeking in May 1900 in particular provoked great celebrations of imperialist fervour in Britain. By June 1900, British troops had pushed deep into Boer territory and a series of British victories, which included the capture of Pretoria, Bloemfontein and Johannesburg, forced President Kruger into exile. He escaped to Europe where he travelled extensively in an attempt to gain support for the Boer cause. So as a conventional military affair, the war was over by June 1900, just seven or so months after it had begun.

But the conflict was to drag on as a guerrilla war for nearly two more years, with Boer forces mounting attacks on British positions throughout the captured territory. Lord Kitchener, the commander of the British forces, countered these by ordering a war of attrition that focused on burning Boer farms and homesteads in order to starve the enemy into submission. Whole Boer communities suspected of supplying or harbouring these guerrilla forces were detained in concentration camps that soon became infamous for their bad sanitary conditions, with as many as 20,000 Boers, mostly women, children and the elderly, dying in them. The repressive policies of the British aimed to break the spirit of the Boer people.

Although this was never achieved, Boer commanders were finally forced to the negotiating table with the Treaty of Vereeniging signed in May 1902. The Orange Free State and Transvaal were brought into the British Empire, but important concessions were granted to the Boer community that included a large amount of political autonomy. Eventually, the various and separate colonies of southern Africa were united in 1910, creating the Union of South Africa. Britain had needed some 400,000 soldiers to win the Boer War. These had faced an enemy that had never numbered more than 80,000.

A powerful British colonial presence, although in this case an informal one, was also challenged in China with the Boxer Rebellion. Britain's interests in China had begun in the 1840s when it had occupied Hong Kong after the first Opium War, and a treaty of 1898 had continued Britain's lease there until 1997. But other less formal agreements had subsequently led to the spread of British and European commercial influence to many other parts of China, and by the 1890s various European countries controlled much of the Chinese coastal trade and rail network.

The rebellion against this burgeoning foreign influence initially broke out in 1898 in the north of the country under the leadership of the Society of Harmonious Fists, an organisation commonly known as the Boxers, which was pledged to the expulsion of all Europeans from China. The Boxer Rebellion quickly spread from the north and it received the tacit support of the Empress Dowager whose political acumen had made her the most powerful person in China for forty years. With her support, the rebellion spread south with the mass expulsion of foreigners and the massacre of hundreds of Chinese Christian converts. In the summer of 1901, the rebellion had spread to Beijing where in June the German ambassador was assassinated and the area given over to the foreign legations besieged.

By August 1901, a multinational task force from six nations, including the USA and, importantly, the rapidly industrialising Japan, had arrived to quell the rebellion and relieve the foreign legations in Beijing. Consequently, the

Imperial Court was forced to flee to the ancient city of Xian where representatives of the Empress Dowager's government were obliged to sign an International Protocol later in the year. In this protocol, the Chinese government accepted responsibility for the rebellion and agreed to pay a large amount in reparations.

The severity of the treaty heightened anti-foreign feeling throughout China, with many Chinese subsequently coming to support Sun Yat-sen and his Nationalist Party. Within a decade, this had forced the collapse of the Manchu dynasty that had ruled China since the seventeenth century. The Boxer Rebellion was also important because it gave Japan an economic and political foothold in Manchuria on mainland China that remained the focus of its campaign for an overseas empire for the next forty-five years.

The USA at the Turn of the Century

While Britain fought in southern Africa and the Far East, and contemplated the emergence of an increasingly robust Germany, the entry of the USA into the new century was rudely interrupted by the assassination of President William McKinley by a young anarchist in September 1901. McKinley fought hard to survive, but succumbed to his injuries after eight days and was replaced by Theodore Roosevelt who, at the age of forty-two, became his country's youngest-ever president.

Roosevelt remained in office until 1908 and presided over a nation of enormous contrasts between the old and the new, the antiquated and the modern. Roosevelt spent much of his time in office trying to sort out the problems that this conundrum brought, and subsequently, in the process, greatly strengthened the power and authority of both the office of the president and of the federal government over the separate state legislatures. In doing so, he also challenged the large industrial trusts that had grown up in oil, steel, construction and the railways in the late nineteenth century and so helped create the economic and political framework that, over time, was to make his country the century's most powerful nation.

It was during this time that the USA began to give notice of the enormous role it was likely to play in the new century. Like Britain in the nineteenth century, this was most obviously shown by massive urban and industrial expansion. Cities like New York, Chicago, Los Angeles and Detroit became some of the biggest in the world, and industrial centres, especially in the north-east where there was a rich supply of iron ore and coal, churned out all sorts of different industrial products.

The country did, however, have to cope with the aftermath of one of the worst-ever-recorded earthquakes that destroyed much of San Francisco in April 1906. However, the city was rebuilt in record time and this was later to be celebrated at the Panama-Pacific International Exposition that took place in the city in 1915. This massive world fair was staged ostensibly to highlight the completion of the Panama Canal, one of the world's biggest-ever engineering efforts that had been overseen by US engineers and financed by US banks. This linked the Atlantic and Pacific Oceans and had taken place in August 1914, only days after the outbreak of World War One. The canal was to remain under US control until 1999. But the exposition was also used to showcase the recovery of California and the city of San Francisco from the ruin of 1906, and so, by inference, suggest the power and strength of the country itself. In the years before 1914, the USA was beginning to rival older, more mature economies across the Atlantic. It was not long before it was to surpass them.

This growth fuelled the largest migration of people in the history of the world, with some thirteen million people sailing across the Atlantic between 1900 and the beginning of World War One. These came from all parts of Europe and elsewhere in search of their fortunes in the New World. Most of those among these disparate groups that flooded to the USA didn't find their fortunes and ended up in the sweatshops, factories, mines and warehouses that dotted the industrial, urban landscape. Some, in fact, decided to return to Europe and others became migrant workers, moving back and forth across the Atlantic, returning only to earn money in order to secure a better future in Europe. But most did stay and it was these men and women who were to give US society such diversity throughout the century.

It was also the beginning of what became the Great Migration, the massive relocation of more than six million African Americans who moved north from the old slave states of the South over the next four decades. In 1909, the NAACP, the National Association for the Advancement of Coloured People, was set up in response to race riots the previous year in Springfield, Illinois, the home town of Abraham Lincoln. It set out to challenge the discrimination and prejudice in law that many still felt. The NAACP and other civil rights groups were to have a marked effect on the development of the USA, especially later in the century when Martin Luther King led the great civil rights movement of the 1950s and 1960s.

It was not only within its own borders that the USA was to give notice of its new aspirations. Under McKinley and Roosevelt, the USA acquired new colonial possessions in the Pacific and the Caribbean that included the Philippines, Puerto Rico and Guam as well as considerable rights in Cuba, and it was also to wield huge economic and strategic influence in Panama as a result of the canal. Neither was Roosevelt frightened of squaring up to the powers of the Old World and faced altercations with Germany, Britain and Spain during his time at the White House.

Germany under Kaiser Wilhelm II and Russia at War and in Revolution

With the USA beginning a process that would eventually see it politically and economically dominate the century, the old powers of Europe were continuing to deal with the threat posed by a new, vibrant and unified Germany. Originally, this dominance had been due to the efforts of Chancellor Otto von Bismarck, the 'Iron Chancellor', who led Germany for twenty years after unification in 1871. The emergence of Germany as an industrial and military power dominating continental Europe had provided the central narrative to European affairs over the last thirty years of the nineteenth century, and this was not a situation that had changed after the sacking of Bismarck in 1890, soon after the succession of Wilhelm II. The new Kaiser quickly embarked on a series of new diplomatic and strategic policies that aimed to transform Germany into a global power, and in 1897 his government outlined his new plan of *Weltpolitik*, or 'world politics'.

Wilhelm II had become frustrated by the constrictions of a foreign policy directed only in relation to Germany's geographical position in central Europe. As a result, Germany's new status on the world stage was imagined increasingly through the acquisition and expansion of an empire in Africa, China, the Middle East and elsewhere, and it was clearly seen that this new ambitious policy necessitated the construction of a large navy, which he hoped would soon rival the Royal Navy of his grandmother.

Relations between Germany and its nearest rivals were not helped by the Kaiser's plans to push German influence down into the Ottoman lands that linked Europe with the Middle East. With its capital in Istanbul, its lands stretched westwards into the Balkans and Eastern Europe, southwards into Egypt, Arabia and North Africa and eastwards towards the Caspian Sea. However, its poor political state in the nineteenth century had led it to become known as the 'sick man of Europe'. At the same time, its lands were becoming increasingly important strategically because of the growing promise of oil in the Middle East and Persia, and the Kaiser was determined that Germany would claim its stake there. Matters were further complicated by the success of the

Young Turks rebellion in 1908, which gave much more influence within the old empire to pro-Turkish nationalists.

Consequently, the two governments discussed plans for rail and pipeline links and German firms were encouraged to expand into the area. This German incursion into Ottoman land worried both Britain and France who had both long resisted foreign intervention in the eastern Mediterranean and the Middle East. In Britain's case, this was because of the need to maintain the security of the sea route through the Suez Canal to British possessions in India and to secure vital interests in Persia and Mesopotamia. This was, after all, why Britain had gone to war with Russia in the Crimea in the 1850s. The importance of the region to Britain was also affected by Churchill's decision at the Admiralty in 1911 to change the fuel of the Royal Navy from coal to oil, much of which came from Persia.

The expansion of German influence into the Turkish lands of the Ottoman Empire also worried Russia, which at the beginning of the new century remained by far the most politically backward of the six Great Powers. Slavery in the form of serfdom had only been abolished in the 1860s and, throughout his empire, Tsar Nicholas II, who had come to the throne in 1894, kept an iron grip on control. Russia was also less developed industrially than its western rivals and, although this was beginning to change, most Russians at the turn of the century still lived as peasants in the countryside.

Russia's weakness was confirmed in 1904-05 when it was soundly beaten in the Russo-Japanese War. The war had originated over rival claims on the Chinese mainland and in Korea, and began with the Russian Pacific fleet being destroyed while at anchor at Port Arthur. An inability to deploy adequate troops, despite the construction of the Trans-Siberian railway that was completed in 1904, led to a series of Japanese victories that stunned not only the Russian aristocracy that ran the Russian military but also observers from across the rest of Europe.

To avenge these defeats, Russian military commanders persuaded the Tsar to order the Russian Baltic Sea fleet to set sail for the Pacific on the six-month journey halfway around the world via the Cape of Good Hope. But the Baltic fleet was also decisively defeated, this time at the Battle of Tsushima, and Russia was forced to seek peace. The peace treaty was mediated by President Roosevelt and it brought an end to the conflict in September 1905. This left Russian imperial claims in the Far East severely damaged.

The humiliating defeat to the Japanese highlighted the industrial and administrative weaknesses of Russia's autocratic regime. It also fuelled a political crisis that turned out to be the forerunner to far more decisive events in 1917. This crisis was the first Russian Revolution of 1905 that broke out in St Petersburg, the Russian capital, following 'Bloody Sunday'. This was the name given to the events of Sunday 22 January 1905 when cavalry troops opened fire on thousands of demonstrators protesting about not only the progress of the war in the Far East but also the government's economic and political record. 'Bloody Sunday' followed a series of bad harvests and the government's refusal to adopt constitutional reform. About 1,000 demonstrators lost their lives, with many more injured or arrested.

But the demonstration caught the mood of the nation and provoked a series of strikes, riots and mutinies that lasted through the spring and summer of 1905. With his country in revolt, the Tsar was forced to implement a series of reforms that heralded in the first steps of constitutional reform. Under a new constitution in October, a parliament of sorts, called the *Duma*, was set up and a prime minister was for the first time appointed to look after certain affairs of state. But these reforms were really no more than a short-term expediency, with real power in Russia retained by the Tsar and the aristocracy. Having reclaimed the support of the middle class through its limited representation in the *Duma*, a representation that was whittled away almost as soon as it was given, the Tsar slowly reclaimed authority over the country.

Many were imprisoned or exiled for their roles in the abortive revolt as Russia returned to the autocracy that had changed little since the Middle Ages. In 1907, the *Duma* was dissolved just a year or so after it had come into existence, leaving the revolutionaries and reformers to bide their time. This was to come a decade later after more military fiascos and defeats in World War One. When it did eventually come in 1917, it brought to power a regime that was to have such a central role in the history of the rest of the century.

The Alliance System and the Deepening Divide with Germany

Following the Franco-Prussian War and the capture of Alsace and Lorraine, Bismarck had always worried that one day France might unite with Russia in an anti-German alliance. As a result, he had set about creating a series of alliances and treaties that aimed to protect Germany from this eventuality. The first of these had been signed in 1879 and bound Germany to Austria-Hungary, a massive but decaying empire dominating much of central and south-eastern Europe. In essence, this treaty was a defensive one for both sides, protecting Austria-Hungary in the Balkans and Germany further north. Russia had always been jealous of Austro-Hungarian land in the Balkans where the population fostered historic and ethnic ties with Russia. Three years later, Italy joined Germany and Austria-Hungary to create the Triple Alliance.

Bismarck's greatest fear was that Germany would be forced to fight a war simultaneously on two fronts and, in order to stop this, he had entered into a secret treaty with Russia in 1887. However, the relative security of this position was given up by the new young Kaiser when the agreement was allowed to lapse in 1890. As a direct consequence, France and Russia, both of whom were unwilling to become diplomatically isolated, signed a pact that became active in early 1894.

So by the last decade of the nineteenth century, Europe had split into two separate and opposing military camps, with each linked by a series of secret and non-secret alliances and treaties. On the one hand, there were the central powers of the Triple Alliance that gathered under the leadership and growing strength of Germany. On the other, there was the diplomatic alliance between France and Russia. In particular, tension remained high between Russia and Austria-Hungary in the Balkans, and between France and Germany over the question of Alsace and Lorraine.

At the beginning of the new century, the British government was slowly coming to the conclusion that the era of nineteenth-century British dominance was coming to a close, and that 'Splendid Isolation' no longer remained a policy that guaranteed safety. In particular, German industrial growth and its military and colonial expansion through *Weltpolitik* were seen as direct challenges to British interests around the world.

Wilhelm II's clear support for the Boers in the war in South Africa had worried diplomats and politicians in London, and by 1900 Germany had replaced both France and Russia as Britain's most obvious natural rival. Increasingly, it was believed that an alliance, as well as the maintenance of the Royal Navy's superiority that had maintained British integrity since the time of Nelson and Trafalgar, was necessary to preserve peace and national security.

British isolation was first broken in an agreement signed with Japan in January 1902 that looked at respective spheres of interest on mainland China. Britain's main aim was to exclude European rivals, and especially Germany, from the lucrative trade there while Japan wanted to remain friendly and extend trading links with Britain, which remained the most powerful nation in the Far East. Britain had extended its lease over Hong Kong in 1898 for a further ninety-nine years, and British traders had huge interests in commercial *entrepôts* such as Canton, Shanghai and many other similar ports along the Chinese coast. In Tokyo, it was thought that an alliance with Britain would allow Japan a gateway to the enormous markets inland that lay behind these ports.

However, it was in Europe, and not in Asia, that the attention of the British government was primarily focused and, as the first few years of the century unfolded, it found itself becoming more and more concerned with German belligerence. Germany was not only dominating continental Europe, as it had done since the 1870s, but was also beginning to look further afield. In this way, it began to pose a direct threat to the British Empire, and this was most obviously expressed through the expansion of the German navy from its bases at Kiel on the Baltic and Wilhelmshaven on the North Sea. In the early years of the century, German naval parity was still a long way off, with its fleet being not much more than a third of the size of the British one. However, German naval shipyards were churning out ships at a rapid rate and this caused huge concern at the Admiralty in London.

The eventual result of this growing concern over Germany, and the colonial and trading repercussions that were brought about by *Weltpolitik*, was the *Entente Cordiale*, a series of agreements and protocols signed in 1904 between Britain and France that categorically confirmed Britain's abandonment of 'Splendid Isolation'. Britain could not let the Kaiser succeed in his plans and so was very much pushed towards France in order to maintain its leading position in the Great Power hierarchy. The *Entente* did not lead to any formal treaty or alliance, but nonetheless was to have the most enormous political and psychological importance on European international relations in the decade running up to World War One. Ostensibly, it concerned agreement over a number of colonial issues, including problems in North Africa over rival claims in Egypt and Morocco, and it ended a series of colonial rows that had marred Anglo-French relations in the 1890s that, among other things, had nearly ended in war in Sudan in 1898.

However, the real importance of the *Entente* was the seal of friendship and partnership that it brought to relations between these two traditional enemies. This was to endure two world wars, the threat to continental Europe from Soviet communism and the veto by de Gaulle of Britain's membership of the EEC in the 1960s. But initially, in the run up to world war in 1914, its importance lay in the alliance it formed against Germany.

Germany's primary concern since unification in 1871 had always been to maintain its military ascendancy over France. This ascendancy had first been challenged in the 1890s by France's alliance with Russia, but this new *rapprochement* with Britain was a much more serious affair. As a result, the Kaiser and his staff determined to seek out an opportunity to split this new relationship and destroy the budding *rapprochement* of 1904 before it became too permanent.

Germany hoped to engineer this rift by isolating France diplomatically over the question of Moroccan independence. In March 1905, the Kaiser visited the Moroccan Sultan in Tangiers while on a cruise in the Mediterranean and made clear Germany's support for Moroccan independence. He also demanded an international conference to consider the legality of French and Spanish claims there. German insistence resulted in this conference being convened in the southern Spanish town of Algeciras at the beginning of 1906.

All the major powers were invited, and Germany hoped that the conference would lead to the diplomatic isolation of France. But at the conference, Britain defended French claims in Morocco and made it clear that it stood by its commitment to the *Entente Cordiale*. Indeed, it was Germany that was to leave Algeciras outmanoeuvred and isolated, receiving support from only Austria-Hungary. As a result, the first Moroccan Crisis and the Algeciras Conference that followed had the very opposite effect to the one that the Kaiser and his advisers had hoped. The *Entente Cordiale* between Germany's two main rivals was, as a consequence, strengthened rather than weakened.

Kaiser Wilhelm II had travelled to Tangiers convinced that he could split the nascent bond between Britain and France that had come into existence in 1904. But the Algeciras Conference clearly showed that, however informal it might be, it was an agreement that Britain intended to honour. To a great extent, this was due not to any great commitment that Britain felt towards France that had, after all, been Britain's traditional enemy for hundreds of years. Instead, it stemmed from the increasing concern felt in London towards German military and diplomatic expansion. From the German point of view, the failure to split Britain from France at Algeciras meant that the alliance with Austria-Hungary took on even more importance.

After the Algeciras Conference, the split between the two camps grew even wider, with Britain tentatively committing itself to the alliance system that had grown up since the 1880s. British involvement deepened a year later when, in August 1907, a protocol with Russia was signed that agreed spheres of influence in Persia and Afghanistan. In theory, at least, this Anglo-Russian agreement was not concerned with European matters, and so was not therefore anti-German in nature although the two did combine to combat increased German influence in the crumbling Ottoman Empire.

But the Kaiser and his government in Berlin saw it in exactly those terms and their reaction to it was to bring about a new intensity to the mistrust and rivalry that had been simmering since the late 1890s. The Anglo-Russian agreement thus concluded the series of treaties and understandings that had begun in the 1870s, and completed the split of Europe into the two armed camps that were to fight World War One.

The Anglo-German Naval Arms Race and the First Bosnian Crisis

The most obvious manifestation of this rivalry was the naval arms race that developed between Britain and Germany. Germany knew of the importance that Britain attached to its naval superiority and was aware of the two-power principle that had been formulated in the 1890s. This stated that Britain should never allow the Royal Navy to become weaker than the combined strength of the navies of its next two most powerful rivals. From the beginning of the century, this was directly challenged by the massive programme of German naval expansion ordered by the Kaiser.

In response to this German threat, HMS *Dreadnought* was launched in February 1906. With its maximum speed of twenty-one knots and with its revolutionary new firepower and massive steam turbine engines, it was actually the sixth ship, dating back to Tudor times, in the Royal Navy to have been so named. But this sixth version was to give its name to a whole new class of battleship. Its launch also led to the intensification of the Anglo-German naval rivalry, with naval leagues and associations set up in both countries to press for further expansion. In 1908, the German Reichstag passed a law authorising the construction of four dreadnought-class ships a year for four years. This seemingly direct challenge to British naval supremacy in turn led to an increase in ships ordered by the British government. As this naval scare reached its peak in 1909, the British government for the first time admitted the very real threat of a surprise German naval attack.

In 1906 and 1907, the Liberal government had authorised the building of two dreadnoughts. But as the Bosnian Annexation Crisis unfolded in 1908 and tension throughout the whole of Europe intensified, the Admiralty in London demanded the construction of eight dreadnoughts a year to preserve British naval superiority. This was supported by public opinion that rallied around the music hall refrain of 'We want eight and we won't wait.'

In the end, the cabinet decided to build four dreadnoughts immediately, but put aside enough money to pay for another four if they became necessary. Similar nationalistic sentiments were being expressed across the North Sea in Germany where huge shipyards were geared up to maximum output. This Anglo-German naval rivalry was to continue until the start of the war five years later, by which time both powers had amassed huge fleets of both military and merchant ships.

As the arms race between the Triple Alliance of Germany, Austria-Hungary and Italy and the Triple Entente of Britain, France and Russia intensified, a series of regional conflicts threatened to drag the six Great Powers into a general war. The first of these arose in Bosnia, which for 400 years had been ruled from Istanbul. But the disintegration of the Ottoman Empire at the end of the nineteenth century had led to an increase in Austro-Hungarian influence in the region and Bosnia, as a consequence, was made a protectorate of Austria-Hungary in 1879. But an anti-Austrian uprising in 1908 persuaded ministers in Vienna that its status should be formalised and, consequently, it was formally annexed, becoming an integrated part of the Austro-Hungarian Empire.

This move outraged Russia that had strong ties with both Bosnia and neighbouring Serbia, and it felt bound to protect the large Slav population there. It also feared that Austrian expansion into the area threatened traditional Russian interests around the Black Sea and the eastern Mediterranean. Eventually, in the face of the threat of German aggression, Russia was forced to back down and grudgingly had to accept the annexation in 1909. However, the Bosnian Annexation Crisis had led to a great deal of rancour across Europe, and it helped to ratchet up diplomatic pressure on all sides. This, in turn, increasingly drove the two armed camps still further apart.

The People's Budget and the Constitutional Crisis in Britain

By 1909, the cost of maintaining British naval superiority was becoming more and more expensive and this was clear to David Lloyd George, the chancellor of the exchequer, as he worked on his Budget. He had already legislated for a number of costly social reforms, including the provision of old-age pensions in 1908, and he resolved that these reforms would not be jettisoned to pay for new ships.

Therefore, he devised a radical and far-reaching programme that came to be known as the People's Budget. This created a super tax for all those earning over £5,000 a year and introduced a land duty that taxed the very essence of aristocratic society. Death duties were raised and new taxes were introduced on new commodities such as petrol and cars. The People's Budget was introduced into the House of Commons in April 1909, but the debate over its provisions was so fiercely contested that it was not finally rejected by the House of Lords until November, a full six months later. This was by an assembly dominated by Conservative peers. The budget was not the first bill to have been rejected by the Lords, and Asquith and his cabinet now met to discuss how to react to this further snub.

As a result, they decided to call a general election over the issue, with the country going to the polls in January 1910. This was to begin a constitutional crisis that was not resolved until the following year. The result of the election was a disappointment for the Liberals. They returned only a fraction more MPs than the Conservatives, with the balance of power held by some seventy Irish MPs. The majority of these eventually struck a deal with the Liberals, but only after extracting promises from Asquith that time in the new parliament would be given over to the question of Irish Home Rule. This had not been seriously debated since the time of Gladstone's third government in the late 1880s.

So due to this support, Asquith was once again returned to Downing Street where he rejoined battle with the House of Lords, and in April 1910 was ready to put legislation before the House of Commons that in essence demanded three basic changes to the constitution. Firstly, he wanted to see the right of veto of the upper house on financial bills ended immediately. Secondly, he wanted to see any bill that had been sent to the Lords three times in a year passed as of right and, thirdly, he wanted to see the life of a parliament reduced from seven years to five.

Asquith's proposals were still being discussed when King Edward VII died in May 1910, with debate and argument continuing through the year in a series of constitutional conferences. But by November 1910, Asquith had had enough, informing the new king, George V, that he intended once again to go to the people, and demanded that the king agree to the creation of enough Liberal peers to force through his legislation if he was again returned as prime minister. In December 1910, the second general election of the year was held and this returned a House of Commons that remained largely unchanged.

Once again, Asquith returned as prime minister and the Parliament Act passed through the House of Commons in May 1911. Asquith informed the Conservative leaders in both Houses that the king had given him an undertaking to create over 270 Liberal peers if the Conservative majority in the Lords once again rejected his proposals. Some Tory peers determined to fight on, but most accepted the inevitable. As a result, the Parliament Act passed into law in August 1911, with all this political change at Westminster being accompanied by an atmosphere of heightened class tension in the years running up to the war, a deteriorating situation best illustrated by the Tonypandy Riots in the Rhonda Valley in South Wales in 1910 and 1911.

Catastrophe
The 1910s

July 1911
(The Second Moroccan Crisis at Agadir)

to

July 1920
(The End of the Russian Civil War in Europe)

The Second Moroccan Crisis and the Three-Year Slide towards War

The Assassination of Archduke Franz Ferdinand and the Outbreak of War

The Battles of the Marne and Ypres, and the Other Fronts in 1914

The War in 1915: Stalemate and the Gallipoli Campaign

The Battle of Verdun, the Eastern Front in 1916 and the Battle of the Somme

The Government of Lloyd George and the Rest of the War in 1916

The Expansion of the War in 1917

The Bolshevik Revolution of 1917

The War in the Ottoman Empire and Lawrence of Arabia

The Failure of the German Offensives of 1918 and the End of Hostilities

The Treaty of Versailles, the Other Peace Treaties and Britain in 1918

Revolution in Germany and the Russian Civil War

The Second Moroccan Crisis and the Three-Year Slide towards War

As the constitutional crisis in Britain was continuing through the summer of 1911, another international crisis threatened to plunge Europe into full-scale war. Once again, the focus of crisis was Morocco where Germany claimed that France had not lived up to the agreements and protocols laid down in 1906 after the Algeciras Conference. As a result, the Kaiser had ordered his admirals to send a gunboat, the *Panther*, to the port of Agadir on the Atlantic coast, and demands for compensation were sent to the French government in Paris.

As the Agadir Crisis unfolded, British public opinion again took on a very anti-German outlook, with vital British interests in Gibraltar and the Mediterranean clearly compromised by the German naval presence in Morocco. This sentiment was echoed by the British government, with Lloyd George, the chancellor of the exchequer, using his Mansion House address in July 1911 to issue a stern warning to Germany. As the crisis deepened through the summer of 1911, negotiations continued between France and Germany, with both clearly informed that Britain would not tolerate the continued presence of the German navy in Morocco.

Eventually, after war had nearly broken out on a number of occasions, an agreement was reached by which Germany accepted French claims in Morocco in exchange for a small concession in the French Congo. Europe had again stood at the brink of war before coming to an agreement of sorts through compromise. Some three years later, time was to run out and a further compromise could not be found. The world then was finally to go to war.

However, this did not come until after what was seen at the time as a period of peace, prosperity and technological improvement for the people of Europe and the Western world that was unparalleled in history. Life for many, though not all, had been improved dramatically through advances in medicine, sanitation, housing and welfare, and new recreational developments such as the cinema and, increasingly, organised sport were entertaining people in a way unimaginable even a generation earlier.

New methods of mass production that characterised twentieth century industrial production were also beginning to revolutionise the world, with the factories of Henry Ford in Detroit, where the moving assembly line was introduced in 1913, in particular gaining a reputation for their efficiency, speed and competitiveness. Equally revolutionary were developments in California where the soft light and pleasant temperatures were soon to make the Los Angeles suburb of Hollywood the centre of the film industry. From modest beginnings grew a film and television industry that influenced and recorded every aspect of the century. Hard-fought victories were also being won politically, and these led to extended franchises, increased trade union activity, improved social liberty and an increase in protection for civil rights.

This all appeared to suggest that the science and technology that had driven late nineteenth-century capitalism was continuing to create a better and more prosperous world. In April 1912, just a few months after Roald Amundsen and four team members had successfully beaten Captain Scott and his team to the South Pole, this seemed to come together with the launching of the luxury steam liner, RMS *Titanic*, a marvel of modern engineering and the world's largest ship. But only five days into her maiden voyage, the *Titanic* sank in the cold and icy expanses of the North Atlantic. Her sinking, with the loss of over fifteen hundred lives, was perhaps a portent of things to come.

For within three years of the second Moroccan Crisis in July 1911, the hope and optimism of the young century had evaporated on the battlefields of World War One, with the science and technology that had shaped the West's rise now seemingly plotting its downfall. The machines of modern warfare had been developed hugely in the nineteenth century, and certainly as far back as the American Civil War thousands had been killed in battle by modern weaponry such as heavy artillery and the machine gun. Tactics, too, had begun to change, with Strasbourg a few years later becoming the first modern city to have its civilian population deliberately targeted by artillery when it was pounded by the Prussians in August 1870. However, nothing that had gone before was to prepare the world for the destruction and death tolls of 1914-18.

The Bosnian Crisis in 1908 and the second Moroccan confrontation at Agadir had brought the Great Powers close to conflict, but on both occasions they had stepped back from the brink of war. However, although war had been averted in both cases, no long-term solution to the fundamental problem dogging Europe had been found. This problem concerned the balance of power and influence both in Europe and in the colonies, and in particular old animosities persisted between Russia and Austria-Hungary in central and south-eastern Europe and Britain, France and Germany in the West.

As Europe teetered towards the abyss of war, a similar foreboding and catastrophe faced the dynasty that had ruled China for two hundred and fifty years. War against Japan in 1894-95 had shown clear deficiencies in government and army organisation, and these had again been highlighted by the ease with which foreign troops had invaded the mainland during the Boxer Rebellion. By 1911, when revolution finally broke out, the Manchu Dynasty was clearly riddled with inefficiency and corruption, and no amount of constitutional promises was going to save it.

The revolution against the Manchus began in the industrial city of Wuhan on the Yangtze River in central China. It soon spread and, as China edged towards civil war, Sun Yat-sen, the leader of the Nationalist Party who had spent sixteen years in exile in Europe and North America, returned to take charge. China now split into two factions, with Sun Yat-sen's forces dominating the south while the army under the command of General Yuan in the north remained loyal to Puyi, the boy emperor. However, a compromise was agreed between the two leaders and Puyi was forced to abdicate. But unity was short-lived and China was to suffer numerous internal battles over the next fifteen years. In particular, these focused on the struggle between the Nationalists and the Northern Warlords. It was not until 1927 that Sun Yat-sen's successor, Chiang Kai-shek, was able to defeat these various warlords and restore some semblance of order and unity to the country.

When war in Europe eventually broke out, as it did in the Balkans in 1912, none of the six Great Powers were directly involved in the fighting. However, all had vested interests in the region, and the outcomes of the two Balkan Wars in 1912 and 1913 had a direct bearing on events leading to the Great War a year later. As a prelude to the first Balkan War in March 1912, the governments of Serbia, Romania, Bulgaria and Greece united under the title of the Balkan League in an alliance against the Ottoman Empire. In October 1912, this force attacked Ottoman territory from the west and was soon at the gates of Istanbul. To all intents and purposes, this expelled the Ottoman Empire from continental Europe for the first time in five hundred years, and a conference in London soon after formalised this victory.

However, the conference also created the new state of Albania to block Serbia's access to the Adriatic Sea. This was done at the insistence of Austria-Hungary, a move deeply resented by Serbia and one that only further increased tension between the governments in Belgrade and Vienna. The peace brought by the London Treaty, therefore, proved to be no more than an interlude, with fighting breaking out once again in the Balkans within a month. This was when Bulgaria, unhappy with the London agreement, attacked Serbia. However, Greece, Romania and the Ottoman Empire soon came to Serbia's defence and the Bulgarians were quickly routed.

Although Greece, Romania and the Ottoman Empire all gained from this second Balkan War, it was Serbia in particular that was to profit, nearly doubling in size geographically and able in the summer of 1913, as a result, to field an army of some half a million men. Austria-Hungary had always seen Serbia as its major rival in the region, and this had been a major reason why adjoining Bosnia, with its capital Sarajevo, had been annexed in 1908. But many ethnic Serbians lived in Bosnia, and so Austria-Hungary now grew increasingly concerned for its own security in the region. As a result, officials in Vienna eagerly looked for an excuse to clip Serbian wings. Serbia, meanwhile, grew stronger in the knowledge that it enjoyed a treaty of protection with Russia.

This tension between Serbia and Austria-Hungary had also been increased by the creation of a Serbian-based, anti-Austrian terrorist group in the Balkans dedicated to the development of pan-Slav nationalism in the region in general and to Bosnian independence in particular. This group was Black Hand and its operations were directed by the secretive Apis, a colonel in the Serbian army. Black Hand drew support from many students and radicals although it also received at least some unofficial support from the Serbian government and its military. It was active throughout the Austro-Hungarian Empire in the years leading up to the outbreak of war in 1914 and was responsible for a series of bombings and assassinations, which included one on the life of Emperor Franz Joseph himself in 1911. This was yet another reason why many infuriated Austrian officials in Vienna were impatient to deal with what they saw as an increasingly belligerent neighbour in Belgrade.

The Assassination of Archduke Franz Ferdinand and the Outbreak of War
Indeed, it was a nineteen-year-old Black Hand member, Gavrilo Princip, who on 28 June 1914 fired the shot that started the five-week-long chain of events that led to the outbreak of World War One in August 1914. The victim of his assassin's bullet was Archduke Franz Ferdinand, the nephew of the Emperor Franz Joseph and the heir to his throne. The archduke, who was on that day celebrating his fourteenth wedding anniversary, was shot while on a state visit to Sarajevo, the Bosnian capital, and was to die along with his forty-six-year-old wife, Sophie, who may have been pregnant at the time. Luck was to play a massive part in making Princip one of the most infamous assassins in history.

The archduke and his wife had only just arrived in Sarajevo when a grenade, thrown at their car by one of six other members of Black Hand who accompanied Princip, bounced off the car's rolled-up canvas roof and exploded close by, injuring several members of the archduke's party driving along in the following cavalcade. The archduke, however, was uninjured and, although shaken by his ordeal, insisted on continuing with his official duties that included an appointment at the city hall. In the afternoon, having concluded his official duties, he ordered his driver to take him to visit the officers injured in the morning's bomb attack, and it was on this journey that fate was to play its part.

On the way to visit the injured officers, the archduke's driver took a wrong turn and, realising his mistake, stopped in order to turn around, a manoeuvre made all the more slow as the car had no reverse gear and had to be pushed. However, by chance this was to take place in front of Princip who had stayed in the city after the morning's failed bombing in the hope that another opportunity would present itself. Princip was still armed with a pistol that he now used to shoot both the archduke and his wife. Both were to die from their wounds almost instantly. Princip was quickly apprehended and taken off by the Austrian authorities. He died of tuberculosis in an Austrian prison in April 1918, seven months before the end of the war that he helped to start.

In the early first weeks of the July Crisis that followed – the thirty-seven-day-long crisis that separated the assassination from the outbreak of war – the government of Emperor Franz Joseph in Vienna made it clear that it held its counterpart in Belgrade responsible for the events of 28 June 1914. Meanwhile at the same time, international tension began to build as the major powers, separating into armed camps based on previous treaty obligations, began to contemplate war.

On 23 July 1914, Austria-Hungary finally delivered its ultimatum to Serbia, issuing a set of ten punitive demands that aimed to destroy its southern enemy. Serbia, however, after having taken the advice of Russia, its closest ally, which itself was unwilling to commit to a war in the Balkans, accepted these almost in their entirety, rejecting only one, Clause 6, which was concerned with the integrity of the Serbian justice system. This would have involved Austrian officials taking part in the internal inquiry into whether there had been any Serbian government involvement in the assassination. On this pretext, Austria-Hungary broke off negotiations and on 28 July 1914, exactly a month after the assassination, declared war on Serbia. Due to both the intense tension that had been building up in Europe since the beginning of the century and the various treaties and alliances that had been signed since Bismarck's time, all the other Great Powers, with the exception of Italy, had joined the war within a week.

Germany was the first into the fray when, reacting to Russian mobilisation, it declared war on Russia on 1 August 1914, turning a regional Balkan conflict between Serbia and Austria-Hungary into a Europe-wide war. German strategy since the beginning of the century had been based on the Schlieffen Plan that argued that Germany could not expect to win a war waged on two fronts. The Schlieffen Plan argued that Russia would take some six weeks to fully mobilise its forces and so France, Russia's ally in the West, should be dealt with first. The Schlieffen Plan went on to conclude that since the common border between France and Germany was heavily defended, any attack on France should be launched through neutral Belgium.

In line with this, Germany declared war on France on 3 August 1914, and a day later, German troops drove deep into Belgium, attacking the heavily fortified city of Liège. Britain had treaties with both France and Belgium and was, as a result, dragged into the conflict, joining Russia and France in their battle against the Central Powers. A general war, which had nearly broken out on a number of occasions in the previous years, had at last arrived.

Liège soon fell and Brussels followed suit within three weeks. Stories of German atrocities in Belgium further inflamed public opinion in France and Britain where recruiting stations were set up to deal with the thousands eager to enlist. Further to the south and east, stiff resistance initially thwarted German advances, but, after this initial stalemate, the German army went on to record a number of early victories. In particular, it succeeded in driving back the British Expeditionary Force, the BEF, at Mons on 23 August. The Schlieffen Plan, which depended on the successful advance through Belgium and northern France before encircling Paris, seemed to be going to plan.

The war against Russia, though, had begun less successfully, with early tsarist victories in both Austria and Prussia persuading German commanders that its army in the East needed strengthening. Consequently, early Russian successes were soon reversed, with important German victories in battles at Tannenberg in the last week of August and the Masurian Lakes in mid-September. These proved a huge blow to the Tsar and his commanders in the field, who were already arguing among themselves. Russia was by far the most economically backward of the Great Powers, and in both battles vast amounts of equipment, arms and men were lost. In retrospect, Russia was never able to make up for these early losses, and it was to lurch from crisis to crisis over the next few years until Lenin took the newly proclaimed communist state out of the war in 1917.

However, one of the main results of the early Russian victories in August had been that it forced a watering down of the Schlieffen Plan in the West. The transfer of troops to the Eastern Front forced German commanders to cancel the planned westward sweep that was intended to encircle Paris, which had been a key principle of the original plan, and push southwards instead. This was not a lesson missed by Hitler who, twenty-six years later, ordered his generals to make the capture of Paris their main military priority. In August 1914, the young Austrian who was to lead Germany in World War Two was in Munich celebrating early German victories. He was soon to join a Bavarian regiment in the German army, serving with distinction for the next four years. He was to win the Iron Cross for bravery twice before a gas attack left him temporarily blinded and hospitalised in 1918.

In response to the German advances east of Paris, the French leadership ordered its army to pull back from the borders of Alsace and Lorraine where it had concentrated since the opening days of the war. Meanwhile, further north fighting had led to heavy British and French casualties at Verdun and Mons. With German confidence high, an early Allied victory was imperative if France was to be saved.

The Battles of the Marne and Ypres, and the Other Fronts in 1914

This victory came early in September with the Battle of the Marne, the first great set battle of the war on the Western Front, where the French army under General Joffre drove the German army back northwards towards the Belgian border. However, victory was only won after reinforcements from Paris, forty or so miles away, had been rushed to the front, with many arriving in about six hundred hastily requisitioned Renault taxis that had been seconded from the streets of the French capital. The four thousand or so soldiers that these taxis brought turned the battle in France's favour and stopped the month-long German advance.

The significance of the Battle of the Marne was not in the amount of land recaptured by the French but rather in the fact that it made an early German victory in the West impossible. In essence, it meant that the Schlieffen Plan had failed, that France had not been knocked out of the war and that Germany would have to fight a war on both fronts. By the end of the Battle of the Marne, the war had lasted for only about six weeks but already half a million men had been killed, wounded or captured.

After the Marne, each side turned their attention northwards in the race for the sea, a series of manoeuvres in which both sides tried to outflank the other, and heavy fighting was particularly experienced at the first Battle of Ypres where troops from the BEF suffered huge losses. But the defence put up by those troops at Ypres saved the seaports of northern France from German occupation and, in time, this allowed more British troops to be landed on continental Europe.

After Ypres, both sides settled down to a war of attrition in which the artillery and the machine gun, the rain and the mud, the trenches and the barbed wire defined the nature of the miserable war that followed. By the end of the year, a line of trenches stretched three hundred miles across Western Europe from the English Channel to the border of Switzerland. For four years, these were to be patrolled by soldiers on both sides who were commanded by generals who remained convinced that victory would come from massed frontal infantry charges, 'over the top' and across No Man's Land, in order to allow for a decisive breakthrough. This central tactic dictated battle plans until 1918, with the most staggering loss of life as a consequence.

Both sides early in the war also struggled with supplies of shells and men, and neither side was really able to solve these logistical issues until 1916. With the development of trench warfare and the machine gun, the odds became stacked heavily in favour of the defenders of these trenches. The war that many had hastily predicted would be over by Christmas was only just beginning. Meanwhile, in Britain parliament passed DORA, the Defence of the Realm Act, which aimed to help win the war by introducing a number of measures that curtailed civil liberties and increased government authority. By the end of 1914, nearly two million men on the Western Front alone had been killed or injured.

One of the major reasons for the failure of the German attack in the West was the early success, especially in East Prussia, of the Russian army in the East. This had not only persuaded the German High Command to strengthen its forces there but also to recall General Paul von Hindenburg from retirement. Hindenburg was to play a central role not only in the war but also in the peace that followed. He was elected president of Weimar Germany in 1925, and such was his standing that Hitler only felt confident enough to pronounce himself Führer after Hindenburg's death in 1934.

By the end of September 1914, Hindenburg's army had overturned early Russian victories, and superior German road and rail communications were beginning to have an impact. A few weeks later, the last remaining Russian troops were driven from East Prussia while at the same time the Central Powers were enjoying the success of an Austro-Hungarian advance into Serbia that eventually saw Belgrade fall in December 1914. Well over a quarter of a million were to die in this campaign alone.

Battle was also engaged at sea, with the German navy keen to challenge British naval supremacy. The main tactic employed early in the war was the use of mines and submarines to attack British shipping, and especially British merchant shipping, in an effort to starve Britain out of the war. Further from home, the two navies chased each other around Cape Horn into the South Atlantic before meeting in the Battle of the Falkland Islands. An emphatic British victory led to the sinking of the German fleet with the loss of some 2,000 German lives. By the end of 1914, British naval superiority had been reasserted, for the time being at least.

As the year drew to a close, the war that had begun as a regional conflict in the Balkans had spread across the world. In the Far East, in southern and East Africa and in the southern Atlantic, the two feuding alliances fought each other, with colonial territories and peoples dragged into a European war far from Europe. More important to the central balance of power, however, was the entry into the war at the end of October 1914 of the Ottoman Empire on the side of the Central Powers. Britain in retaliation annexed Egypt and Turkish Cyprus, and moved to defend the Suez Canal, a vital link with its empire in India, its possessions in the Far East and, of ever-increasing importance, its oil supply.

The War in 1915: Stalemate and the Gallipoli Campaign

The new year began with much of the carnage continuing on the various fronts that had been opened in 1914. On the Western Front, the two sides pounded each other relentlessly while in the East both sides suffered the terrible effects of the Russian winter. This came before the Central Powers won considerable gains through their summer campaigns. For the French, British and Russian leaders in charge of the Allied war effort, the entry into the war of the Ottomans had presented an added problem. It had cut off entry into the Black Sea through the Dardanelles, thus isolating Russia from its Western Allies.

So, early in 1915, Allied leaders were faced with the important tactical and strategic decisions of how to best deploy their forces. On the one hand, they needed to preserve their position on the Western Front while, on the other, they needed to reopen the Dardanelles and relieve Russia. In addition, a generous offer of land in Austria, Turkey and in the colonies was offered to Italy by the Allies in April 1915 if it agreed to enter the war within a month. The Central Powers also had decisions to make. They needed to decide how best to split their forces between the Western and Eastern Fronts.

Although the Allies were to spend many months of 1915 trying to force a way back into the Black Sea, their early efforts focused on the battlefields of

Belgium and northern France. Battles at Artois and Champagne resulted in losses for both sides, but little land was actually captured or lost, with ever-improving machine gun technology ensuring that defenders in their trenches always retained the upper hand. The spring campaigns concluded with an Allied offensive in the north at Ypres. This battle was particularly significant because it was the first in the war in which gas was used. Gas was a weapon that became particularly feared in the trenches of Flanders. The two exhausted armies took part in little fighting through the summer with each content to regroup and resupply after the enormous efforts of the spring.

This quasi-ceasefire was shattered in the early autumn when a second Allied offensive again tried to push through at both Artois in the north, near the border with Belgium, and further south in the Champagne region. Again little was achieved although heavy British losses at Artois resulted in the dismissal of General French, who had commanded the BEF since the beginning of the war. His replacement was General Douglas Haig. But Haig's arrival did little to alter the stalemate on the Western Front, and the two opposing armies ended 1915 occupying pretty much the same positions that they had held at the beginning of the year.

One major tactic that the German leadership continued to employ through the first part of 1915 was the submarine campaign in the North Sea and the North Atlantic against the Royal Navy and Britain's merchant fleet. However, neutral and passenger shipping sailing to Britain was also attacked, and in early May, despite US warnings, the British liner, RMS *Lusitania*, was sunk off the southern coast of Ireland. Among the dead were over 120 US citizens, causing a backlash from the USA that forced Germany to suspend its submarine campaign against passenger ships. However, the effect that this had on US public opinion was of far greater long-term importance, turning it against the Central Powers although it would still be nearly two years before the USA entered the war.

On the Eastern Front, the war continued with a series of German victories, most notably again at the Masurian Lakes where nearly 100,000 Russians were captured. These included many soldiers who went into battle unarmed because of the lack of supplies reaching the front. However, German advances were eventually halted and similar reverses were also gained over Austro-Hungarian forces further south. But these Russian successes proved only temporary and, with the German leadership in Berlin demanding the war in the East be given priority, the German army again advanced into Russia through the summer.

Poor leadership and bitter infighting within the Russian hierarchy was blamed for many of these ensuing losses, and these forced the Tsar to take personal charge of his army in September 1915. However, this did little to alleviate the problems that the lack of a modern army and industry had created, and for much of the rest of the war many Russian soldiers remained badly armed and badly trained. War on the Eastern Front was far more mobile than the one being waged in the West, but it was not as a consequence any less bloody, with millions from Germany, Austria-Hungary and Russia losing their lives there.

While the carnage on the Western and Eastern Fronts continued, Allied politicians decided to try and retake the Dardanelles, and in the process knock the Ottoman Empire out of the war. This was vital if a supply route to a beleaguered Russia in the East was to be re-established. The plan was principally the idea of Winston Churchill who at the time was serving as First Lord of the Admiralty in Asquith's government. The failure of the campaign in the Dardanelles, however, forced his resignation from the cabinet at the end of the year. He was to spend much of 1916 serving as an officer on the Western Front before returning to politics in 1917.

Churchill had envisaged a weak and dispirited response from the Ottomans and the almost immediate capture of the Dardanelles. This would, in turn, have allowed the capture of Istanbul across the Sea of Marmara, the gateway to the Bosphorus and the Black Sea. However, early Allied hopes were soon dashed and repeated attempts to take the Gallipoli Peninsula, which overlooked and protected the Dardanelles Straits, were rebuffed by stiff Turkish defence.

After two serious attempts through the summer of 1915, a general withdrawal was ordered in August. The Gallipoli campaign was an unmitigated disaster that ranked as one of the most humiliating defeats in British military history, with 22,000 British soldiers losing their lives in the Dardanelles. In addition, 27,000 French troops died while around 10,000 men from Australia and New Zealand also gave their lives. On the Turkish side, nearly 60,000 soldiers died defending the peninsula. Many have subsequently blamed the losses at Gallipoli on the logistical mistakes and inept leadership of the generals in charge. The last Allied troops finally left the Gallipoli peninsula at the beginning of 1916.

The success of the Ottomans in Gallipoli, which kept in power the Young Turks government in Istanbul, was to have the direst effect on the Armenian people who between 1915 and 1918 were subjected to a sustained attack that has been described at the first modern genocide. The Armenian Massacre, in which over a million were to lose their lives, was a move that aimed to ethnically cleanse the Ottoman Empire of the Armenian people who made up about 10% of its total population. Many were to die on forced marches eastwards across Asia Minor to the barren deserts of modern-day Syria and Iraq.

By the end of 1915, war was being fought on the Western Front, the Eastern Front, in the Balkans, Egypt, southern and East Africa, the Middle East and at sea. However, none of the disputes that had begun the war fifteen months earlier had been resolved and deadlock remained. As it dragged on, still more men were to lose their lives, mown down and blown up by the weapons of destruction that the war had spawned. By the end of 1915, hundreds of thousands had lost their lives or been injured in the Great War. In 1916, still more were to join them.

The Battle of Verdun, the Eastern Front in 1916 and the Battle of the Somme
Both sides began 1916 looking to make early advances on the various fronts of the conflict. The most important of these was in the West and it was here that the German generals were most anxious to make progress. In simplest terms, they knew that the campaigns of 1915 had killed so many young French soldiers that France was suffering a severe manpower crisis. They also knew that Britain had brought in compulsory conscription in January 1916 and that this would soon fill the gap. They concluded then that this advantage, their window of opportunity, would last only a short time, and so they needed to hit hard and quickly.

Consequently, they chose to launch their attack near the strategically important ancient city of Verdun on the River Meuse, close to the border with Luxembourg. This was almost halfway along the 300 miles of the Western Front that stretched from the English Channel to the Swiss border, and the German generals in charge knew that victory here would open up the road to Paris.

The Battle of Verdun began towards the end of February with an enormous German artillery bombardment on the French trenches, with over a million shells fired at the city on the first day alone. As a result, early German gains were considerable and this resulted in General Pétain, the subsequent leader of Vichy France during World War Two and a man who had already earned himself a reputation as a shrewd tactician, being sent to the city to organise its defence.

A second German attack was launched in early March, but as wave after wave of German soldiers were driven back, the motto 'Ils ne passeront pas – They will not pass' became the rallying cry for the whole of France. A third offensive in April and May lasted six weeks, with the German army attacking on both sides of the city, but again they were stubbornly pushed back. Further attacks continued through 1916 in the hills and valleys surrounding Verdun, but by the summer other considerations were beginning to engage the strategists directing the German war effort. Before the last shot was fired at Verdun in December 1916, about a million men had been killed or injured. Meanwhile, as the body count on both sides steadily rose, thousands more showed the symptoms of the newly diagnosed condition of shell shock.

One major reason for the failure of the German offensive in the West was the success of the Russian army in the East. These renewed attacks had been requested by the French to relieve pressure at Verdun. As a result, thousands of troops had to be rushed eastwards to shore up the Eastern Front where a resurgent Russian army was once again making progress against both Germany and Austria-Hungary.

But this success was not maintained for long in the north and German forces soon regained lost territory near the Lithuanian border. But further to the south, the Russian advance continued through the summer with a series of victories under General Alexei Brusilov driving Imperial Russian troops deep inside the borders of the Austro-Hungarian Empire. By early autumn, this June Offensive had brought Austria-Hungary to its knees, and Germany was forced to send still more troops from the Western Front to help its ally stay in the war. Brusilov and his men had proved themselves highly competent, but unrest in Moscow and Petrograd, which had changed its name from the German-sounding St Petersburg in 1914, and a lack of supplies and manpower meant that their efforts were eventually doomed to fail.

A major reason for this unrest was the scandalous behaviour of Grigori Rasputin, the self-styled Siberian mystic whose faith-healing powers over Prince Alexei, a haemophiliac and the royal couple's only son, had endeared him to the Tsarina Alexandria since 1907. Rasputin's influence on government had grown after the Tsar had moved to the front to personally take control of his armies, and rumours about his abhorrent behaviour were widely reported in elite Russian society. It was also popularly believed that he was a German spy and that he was using his influence over the Tsarina, who was perhaps his lover as well as being German herself, to sabotage the Russian war effort.

Many conservative elements within the ruling elite came to believe these rumours and, consequently, a plot to assassinate him was hatched by several leading noblemen in December 1916. Rumour and legend has it that Rasputin was lured to a country *dasha* near Petrograd where he was first poisoned. When this poison did not work, he was then shot although once again Rasputin refused to die. His assassins then bundled him up in a carpet and threw his bullet-ridden body into the freezing water of the River Neva where he drowned. Before Rasputin's death, however, the Russian advance had ground to a halt, and within a few months the Tsar had been forced from power. Less than a year later, the Provisional Government that replaced him had also fallen and Lenin had proclaimed the Bolshevik Revolution.

Plans for an all-out Allied attack on the Western Front had been agreed at an Allied conference at the end of 1915, but this had been delayed because of the German offensive at Verdun. Eventually, Russian successes in the East and stiff resistance by Allied forces at Verdun allowed it to be launched in June 1916. This offensive was to become the Battle of the Somme, named after the river in northern France near the border with Belgium some seventy miles north of Verdun, and was fought within a sector of the front forty miles wide. This was to last over four and a half months and was to be the bloodiest battle of the war.

As with the German offensive at Verdun, the Battle of the Somme was preceded by a week-long artillery bombardment that devastated the landscape for miles around. On 1 July 1916, this artillery barrage ended and the assault began, with the French maintaining their position south of the river while the British attacked to the north. This charge 'over-the-top' continued all day until some 20,000 British troops lay dead in No Man's Land, cut down by German machine gunners as they reached the miles and miles of barbed wire that a week of artillery fire had failed to destroy. A further 40,000 lay injured on the battlefield. These losses constituted the largest-ever one-day loss of men in British history.

Despite these horrendous losses, the battle continued week after week, with British and French soldiers slowly winning ground from their German counterparts. This forced the German leadership to reinforce their lines with troops from Verdun, and Allied progress continued through much of the summer.

In September 1916, tanks were used in battle for the first time in a major new offensive ordered by General Haig. In reality, however, these new instruments of war, which were to play such an important role in World War Two, were largely ineffective, with many breaking down in the heavy mud of the battlefield. Eventually, the battle ground to a halt in the middle of November in the mud and the rain of late autumn. Despite the loss of some 600,000 men, the Allied advance never managed to gain more than ten miles of enemy territory.

Although the Battle of the Somme did not inflict the major defeat of the

German army that had been its main objective, it did relieve the French army further south at Verdun. The Somme offensive was also crucial to the eventual outcome of the war because of the scale of casualties it inflicted on Germany. Although the 600,000 German soldiers killed or wounded in the battle was a similar number to those lost by the Allies, they were men that the Germans could not afford to lose. In a war where the soldiers were the raw material of battle, Germany, especially after the entry into the war of the USA a year later, was to run out of men quicker than its enemy.

General Haig, who had ordered the continuous frontal attacks on the German trenches for so long, suffered furious criticism in the British press for his actions, while the prime minister, Asquith, was forced to resign in December 1916, partly at least because of the carnage at the Somme. Asquith was replaced by David Lloyd George who himself had replaced Lord Kitchener in June 1916 as minister of war. Kitchener, whose moustachioed face and pointing finger had become famous on recruiting posters all over Britain, had drowned off the Orkneys when the ship carrying him on a mission to see Tsar Nicholas had hit a German mine.

The Government of Lloyd George and the Rest of the War in 1916
Lloyd George set quickly to his task and recruited businessmen and trade unionists from outside politics to help in the war effort. The campaign to recruit women into the service of their country was also stepped up, with many now taking over jobs that before 1914 had been reserved for men. This contribution to the war effort helped in part at least to secure improved voting rights after the war. Lloyd George also waged a war on drunkenness, which he called an enemy of the nation, by tightening up licensed opening times. This, he hoped, would help in achieving the increase in production that was so sorely needed. The strict licensing laws of Lloyd George's wartime Liberal government remained in force for most of the century.

One incident that had damaged the reputation of Asquith and his government was the Easter Rising in Dublin. This began on Easter Monday 1916 when Irish nationalists took over the General Post Office in the centre of the city and read out a proclamation from its steps declaring Irish independence. Many of those who joined the Rising were members of the Irish Volunteers, a paramilitary force founded in 1912 during the Home Rule Crisis. Many others were from Sinn Fein, an older association founded in 1902. Irish nationalists had been frustrated by the British government decision to postpone any further Irish Home Rule legislation until after the war.

However, the Rising was easily defeated, with the Post Office and other landmarks around Dublin taken by the nationalists back under British control within a week or so. By the time of the surrender, this had led to the deaths of just over 400 people. But within a few days of the surrender, the leaders of the Easter Rising had been made into martyrs by the violence of the British response. Fifteen were hung for their part in the disorder as thousands more were rounded up around the country. Eamon de Valera, a future prime minister of Eire, had played a leading part in the Easter Rising and was only saved from the hangman's noose by virtue of his joint US citizenship. He was sent to prison in England instead. The severity of the response rekindled an age-old hatred of British excesses, and led to a sharp increase in support for Irish nationalism, with thousands in the immediate aftermath flocking to join organisations that campaigned for independence.

While the Somme and Verdun on the Western Front were claiming the lives of thousands of men, other great campaigns on the Eastern Front, the Italian Front, in the Balkans and in the Middle East were killing still more. Through the summer of 1916, Austro-Hungarian and Italian troops again met at Isonzo. However, despite joint casualties approaching 250,000, neither side was able to wrest the initiative. In the Balkans, Allied forces holding land around Salonika in Greece were reinforced in July by a Serbian army of over 100,000 men. A campaign was mounted to break out northwards into the Balkans, but little headway was made after battle was joined in August against a joint German-Bulgarian army. As on the Western Front, the huge loss of life failed to move the front more than a few miles.

In the Middle East, the war was being fought in the Caucasus, Mesopotamia, Egypt, Palestine and the peninsula of Arabia. In the Caucasus, the year began with a Russian offensive against the Ottomans. Attack was followed by counter-attack as both sides vied for superiority before a general retreat quelled fighting for the winter. Again the front changed only a matter of miles after nine months of fighting. In Mesopotamia, which was becoming increasingly important due to oil, an Anglo-Indian army was besieged at Kut, one hundred miles south of Baghdad on the River Tigris, and suffered casualties that numbered over 20,000 before starvation and disease forced its surrender in April.

From Kut, the Turkish army moved southwards into the vast peninsula of Arabia while further west in Egypt, British forces moved eastwards across the Sinai Desert, meeting only sporadic Ottoman resistance. This was until August when a concerted German-Ottoman attack destroyed the British-run railway link with the Mediterranean, persuading Allied generals in Cairo to redouble their efforts to recapture Palestine. As the year ended, the Allies were able to once again restore their ascendancy.

With the Ottomans in retreat, T. E. Lawrence was sent from Cairo to Jeddah in December 1916 to help foment a local Arab revolt against Ottoman rule that had begun in the summer. Lawrence had been in the region since 1910 working as an archaeologist, and had joined the British army at the beginning of 1914 in order to help perform a military survey of the region. In a war of such horror, the story of Lawrence of Arabia and his relation with the Arab army of Hussein bin Ali, Sharif of Mecca and, after 1917, King of Hejaz, was to inspire a sense of romance far removed from the carnage of the Western Front.

In May 1916, the fleets of the two major protagonists faced each other for the only time in a major naval confrontation at the Battle of Jutland. British and German naval rivalry had been a major source of tension in the run-up to the war, and since 1914 the Kaiser had been determined that his fleet should destroy the Royal Navy's Grand Fleet in an open confrontation in the North Sea. He was adamant that this was the key to the defeat of Britain.

Battle was engaged on the afternoon of 31 May 1916 after the position of the German fleet was discovered by intercepted radio messages. Early skirmishes resulted in the German fleet gaining the upper hand, and for two hours the British flotilla was chased northwards. At about 6pm, the British had reached their main fleet of dreadnoughts and cruisers, and for an hour the massive navies of the world's two strongest military powers pounded at each other in open battle. Both sides suffered heavy losses before night fell and battle was discontinued. Battle was again briefly engaged at dawn the next day before each admiral commanding sailed his fleet back to the safety of a home port.

In terms of ships and lives lost, it was the British fleet that was to suffer the most in the Battle of Jutland. However, it was not destroyed and, as a result, was able to continue to patrol North Sea waters. This, in turn, forced Germany at the end of January 1917 to return to a policy of unrestricted submarine warfare against merchant shipping supplying Britain. This had been suspended after the sinking of RMS *Lusitania* in May 1915. This eventually led to the entry of the USA into the war in April 1917.

By December 1916, some five million soldiers and sailors had lost their lives in the conflict that some had confidently predicted would be over by Christmas 1914. The war that many in 1913 had felt Europe needed in order to redefine internal relations and Great Power spheres of influence had turned into a war of carnage unparalleled in history. Machine guns and mustard gas, tanks and submarines, Zeppelins and aeroplanes were all playing their part in making World War One a battle of technology and, in that respect, it was the first of scores of such conflicts that littered the twentieth century. On 30 December 1916, Allied politicians, on the advice of senior members of the military who promised a major breakthrough in 1917, rejected proposals from the Central Powers for a negotiated peace, feeling that the terms offered were too conciliatory. As a result, the war and its killing moved into its fourth year.

The Expansion of the War in 1917
With the continuation of the war into 1917, both the USA and communist Russia were to make their mark on the century that they were to dominate. In April 1917, the USA entered the war against Germany after a year of deteriorating relations while in October the Russian empire fell to the Bolsheviks. Firstly in their isolation in the 1920s and 1930s, then in their joint struggle against Nazism and the fascist right in World War Two, and finally during their subsequent four-decade-long struggle against each other through the years of the Cold War before the final collapse of communism in the early 1990s, the story of these two superpowers in many ways was to define the rest of the century.

One of the reasons that the armistice proposals of the Central Powers had been rejected in December 1916 was that the Allied generals were able to persuade senior politicians that they were on the brink of a clear-cut victory on the Western Front. But any advance by Allied forces that might have brought this about was delayed by a clash over strategy between senior French and British generals, and so this much anticipated attack was only finally launched in April 1917 with Canadian troops taking the Vimy Ridge near Arras. It was Canadian poet John McCrae's popular 1915 poem, 'In Flanders Field', which referenced the red poppy that was to become the symbol of remembrance after the end of hostilities.

At the same time, repeated French offensives were thwarted at great cost and, with morale at a low ebb, mutiny broke out within the French army that was still coming to terms with the losses suffered at Verdun and the Somme the previous year. General Pétain, the hero of Verdun, managed to quell the mutiny within a fortnight or so and, incredibly, news of the mutiny was kept from Germany by a highly efficient French news blackout.

General Pétain's new job as leader of the French army was made all the more difficult by the defensive withdrawal of the German army to the so-called Hindenburg Line, thirty miles or so behind the line of trenches established in 1916. This meant that a shorter Western Front could be defended by fewer troops allowing more to be sent to the East in order to knock Russia out of the war. Although French forces captured some ground to the south of the Hindenburg Line and the British some to the north, it remained pretty impregnable throughout the year. This proved to be increasingly frustrating for Haig and Pétain, and later also for General John Pershing, the commander of the American Expeditionary Force, which joined Allied forces on the Western Front at the end of the year.

Another worry for the British government was the success of the German submarine campaign against merchant shipping bringing essential food and raw material supplies to Britain. German experts predicted that if levels of British losses at the beginning of 1917 were maintained, Lloyd George's government would be forced out of the war within six months. However, the entry of the USA into the war in April 1917 began to remedy the situation as did the adoption of the convoy system. This turned the battle for maritime superiority once again back in the Allies' favour, with merchant shipping now increasingly safe on the North Atlantic trade routes. The number of British and US destroyers on patrol in the North Atlantic was also increased, leading to major losses for the German submarine fleet.

The war in the West in 1917 continued through the unseasonably wet summer with a major offensive launched in July concentrating on an assault in the north. This was the third Battle of Ypres, also known as the Battle of Passchendaele, which looked to retake Ypres before pushing on to take the village of Passchendaele itself, some seven miles further to the east. This was to be the first battle in which Britain was able to really capitalise on its growing aerial superiority. Before the launch of the battle, high ground to the south of the city was taken in the Battle of the Messines Ridge in June. This gave the Allies a morale-boosting victory after the problems of earlier in the year. In time, the Battle of Passchendaele was to become infamous for the mud and the rainy conditions in which it was fought, with images of the battle, and stories from it, coming to symbolise as a kind of evocative shorthand the atrocity of the whole war itself.

The battle for the city of Ypres itself began after days of artillery fire, but German defences were well organised and Allied losses were again heavy. As the fighting continued into the autumn, there was to be no let-up to the violence and bloodshed. For the first time in the war, Germany used mustard gas that tore into the skin and choked the lungs of Allied troops. Mustard gas was a major development in gas warfare as it lingered much more effectively than other gasses that had been tried, by both sides, since 1915.

The battle was finally concluded in November with the Canadian capture of the village of Passchendaele itself. In achieving this, Allied forces lost over 300,000 men, with Haig again coming in for sustained criticism for his willingness to sacrifice his soldiers through frontal assault, a task that had been made all the more difficult due to the mud and the rain. The German defenders of Passchendaele lost a similar number.

Allied commanders were keen to follow up this victory in and around Ypres and Passchendaele, and so ordered a further offensive fifty miles or so to the south. The objective of this was the city of Cambrai, which lay twenty miles north of the Somme and which was an important railhead supplying the German forces at the front. Again artillery was massed for the preliminary onslaught, but the battle differed from any other that had gone before as for the first time tanks were to lead the initial attack. Over 300, in fact, drove through No Man's Land and over the barbed wire protecting the enemy trenches that had stopped so many 'big pushes' of the past. Initial gains were substantial, but soon the tanks began to break down in the mud and mire of the battlefield, and the Germans were able to reorganise their defences.

The various offensives on the Western Front in 1917 were supposed to have coincided with a similar all-out attack by the Italian army to the south. However, this was not launched until May, with the tenth Battle of Isonzo lasting for three weeks before ending inconclusively. Two months later, battle was again rejoined at Isonzo, with Italian generals determined to make a telling breakthrough. This eventually occurred in August 1917 and, with Austria-Hungary near to collapse, help was sought from Germany.

This help eventually arrived in October and a counter-offensive was launched. At this twelfth Battle of Isonzo, German reinforcements made an important difference and territory lost through the summer campaign was once again recaptured. As a result, British and French troops were rushed to the Italian front to support a demoralised Italian army, and at a crisis conference, which was hastily convened at Rapello, it was decided that an Allied Supreme War Council should be set up in order to run the war effort more efficiently.

The USA entered the war on 6 April 1917 led by a president whose re-election campaign slogan the previous autumn had been 'He kept us out of war', a reference not only to war in Europe but also to the one that was brewing with Mexico after various heated border disputes. Woodrow Wilson's rapid U-turn was brought about by two reasons that finally made war against Germany inevitable. The first was that Germany had returned to the policy of torpedoing neutral shipping supplying Britain. This was a policy that had been suspended after the sinking of RMS *Lusitania* in 1915, but one which had been reintroduced in January 1917. This led to a number of US ships being sunk and led Wilson in early February 1917 to cut off diplomatic links with Germany.

The second was the interception of the Zimmermann Telegram, a telegram from the foreign office in Berlin to the German ambassador in Mexico. It was intercepted by British agents and was quickly passed on to the State Department in Washington. In the telegram, the German ambassador was instructed to offer Mexico the return of New Mexico, Arizona and Texas in exchange for Mexican support in a war against the USA. Although the authenticity of the telegram was later questioned, it was enough to persuade Wilson and US public opinion that war was necessary.

The USA did not officially become one of the Allies and reserved the right to negotiate a separate peace. Its forces, therefore, operated outside of the Allied command structure and were assigned their own areas of control. In June 1917, the first US troops began to arrive in Europe, and in October, the month that revolution in Russia ended the war in the East, these men, the Doughboys, saw their first fighting.

The Bolshevik Revolution of 1917

Another incident that severely hampered prospects of an Allied victory in 1917 was the collapse of the Romanov dynasty that had ruled Russia and its empire for over 300 years. In September 1915, Tsar Nicholas II had taken personal command of his army, but his leadership had done little to improve its overall performance and by the end of 1916 Russia faced defeat.

Victories had been few and far between throughout the war, while in Petrograd and Moscow the bizarre and outrageous behaviour of the Tsarina and Rasputin had destroyed any last semblance of loyalty that the Tsar might have enjoyed from his people. This catastrophic situation continued into 1917, with mutinies breaking out along the Eastern Front where thousands of Russian troops remained underfed and underarmed. At home, protests against the war, and against the crippling inflation and high taxation that it had brought, grew daily.

The initial revolution against the Tsar was led by a mixture of liberals, aristocrats and military figures who believed that the war could still be won if

Russia was led by a government not bound by the constraints of an autocracy. It began in March 1917 and was preceded by a series of riots and strikes that centred on Petrograd and Moscow. In order to put down this unrest, soldiers were ordered to fire on demonstrators who had taken to the streets. It was an order given directly by the Tsar, but it was one that the *Duma* refused to back.

By this stage, time had run out for Nicholas who within a week had been forced to abdicate. He was replaced by a Provisional Government drawn from leading members of the *Duma* and the military. Initial support for the Provisional Government was almost universal, with it becoming particularly popular with the ordinary people of Russia who had suffered for so long under successive tsars. New wage agreements were soon agreed and civil liberties that had been ignored in Imperial Russia were now guaranteed.

However, the Provisional Government soon came into conflict with another organ of power that claimed authority over the city of Petrograd. This was the Petrograd Soviet, a communist council of workers and soldiers elected to run the city. In the weeks that followed, it became clear that this had a completely different political agenda from that of the Provisional Government. This led to it taking an increasingly aggressive stance towards the Provisional Government that came to be dominated by Alexander Kerensky who, first as war minister and then as prime minister, saw the initial popularity of his government decline through the summer of 1917. This unpopularity increased when it became clear that Kerensky intended to continue the war that had for so long been associated with the Tsar, his wife and Rasputin.

Soon after the initial revolution, the Bolshevik-dominated Petrograd Soviet defied the Provisional Government by issuing Order No. 1, which stripped all officers of their authority and called upon each regiment to elect their own soviet from the ranks. In the aftermath of this and many other acts of defiance by the Bolsheviks, discipline in the Russian military, which for long had been teetering on the brink of mutiny, collapsed.

At the same time, peasants all over Russia were rising up against the landlords and landowners who had ruled their lives for so long. These agrarian uprisings continued through the summer of 1917 and, given the predominantly agrarian nature of Russian society, were far more important at the time than the ones going on in the cities. As a result, thousands of mutinying peasant soldiers and sailors spent their summer rushing home to join their families in order to secure land that this initial revolution had brought. This was to hamper the war effort still further.

To further undermine Kerensky's increasingly unpopular government, the

German government agreed to allow the leader of the Bolshevik Party, Vladimir Ilyich Lenin, to pass through German territory in a sealed train on his way back to Petrograd, via Finland, from exile in Switzerland. The German government hoped that the return of such an important Marxist revolutionary would further undermine Russia's military capability. In Petrograd, Lenin was soon joined by fellow revolutionaries such as Trotsky and Stalin.

By September 1917, the whole Russian military seemed close to collapse, with a German offensive even threatening Petrograd itself. At home, Kerensky faced a right-wing coup led by disgruntled elements in the army and, fearing revolution and violence in the capital, rashly removed himself to Moscow. With Kerensky now far from the epicentre of Russian political life and prompted by further military defeats and economic despair, Lenin was ready to make his claim on power.

On 7 November 1917, Lenin came out of hiding and proclaimed the Bolshevik Revolution. However, Russia at the time was still using the Julian, and not the Gregorian, calendar and so at the time Bolsheviks recorded the date as 25 October 1917. On the same day, the Red Guards, the military wing of the Bolshevik Party, were ordered to storm the Winter Palace, the old home of the tsars and now the seat of the Provisional Government in Petrograd. Sensing a groundswell of support for his anti-war stance, Lenin promised the Russian soldiers, peasants and proletariat who were flocking to the revolution 'land, peace and bread'. Private land ownership was abolished and control of the factories was given over to the workers. The following day Lenin was elected Chairman of the Council of People's Commissars while Trotsky was elected Commissar for Foreign Affairs. Trotsky also remained Lenin's unofficial right-hand man.

One of Lenin's first acts was to open negotiations with the Central Powers that led to the armistice ending the war in the East. At the Treaty of Brest-Litovsk four months later, Lenin and Trotsky were forced to hand over large tracts of Imperial Russian soil in order to preserve this peace. However, civil war had broken out by that time and Lenin had little choice but to agree to the treaty. After the treaty, Trotsky, as leader of the Red Army, turned his attention to defeating the Whites, the army of counter-revolutionaries that had been set up in December 1917.

The War in the Ottoman Empire and Lawrence of Arabia

The elimination of Russia from the war in 1917 freed up thousands of Ottoman troops from the front in the Caucasus, and these were sent to the Middle East to bolster an increasingly desperate battle for Ottoman survival. In January 1917, British troops had finally taken control of the Sinai Desert and this force was soon marching northwards towards Gaza. Orders were issued from Cairo to take Palestine as soon as possible and an initial attack was launched in April. But Ottoman reinforcements thwarted this, and others, through the hot summer months.

Among other things, this resulted in the appointment of General Edmund Allenby as Allied leader in Palestine with express orders to take Jerusalem before the end of the year. Allenby was aided in his fight by the Arab army led by King Hussein and Lawrence of Arabia, and Gaza, Jaffa and Jerusalem were all duly captured by December 1917. Allenby had carried out his orders and the liberation of Palestine could be added to that of Mesopotamia, whose rich oilfields were captured by British, Indian and Arab forces in the autumn.

Allenby's conquest of the Middle East had been preceded by the remarkable success of Lawrence of Arabia and the Arab forces under King Hussein on the Arabia peninsula in 1917. Lawrence's campaign began when he was sent from Cairo to Jeddah to help foment the Arab revolt there that had broken out in 1916. Dressing as a local Bedouin and using his considerable knowledge of the region, its culture and its language, Lawrence set about constructing a force that could tie down as many Turkish soldiers as possible.

Concentrating his attacks initially on the Damascus to Medina railway, Lawrence and his guerrilla army soon gained a reputation for bravery and courage and, as a result, was soon to become something of a celebrity, a status that was increased after the capture of the Red Sea port of Aqaba in July 1917. Marching with his men across the infamous Nefud Desert through the heat and humidity of the Arabian summer, Lawrence caught the garrison there by surprise, attacking from the rear with the Turkish guns fixed and pointing out into the Red Sea. After the capture of Aqaba, Lawrence and his Arab force struck north and were to become the right flank of Allenby's Palestine Army.

After the capture of Jerusalem, some of Allenby's men were transferred to the Western Front to help thwart the last great German offensive of the war. As a result, progress northwards through 1918 slowed down and it was not until September that Damascus was captured. But the Turkish army was by then in full retreat, and within a month any remaining Ottoman resistance in the Middle East had evaporated. By the beginning of October 1918, Allied ships had anchored off Istanbul while a general armistice ending the war with the Ottoman Empire was being dictated to the Sultan and his advisers.

The terms of this peace had been decided in 1916 in a secret agreement between Britain and France. This Sykes-Picot Note, named after the British and French diplomats leading the negotiations, had awarded the northern Ottoman provinces of Syria and Lebanon to the French while the British received Transjordan, Iraq and Palestine. The agreement largely ignored the promises that Lawrence had been authorised to make to the Arabs in 1916 in return for their support. Lawrence, who had spent two years in the desert with his Arab allies, felt particularly let down by what he saw as the injustice of this example of European diplomacy when it was confirmed after the war at the conference table in Paris.

The post-war Middle East settlement was further complicated by the Balfour Declaration of November 1917. The declaration promised, in a letter from Arthur Balfour, the British foreign secretary, to Lord Rothschild, the leader of the Zionist movement in Britain, British support for the eventual creation of a Jewish state in Palestine. Soon after the end of the war, trouble erupted between Zionists and Palestinians in the region that was to last for the rest of the century.

The Failure of the German Offensives of 1918 and the End of Hostilities
At the beginning of 1918 and despite these setbacks in the Middle East, Ludendorff and Hindenburg, the generals in charge of the German war effort, had seen off the great Allied offensives at the Somme and Ypres, and they had defeated Imperial Russia. The favourable peace in the East that this brought left German generals confident that, despite the entry of the USA, the war in the West could still be won. However, Germany was not without its own problems, with low morale at home particularly worrying its leaders. This was primarily due to the success of an Allied naval blockade and the effect that the increasingly unreliable support from Austria-Hungary, Bulgaria and the Ottoman Empire was having on domestic public opinion.

Ludendorff and Hindenburg also knew that the US build-up would eventually tell against them, and so both came to the conclusion that Germany's best hope of victory in the West was to mount one last 'big push' early in 1918. In fact, this last great German effort, which in Germany was called the *Kaiserschlacht*, or Kaiser's battle, was to consist of a number of separate offensives during the first six months of the year. The first began on the morning of 21 March 1918 with an all-out attack on British positions near the

Somme. The second Battle of the Somme took the British by surprise and initial German gains were substantial. British reinforcements were rushed to the battle site and British commanders appealed to their French counterparts for help.

However, a difference of opinion between French and British generals prosecuting the war could not be overcome and only a few French reinforcements were forthcoming. This difference of opinion centred on the importance that French generals, led by Pétain, gave to the protection of Paris. In early March, the French capital had been the target of German long-range artillery guns firing from positions only sixty miles away. This had caused panic in Paris and persuaded Pétain that the threat to the French capital was indeed very real. However, this view was countered by the British, led by Haig, who argued that if the Battle of the Somme was lost, Paris would be in a lot more danger from an attack launched from a lot closer.

In April 1918, this disunity was finally resolved after three and a half years of fighting when Marshal Ferdinand Foch was appointed as the commander-in-chief of Allied forces. Foch immediately reversed the earlier decision of Pétain and ordered French reinforcements to the Somme. By this time, the German assault was already losing momentum and the added presence of the French troops now brought it to a halt. In the meantime, combined British, French and German casualties for the battle approached half a million men.

The second great offensive of the *Kaiserschlacht* was launched at the beginning of April and struck at British positions in Belgium to the north. German advances were quick and decisive, and recaptured, in total, ten miles of territory that included the Messines Ridge near Ypres that had been taken by Canadian troops in June 1917. However, the breakthrough to the Channel ports, which had been the primary objective of the offensive, was never achieved and the Allied supply line remained intact. Meanwhile, tens of thousands of US troops were arriving on the Western Front daily.

The third German offensive of 1918 was launched at the end of May and struck at British positions fifty miles south of the Somme. This was the third Battle of Aisne. Again the initial offence was successful, and within three days German divisions had swept past the River Aisne and were on the banks of the Marne, only forty miles or so from Paris. But here they were met by General Pershing and troops from the American Expeditionary Force, which soon after launched its own offensive further north. By the beginning of June, joint US-French action had stopped the German advance and, in some cases, territory initially lost had already been won back. By the middle of June 1918, the impetus of the German attack had completely petered out as a series of Allied counter-offensives were launched up and down the central section of the Western Front, from the Somme to Verdun.

A final desperate German advance on the Western Front was launched on the night of 14-15 July 1918. This was the second Battle of the Marne. Ludendorff's plan was to divert French troops from the north by attacking around the Marne region, which threatened Paris, and then launch a second offensive in the north in order finally to take the Channel ports. But information about troop movements, gathered from aerial reconnaissance flights over German positions, meant that Allied artillery could be used to accurately shell the German advance, and little ground was made before this last effort was snubbed out by French and US troops. By this stage in the war, more than 300,000 US troops were arriving at the front each month, and the Allies were winning the battle for the sky.

The French and US success at the second Battle of the Marne had turned the tide of the war and made an Allied victory inevitable. Ludendorff had concentrated on a major breakthrough before too many US troops arrived. But the 'Big Push' of early 1918 had not given him the decisive victory that Germany needed, and he knew that his failure at the Marne was the beginning of the end. All he could do was draw back to heavily fortified positions along the Hindenburg Line and struggle on in the hope that a favourable peace would be offered by the Allies.

Early in 1918, the German submarine threat had also been contained although right up until the end of the war heavy Allied losses at sea were recorded. German admirals had planned one last great battle against the Royal Navy in October 1918, but their plans were foiled by widespread mutiny on and after 29 October 1918. The fleet was impounded at the end of the war and taken to the Orkneys while its fate was considered at Versailles. Seven months later, Allied politicians in Paris decided that the fleet should be taken from Germany as part of the peace settlement. However, rather than hand over his ships, the German commander of the fleet ordered his sailors to scuttle them. As a consequence, over seventy ships, some of which were the biggest of their class in the world, were sent to the bottom of the sea at Scapa Flow just off the Orkney coast.

While fighting was still going on at the Marne, the last great Allied offensive of the war began. Attacking in the north, a well-supported French offensive made quick progress and by the beginning of August the German army was in full retreat. Within the month, it was stretched defending even the Hindenburg Line as the American Expeditionary Force won its first major solo encounter of the war at the Battle of Saint-Mihiel. This recaptured territory had been in

German hands since the start of the war. The arrival of troops from the USA, the Allied dominance of the air, the collapse of the German navy and the superior artillery power of the Allies through the summer of 1918 were all clear indications that the end was near.

Foch planned to end the war with a two-pronged offensive that would see US and French troops advancing in the south near Verdun while British forces attacked German positions further north on the Belgian border near Lens. If both offensives were successful, Foch forecast that German supply routes would be broken and the war ended in a matter of weeks. However, German resistance, especially in the south, remained strong and Allied progress was slow. For a month, US and French artillery positions pounded well-defended German trenches around Verdun, but little territory was won. Further north, British efforts to break through the Hindenburg Line were also thwarted by brave and tenacious German defence. Meanwhile, thousands more on both sides continued to lose their lives.

By this time, the war in the air was becoming more and more important, with both sides having realised the need to control the skies. As a result, huge sums had been spent not only on production but also on aircraft development. Initially, aerial warfare was primarily concerned with reconnaissance and observation, with reports from the air and aerial photographs helping to improve the precision of artillery attacks as well as helping in other areas of intelligence gathering such as data about troop locations and rail movements.

However, in July 1915 the modern fighter was born when the Germans developed a way of synchronising the shooting of a machine gun with the turn of a propeller, allowing the pilot for the first time to shoot forward. This gave the Germans a massive advantage for a year or so, and this was most famously exploited by the Red Baron, Manfred von Richthofen, who became notorious as a top German flying ace. Richthofen, a Prussian aristocrat who in 1915 had painted his aeroplane red, the colour of his old cavalry regiment, was responsible for shooting down some eighty enemy aircraft. He was himself killed while flying over northern France in April 1918, the same month that the various outfits flying for Britain were consolidated into the RAF.

By the end of October, the immense numerical and logistical superiority of the Allied forces began finally to tell and the final breakthroughs on the Western Front were made. By the beginning of November, artillery and aerial attacks on railway links with Germany had cut off supplies to the front. The Kaiser and his military hierarchy had hoped that their rearguard action through the autumn would force the Allies into offering a negotiated settlement, and at the beginning of October 1918 Prince Max of Baden, Germany's new chancellor, had written to President Wilson asking for an armistice based on the president's Fourteen Points. This was Wilson's blueprint for the post-war world that he had outlined in an address to Congress in January 1918. In particular, the Fourteen Points had envisaged a fair and lasting peace as well as the creation of a League of Nations that could police the world community so as to stop another catastrophe such as World War One ever breaking out again.

However, in the autumn of 1918 it was clear that this was not going to happen, and Allied commanders and politicians, including Wilson, insisted that any settlement would not be negotiated while the Kaiser and his generals remained in charge. As a result, Ludendorff resigned as commander-in-chief of the German army on 26 October in order to allow ceasefire negotiations to begin. These negotiations had hardly begun in the early days of November when riots and mutinies broke out all over Germany, which was proclaimed a republic on 9 November 1918. A day later, Kaiser Wilhelm II fled to the Netherlands, where he was to live in exile until his death in June 1941 only a few weeks before the Nazi invasion of the USSR.

Meanwhile, a German civilian delegation arrived in France to negotiate terms with Marshal Foch, and on 11 November 1918 armistice terms were agreed. At 11am, this agreement was signed in Foch's railway carriage in its siding in the Forest of Compiègne. Thus, at the eleventh hour of the eleventh day of the eleventh month, hostilities officially ceased. Twenty-two years later the same carriage was placed in the same siding and surrounded by the flags and paraphernalia of the Nazi state. It was to be in this same carriage that French representatives were made to officially accept the surrender of France after the Nazi *Blitzkrieg* of May and June 1940.

The terms of the 1918 armistice called for the unconditional surrender of Germany and its immediate evacuation of contested territory. Alsace and Lorraine were to be immediately returned to France. By this time, Allied ships had steamed through the Dardanelles into the Sea of Marmara, taking control of Istanbul, the Bosphorus and the Black Sea shipping routes. Hostilities had ended a week earlier on the Italian front while a month before that an armistice had brought peace to the Balkans. Finally, a small guerrilla force of Germans offered their surrender in East Africa twelve days later on 23 November 1918. This formally brought an end to the hostilities that had plagued the world since the assassination of Archduke Franz Ferdinand in June 1914.

In late July and early August 1914, seven countries had gone the war. Four years later, they had been joined by another twenty-three. In total, some sixty-five million men were involved in the fighting that killed ten million and wounded a further eight million. It was said that World War One was to be the war to end all wars. However, just twenty-one years later an even more ferocious and costly one was to break out between many of the same belligerents.

The Treaty of Versailles, the Other Peace Treaties and Britain in 1918

In June 1919, six months after the signing of the armistice, the Allied victors gathered together at the Palace of Versailles to the west of Paris to sign off on the post-war peace. Two issues dominated proceedings at Versailles. The first of these revolved around how Germany and its allies should be dealt with while the second looked at how to construct a post-war peace that would never allow a world war to break out again.

Delegates from seventy countries met at Versailles although the views of the leaders of USA, France, Britain and, to a lesser extent, Italy held sway. The USA was represented by Woodrow Wilson, France by Georges Clemenceau, Britain by David Lloyd George and Italy by Vittorio Orlando. Representatives from Germany and Lenin's new Bolshevik Russia played no important role in the proceedings.

At the heart of Wilson's vision was a just peace for Germany and the creation of a League of Nations organisation capable of policing any difficult international crisis in the future. This had been a central tenet of the Fourteen Points that he had put forward at the beginning of 1918. But the seventy-eight-year-old Clemenceau had lived through two German invasions of his country and remembered the harsh peace of 1871. As a result, he, and certainly French public opinion, were not in the mood for compromise, insisting that Germany was responsible for the war and that it must be made to pay. He was supported to a large extent by Lloyd George, who, although he was to soften his attitude towards Germany later, had won the Coupon Election of December 1918, partially at least, due to his harsh stance against Germany. In the election, he had called for the Kaiser to be hanged and demanded that Germany be squeezed until 'the pips squeak'. The Coupon Election was also important because it resulted in the election of Britain's first female MP, Constance Markievicz, although, as an Irish republican, she was never to take her seat at Westminster. So Britain was not to have its first female sitting MP until Lady Nancy Astor was elected member for Plymouth Sutton in a by-election the following November, an election precipitated by her husband's elevation to the House of Lords.

Clemenceau went on to argue that Germany should be made so weak that a third invasion of France could never be launched. Orlando, for his part, was more interested in championing Italian territorial claims in the Austro-Hungarian Empire that had been offered by Britain and France in return for Italian support in 1915. In the end, Clemenceau was largely to get his way, with both reparations from Germany and the emasculation of Germany's armed forces becoming central features of the Treaty of Versailles. As a result, Wilson was to return to the USA having seen his vision of a post-war world rejected by his European allies.

On 28 June 1919, the fifth anniversary of the assassination of Archduke Franz Ferdinand, the Treaty of Versailles was signed and hostilities formally ended. The League of Nations was created, but Germany and Bolshevik Russia were excluded. The German army was limited to a size of no more than 100,000 and it was forbidden to have an air force. Its navy was also dramatically reduced in size and it was banned from possessing any submarines. The treaty also created a demilitarised buffer zone thirty miles deep in the Rhineland on the German border with Belgium and France. This would remain under Allied control for fifteen years. Germany also lost some territory to France and Belgium in the West, and to Poland in the East.

Crucially, a so-called Polish corridor was driven through East Prussia to give Poland access to the Baltic Sea, and the city of Danzig was made into a free city under the control of the League of Nations. It was this corridor that was to be the focus of so many problems in the late 1930s. Germany also lost all of its colonial possessions, with the bulk in Africa going to Britain and France. In the Far East, Japan staked its own claim. Also, a war guilt clause was written into the agreement, Clause 231, that laid responsibility for the war squarely with Germany. As a result, Germany was forced to pay reparations for the destruction that four years of war had brought. In the years to come, Hitler's opposition to the most vindictive of these clauses was a major reason for his rapid rise to power.

Rather than accept a document that condemned their country to economic chaos and political servitude, the cabinet of the new republic resigned, leaving Friedrich Ebert, the new president, to agree to the terms. However, Ebert first made a bitter attack on the treaty provisions, reminding the Allies that the armistice of the previous November had been signed on the understanding that Wilson's Fourteen Points would form the basis of the peace treaty. But Ebert, who had himself lost two sons in the war, knew that starvation, famine and disease were still killing thousands of his countrymen and that the only chance of ending the misery lay with him agreeing to the terms dictated at Versailles. Therefore, having checked with Hindenburg that the Germany military was unable to restart the war and having failed in a last ditch attempt to have some of the most vindictive clauses removed, Ebert and Gustav Bauer, his new chancellor, informed the Allied delegates that Germany would sign the treaty.

Opinion in France inevitably differed enormously from that in Germany, and Clemenceau was soon defeated in the 1920 presidential election at least in part for what was seen as leniency in the treaty that he had negotiated on their behalf. Other treaties formally ended the war with Austria-Hungary and the other minor belligerents in Europe, bringing into existence a number of new nations in central and southern Europe. Most of these adopted liberal democratic systems of government.

A lasting peace settlement with the Ottoman Empire took longer to negotiate after a nationalist uprising in the early 1920s ejected a Greek army from European Turkey, threatening the armistice truce of 1918 and the subsequent treaty that had been signed in Paris. But Mustafa Kemal, the leader of the uprising, quickly made it known that he accepted most of the terms of the original agreement, and was not looking to restart the war. Faced with the possibility of reigniting a war in the Balkans, the Allies agreed to lessen their demands in the region and a final peace treaty was signed in the summer of 1923. Kemal then turned his attention to getting rid of the Ottoman Empire and establishing in its place the new state of Turkey.

In July 1919, Wilson returned home to present his proposals concerning the League of Nations and the peace treaty to Congress. However, he found that his country did not hold his idealistic views about world peace, but wanted instead to return to the state of isolation from the Old World that had served it well for so long. Consequently, Congress voted against the treaty and the USA was never to join the League of Nations.

Wilson was replaced at the end of the year by Warren Harding who ran his election campaign on his pledge to return the USA to 'normalcy', a word he coined himself. Harding was elected with an overwhelming majority. Wilson, however, was not to take part in the election, having collapsed a few weeks after returning from Paris. He was never to return to active politics before his death in 1924 although this was not before he was awarded the Nobel Peace Prize for his efforts in Paris. It would not be until after the bombing of Pearl Harbour in 1941 that the USA was to totally abandon its position of isolation.

In Britain, Lloyd George faired better than Wilson and remained in power as the leader of a coalition government for another four years after his December

1918 election victory. Crucially, however, seventy-three Sinn Fein MPs were returned in 1918, inevitably forcing the question of Ireland to the centre of the political agenda. Lloyd George's personal popularity was high and he and his cabinet used this to pursue a series of reforms, which included the immediate building of 200,000 new council homes for soldiers returning from the trenches. This was one of many schemes that aimed to help ex-servicemen readjust to civilian life.

One incident, however, that brought Britain no honour was the massacre at Amritsar in India of over 300 demonstrators, many of whom were women and children. Another 1,500 were injured in the incident in which troops under the command of General Reginald Dyer opened fire on an unarmed crowd caged inside a walled park. Many Indians had died on the battlefields of the Western and Middle Eastern Fronts, and reaction against British rule was made particularly acute by the response of the House of Lords. Despite the fact that Dyer had been forced to resign his commission, it passed a motion congratulating him on his action. The Amritsar Massacre galvanised support for Mohandas Gandhi whose campaign of civil disobedience began soon after.

Revolution in Germany and the Russian Civil War

In December 1918, Germany was in ruin and close to anarchy. A new republic had been set up just before the end of the war, but its hold on power was weak and it seemed only a matter of time before a communist revolution turned Germany into another Bolshevik state. In Berlin, a left-wing mutiny seemed to confirm this. With Germany near to civil war, and with soviets being set up in factories and barracks all over the country, Ebert knew he had to act.

The revolution that inspired the mutiny was led by Rosa Luxemburg and Karl Liebknecht, two communist revolutionaries who had founded the Spartacist League before the war. The Spartacist Revolution raged for the next few months and forced the government to remove itself from Berlin to the city of Weimar where the constitution for the new republic was written. Eventually, Ebert was able to restore authority, but not without the support of the *Freikorps*, an anti-communist collection of ex-soldiers who had little time for the politics of the new republic. Before the revolution was finally put down, over 1,000 revolutionaries had lost their lives. Among those killed were both Luxemburg and Liebknecht.

A year later in March 1920, the *Freikorps* launched its own revolution, trying to overthrow the new Weimar Republic government, which it saw as pro-communist. This attempt was also thwarted and its leader, Wolfgang Kapp, imprisoned. The Spartacist Revolution of the left and the Kapp *Putsch* of the right weakened Germany still further and set in motion an economic and political crisis that was not resolved until after the intervention of the USA in 1924.

In the aftermath of the war, life in Bolshevik Russia was also harsh, with supplies of food and fuel that had been scarce during the war now becoming non-existent. Lenin's hold on power remained weak throughout 1918, and it was inevitable that groups loyal to the Tsar and the Provisional Government, as well as other revolutionary parties, would try to overthrow him. In 1918, the civil war intensified and for a long time it seemed likely that the communist revolution would not survive. The anti-Bolshevik White armies attacked communist strongholds from positions in Siberia, the Caucasus and the Ukraine, and from December 1918 they could rely on supplies of men and armaments from the Western Allies.

By this time, the success of the Whites had also led to the assassinations of the Tsar, the Tsarina and their five children at the country estate in the Urals that had served as their prison. Records released after the collapse of the USSR suggested that this was not carried out on Lenin's order. Rather, the executions in July 1918 were unauthorised actions by a group of radicals desperate to prevent the restoration of the Romanovs. For years during the Soviet period, the fate of the royal family remained shrouded in mystery. However, DNA tests on bodies found in the Urals and exhumed in 1991 proved that they were the Tsar and his family, ending a mystery that had run for three-quarters of a century.

However, despite these White advances through 1918, Trotsky was able to turn the Red Army into a formidable fighting force that by the spring of 1919 was ready to counter-attack. A major key to his success was the continued support of the peasants whose land seizures before November 1917 had been quickly ratified by Lenin's government and who instinctively distrusted any promises made by the Whites. Allied support for the Whites was soon withdrawn and, with millions dying from disease and starvation, the communists slowly secured control.

Millions more were to die before this control led to any meaningful improvements in agricultural production that allowed the people of Bolshevik Russia to be fed. By July 1920, the bulk of the fighting had finished although the war itself did not end until October 1922 when a Japanese army of occupation was finally expelled from Vladivostok. The immediate threat to the fledgling communist state had been thwarted. However, Lenin, Trotsky, Stalin and their comrades had a lot of work to do if their grip on power was to be made secure.

Boom and Bust
The 1920s

July 1920
(The End of the Russian Civil War in Europe)
to
October 1929
(The Wall Street Crash)

The Post-War World and the Emergence of Two New Superpowers

The Development of Modern Japan and the Rise of Fascist Italy

The Establishment of Turkey, Saudi Arabia and Iran

Crisis and Recovery in Weimar Germany

The League of Nations and the Treaty of Locarno

Post-War Britain at Home and Abroad

Stalin's Rise to Dictatorship and the Five-Year Plans

China in the 1920s and the World in 1929

The Post-War World and the Emergence of Two New Superpowers

The new decade began with the world still trying to deal with the economic and political devastation that years of fighting had brought. The result of this for millions in the early years of the decade was continued misery, famine and discord, and matters were not helped by the aftermath of an influenza pandemic that killed over twenty million worldwide, more than twice as many people as had lost their lives in the war itself. This medical catastrophe was to some extent, however, offset by the introduction of the BCG vaccine, which was made available in 1921. This was to inoculate a new post-war generation of children against the scourge of tuberculosis that had been the world's greatest killer for centuries.

The war had also had the most profound psychological effect on a world that had seen four years of devastation and destruction, and much of the optimism and hope that had been a feature of the earlier years of the century were lost for good. As the new decade began, this change affected every aspect of life from politics to popular culture.

The problems facing the new communist regime in Russia, where civil war continued, were particularly acute. For most citizens of the fledgling communist state, the most obvious manifestation of this was the famine of biblical proportions that continued long into the decade. On the other hand, the experience of the USA was very different. It had remained unscathed economically and physically by the war, and it used the 1920s to capitalise on this good fortune. It emerged from World War One as the world's richest nation, and it spent the decade cementing the position of commercial pre-eminence that this brought. Despite these very different experiences and despite spending most of the decade isolated from the international community, both the USA and the USSR, which officially came into being in December 1922, began in the 1920s to show signs that suggested the dominant role each was to play for the rest of the century.

Consequently, the decade following World War One was the one in which the Old Order of the nineteenth century began to lose its power and position of pre-eminence. The war had changed the world irreparably, bringing into being new countries from the ashes of the old empires of Europe and the Middle East. Britain and France retained their empires and, indeed, gained from the defeat of Germany and the Ottoman Empire. In fact, the British Empire reached its geographical zenith during the 1920s and 1930s. But both were hugely weakened by the 1914-18 war, and were forced to spend much of the 1920s trying to re-establish their positions as world leaders that the war had challenged. One reason why they were able to do so was, at least in part, due to the reluctance shown by the USA in taking an active role in international affairs.

In the USSR, Lenin's first objective after winning the civil war was survival. Millions had died in six years of war, and millions more were suffering from the terrible poverty and famine that had arrived in its wake. This poverty and famine threatened the very existence of the Bolshevik experiment, and so Lenin's primary aim soon became focused on the reinvigoration of the economy and the elimination of the most chronic aspects of this distress. Only after this, it was argued, would it be possible for the USSR to successfully implement the theories of Karl Marx and create the world's first communist state.

In order to do this, he replaced War Communism, the violently harsh system of economic and political organisation that had been used since 1917, with the New Economic Policy. This was introduced in March 1921 after a series of riots in Petrograd and Kronstadt had threatened to begin a new revolution, this time against the Bolshevik vanguard led by Lenin. The NEP was a step back from Marxist doctrine and it ushered in a return to a limited form of capitalism and private ownership. As a result of his decision, Lenin faced stiff opposition from many sections of the party, but he insisted that the NEP was necessary if the USSR was to survive.

Lenin argued that War Communism had been necessary in time of war, but that the USSR now needed a period of economic, and especially agricultural, expansion that could best be brought about if the peasants were allowed access to the market place. The NEP scrapped the oppressive and centralised policies of War Communism, and replaced them with a number of concessionary policies that aimed at enhancing growth.

Lenin insisted that the 'commanding heights of industry', which included heavy industries such as coal, iron and electricity production, remained under the strict control of central government, but other areas of the economy were freed. Internal trade was opened up, and the peasants were allowed once again to sell their surplus produce for profit, for which they paid a tax to the state. In order to make this free market work, merchants were also allowed to deal more openly and small traders were freed to own private businesses. Some smaller banks were also given back their independence.

The NEP led to the growth of a small bourgeois class of traders who were to grow rich from the business that was allowed to flourish until 1929. It also saw the growth of the Kulak class of rich peasants. It was this class in particular that Stalin was to persecute a decade later during the great collectivisation programmes of the 1930s. The major objective of the NEP was to restore the economy by boosting agricultural production, and pre-war levels were reached by 1926. This, at least, ensured the immediate survival of the USSR.

During these years of crisis in the USSR, the USA was enjoying a period of unprecedented prosperity. Its economy had grown massively during the war and this continued into the 1920s, with mass production bringing about a consumer boom that was marvelled at around the world. The USA dominated world trade and its enormous prosperity seemed even greater when compared with Europe, which was still suffering so greatly from the effects of the war.

The reason for this boom was the global growth in demand for goods made in the USA. At the centre of this demand was the car that in the 1920s became globally widespread, popular and, most importantly, cheap, but demand for other consumer goods also increased incredibly through the decade. Politicians in Washington may have rejected Wilson's vision of the USA at the heart of the world community, but its commercial leaders were determined that this would not stop US business from being at the heart of world trade. It was also a good decade for US banks that lent hugely to Europe for post-war reconstruction. Much of this, however, was in fact reinvested back into the US economy by European businessmen and governments determined to cash in on the huge profits to be made on the stock markets on the other side of the Atlantic, creating a credit bubble that was eventually to burst in October 1929.

The success of the American Dream was symbolised by Charles Lindbergh who in 1927 became the first pilot to fly solo across the Atlantic Ocean when he took thirty-three hours to fly from New York to Paris. Eight years earlier, the British adventurers, John Alcock and Arthur Whitten Brown, had been the first to cross the Atlantic when they flew from Newfoundland to Ireland.

But not everyone was to enjoy this boom. Many families in the South, where there was little industry, still lived below the poverty line, and many workers in the cities lived in ghettoes and had to work long and hard for their money. The 1920s was also the decade of prohibition, which came into being as a result of the Eighteenth Amendment to the US Constitution that was passed in January 1919. One massive side effect of this was the growth in organised crime that allowed gangsters such as Al Capone to grow rich on the sale of illegal alcohol. Bootleggers smuggled this in from Canada and Mexico, and thousands of illegal bars, or 'speakeasies', selling alcohol and playing jazz, opened up all over the country.

By the end of the decade, Capone's Chicago business was making him around $US60 million annually while at the height of his reign, between 1927 and 1930, some 500 gangland murders were reported. The most infamous of these came in 1929 with the Valentine's Day Massacre when Capone's henchmen killed seven members of a rival gang. But Capone had such power and influence in Chicago that he was never convicted for any crime connected with this gang warfare. Instead, he was convicted of tax evasion in 1931 and was sent to prison for ten years, much of which was spent at Alcatraz. He was released for health reasons in 1939 and retired to Florida where he died in 1947.

It was also the decade when Hollywood came of age, with rival studios making bigger and more complex films. The most glamorous of these studios was United Artists that was set up in 1919 by Charlie Chaplin, Douglas Fairbanks, Mary Pickford and D. W. Griffith. The Academy of Motion Picture Arts and Sciences was founded in 1925 and the first Oscars were presented a year later. In 1927, Al Jolson starred in the first 'talkie', *The Jazz Singer*, while a year later Mickey Mouse made his first appearance in the film *Steamboat Willie*. It was also the decade in which CBS and NBC, the country's major television networks for most of the century, were set up. These followed the first television transmission that had been made in London in 1926 where the BBC, initially as a private company, had been founded in 1922.

The Development of Modern Japan and the Rise of Fascist Italy

A major market for US goods in the boom years of the 1920s was the Pacific Rim where the USA had expanded both economically and politically since the 1890s. Japan was its main rival there, and by the 1920s its economic development had advanced so quickly that it could claim to be one of the world's five most industrialised nations.

In the 1920s, Japan was nominally a democratic country with a succession of weak governments voted in by universal franchise. However, in reality it was the emperor and the army that retained much of the power and political authority that they had always traditionally held. In 1921, Emperor Hirohito took over the reins of government from his ailing father and, as regent, ruled until 1926 when he succeeded to the most ancient throne in the world. After World War Two, Hirohito was allowed to remain as emperor, but was forced by the Allies to renounce his claim to divine status. He continued to rule as a constitutional monarch until his death in 1989.

Japan dominated Asian trade and its position of pre-eminence was heightened by internal turmoil in China that lasted until Chiang Kai-shek's defeat of the Northern Warlords in 1927. Later during the Depression, it was here in China that Japan looked to restore its fortunes, having been denied markets on the other side of the Pacific by US economic protection.

Italy's experience of capitalism and liberal democracy was very different from that of the USA, and in 1922 it became the first of many European countries to fall to the lure of fascism. Italy was a victor in World War One, but had been left bitterly disappointed with its treatment at Versailles. This seething resentment in the years that followed was fanned by an economic crisis brought about by crippling inflation and industrial unrest, and a spate of strikes through 1919 and 1920 weakened the economy still further. In some cities, especially in the industrial north, workers' soviets were set up in a number of factories.

A series of coalition governments were unable to bring about an upturn in fortune and, as the country slumped further and further into decline in the same way as Germany would do a decade later, Italy seemed close to revolution. On the left stood the socialists and the newly formed communist party while on the right massed a number of different parties that included the Fascists led by Benito Mussolini. Both sides of the political divide prepared themselves for the battles ahead.

Mussolini was the son of a blacksmith who had grown up to become a schoolteacher and then a journalist. He began his political life as a socialist and in 1912 came to edit a left-wing newspaper in Milan. However, the anti-war stance of the socialists in 1914 appalled Mussolini's nationalist tendencies and he soon left the movement. He joined the army and served until he was wounded in 1917. After leaving the army, he went back into journalism, starting up his own right-leaning nationalist newspaper. In 1919, he and other Milanese veterans founded the Fascist Party, taking the name from the Latin word *fasces*, which was the ceremonial bundle of wooden sticks that symbolised the authority of ancient Rome.

Enthusiastic support for their programme of economic expansion and ultra-nationalism meant that the Fascists soon came to dominate the political right. By 1922, they had also gained the support of important industrial and business interests that saw Mussolini, amid a political situation that approached anarchy and civil war, as a weapon that could be used to combat the growing threat of communism and socialism. Mussolini had also secured the hugely influential backing of the Roman Catholic Church, and his decision to uphold the rights and claims of the monarchy brought support from King Victor Emmanuel III.

As support for the Fascists grew through 1922, a general strike was called by left-wing parties who hoped to demonstrate the country's opposition to

Mussolini's rightist fundamentalism. However, Mussolini decided to face this challenge head-on, organising the March on Rome in which 50,000 black-shirted fascists took part. At the same time, other fascist groups all over the country staged massed demonstrations in support.

For a while, it seemed likely that the marchers would be dealt with by the army, but the king refused to order the state of emergency that would have given the military the power to put down the revolt. Instead, he invited Mussolini to form his own government. Mussolini, who had been waiting anxiously in Milan for news of events in Rome, arrived triumphantly in the capital soon after by train. He promptly took the title, *Il Duce*, the leader, and went on to lead Italy until, apart from a short interlude in 1943, his death in 1945.

Within a few years, many other countries in Europe had followed the Italian lead and turned to fascism. At its core, it stood for strong internal government, fervent nationalism, a deep-seated belief in economic self-determination and the development of a strong military base within the state. Fascism came to challenge the liberal democratic beliefs that as a political creed had evolved to dominate Western civilisation since industrialisation. The fascist challenge for world supremacy was to dominate international affairs for the next two decades.

After coming to power, Mussolini set to work destroying any opposition. Pressure was put on socialists, communists and liberals and, as violence in the streets escalated, the democratic process finally came to an end with the murder of Giacomo Matteotti in 1925. As leader of the socialists in the Italian parliament, Matteotti had been an outspoken critic of Mussolini and his fascist regime and investigations into his death pointed towards the complicity of a fascist Blackshirt hit squad.

In protest against the fascist cover-up, opposition deputies withdrew from parliament and demanded a full inquiry into the death. But they remained disunited and fragmented in their criticism of the Fascists and this allowed Mussolini to round on his critics and pick them off one by one. Within a year, this had forced any serious opposition underground, allowing Mussolini to build a dictatorship in a very similar way to Hitler eight years later.

Mussolini soon turned his attention to rebuilding Italy, and gained huge popular support for his public works programme, his emphasis on military rejuvenation and his commitment to law and order. Mussolini's grip on power was further strengthened in 1929 when he signed the Lateran Treaty with Pope Pius XI. The treaty ended the hostility between the Vatican and the Italian state that had existed since Italian unification in 1861.

The Establishment of Turkey, Saudi Arabia and Iran

While Italy and many other European countries and their colonial dependencies were struggling in the aftermath of world war, others were using the experience to wrestle independence. One such country was Turkey that had been deeply affected by its wartime experience. The Ottoman Empire had lost the war and, as a result, had been forced to give up land to the victors of 1918. But in 1922, the Turks, under the leadership of Mustafa Kemal who earlier as a junior officer had distinguished himself in the Ottoman defence of Gallipoli, defeated the occupying Greek army in Anatolia and Eastern Thrace, and nearly came to blows with British and French forces who were stationed at Chanak protecting the Dardanelles.

The events surrounding the Chanak Crisis weakened Lloyd George's grip on power and forced the Allies back to the negotiating table. The result of this was the Treaty of Lausanne in July 1923, which superseded the Treaty of Sèvres that had been agreed upon at the Paris Peace Conference. In this new treaty, the Turks agreed to give up all claims to land not populated by ethnic Turks and, in return, the Allies agreed to recognise the Republic of Turkey. Kemal had led the movement towards independence since 1920 and was elected Turkey's first president, a post he held until his death in 1938.

Kemal ruled as an autocrat and was ruthless in his efforts to transform Turkey into a modern state based on a Western and capitalist model. But progress was not always quick, and Kemal was forced to nationalise many crucial industries in his pursuit of modernisation. In his bid to emulate the USA, Western clothing and business techniques were adopted, and any opposition from traditionalists was systematically repressed. A nationwide programme of education for young and old was developed while Islam was disestablished as the state religion. Secularisation was encouraged and at one time the wearing of veils by Muslim women was made illegal. Such was his importance as a national leader that in 1934 Kemal accepted the title of 'Ataturk', the father of the Turks.

Another country born out of the ashes of the Ottoman Empire was Saudi Arabia whose oilfields were to become so politically and economically important during the century. Since the sixteenth century, the Arabian Peninsula had been ruled from Istanbul, but as the power of the Ottomans had declined through the nineteenth century this rule had become only nominal. Various tribal groups had fought to take control and by the beginning of the twentieth century, Ibn Saud, the king of the Wahabi tribal dynasty, had gained authority over the Nejd, Hasa and Hejaz regions of western and central Arabia.

Through much of the first two decades of the century, Ibn Saud had waged a guerrilla campaign against continued Ottoman presence. However, he had not joined Lawrence of Arabia during World War One because of his rivalry with Sharif Hussein bin Ali, Lawrence's ally against the Ottomans who had proclaimed himself King of Hejaz in 1917. Ibn Saud and Hussein had first fought against each other in 1910 and, after the war, this rivalry was renewed, with Ibn Saud winning by about 1925. In 1932, Ibn Saud changed the name of the land over which he ruled to Saudi Arabia and went on to conclude a series of treaties and agreements that confirmed its existence. Oil was discovered in 1936, confirming its political and economic importance. Ibn Saud finally died in 1953, having created a country of major international importance in much the same way as Kemal had done in Turkey.

Another key Islamic nation to gain freedom in the 1920s was Iran whose political and economic influence through the century was also very important. Since antiquity, Iran had existed as Persia, but after the Mongol invasions of the thirteenth century this entity had been divided. Persia was once again reunited in the sixteenth century and over the next 300 years was ruled by a number of different dynasties before coming under the influence of Russia and Britain during the nineteenth century. In 1907, the Anglo-Russian Entente had formally agreed spheres of influence in Persia with a neutral area dividing these. Crucially, oil was discovered in Persia a year later.

In 1921, Colonel Reza Khan was able to unite the army and lead a rebellion against the Persian government that had accepted the continued influence of communist Russia in the north and Britain in the south. The government he came to dominate elevated him to the position of Shah of Persia in 1925. The Shah then embarked on a programme of modernisation similar to that being followed by Kemal in Turkey, changing Persia into Iran in 1935.

Like Kemal, the Shah was deeply influenced by Western models of economic organisation and fought bitterly to defeat the traditionally powerful Shiite religious leadership. This leadership was not to regain control of Iran until after the Iranian Revolution of 1979 and the return of Ayatollah Khomeini. Reza Khan was forced from power in 1941 by Britain and the USSR who both suspected him of being pro-German. He was replaced by his son who ruled Iran until Khomeini's return.

Crisis and Recovery in Weimar Germany

As these various states in the Middle East moved towards independence, Germany, like so many other countries around the world, was in turmoil.

However, unlike Italy where this turmoil led to the successful elevation of Mussolini, Germany's first brush with fascism did not lead to the overthrow of a fragile liberal democratic government. Instead, it led to a failed coup attempt in Munich in November 1923, and to the imprisonment of Adolf Hitler. This was the Munich Beer Hall *Putsch* that was to play such an important part in Nazi propaganda and mythology when eventually Hitler did gain power a decade later.

Hitler's *Putsch* was provoked by a series of crises that had plunged Germany into despair. In 1919 and 1920, the government of the fledgling republic had been able to put down revolutions launched by both sides of the political divide, but nonetheless still retained only the weakest grip on power. Things changed very little over the next few years, with the country lurching from one crisis to another.

The commitment of the German people to the Weimar Republic always remained questionable, and the government's plight was further hampered by the widespread belief that the liberal politicians behind the Weimar Republic were responsible for accepting the harsher clauses of the Treaty of Versailles. These critics argued that the German army had not lost the war, but that it, and the German people, had been stabbed in the back by anti-German elements that had agreed to the armistice. This 'stab in the back' theory fuelled support for those parties that railed against the new republic and its representatives.

The most obvious crisis facing Germany was economic. Reparations had been set by the Inter-Allied Reparations Commission in January 1921 at cripplingly high levels, and within a year Germany was edging closer and closer towards bankruptcy. As a result, German diplomats made overtures to the French government at the end of 1922, hoping to suspend payments until the German economy had recovered. But the French refused to negotiate in any way and, when the 1922 payment was not paid in full, French soldiers marched into the industrial Ruhr region to secure raw materials and plant machinery as payment. The German government ordered its workers to strike in protest, and German industry was plunged even further into depression. The occupation of the Ruhr in March 1923 caused the collapse of the German mark and began a period of hyperinflation. Paper money lost its worth and it soon took a suitcase of banknotes just to buy a loaf of bread.

The economic and political crisis following the French occupation of the Ruhr led to an increase in support for a small, Bavarian, ultra-nationalist party based in Munich that focused its vitriol on the Treaty of Versailles. This party was called the National Socialist German Workers Party, or Nazi Party from the German abbreviation, and it blamed Versailles squarely on a Jewish-inspired communist conspiracy. The Nazis were led by Adolf Hitler who had been sent by his army superiors to spy on the party in the months following his release from hospital where he had been since being temporarily blinded by a gas attack in October 1918. But he had been so impressed by what he had heard that he had joined in September 1919, and soon used his energy, political skills and oratory to take over as leader.

By 1922, Hitler had made an important ally in General Ludendorff, Germany's second most important military leader in World War One who since 1918 had been actively supporting a number of nationalist and quasi-military associations in the Munich area. Hitler hoped that he could use this link to bring the Nazis to power, but his was not the only right-leaning party active in German politics at the time and certainly it was not the strongest.

So as the year of economic crisis after the French occupation of the Ruhr played out, Hitler's main fear was that one of these other right-wing groups might take advantage of the crisis and launch a bid for power of their own. For this reason, Hitler took the decision to try to outmanoeuvre his other rivals by launching his Nazi coup first. He hoped that this would emulate Mussolini's March on Rome the previous year with a groundswell of public support allowing the Nazis to take Munich and Bavaria, before moving northwards towards Berlin and the rest of Germany.

On 8 November 1923, Hitler launched his abortive *Putsch* at a beer hall meeting in Munich where the leaders of the Bavarian government were addressing an audience of about 2,000 supporters. Hitler and his brownshirted stormtroopers, the SA, burst in and surrounded the audience, proclaiming a national revolution. He forced the leaders present, many of whom he had been in league with against the federal government over the previous few months, to publicly offer their support. However, in the confusion that ensued, some of these men were able to escape through the Nazi cordon that had been put around the hall, and they quickly returned to their offices where the military and police response to the *Putsch* began.

The next day, Hitler and Ludendorff stood at the head of a large Nazi crowd that marched on the Odeonsplatz, one of Munich's main squares. They were met there by the Bavarian police force that Hitler hoped would mutiny and come over to the Nazis. However, their leaders, who had also been involved in discussions with Hitler and Ludendorff in the weeks running up to the *Putsch*, decided not to support the Nazis and instead gave orders to open fire, killing fourteen Nazi marchers. Hitler escaped but was arrested the following day.

Among those wounded was Hermann Goering who was to play such an important part in the Nazi state ten years later. Heinrich Himmler, who in 1929 became the leader of the SS, was also present.

The Nazis' first attempt at power had ended in a humiliating defeat and provoked little comment at the time outside Bavaria. Hitler was sent to prison for leading the *Putsch* and served nine months of a sentence that should have lasted five years. At the beginning of the trial, he was despondent, believing that his chances of power had been dashed forever. But when news reached him that the *Putsch* had hugely increased Nazi support in the area locally, he once again grew in confidence, turning on the judges with his barbed tongue and prophetically predicting that history would tear up their judgement. While in prison, Hitler earnestly dictated his thoughts to Rudolf Hess who was already a devoted follower. The results of their labour was *Mein Kampf,* Hitler's blueprint for the rejuvenation of a new Germany and his testimony to Nazism.

The Nazis' first attempt on power was in fact of little consequence, and Hitler had nowhere near the support that Mussolini had enjoyed in Italy during the March on Rome. The Nazis in 1923 remained no more than a small regional party, but Hitler learnt his lessons from the Beer Hall *Putsch* and in its aftermath became determined that he would come to power by legal means. He eventually did this in January 1933 with devastating effect.

More worrying at the time to the government in Berlin was the continuing crisis in the Ruhr that had destroyed German industry and led to hyperinflation. This was the culmination of a post-war economic malaise that was not resolved until 1924, and this was largely due to the work of Gustav Stresemann who was chancellor for only four months between August and November 1923 but who remained as foreign minister until his death in 1929. Stresemann was the ablest and most successful politician of the Republic, and between the end of 1923 and 1929 was responsible for an amazing reversal in the fortunes of Weimar Germany.

Stresemann began this reversal by launching a new currency in November 1923 that calmed internal inflation and paved the way for a massive increase in foreign loans and investment so desperately needed. This investment led to, among other things, the opening of a Ford factory in Berlin in January 1925.

Also, it was Stresemann who successfully negotiated the Dawes Plan, which was signed in August 1924 and which greatly helped Germany's recovery by reducing reparation payments, while he was also instrumental in agreeing a large loan to aid recovery and in negotiating the withdrawal of French forces from the Ruhr. The Dawes Plan, which was named after the US banker who oversaw its implementation and who was to go on to serve as vice president between 1925 and 1929, helped Germany recover from the horrific depression that had ravaged the country since 1918, and allowed it to enjoy a position of relative prosperity in the years up to 1929. As a result of Stresemann's diplomacy, French troops finally left the Ruhr in 1925 and Germany was accepted into the League of Nations in 1926. The relative political and economic success of the Weimar Republic in these years was further rewarded in June 1929 when the Young Plan reduced German reparations by another 75%.

The League of Nations and the Treaty of Locarno

The League of Nations had formally come into being in January 1920 and was based in the Swiss city of Geneva that for a century had been renowned for its neutrality. It had been the scene for the original Geneva Convention in 1869 that had attempted to legislate the rules governing war. The League was one of the most important results of the Paris Peace Conference, but its chances of success were immediately hampered when President Harding, Woodrow Wilson's successor, declared that the USA would not join and that it was his intention to lead his country back to a position of isolation.

The major aim of the League was to stop another war and, to do this, it concentrated on promoting co-operation between member states. Its major functions included settling disputes, encouraging disarmament and providing a collective security network in which members worked together against belligerent nations. The League had a number of early successes in the early 1920s with its intervention preventing an escalation of tension in the Balkans, Scandinavia and South America, and it was also responsible for a number of disarmament treaties. Despite these successes, doubts remained about how well it would be able to cope with a major crisis, and these doubts were eventually proved correct when the League failed to deal with a series of violations in the 1930s.

The League comprised three major organs. The first was the Assembly that met at least annually and in which each member was represented. The second was the Council whose role was similar to that of the Security Council of the United Nations. Britain, France, Japan and Italy had permanent seats in this council, and they were joined by other countries elected periodically. The third organ, the Secretariat, implemented the decisions of the Assembly and the Council, and administered the various bodies that were run by the League. Most notable among these were the International Court of Justice based in The Hague and the International Labour Organisation. Despite the League being unable in the 1930s to fulfil the ambitions of its founders, it did give a platform for dialogue in the 1920s and was an important development in international affairs.

World War One had shocked the world and resulted in, as well as the League of Nations, a number of other treaties and agreements in the 1920s that attempted to make another war impossible. An early agreement was the Four-Power Treaty, signed in December 1921, and this was followed by the Five-Power Treaty the following February. These were agreed during the Washington Naval Conference that represented a watershed in diplomatic history. In the first of these treaties, Britain, France, the USA and Japan agreed spheres of influence in the Far East, while in the second the same four powers and Italy agreed to a disarmament treaty that greatly reduced the naval firepower of each country. This treaty was extended in 1930 with the Treaty of London, but this was violated by Japan in 1934. In 1924, the Geneva Protocol, organised by the League, aimed to make starting war an international crime, and in August 1928 over sixty countries signed the Kellogg-Briand Pact that renounced war as a means of settling international disputes. These included the USA, the USSR and all the other major powers.

But the most important agreements of the 1920s were signed at the Swiss town of Locarno in 1925, with the treaties signed there leading to a period of stability and progress in Europe that had not existed since the late nineteenth century. Delegates met at Locarno to work out problems between Germany and the victors of 1918 that for seven years had remained unresolved, and the most important agreement led to a treaty between Germany, France and Belgium, guaranteed by Britain and Italy, that finally set Germany's western border. A similar agreement that fixed its eastern border was signed by Germany, Poland and Czechoslovakia. In addition, all signatories agreed to settle any future disputes without recourse to aggression.

The Locarno Treaties finally brought peace to Europe after World War One, and it was followed by a period of prosperity that is sometimes called the 'Locarno Honeymoon'. Europe's economies soon felt the benefits of the improved political situation that, among other things, saw Germany welcomed into the League of Nations in 1926. For their efforts at Locarno, Gustav Stresemann and Aristide Briand, the French foreign minister and previous prime minister, received the Nobel Peace Prize.

Post-War Britain at Home and Abroad
British support for the Locarno Treaties was instrumental in ensuring that the most significant piece of diplomacy of the decade became a reality. Britain had

been weakened by war, and there could no longer be any doubt that the USA had become the world's premier industrial nation. But despite this, Britain retained a huge empire and, with France, dominated the League of Nations. Britain was in relative decline when compared with the USA. But its relative position to the rest of the world remained strong.

The most pressing problem faced by Lloyd George and his cabinet in 1920 was undoubtedly over the question of Ireland. Negotiations over Home Rule implementation had been postponed for the duration of the war, but the Easter Rising in 1916 had led to a massive increase in the clamour for Irish independence and this had intensified after the end of hostilities in 1918. As a result, Sinn Fein was to become the main nationalist party in the December 1918 election in a massive landslide victory that was to change the whole political landscape of southern Ireland. This was primarily because the Sinn Fein MPs refused to take their seats in Westminster, but instead set up their own Irish parliament, the *Dail*, in Dublin. At the same time, the Irish Republican Army launched a guerrilla war that led to a state of near civil war.

The British government's response was the Government of Ireland Act that set up separate parliaments in the north in Belfast and in the south in Dublin, although it soon became clear that the only parliament in the south with any credibility was the rival one set up by Sinn Fein. In light of this, British and Free Irish diplomats negotiated a new agreement during an IRA ceasefire in 1921. The result of these negotiations was the Irish Free State that became a self-governing dominion of the British Empire. Six of the nine counties that made up Ulster remained outside the Free State and became the province of Northern Ireland. This continued to be part of the United Kingdom and was ruled by the parliament in Belfast.

But this deal, brokered by Michael Collins, an influential member of the IRA and Sinn Fein who had led the negotiations with the British government, did not please all factions within the nationalist movement. The result was a civil war between supporters of Collins, who supported the deal, and those of Eamon de Valera, who believed that the armed struggle against British rule should be continued until the whole of Ireland had been liberated. The civil war was bitter, but was quickly won by the pro-agreement faction. However, this was not before the assassination of Collins who had become a leading member of the Irish Free State's new government.

Links with Britain were weakened through the 1930s when a de Valera government finally came to power and the country's name was changed to Eire in 1936. During World War Two, relations between Eire and Britain were strained by the former's neutrality, and in 1949 links with the British Empire were formally severed.

Britain also had trouble in other parts of its empire, and this was particularly the case in Egypt and India. In Egypt, opposition to British rule had led to riots and disturbances after the war, and in 1922 it was granted independence although close links were maintained between Britain and the government of King Fuad who had been the sultan under British rule since 1917. In the same year, Howard Carter discovered the tomb of King Tutankhamun, perhaps the most famous and certainly the most spectacular archaeological discovery of the century. Britain retained the right to station troops in Egypt although this right was given up under the Anglo-Egyptian Treaty of 1936, except in the Suez Canal Zone where Britain retained a military presence until the Suez Crisis in 1956.

In India, Mahatma Gandhi had begun his first campaign of civil disobedience in the aftermath of the Amritsar Massacre although this had been called off after it led to violence in 1922. A series of campaigns and prison sentences for Gandhi punctuated the 1920s before he set off on a 250-mile symbolic march to the Indian Ocean in April 1930 in order to produce salt. Both he and the British authorities knew that this was a monopoly right of the government, but such was the success of the march that it provoked the second great wave of the civil disobedience.

Gandhi's moral and physical courage did much to force concessions from the British government, and eventually this led to the Round Table Conferences of 1930 and 1931, which were attended by many Indian nationalist leaders, the Round Table Conference of 1932, which was not, the Government of India Act of 1935 and the promise of independence after World War Two. This was made by Churchill in exchange for Indian support for the war in Burma and the Far East.

Britain's white dominions were also showing signs of wanting more independence. South Africa, with its large Afrikaner population, and the Irish Free State wanted more freedom to break with Britain over foreign as well as domestic affairs, and Australia and New Zealand were also demanding more independence. As a result, representatives met in 1926 at the Imperial Conference, under the chairmanship of Arthur Balfour, the ex-British prime minister, in order to air grievances and plan for the future.

As a result of negotiations at the conference, it was agreed that South Africa, Australia, the Irish Free State, Canada and New Zealand were to be equal and free countries in charge of their own domestic and foreign agendas. They all also agreed to join the British Commonwealth of Nations. This new constitutional arrangement was enshrined in the Statute of Westminster, an act of parliament that passed into law in December 1931. So began a new period in British imperial history, with the Commonwealth, which between the 1940s and 1960s expanded to include many newly independent nations from Asia and Africa, continuing to play an important cultural and political role for the rest of the century.

Britain was led by a mixture of political parties through the 1920s although the first Labour Party government in 1924 was perhaps the single most important historical event. The decade began with Lloyd George as prime minister, and he was to remain at Downing Street until October 1922 when an election victory returned the Conservatives under the leadership of Andrew Bonar Law. Lloyd George had increasingly run into problems holding together the various factions that made up his coalition government, problems that stemmed from his split with Asquith during the war. This inability to reunite the Liberal Party led to its steady decline in the interwar period and beyond, and it was never to hold power again, losing its position as the second party of government to Labour. Lloyd George was also harmed by a scandal in the summer of 1922 over the sale of honours that tainted his reputation.

Bonar Law had led the Conservatives, with the exception of a few months in 1921-22, since 1911, but was struck by illness within months of taking office, resigned and was replaced by Stanley Baldwin, his chancellor of the exchequer. He had only been in charge at Downing Street for just over 200 days, making him the shortest-serving prime minister of the twentieth century. He was also the only British prime minister ever not to have been born in the British Isles. He was born in Canada.

Like Lord Salisbury before him, Baldwin was to serve as prime minister three times. Baldwin immediately decided to call another general election over the question of protection. Both the Liberal and Labour Parties disagreed with Baldwin over the issue, which meant raising high tariff barriers on foreign imports, and both campaigned instead for free trade. In the election of November 1923, the Conservatives returned 258 MPs. However, protection was clearly rejected by the electorate, which returned 191 Labour members and 158 candidates from the Liberal Party.

It was clear that the Conservatives, the largest party, could not remain in office because any legislation enacting protection would be voted down by the combined strength of Labour and the Liberals. Therefore, George V summoned Ramsay MacDonald, as the leader of the second largest party in parliament, and in January 1924 invited him to form a government. MacDonald had first become an MP in 1906, but had left Westminster politics during the war. He had failed in his first attempt to re-enter national politics in 1918, but was more successful two years later when he was returned as MP for Aberavon. Such was his power and reputation within the party that he was soon elected leader and became leader of the opposition. By the end of the century, he had only been followed by a further four Labour prime ministers: Clement Attlee, Harold Wilson, James Callaghan and Tony Blair. Again, like Lord Salisbury, MacDonald became his own foreign secretary.

Despite MacDonald's reputation within the party, his first Labour administration only managed to survive until November 1924. This was primarily because it suffered a series of setbacks with the trade unions that had hoped that a Labour administration would do more for the rights and conditions of the working class, and strikes by dockers and transport workers particularly soured relations. However, MacDonald was able to pass a number of important pieces of social legislation concerning education, old-age pensions and housing, and British support for the Dawes Plan was important in bringing about its successful implementation.

The fall of the first Labour administration came at the end of the year when the Conservatives and Liberals united over the Campbell Affair. This came about when a communist weekly newspaper editor was charged, under an arcane law, with inciting mutiny after he had urged soldiers sent to break up strikes not to fire on striking workers. But when he was set free, the matter was taken up in the Commons, with a majority of over sixty voting for an inquiry into the affair. This was taken by MacDonald as a vote of confidence in his government and an election was called for November 1924. MacDonald hoped that the people of Britain would return his party with an increased vote so that he could form the first majority Labour government.

However, an anti-communist scare set off by the publication in the British press of the Zinoviev Letter, which linked the labour movement in Britain to the new Soviet regime in Moscow only days before the election, massively harmed MacDonald's chances in the run-up to polling and Baldwin was returned to Downing Street for a second time with an overall majority. His ministry lasted until just before the Wall Street Crash in 1929, and coincided with a period of relative diplomatic calm abroad that was particularly the case after France and Germany had formalised peace at Locarno.

But the period was also one of uncertainty at home, with unemployment and a weak economy threatening his government throughout its five years. This was a situation that was not helped by the Budget of April 1925 when the new chancellor of the exchequer, Winston Churchill, returned Britain to the Gold Standard, in a last attempt to restore the pre-war world of stable currencies and balanced budgets. The economic crisis also led to the General Strike of May 1926. The strike began with a disagreement in the coal industry over the best way to modernise in response to the fall in exports that had been troubling the industry since the end of the war. The mine owners blamed Britain's lack of competitiveness on high wages and wanted to extend the working hours expected of each miner. The miners, on the other hand, believed that greater productivity would only come through greater efficiency brought about by a huge programme of investment. This was a strategy the mine owners were not willing to fund.

Crisis point was reached in the summer of 1925 when cheap German coal from the recently reopened Ruhr coalfields flooded the British market. As a result, hard-pressed mine owners announced that they intended to reduce wages while at the same time increasing working hours. In response, the miners gained the backing of the Trades Union Congress that was well aware of the importance of their struggle. The miners were a large and influential group of workers, and the TUC leadership concluded that the well-being of many other workers in many other industries rested on their success.

Crisis was averted when Baldwin announced that he had ordered a Royal Commission to look into the industry, and that he had made provisions for a subsidy to cover wage cuts during the nine months before its report was to be published. In anticipation of this report, both sides backed down and an uneasy truce was followed through the winter.

The findings of the commission, which were published in March 1926, were quickly rejected by both sides, and for six weeks no amount of negotiation could force a compromise. At the end of April, the mine owners announced that wages would have to be cut and the miners in response announced that they would strike. The TUC fully backed the miners, and announced that a general strike would be called if the mine owners and their supporters in the ruling Conservative government did not back down. When this did not happen, the General Strike began on 4 May 1926.

It immediately gained the mass support of the British working class, with some three million workers from most industries heeding the TUC's call and striking in support of the miners. The government took the view that the strike was not a valid industrial dispute, but rather was a revolutionary attack on the integrity of the country and its institutions. As a result, Baldwin refused to join talks with the TUC, and called out the armed forces to replace striking workers in essential industries.

Emergency contingency plans that had been worked out months before were put into place as support around the country polarised between the two camps. The strike continued for eight days and was called off by the TUC after a rushed report by Sir Herbert Samuel, who had been responsible for the Royal Commission a year earlier, suggested a short-term settlement based on a return to the subsidy. This would mean no wage reductions until after major reorganisation and modernisation.

The TUC's decision to call off the strike was criticised by the miners because no guarantee had been made that the government and the mine owners would act on Samuel's initiative. With no assurances in place, the miners refused to go back to work, and their dispute with the owners lasted until December when poverty and destitution forced them to give in. The strike had been costly both in its damage to the economy and to the reputation of the country. One important result of the strike was the Trade Disputes Act that aimed to make a future general strike impossible. In retrospect, the strike was to have an adverse effect on Baldwin's government, with large sections of the working class feeling alienated by its response and voting Labour at the next election in 1929.

Stalin's Rise to Dictatorship and the Five-Year Plans

In January 1924, Lenin died having never recovered from a stroke that he had suffered the previous year. Such was his importance as the architect of the revolution and as a patriarch of the party that within a week Petrograd had been renamed Leningrad and his body had been placed on public display in a mausoleum in Moscow's Red Square.

After his death, the power struggle that had been prompted by his stroke and his political incapacitation the previous year intensified, eventually leading to the emergence of Stalin as dictator of the USSR later in the decade. But this rise to power was far from a foregone conclusion and Stalin in 1924 had many capable rivals. Principal among these was Leon Trotsky who had worked closely with Lenin during the revolution and who had been in charge of the Red Army during the civil war.

Lenin had foreseen this rivalry when in December 1922 he had laid out his opinions in a long letter, his Testament, addressed to the Party Congress. But Lenin had fallen ill soon after writing this, and the Politburo chose not to act and inform the Congress of Lenin's principal suggestion. This was that Stalin should be sacked before he became too powerful, and this was mainly because many influential members of the party were worried that sacking Stalin would concentrate too much power in the hands of Trotsky, therefore threatening their own positions in government.

As a result, the Politburo voted to retain Stalin in his post as general secretary of the Bolshevik Party and it was from this highly influential base that Stalin was able to manoeuvre over the next four years. While others worried about doctrine and speech-making, Stalin concentrated on using the considerable powers at his disposal to secure appointments and positions of authority for his supporters at all levels of the state and party machinery.

The first element of the party that Stalin needed to defeat was the left that was led by Trotsky. This faction wanted to concentrate the energy of the country on fomenting world revolution. They also disagreed with the continuation of the NEP, which, they argued, concentrated too much on agriculture to the detriment of industrial development. Stalin and the right of the party meanwhile developed an alternative to world revolution that they called 'Socialism in One Country'.

They argued that the party should concentrate on the development of the USSR, and that the capitalist countries of the West would not attack the USSR if it were economically and militarily strong. 'Socialism in One Country' was vigorously championed by Stalin and his allies, and key members on the left were forced to resign from the Politburo in 1925. Their places were taken by men who owed their positions to Stalin, and Trotsky himself was expelled from the party in 1927. He was exiled from the USSR in 1929, beginning a nomadic life that eventually ended in Mexico where he was assassinated by Soviet agents in August 1940.

Stalin could now turn his attention to the defeat of those on the right. In 1927, he began arguing that the NEP had run its course and that a new approach to industrial and economic planning was needed. He argued for vigorous centralised planning of the economy and a squeeze on the rich peasant class that had re-emerged since the end of the civil war. The right opposition tried to argue against him, but Stalin now had a majority in the Politburo and they too were forced from power.

By 1928, effective opposition to Stalin had to all intents and purposes been snuffed out. But even after this, Stalin remained paranoid about opposition and threats to his leadership, and hunted down any possible signs of dissent right up until his death in 1953. In terms of sheer numbers, this meant that many more people died under Stalin's rule in the USSR than did under Hitler's twelve-year reign of terror in Nazi Germany.

Once Stalin's authority was secured in 1928, he could turn his attention to the problems that were to dominate internal policy for the next twenty-five years. Central among these were industrialisation, collectivisation and the maintenance of order within the party and state. Industrialisation was needed if the USSR was to catch up with the West. Collectivisation was needed to subdue the peasants and create a modern and efficient system of food supply for the urban proletariat, and the maintenance of order within the party and state was needed to preserve the achievements of the 1917 revolution and Stalin's often somewhat rewritten place in it.

Stalin's plan for industrial expansion was based on the Five-Year Plans, the first of which began in October 1928. However, it was immediately decided that the goals of the plan could be achieved within four years, and quotas and expectations were adjusted accordingly. In order to pay for this industrialisation, which in essence meant building many industries from scratch, Stalin ruthlessly looked to the peasant class of farmers who had prospered so much through the years of the NEP. At the heart of his plan was collectivisation with upwards of twenty villages gathered together into collective farms and told what to produce by state planners who in turn took their orders from Moscow. No payment was made if production was affected by failed harvests, and heavy penalties, including in some cases the use of summary execution, were imposed for hoarding.

A major aim of the collectivisation process was the elimination of the Kulaks. These were the richest class of peasants who had profited most from the NEP. The Kulaks were thrown off their land but excluded from the collective farms. Many were forced into the Siberian labour camps run by the Gulag, an organisation founded in 1930 in order to tighten repression and state control, with about a million dying as a result. Collectivisation was meant to pay for the mass industrialisation programme that was at the heart of the first Five-Year Plan. But it led to chaos in agricultural production, with widespread inefficiency and corruption meaning that less food was getting to the cities than ever before. However, no one dared to question its probity because of Stalin's fixation with it, and collectivisation continued even after it had resulted in a massive famine in 1933, centred on the Ukraine, which killed about two million people.

The industrial drive of the first Five-Year Plan began with an attack on a section of the community, the professionals and specialists such as engineers and architects that Stalin felt had not served the revolution with enough vigour. The early success of the Five-Year Plan was used as proof of their previous disloyalty, despite the fact that the point at which the plan began was so far behind that of the developed economies in Western Europe and the USA that any early improvement was bound to be impressive.

Huge dam, canal and electrification projects drew inevitable publicity, and new cities grew up in coal and iron ore regions in the Ural Mountains and further south in the Don Basin. The human costs of this rapid expansion were, as with collectivisation, huge, but again few were willing to question the man whose paranoia was about to unleash the purges of the 1930s.

The second Five-Year Plan was aimed at boosting consumer production, but came at the height of the show trials of the Great Purge. Consequently, managers and planners fell over themselves to fudge returns and create the image of success, prosperity and improvement. In theory, therefore, the USSR was expanding rapidly and efficiently. In reality, Stalin's Terror was to create an inefficient and corrupt bureaucracy, the legacy of which was to dog Soviet leaders in the future from Khrushchev to Gorbachev. It also meant that after the collapse of the USSR at the end of the 1980s, the citizens of the fifteen emerging republics were to continue to suffer from the mistakes that three generations of Soviet repression, intimidation, false imprisonment and misrule had brought.

China in the 1920s and the World in 1929

The same could perhaps be said of the people of China who laboured under the rule of Chairman Mao for twenty-eight years. He came to power eventually in October 1949, but not before thirty years of fighting against the Northern Warlords, the Japanese and the Nationalists who all vied for power in the aftermath of the collapse of Imperial China in 1911.

Power for a short time was held by an army elite, but by 1918, Sun Yat-sen, the leader of the Nationalist Party who had been instrumental in the collapse of the old regime in 1911, was having some success in expanding from his power base in the south. From there, he appealed for foreign aid from the West, but when this was not forthcoming, he sent Chiang Kai-shek, a young and ambitious officer in his army, to Moscow for talks with the new communist regime there. Chiang's visit was a success and on his return he worked with Soviet advisers to formulate a strategy for the battle ahead. In 1924, Sun Yat-sen announced that as part of this strategy, the communists under Mao would join in an alliance with his forces against the Northern Warlords who by the early 1920s had come once again to dominate northern and central China.

Chiang took over the party leadership in 1925 on the death of Sun Yat-sen and immediately ordered plans to launch the Northern Expedition. This drove his army northwards towards his enemy's strongholds around Beijing, which was finally captured in 1928, and the warlords were forced to accept the authority of Chiang's government in Nanking. Chiang's support came mostly from business and commercial interests whose profits were being ruined by the outmoded, violent and antiquated policies of the warlords.

The communists, on the other hand, were supported by the peasants who increasingly flocked to them, attracted by the promises of land and liberation. Indeed, support from the peasants grew so quickly that by 1927 Chiang was clear that it was the communists, and not the warlords, who now posed the main threat to his rule. So as a result, he severed all links with his former allies and ordered a crackdown that led to the deaths of some 250,000 communists and trade unionists. In the early 1930s, the power of the Nationalists forced Mao and the communists to embark on the Long March. However, the peasants never forgot the communists' commitment to them, and eventually it was Mao, and not Chiang, who in the end was to rule over them.

At the end of the decade, Britain still remained the world's greatest colonial power and retained an empire on which the sun never set. France, too, held onto a pre-eminent position in world affairs, but the USSR under Stalin and the USA under three different Republican presidents were also beginning to stake their claim to superpower status. Japan was beginning to extend its influence in the Far East although Europe still dominated the political landscape as it continued to do for much of the century. Indeed, it was the expansionist policies of Germany at the heart of Europe that were soon once again to plunge the world into war.

In Europe, North America and in the British dominions, capitalism and liberal democracy flourished throughout the decade that followed World War One. But soon events that followed a disaster in New York in October 1929 threatened their very existence. This disaster led to a trade depression that ruined millions of lives across the world and destroyed the very credibility of the capitalist, liberal democratic creed. This disaster was the Wall Street Crash that broke the peace that had characterised the last years of the decade. Thus, there began, almost halfway between 1918 and 1939, the long and tortuous journey towards a new and even costlier world war.

The Road to War
The 1930s

October 1929
(The Wall Street Crash)
to
September 1939
(The Invasion of Poland)

The Wall Street Crash, the Great Depression and Roosevelt's New Deal

The Rise of the Aggressor States and the Invasion of Manchuria

The Rise of Hitler and the Nazification of Germany

China and the Long March

The Response to the Rise of Hitler and the Invasion of Abyssinia

The Great Purge in the USSR

The Spanish Civil War 1936-39

The Abdication Crisis and the Adoption of Appeasement

War in the Far East and the Anschluss between Austria and Germany

German Claims in Czechoslovakia and the Munich Conference

Nazi Pressure on Poland and the Coming of War

The Wall Street Crash, the Great Depression and Roosevelt's New Deal

The first few years of the 1930s were dominated by the Great Depression that followed the Wall Street Crash. Soon people across the world became weary of the unemployment and the poverty that this brought, and they came to question the political and economic systems that had allowed them to happen. This, in turn, brought about a crisis in confidence for the liberal democracies that had emerged so victoriously from World War One and that had so successfully managed to contain the growth of communism in the 1920s.

Fuelled by the massive growth of the US economy, these democracies had by the end of the decade enjoyed a period of enormous economic prosperity and political stability. However, the confidence and self-belief in liberal democracy and in capitalism that this had brought soon came to an abrupt end and, as the Depression deepened, millions began to listen to those who offered new and different messages of hope. Although these challenges were to come from both sides of the political divide, it was generally those from the right that were to prove most successful. The right believed in strong totalitarian, nationalist government, backed up by a powerful military that offered total loyalty to an omnipotent leader.

In particular, this looked to the example of Adolf Hitler and Nazi Germany, and its success was so great that as many as fourteen countries in Europe that had been ruled as liberal democracies in 1919 had succumbed to some type of new fascist organisation by the time of the Munich Agreement in 1938. This movement to the right also occurred in the Far East where the successful imperial expansion of the militarists swept Japan onto the Asian mainland. These parties of the right became popular because they offered visionary images of national rebirth and rejuvenation. They offered promises of military conquest, new empires and the restoration of national pride. But most of all, their initial appeal lay in their ability to deal with the ravages of the Great Depression.

The origins of the Wall Street Crash can be found in the artificial nature of the boom that had been enjoyed by the USA throughout the 1920s. Banks had lent to almost anyone and, so long as the boom persisted and confidence remained high, all continued to be well, with many mortgaging all they possessed so as not to lose out on the enormous profits on offer. However, all this changed on 24 October 1929 when analysts and investors at the Stock Exchange on Wall Street in New York began to worry about the future of a number of large companies. Eager to realise early profits, many of these investors began to dump their stock in these companies, creating a panic from which the world was not to recover for a decade.

In the week that followed, thousands more joined the frenzy, desperate to sell fast-depreciating stock and, as prices continued to plummet, millions of investors, both corporate and individual, were left bankrupt. The effects of the Wall Street Crash were soon also to be felt outside the USA, with the world economy literally grinding to a halt. Capital from the USA had been crucial in helping rejuvenate markets and confidence in Europe in the aftermath of World War One, and millions of US dollars had been lent in the form of short-term loans. Crucially, though, much of this loaned money had not been used to rebuild broken economies within Europe. Bankers and governments in many countries had chosen instead to reinvest it back into the booming US economy, happy to be a part of the speculative boom on the other side of the Atlantic.

After the Crash, and taking their lead from the USA, these governments now shrank back into the protection of isolated economic nationalism. Eager to protect their economies and their people from further losses, tariffs on foreign goods were quickly raised and restrictions on the employment of foreigners and the export of domestic capital were hastily adopted. This soon created a downward spiral in world trade and, as the Depression deepened, the world economy became increasingly driven by fear and uncertainty. The political and economic system that had claimed to guarantee prosperity, progress and peace in the 1920s now seemed ever more at a loss to answer the needs of the 1930s.

The Crash led to a shortage of capital in the USA that forced US banks to recall money lent to Europe during the previous decade. Among those countries most badly affected by this was Germany whose size and position at the heart of Europe meant its economic well-being was of central importance. Germany was soon deep in depression, dragging down with it the economies of the rest of central Europe. Britain and France, who depended on German reparation payments to repay their US loans, were also immediately affected. Their relative decline led, in turn, to a reduction in their ability to import, devastating the economies of their imperial dependencies and dominions.

Between 1929 and 1931, the world slipped deeper and deeper into the Great Depression as the volume of world trade was cut in half. Various attempts to solve the problem were made, and in 1931 President Hoover announced the suspension of war debt repayments for one year to allow those countries in Europe on the brink of bankruptcy time to sort out their problems. However, when it became clear after this period that these debtor nations were still in need of help, the US government steadfastly refused to join negotiations in Switzerland to discuss the economic future, and, when six of these nations defaulted from payment in December 1932, the USA retaliated by making it illegal for US citizens and institutions to invest in government bonds issued by these countries.

In economic terms, the response of governments around the world to the Great Depression tended to follow the accepted economic rules of the day. Governments were expected to implement deflationary policies that demanded the maintenance of stocks of hard money in the form of gold reserves. This meant that budgets had to be balanced with no more being spent than was earned. In order to achieve this, cuts had to be made and these most usually hit public spending hardest. Millions of people with no jobs now found themselves with no, or at least much less, social welfare.

It was generally accepted that these policies should be followed until the economic storm had been weathered and confidence once again restored. Deflationary economic policies in times of slump had been followed since the rise of the industrial capitalist economies in the nineteenth century, and most governments across the world saw no alternative but to follow them at the beginning of the Great Depression. Generally, this was done with the most spectacular lack of success.

One of the first politicians to look for new solutions was President Franklin D. Roosevelt who unveiled his New Deal in 1932. Roosevelt was a pragmatist and was willing to experiment with a number of approaches to aid recovery. He collected together a team of experts from all walks of life who advised him to increase the power of the government to plan the economy in order to deliberately unbalance the budget. This was done to create jobs. Claiming that the USA 'had nothing to fear but fear itself', he presided over a flood of Congressional bills in the first hundred days of his administration that aimed to restore confidence in the system that had let so many down since 1929.

At the same time, the USA had to deal with the Dust Bowl, a series of dust storms that decimated the mid-West prairie states throughout the decade. The land in these states, which had in the nineteenth century been called the Great American Desert, had been increasingly brought under the plough in the 1920s, and record wheat harvests had been recorded in 1931. However, this had also resulted in over-farming, with the loss of a secure and fertile topsoil coinciding with a series of droughts that lasted until 1939. The result of the Dust Bowl was that millions were forced to flee the region, with many migrating westwards to California where they were not always welcome.

As a result of the various problems that faced the USA after the election of Roosevelt, a great number of government-financed organisations, which came to be known as alphabet agencies, were set up. These were given federal money to spend on public works aimed at reducing unemployment. After an initial scare connected with a number of bank closures in early 1933, the efforts of alphabet agencies such as the Tennessee Valley Authority (TVA), the Civilian Conservation Corps (CCC) and the Civil Works Administration (CWA) were eventually successful in putting millions back to work.

A second New Deal was launched in 1935 to deal more specifically with social legislation, and this led to conflict between the administration and the Republican-dominated Supreme Court that resented the continued intrusion of the federal government. Despite these problems, which Roosevelt faced head-on during his second term of office, the New Deal did much to restore confidence, sending thousands back to work and beginning a recovery that was completed during World War Two.

The theoretical and academic foundation for this new interventionist economic practice was provided in 1936 by the British economist John Maynard Keynes. Keynesian economic theory, which was to have such an important impact on post-war, Western economic planning, attempted to see how unemployment, the great social problem of the day, could be defeated. Keynes argued that neither communism nor fascism could do this. Capitalism could, he reasoned, but needed to be adapted in order to eradicate problems connected to the trade cycle, particularly concerning unemployment. This could only be achieved through far greater government intervention.

In the summer of 1931, long before Keynes had published his ideas or Roosevelt had been elected to enact the New Deal, another crisis threatened to plunge Europe even further into depression. This was an exchange crisis that began in May when French bankers withdrew credit from Austria's largest private bank because certain loan obligations had not been met. Fearing that the collapse of the bank would undermine the whole Austrian state, the government acted quickly and ordered that all remaining assets in the bank be frozen.

This led to widespread panic throughout central Europe, with both investors and governments concerned that a general freeze on assets in banks across the region would be introduced. Many investors rushed to withdraw their money and, in order to stem this flow of capital, interest rates across Europe were raised. But this failed to have any real effect on the increasing panic, and governments, faced with the prospect of financial calamity, therefore rushed to take decisive action in defence of national economies.

Before long, the governments of eleven central and eastern European countries, led by Germany, had followed the Austrian example and imposed exchange controls on money leaving their countries. Trade that had been stagnant was harmed even more. Economic depressions connected to the trade cycle had been experienced since the beginning of industrialisation and so were nothing new. But the Great Depression in the early 1930s was unique in its depth, severity and length. Central Europe, which had been slipping further and further into depression and despair since 1929, now teetered on the brink of bankruptcy.

So as more and more factories and businesses closed down and more and more people were forced out of work, bread queues and soup kitchens, itinerant beggars and shanty towns became familiar sights in cities across the world. To these problems, demoralised governments simply did not seem to have any answers. So it was not surprising, therefore, that many people, especially in central Europe where the Great Depression had caused the most extreme hardship, were quick to question a system of government that had let them down so badly.

There were others in different parts of the world suffering from the Depression who also questioned the system of government under which they were forced to live. This was the case in India where Britain had been the dominant colonial power since the eighteenth century. Limited autonomy had been given after World War One, but not enough to satisfy the wishes of either the Indian National Congress, which represented the Hindu majority, or the Muslim League, which represented the minority Muslim population. These two groups had come together to form a coalition against British rule in 1916, and this led initially to the widely supported Non-Cooperation campaign of 1920-22.

As the struggle for Indian independence developed through the 1920s, it was the figure of Mahatma Gandhi who had taken a central role. A series of highly publicised confrontations with the British had allowed him to emerge as both powerful and charismatic, and at the end of 1931 he visited Britain for three months to attend the ill-fated second conference on the future of India. Gandhi's visit was a huge success for him personally, and large and enthusiastic crowds followed him around wherever he went. But his negotiations at the conference table were less successful, and he returned to the subcontinent convinced that Britain was not serious about devolving any real authority to the indigenous population.

As a result, he stepped up his campaign of non-violent civil disobedience that infuriated the colonial authorities and led to his imprisonment on more than one occasion. But despite Gandhi's campaigns and the boycott of any further negotiations, the Government of India Act passed into law in 1935. This was the largest piece of legislation ever to pass through Westminster, and gave limited powers to provincial governments although India as a whole remained bound to Britain and its foreign policy was still dictated by London.

This was not enough for many in India who continued to support Gandhi's campaigns although it was not until the onset of World War Two that any further concessions were forced from Britain. These included a pledge made by Churchill's government that dominion status would be given to India after the end of the war. Later, this pledge was extended and the promise of full independence as soon as hostilities ceased was made.

The Rise of the Aggressor States and the Invasion of Manchuria

While Gandhi wrestled with the problem of Indian nationalism, Europe was continuing to struggle with the Depression and the increase in economic hardship that this brought. One inevitable consequence of this was the growth in support for those who advocated alternative political and economic strategies and of these it was the radical right that was to gain the most.

The fascist parties that soon grew up all over Europe promised strong, centralised, dynamic leadership that would cut through the inertia that had plagued the decision-making of the liberal democracies since 1929. The right was to preach an intoxicating manifesto of strong leadership, stirring nationalism and common sense economics, and it appealed to people in all layers of society, all of whom had endured so much in the years that followed the Wall Street Crash.

Certainly, Mussolini's role in this challenge was important, but it was with the rise of Adolf Hitler and the Nazi Party in Germany that it was to find its focus and direction. Firstly as an opposition leader, Hitler vehemently criticised the Weimar Republic, the Treaty of Versailles and the liberal democracies that had dictated the peace in 1919. Then as its legal chancellor from January 1933, he dealt with the restoration of German self-respect and self-esteem. And then finally as dictator of the Third Reich after the death of President Hindenburg in August 1934, it was Hitler's success in the mid-1930s that gave the fascist doctrine its impetus, credibility and momentum.

Both his critics and supporters alike watched in awe as he successfully rekindled national pride and a confidence in the future by ridding Germany of the constraints of Versailles, rebuilding the German economy and restoring national prosperity. All these successes made it very difficult for those who opposed him to argue against his fascist vision when it was so obviously proving successful for those millions of Germans better off under his rule.

Fascism appealed to the lost soul of Germany, offering a place in a bright future for all those willing to pledge their support to Hitler's Third Reich. It appealed to the working class whose jobs and homes had been taken by the Depression. It appealed to the middle classes who had lost all their savings in the financial crises that had bedevilled Germany since 1918. And it appealed to the industrialists and the ultra-conservatives who saw it as a controllable agent that could be used in their fight against communism. Nearly all sections of German society could feel more secure and better off under the Nazis. As Hitler's prestige grew through the decade, international relations became increasingly dominated by the efforts of the liberal democracies, led by Britain and France, to deal with the challenges laid down by the Nazis.

However, the first challenge from the radical right was not to come from Germany but rather was precipitated by Japan on the other side of the world. At the end of 1931, Japan invaded the northern Chinese province of Manchuria, where it had long held imperial ambitions, following the Mukden Incident. This involved the bombing of the railway at the town of Mukden, an act that was organised by dissident and rogue elements within the Japanese military based in Manchuria. This was then blamed on the Chinese army and used as an excuse for invasion.

Japanese interests in Manchuria had first been formally recognised in the Treaty of Portsmouth of 1905 that had concluded the Russo-Japanese War. This allowed Japan to maintain a military presence along the South Manchurian Railway in order to protect important economic investments there, and between 1905 and the onset of the Great Depression at the end of the 1920s Japanese economic involvement in Manchuria had grown rapidly.

This special interest in Manchuria was accepted by the Western allies in the peace settlement after World War One, which saw responsibility for the administration of the Shandong Peninsula, a key commercial region in Manchuria, transferred to Japan. As a result, a spirit of co-operation in Far Eastern affairs symbolised the relationship between Japan and its World War One allies through much of the 1920s. Occasional disagreements had arisen, and the USA in particular looked to build its strength in the northern Pacific as a counterbalance to Japanese naval expansion.

The pursuit of friendly relations with Japan had indeed seemed to many in the West a prudent precaution, given the terrible political state of China itself.

Torn by the ravages of civil war, China was in perpetual chaos and to diplomats and politicians in London, Paris and Washington, a friendly relationship with Japan seemed to be the wisest way of achieving security in the region.

This attitude was shared throughout the 1920s by Japan itself, which had adopted a more conciliatory attitude towards the West, embracing a Western-style system of government and seeming to turn away from the more militaristic and expansionist policies of the pre-war period. However, despite this spirit of compromise, a large section of Japanese society, led by important elements within the military, continued to be suspicious of European and US involvement in eastern Asia, and remained deeply committed to the notion of a large Japanese colonial presence on the Chinese mainland.

Support for this view grew after Chiang Kai-shek's successful campaign against the Northern Warlords in 1928 had brought a certain amount of stability to the Chinese mainland. This had led to an improvement in relations between China and the USA, which in turn threatened Japanese interests on the mainland. Japanese merchants and traders had already seen their routes to lucrative US markets closed, and they now faced the possibility of losing additional markets in China. Many came to believe that Japan was being forgotten by its wartime allies and, with the onset of the Great Depression in the early 1930s that closed many markets to Japanese goods, clamour for a more aggressive foreign policy increased. Supporters of this point of view considered the military occupation of mainland China as a prerequisite to economic recovery.

The Japanese invasion of Manchuria was completed in February 1932 by an army that acted outside the control and authority of the civilian government in Tokyo. The Chinese government immediately appealed to the League of Nations where the Japanese were swiftly condemned although few practical steps were taken to come to China's aid. In Britain, Ramsay MacDonald publicly condemned this breach by a fellow League member, while in Washington, Japan was similarly criticised, but only in weak and vague terms. The USA had relatively little investment in northern China and was keen to restore the peace that had existed for much of the 1920s. Indeed, some diplomats and politicians on both sides of the Atlantic privately welcomed the invasion, seeing it as a way of working out spheres of influence in the Far East that had become blurred since World War One.

A commission was dispatched by the League of Nations to investigate Chinese claims and it concluded a year later that Japan was at fault and that Manchuria should be governed as a mandate of the League. This decision was immediately rejected by Japan and this was followed by its immediate resignation from the League. In practical terms, little more was done to further China's claim and Article 16 of the League's covenant, which stated that economic and military sanctions should be used against aggressive powers, was never implemented. The whole Manchurian incident enormously boosted the power and the prestige of the military in Japan, which increasingly came to dictate their country's political agenda.

The League's inability to act in defence of Manchuria showed clearly that its commitment to collective security, the guiding principle behind the League that demanded that aggressor nations should be punished for their actions by the collective action of all other members of the League, no longer existed. Britain and France, the two countries most closely associated with the League and collective security, were preoccupied by other factors at the time and Manchuria was not high on either's agenda.

Britain was struggling to deal with a monetary crisis that threatened MacDonald's government, while the attention of the French government was focused on delayed reparation payments and the threat of German rearmament. In any case, neither was willing to spend too much time or energy drumming up support for sanctions that, in all likelihood, would only further damage their own ailing economies.

The invasion of Manchuria dealt a mortal blow to the authority of the League of Nations. By showing that a commitment to collective security as a means of regulating international affairs no longer existed, the League was in essence admitting its own impotence. This message was not lost on the leaders of the fascist parties in Germany and Italy. Mussolini's invasion of Abyssinia and Hitler's orders to step up Germany's rearmament programme soon directly challenged the authority of the League in general, and that of France and Britain in particular.

The result of these challenges was the formal abandonment of collective security and the adoption of appeasement. Soon the League of Nations was to crumble from within as nations clambered over each other to do deals with the dictators. The final episode came with the Munich Conference in September 1938 where Britain, France and, in this instance, Italy gave in to Germany's demands and handed over half of Czechoslovakia. This was a country created at the Paris Peace Conference only nineteen years before, but one which was not even represented at the meeting. The invasion of Manchuria began this process and, as such, can be seen as the first in a long line of events that eventually led to world war in 1939.

The Rise of Hitler and the Nazification of Germany

As the League of Nations attempted to deal with problems in Manchuria, the focus of world attention once again returned to Europe where the Depression was still causing the most enormous suffering. This was nowhere more the case than in Germany where the Weimar Republic was in its death throes. Since the onset of the Depression, no single party had managed to command a majority in the Reichstag, the German parliament, and so, with parliament in disarray, a succession of conservative chancellors had each tried to govern using the presidential decree that, under the constitution of the Weimar Republic, could be used in times of emergency.

However, this increased power had been used to little effect, and by the middle of 1932, with the economy still in tatters and with rival Nazi and communist gangs roaming the streets increasingly inclined to take the law into their own hands, Germany was on the brink of revolution. The political health of the Weimar Republic had not been helped by the reluctance shown by most of the main political parties in Germany to come to its defence. Indeed, the agendas of most were best served by its destruction.

The German communists, the KPD, whose support crucially increased in the elections of November 1932, wanted to see Germany's own proletariat revolution and aligned themselves closely with Stalin's regime in Moscow. The traditional conservative parties on the right had always hated the Republic and agitated for the restoration of the monarchy and the return of the political elites of the Kaiser's day. The Nazis wanted a revolution of their own and argued vociferously that the Weimar Republic was an embodiment of the unjust peace of 1919. So it was only the Social Democrats who placed any importance on the maintenance of the Republic, but their position had been weakened significantly after 1930 when they were removed from power for failing to deal with the Depression.

The success of the communists in the Reichstag elections of autumn 1932, when they gained six million votes to secure a hundred seats, greatly concerned the conservative elite who worked with the new chancellor, von Papen, and President Hindenburg. This elite had seen the polarisation of German politics that the Depression had caused and it was convinced that the threat of a communist revolution was indeed real. As a result, von Papen managed to persuade the ageing president that an alliance with Hitler and the Nazi Party, the largest party in the Reichstag with 196 seats, was the best way to ward off this threat. Von Papen assured Hindenburg that he and his conservative colleagues could harness not only Hitler's charisma but also the organisational power and physical presence of the Nazi Party on the streets.

So after much political manoeuvring in the last months of 1932, Hitler came to power as chancellor of the Weimar Republic on 30 January 1933. He was only one of three Nazis in a cabinet of twelve that was dominated by old-guard conservatives. Von Papen assumed the office of vice chancellor and assured the president that it was he who really retained power. But Hitler had other ideas and within eighteen months had masterminded a Nazi revolution that transformed German society and the German state. The speed, military precision and cast iron determination of this *Gleichschaltung*, or co-ordination, took his opponents completely by surprise, with the political genius of this Nazi Revolution lying in the fact that the apparatus and authority of the German state were subsumed into the Nazi Party and, more importantly, into the person of Adolf Hitler.

So opposition to the Nazi Party came to mean opposition to the German Reich and criticism of the Nazi Party or the Nazi leadership came to mean treason. In this way, legitimacy was given to the armed gangs of the SA, and later the SS, that formed the Nazis' own private army, to the laws that persecuted the Jews and other minorities, and to the concentration camps into which all who opposed Hitler were soon to be sent. All this Hitler achieved in a startlingly short time period and from a power base that was in January 1933 still relatively weak.

Immediately after coming to power, Hitler called an election for early March 1933 and, with his propaganda chief Josef Goebbels at his side, made full use of the state apparatus now at his disposal. He turned on all those who opposed his fascist vision, directing his fiercest attacks on those he held responsible for the failure of the Weimar Republic. Blame was squarely placed on the parties of the centre that had dominated Reichstag politics in the 1920s, but he also took the opportunity to warn once again of the threat of an international, Jewish-inspired communist conspiracy committed to the destruction of the Fatherland.

Hitler's premonition seemed to come true when, within a month of coming to power, the Reichstag building, the government building, in Berlin burnt down on 27 February 1933. A young communist sympathiser was found nearby, and Hitler chose to take this as proof of the presence of the communist plot that he had foretold. Redoubling his attacks on the communists, Hitler gained a presidential decree from Hindenburg that suppressed personal liberty and further concentrated the power of the state in the office of the chancellor.

Despite further bullying and intimidation from the SA, the Nazis were only to gain 44% of the vote in the March election, the last of nine Weimar Republic elections that had been held since 1919. This was despite the fact that the rights and movement of opposition party candidates had been hugely curtailed. This could be put together with a further 10% gained by other supportive parties on the right, but still fell far below the two-thirds majority in the Reichstag that he needed to pass the Enabling Act, which he insisted he needed to make Germany safe from further communist threats. The communists, despite all the censorship and intimidation, had still managed to poll 12% of the vote and win eighty-one seats.

The Enabling Act would give him further dictatorial powers for four years, and was finally passed into law on 23 March 1933 when opposition members in the Reichstag finally gave in to a final ultimatum after three weeks of intense intimidation and threats. Ostensibly, these powers were to be used to protect Germany from revolution from the left, but in reality they were soon used to secure the Nazis' hold on power. The first stage of the Nazification process had been accomplished.

At the same time, Hitler began promoting into government those Nazis from the days of struggle upon whom he could rely. Hitler had dictated his book, *Mein Kampf*, to Rudolf Hess while in prison in 1923 and they had remained close during the years of struggle. Hess was to become deputy führer in 1934. Heinrich Himmler had been in charge of the SS since 1929 and was soon given the added responsibility of the Gestapo, the Third Reich's secret police, while Dr Joseph Goebbels continued as Hitler's principal propagandist.

But it was Hermann Goering, the aristocratic and extrovert World War One flying ace, who had been shot during the Munich *Putsch* in 1923, who was to become Hitler's most trusted lieutenant during these early years of Nazi rule. His enthusiasm and single-mindedness as prime minister of Prussia, the largest of the German states, did much to further the Nazification process not only there but also throughout the German Reich. But the Nazification process did not occur only in the senior ranks. All over the country, Germans were encouraged to join the Nazi Party, and soon success and advancement in all walks of life became dependent upon party membership.

Within nine weeks of coming to power, Hitler had cajoled and bullied his way into a position of massive legitimate power from which he could now expand. Using the Enabling Act for his own ends, he began picking off his opponents at will while always making sure that the interests of the army and big business were kept in mind. As Hitler strengthened his grip on power through the summer of 1933, the KPD and the SPD, as well as the trade unions, were all banned.

This descent into dictatorship was perhaps clear to Albert Einstein who was in California when Hitler came to power in January 1933. Einstein returned to Europe in the middle of 1933, but was never to return to Germany where the campaign against the Jews had already been launched. Jewish teachers, for example, were banned from working in state-run schools as early as 1 April 1933, and on the same day the first of many nationwide boycotts of Jewish shops was organised. Einstein was to spend some time in Belgium and Britain before returning to the USA in October 1933. The world's most famous and esteemed scientist was then to take up a post at Princeton University. He was to work there, and for the US government, until his death in 1955.

By August 1933, communists, social democrats and minorities such as the Jews and the Gypsies were being rounded up and sent to the new concentration camps that were being set up across Germany. The first of these had been set up in the town of Dachau, just to the north of Munich, within weeks of Hitler becoming chancellor, and by December 1933 these new institutions of state control had quickly mushroomed to house around 150,000 enemies and opponents of the new state. It soon became clear to von Papen and his colleagues that they had been outmanoeuvred and that the puppet that they had promised Hindenburg had become the puppetmaster. Hitler was well on his way to becoming the dictator of Germany.

Opposition to the Nazi Revolution in 1933 and 1934 was hampered by Hitler's economic success, with many Germans soon beginning to feel the benefits of Nazi rule. The extreme poverty and depravation of the early 1930s did not immediately disappear, but Hitler did at least offer an alternative to the dithering of the last Weimar chancellors. Hitler threw Germany into a series of high-profile public works programmes of which the building of the autobahn system became the most famous. The propaganda films and the radio programmes that reported these projects depicted Germany literally being driven back to work by the will of Adolf Hitler. This was a message that the Nazis got across so effectively, and this in part was due to the sale of cheap mass-produced radios, which was encouraged by Nazi propagandists. So the listlessness and vacillation of the Weimar years were brushed away, as the rest of the world looked on with a mixture of awe, jealousy and fear.

By June 1934, Hitler had largely completed his Nazi Revolution and had done much to restore German economic prosperity. But he knew that this success had been, in part at least, due to the support that the Nazis had received from the army and from the relatively small class of businessmen and industrialists who ran the German economy. These two elements of

German society had remained outside the control of the Nazi Party although both had benefited from the early changes that the Nazi Revolution had brought.

However, during the early months of 1934, some within these elites had begun to fear that the Nazi Revolution was going too far and that Hitler could not control the radical, anti-capitalist element that had always existed within his movement. This element was most strikingly represented by the SA, the brownshirted stormtroopers who had accompanied Hitler at the abortive Munich *Putsch* in 1923 and who had been ever-present during the struggle that had brought the Nazis to power a year earlier.

The SA represented an important, working-class grassroots section of Nazi support that was growing increasingly vociferous in their demands for more radical reform, and much of the debate within the Nazi movement during the first half of 1934 had centred on how this element should be rewarded. As this debate intensified, the generals and the industrialists looked on anxiously to see if Hitler could maintain authority over his party.

Eventually, it became clear to Hitler and his senior advisers that an impasse in this debate had been reached. At the same time, Hitler came to believe that the preservation of the Nazi state rested on the maintenance of good relations with industry and the army, and that the left wing of the party, and the SA leadership in particular, was damaging this.

In typical fashion, he decided to act quickly and decisively and, on the night of 29-30 June 1934, ordered SS units all over the country to round up hundreds of SA members including its leader, Ernst Röhm. About one hundred of those arrested, including Röhm himself, were murdered as in one clinical move Hitler wiped out the one group who posed a threat to his hold on power. He also used the opportunity to order the assassination of many who had crossed him in the past or who might pose a threat in the future.

Among those to lose their lives were General von Schleicher, the ex-chancellor who was seen as too close to Röhm, and Gregor Strasser, the leader of the Berlin Nazis, who had been a leadership rival in the 1920s. Von Papen was also arrested, having made a speech earlier in the month criticising Hitler's government. His life was spared although two of his closest aides were not so lucky. Von Papen was eventually dispatched to Vienna where he became a compliant ambassador. He was arrested and tried at Nuremberg after the war, but was acquitted.

The Night of the Long Knives, as this night of murder was soon dubbed, effectively silenced what little open opposition still remained in Nazi Germany.

It was also the night when Germany lost its innocence. The industrialists and the generals, whose positions in the Nazi state were guaranteed as a prize for their support, could no longer plead ignorance after the actions of that night. Neither could the majority of other German citizens whose lives continued to improve as a result of the economic policies of the Nazis, but whose liberties were increasingly restricted. To many ordinary Germans, this suppression of personal liberty and the persecution of minorities such as the Jews seemed a small price to pay in return for these other improvements.

Millions of Germans, intoxicated by the flags and insignia, the candlelit processions and the uniforms of the Nazis, chose to ignore the evidence of the Night of the Long Knives and follow Hitler and his demonic dream. Those who opposed him, and there were many brave Germans who secretly did so, lived in a police state dominated by the SS and the Gestapo where the threat of deportation to the concentration camps remained a constant fear.

In August 1934, President Hindenburg died and Hitler combined the position of president and the office of the Chancellor into one new position, Führer of the German Reich. By the middle of 1934, Hitler had completed the first stage in his megalomaniac's plan and become both Germany's head of state and its head of government. The Third Reich, which Hitler promised would rule for 1,000 years, had replaced the Weimar Republic. He had Nazified Germany.

China and the Long March

As the attention of Europe focused on the rise of the Nazis in Germany, the full impact of the Japanese invasion of Manchuria began to have its effect on the rest of China. The failure of Chiang Kai-shek's Nationalist government, the Kuomintang, to deal with the invasion divided even further a country that had already experienced a generation of civil war. Chiang faced renewed opposition from the Northern Warlords against whom he had fought in the 1920s, but it was the communists of the Jiangxi Soviet in the south that he particularly feared. Since gaining control of the area in 1930 and 1931, the communists, under the leadership of an ex-schoolteacher called Mao Tse-tung, had managed to win over the support of millions of peasants.

Under Mao's direction, the Jiangxi Soviet had introduced land ownership schemes, reduced taxes and organised Peasant Councils. In short, it had given economic and political power to a social group that for centuries had had none. Chiang was well aware that the peasant class made up over 95% of China's population and that peasant support for the communists gained in Jiangxi might spread to the rest of China. As a result, he had ordered a series of extermination campaigns against the communists that proved generally ineffective until 1934 when his German military advisers suggested a blockade of the entire region. By the middle of 1934, this had severely weakened Mao's forces and Chiang's Nationalist army was preparing for a final offensive.

As the Nationalist forces slowly tightened their stranglehold, Mao and his military commanders began to make hasty plans for a mass retreat from Jiangxi. By October 1934, these plans had been finalised, and an army of 100,000 began what turned out to be a 6,000-mile-long journey across some of the world's most demanding terrain. This epic struggle came to be known as the Long March and was to take over a year to complete, covering an average of fifty miles a day.

Of the 100,000 soldiers who left Jiangxi, only about 30,000 were to survive the Long March and help re-establish the soviet near Yenan in China's remote North West. Many of the 70,000 who died along the way lost their lives fighting the pursuing Nationalist forces. Many more, however, succumbed to starvation, disease and the elements that challenged Mao and his army throughout their epic journey. The Long March certainly saved Mao's Red Army from annihilation, and it gave him a more secure base from which to lead the struggle against the Nationalists and the Japanese during the next fifteen years. It also offered the communist cause an episode of heroism and patriotism that Mao and his leading propagandists were later to use to great effect.

The Response to the Rise of Hitler and the Invasion of Abyssinia

At the same time that Mao and the Red Army were fleeing from the Nationalists, developments in Germany were being watched with keen interest all over the world. As observers around the world looked at this new, strong political phenomenon at the heart of Europe, it soon became clear that the Nazi Revolution had radically altered the social, political and economic composition of an entire continent. The growing success of Hitler's policies, especially in relation to the economy, increased the acute crisis of confidence that many outside Germany had felt since the onset of the Depression in 1929.

In Britain, recovery was slow, with many areas throughout the decade continuing to suffer the blight of mass unemployment. The most badly affected of these were those that had been at the heart of the first wave of industrialisation a century before. In Jarrow, for example, when the marchers began their long march from the North East to London in 1936, unemployment stood at nearly 70%.

But even with such a high level of unemployment, the fascists in Britain under the leadership of Sir Oswald Mosley, a disillusioned radical aristocrat who had resigned from MacDonald's government at the onset of the Depression in May 1930, were to gain little popular appeal. Mosley's one great effort at dissent, a march in October 1936 through a predominantly Jewish area of the East End of London, the so-called Battle of Cable Street, was to end in farce, and he was soon marginalised as British public opinion swung against Hitler and the whole notion of fascism. Mosley was later interned between May 1940 and late 1943 after which he was to spend the rest of the war under house arrest.

France was still badly affected by the Depression, and a volatile political atmosphere, which included a series of riots in 1934, left it rudderless for much of the decade. Successive governments tried to create a broad-based coalition and these included the government of the Popular Front, which was led by the Jewish politician Léon Blum. Blum was later arrested by the Vichy French authorities, and handed over to the Germans. He was sent, as a result, to the concentration camps but survived and was freed in 1945. These various governments tried to solve the economic problems that the Depression continued to bring and unite the country against the forces of fascism that were mustering on three of its main borders. These attempts eventually broke up amid criticism of the role played by Blum's successor, Daladier, at the Munich Conference.

The USA had chosen for a short time between 1932 and 1934 to work with the international community, but soon once again returned to the path of isolation. Many people in the USA had little time for the problems of the Old World from which they had only just escaped. Later in the decade, however, many in the USA came to see the evil of fascism, and more pointedly its threat to US peace and prosperity, and lent support to the British and Allied cause, especially after the collapse of Europe in 1940. But isolation was not really broken until the Japanese attacked the US Pacific Fleet at anchor in Pearl Harbour, Hawaii, in December 1941.

Despite the continuing problems of the Depression, delegates from sixty nations had gathered in 1932 at a League of Nations Disarmament Conference in Geneva. They met to consider how best to secure a reduction in national arsenals in order to preserve world peace. League delegates were joined by representatives from the USA and the USSR, both of which remained outside the League.

However, the Conference was not a success and negotiations were suspended in October 1933 after the Nazi delegation representing Germany walked out over France's refusal to accept its neighbour's demands for military parity. Germany immediately resigned membership of the League, which had been taken up in 1926, and the Conference, which had met for five months in 1932 and eight months in 1933, fell apart. In 1934, it met for only two weeks.

The Disarmament Conference showed clearly that it was France that felt most threatened by the re-emergence of a strong and rearmed Germany. Twice within living memory, France had been invaded by Germany and many of the more restrictive articles of the Treaty of Versailles, including the demilitarisation of the Rhineland and the limitation of the German armed forces, had been included to protect France from future German attack.

But as the decade progressed and as the Depression persisted, there grew a consensus in many important sections of the international community that, despite these French concerns, some elements of the Treaty of Versailles had been unjust and vindictive, and that Germany should be allowed some release from its most severe articles. Hitler now picked up on this atmosphere of conciliation and ruthlessly exposed the inadequacies, uncertainties and weaknesses of those with whom he negotiated. Goebbels worked hard to portray Hitler as a leader who, while a man of peace and honour, was resolute in his determination to reclaim for Germany all that had been unjustly taken away in 1919.

In this new atmosphere, it soon became clear to many politicians in the West that the continued commitment to disarmament and collective security was not going to constrain the new German regime in its offensive against the Treaty of Versailles. These policies, after all, had been spectacularly useless in dealing with Japanese aggression in Manchuria early in the decade.

In March 1935, Hitler repudiated the disarmament clauses of the 1919 treaty, restored conscription and announced the formation of a German air force, the Luftwaffe. He also announced, to the delight of the generals who had been worried about the role of the army in the new Nazi state, plans to expand the German army to half a million men. Hitler was willing to show quite clearly that the weight of international public opinion meant little to him, confident as he was in the power and the strength of the German economy, the German people and the German state.

In light of these developments in Germany, the governments of Britain, France and Italy became increasingly convinced that any accommodation of Germany within the international community would be best achieved if they could negotiate from a united position of strength and unity. As a result, the leaders of the three World War One allies met at the Italian town of Stresa in

April 1935. The Stresa Conference issued a strong condemnation of Hitler's actions and, by guaranteeing the borders of Europe agreed in 1919, attempted to present a common front against further German aggression. It was hoped that this strong and united front would allow them to challenge Hitler's belligerence and get him to a negotiating table so that they could see what he wanted.

In fact, the Stresa Front proved to be the last act of combined European unity against Nazi Germany. Italy had long felt that it had not been rewarded properly as a victor of the previous world war, and these feelings resurfaced in the months that followed Mussolini's diplomatic success at Stresa. With Italy once again at the centre of the world stage, Mussolini searched for another international victory to cement his stature as national leader, a latter-day conquering Caesar. He knew that the acquisition of empire would give him this, and so he ordered the Italian army to prepare for the invasion of Abyssinia, the East African nation bordering Italian Somaliland that had inflicted a heavy and embarrassing defeat on Italian forces in 1896.

During the months that led up to the Italian invasion, the new British prime minister of the National Government, Stanley Baldwin, found himself trapped in a diplomatically awkward position. He and his cabinet wanted as a point of international law to protect the rights of Abyssinia, an independent nation and a member of the League of Nations. At the same time, however, he saw the need to preserve the strength of the Stresa Front in order to counter the threat of increased German aggression.

In June 1935, Britain's position was further complicated by the signing of the Anglo-German Naval Agreement, a pact initiated by the Nazi government that limited the size of the German navy to 35% of that of its British counterpart. Baldwin was quick to take advantage of this new willingness by the Nazi government to negotiate on international issues and, to an island nation like Britain, the agreement offered important security guarantees.

But in his rush to find common ground with Hitler's government in Berlin, Baldwin was to ignore the fundamental principle agreed at Stresa that negotiations with Germany should be conducted collectively. This point was not lost on Mussolini who viewed the agreement as nothing less than a direct violation of the Stresa accord. As a result, he proved much less inclined to listen to Britain over the issue of Abyssinia when a delegation led by Sir Samuel Hoare, the foreign secretary, and Anthony Eden, the minister of League of Nations affairs, visited Rome. This group had hoped to persuade Mussolini that an invasion of Abyssinia would be unwise and reckless.

Mussolini chose to ignore these warnings and in October 1935 ordered a full-scale invasion from Italian Somaliland. The mechanised and well-equipped Italian army, as a result, rolled into Abyssinia and had little problem defeating the massively outgunned forces of the Emperor Haile Selassie. The League of Nations responded quickly to this violation of Abyssinian sovereignty and economic sanctions were immediately imposed. But it soon became clear that these sanctions were not working although Mussolini was later to admit that a ban on the sale of oil and coal, which were excluded from the sanctions list, would have brought him to the negotiating table within a week. These extra sanctions were never included because Baldwin was worried that they might provoke a war for which Britain was unprepared. France remained in a state of economic and political crisis and was increasingly inclined to follow the British lead.

In this way, Italy managed to ignore the League of Nations, just as Japan had done in 1931 and Germany had done between 1933 and 1935, and escape unscathed. By June 1936, sanctions were dropped and the Italian colonisation of Abyssinia was quietly accepted in the vain hope that this would lead to continued Italian support in the struggle against Germany.

The Great Purge in the USSR

In the USSR, the worsening crisis in Europe and the rise of the aggressive right had persuaded Stalin of the benefits of improved relations with the West. As a result, he had sent delegates to the Disarmament Conference in Geneva and in 1934 he agreed to join the League of Nations. However, despite these forages into foreign affairs, which also led to US recognition for the USSR, Stalin remained deeply suspicious of the outside world all his life and travelled abroad only very rarely.

Stalin spent most of his energy on domestic issues and, having dealt with the worst aspects of Soviet economic inefficiency in the early 1930s, turned his attention to cementing his position as leader of party and state. This was done in a series of ruthless purges, which began in 1934 and which lasted throughout the decade, beginning a reign of terror that claimed the lives of millions and touched every city, town and village in the country. In their brutality and inhumanity, Stalin's purges were every bit as appalling as the Holocaust orchestrated by the Nazis a few years later.

This campaign of terror against the Soviet people culminated in the Great Purge that ripped through all sections of Soviet society between 1936 and 1939. This began with a series of dramatic show trials aimed at purging members of the old Bolshevik Party and Red Army hierarchy who had survived from Lenin's day. These trials led to a stream of high-level politicians and military heroes willingly admitting their guilt in public and going to their deaths begging Stalin's forgiveness. Whether motivated by the fear of further torture, a misguided hope for clemency or the belief that an admission of guilt would in some way protect their families from persecution, these confessions were used by Stalin's hand-picked prosecutors to throw their net still wider.

Between 1936 and 1939, over half the delegates who had attended the Communist Party Congress in 1934 and over 70% of the members elected to the party's Central Committee in the same year were executed. Eight generals who had served since the Civil War were shot in 1937 as were all the admirals serving in the Soviet navy. Over half the Red Army's middle-ranking officers were arrested at some time in the period up to 1939.

Many of these men who had faithfully served their country since the 1920s and before subsequently found themselves in front of the firing squad. This decimation of the Red Army was keenly noted in Berlin where military advisers close to Hitler were already preparing plans for the invasion of the USSR that was to push the German empire far into Eurasia. They could not believe that Stalin was weakening his nation's defences so dramatically, and so pointlessly.

But the purges did not only affect the military and those high up in the party hierarchy. They were also to affect many ordinary people throughout the Soviet empire, with millions forced to move to the new centres of industry being developed by the Five-Year Plans. Many more were thrown into new labour camps that were springing up all over Siberia, run by the Gulag. This campaign of terror was directed most violently against the Kulaks, the class of rich peasants that Stalin aimed to eliminate.

It is difficult to determine exactly why Stalin found it necessary to unleash the purges with such fury, ferocity and violence. His authority over the USSR had been absolute since 1928, and there can be no doubt that he could have dealt with any criticism or ideological differences within the communist hierarchy in a far less severe but far more efficient manner. The purges did the most enormous political, economic and military damage, and in the end seemed to serve little apparent purpose. But despite his absolute control over the country, Stalin remained a paranoid figure throughout his life and it was this paranoia that lay behind his motives. Even twenty years later as Stalin lay dying in his Moscow bed, he was having evidence collected that was to be used to launch one final purge against the people of the USSR.

The Spanish Civil War 1936-39

As prosecutors in Moscow began the first trials of the Great Purge, the Abyssinian crisis was leading to the break-up of the Stresa Front. The major result of this was the development of stronger ties between Britain and France while, at the same time, Italy and Germany were pushed closer together. In the 1920s, many foreign policy decisions made in London and Paris had been shaped by a deep fear of communism. By the mid-1930s, this had changed dramatically and restraining fascist and Nazi aspirations was fast becoming the central issue taxing British and French politicians and diplomats.

With the break-up of the Stresa Front and the emergence of this new alliance system within Europe, a focal point for the battle between the Western liberal democracies and the fascist states emerged with the outbreak of civil war in Spain. For ten weeks before hostilities began in the summer of 1936, Manuel Azaña had led a left-wing Popular Front government that had introduced a series of reforms that attacked many traditional elements in Spanish society that included the army, the traditional business elite and the Roman Catholic Church.

During this time, Azaña had earned himself powerful enemies and in July a rebellion broke out in Spanish Morocco led by General Francisco Franco, the colonial army chief there. However, when it became clear that he wasn't gaining the support on the mainland he needed to sustain the coup, Franco turned to the fascist regimes in Germany and Italy for aid. Both were happy to see the spread of fascism onto the Iberian Peninsula and were quick to oblige. Aid came first in the form of air transport that helped Franco transfer his forces from North Africa to Spain, but soon his Nationalist forces were also to gain the full-time support of a detachment from the German Luftwaffe and over 50,000 Italian ground troops.

With this extra support, Franco was quickly able to gain control over much of southern and western Spain. Nationalist successes under Franco's leadership continued through 1937 with the notable exception of the defeat of a predominantly Italian force at Guadalajara. Further German and Italian assistance led to more Nationalist advances, and by the end of 1938 the forces of the Republican government, increasingly starved of Soviet money after 1937, had been split in half by a decisive Nationalist advance through the centre of the country.

These successes particularly weakened the Republicans in Catalonia, and Barcelona, the Catalan capital, fell in January 1939. In the aftermath of this loss, the end was near and Azaña knew it. As a result, he accepted defeat and moved into exile in France. In March 1939, the Nationalists took Madrid and Franco was proclaimed head of state. The Spanish Civil War ended with another decisive victory for fascism, with Franco and his Falangist movement going on to rule Spain until his death in 1975.

The Spanish Civil War was fought with the vigour, cruelty and disregard for human dignity that so often typifies civil war. Mass executions, torture and assassination became commonplace as both sides worked to maintain their power bases. In Nationalist areas, trade unionists and suspected left wingers were summarily executed. In Republican areas, the same fate awaited those who opposed the government in Madrid. Perhaps in excess of 100,000 people lost their lives in this way. These were in addition to over half a million others who were killed on the battlefield.

The most infamous incident of the war, and one which was so graphically illustrated by Pablo Picasso's painting, was the German bombing of the Basque village of Guernica in April 1937. The village was first attacked and left in ruins as wave after wave of bombers pounded this Republican stronghold. But the terror was not over as a series of machine gun attacks were launched from a new wave of dive-bombers, killing most of the fleeing villagers as they tried to hide in the surrounding fields. The bombing of Guernica came to symbolise the savagery and inhumanity of the whole war.

For Britain and France, the Spanish Civil War exploded the notion that an alliance of the Stresa powers against Nazi Germany was a sensible political strategy. Throughout the war, relations between the Axis powers, Germany and Italy, had grown closer and closer while once again Britain and France seemed to have few answers to counter the threat of further fascist encroachment on the continent of Europe.

At the outbreak of the war, they had set up a Non-Intervention Committee that all the main European powers had joined. It was hoped that this would isolate the war in Spain from the wider political and diplomatic crisis afflicting Europe, but Germany and Italy openly ignored the committee and left it two months after the bombing of Guernica. If the Spanish Civil War can be seen in a wider context as a battle of ideologies between fascism and liberal democracy, it is a battle that was clearly won by the powers of the former.

The Abdication Crisis and the Adoption of Appeasement

Britain's international status was not helped by a constitutional crisis at home that shook the country to its core. For a number of years, newspapers abroad, and especially in the USA, had been full of rumours of a liaison between the Prince of Wales and an American divorcée called Wallis Simpson. The two were reported to have spent long periods travelling together through Europe and, although news of this affair had largely been kept from the British public, it was widely reported in London's elite society.

Indeed, as early as 1934 the prime minister was made aware of the prince's intention to marry Mrs Simpson after the formalities of her divorce had been completed. As a result, efforts had been made to overcome this difficult constitutional problem for some time before his succession to the throne in January 1936. One suggestion would have allowed a morganic marriage to go ahead that would have denied Mrs Simpson, by act of parliament, the right to be called queen and deny any children from the marriage any rights to the throne.

However, Baldwin believed that it was the marriage itself, compromising as it did the king's position as head of the Church of England, that was the real problem. But the king, who had built up strong support and loyalty around the country as a result of his travels as Prince of Wales during the worst years of the Depression, remained determined to marry and reaffirmed this commitment to the prime minister at the time of Mrs Simpson's divorce in October 1936. This was steadfastly opposed by Baldwin and most of his senior cabinet colleagues and so, when news of this crisis finally broke in the British press early in December, the king was left with a clear choice between his crown and his fiancée.

On 10 December 1936, King Edward VIII chose the latter, abdicating his throne in favour of his younger brother, the Duke of York. He had been king for less than a year. He spoke to the nation the following day of his decision to marry 'the woman I love', before leaving for France where he wed Mrs Simpson the following year. He was created the Duke of Windsor on the day after he left England, and was to serve as governor of the Bahamas during the war period before settling in Paris on his return in 1945. After his death in France in 1972, his niece, Queen Elizabeth II, made arrangements for his body to be brought back to Britain for burial at Windsor.

The Abdication Crisis came at a time when both Britain and France were diplomatically very much on the defensive. In Abyssinia, in Spain and with the reoccupation of the Rhineland, their vacillation and lack of authority had led to major setbacks. They had endured the 1936 Berlin Olympics, which had been the first-ever major sporting event to be televised live, that Hitler had used so successfully to advertise the success of fascism in general and of German Nazism in particular. This was despite the embarrassment caused by Jesse Owens, the African-American athlete who won four gold medals, and by nine other African-American athletes and sixteen Jewish competitors who also ended up winning medals.

An already grave situation deteriorated still further in November 1936 when three separate incidents confirmed the new spirit of fascist co-operation. Firstly, the Rome-Berlin Axis, which brought Germany and Italy even closer together, was signed. Secondly, the German and Italian governments recognised Franco's Nationalist government in Spain. And thirdly, the Anti-Comintern Pact, which brought together the fascist forces of Europe and the militarists of the Far East, was agreed by Germany and Japan.

So there were clearly a number of problems that faced Neville Chamberlain when he took over from Stanley Baldwin as British prime minister in May 1937. Chamberlain had been a member of the cabinet since 1931 and had seen at close hand the problems that the rise of Hitler and the fascist right had brought. Like Baldwin before him, he was certain that Hitler could be reasoned with, and so he made it his mission to instigate a dialogue that would restore peace between the major belligerents of World War One.

Events in Spain, he argued, were graphic proof of what could happen if diplomacy broke down. As a result, he embarked upon a foreign policy initiative that endeavoured to find out what Hitler wanted, reach a compromise acceptable to both sides and thus create a peaceful and prosperous continent in which both political ideologies could live side by side. This policy of appeasement, begun by Baldwin and accelerated by Chamberlain, was to dominate British and French foreign policy until March 1939 when it was eventually abandoned after the promises made at Munich in September 1938 were broken and German forces marched into Prague.

After the years of vacillation and dithering, Chamberlain soon found that there were many both in Britain and abroad who supported the dynamic and energetic manner in which he, in close partnership with his French counterpart Edouard Daladier from 1938, attempted to conduct affairs with Hitler. Since the onset of the Depression, there had been a general admission by many in Britain, and some in France, that the Treaty of Versailles needed to be revised, and many had come to believe that Hitler's unilateral decision in 1935 to break with the Treaty was not entirely unreasonable. Indeed, many openly admired the manner in which Hitler had rebuilt Germany since 1933, and thought it unjust for the allies of World War One to stand in the way of this German progress.

Nazi propagandists worked hard to develop this image of Hitler claiming back what was rightfully Germany's while, at the same time, portraying him as a man of peace and the father of the nation. This was most graphically portrayed in the 1935 film, *Triumph of the Will*, directed by Hitler's favourite, Leni

Riefenstahl, which chronicled Hitler's triumph at the 1934 Nazi Party Rally in Nuremberg. For Hitler, these were the years when his international prestige was at its height and those who visited him to see the success of the Third Reich included the Duke and Duchess of Windsor and the British prime minister from World War One, David Lloyd George.

In this atmosphere of peace and reconciliation, many chose to support Chamberlain in his belief that it was possible to reason with Hitler and came to see opponents of appeasement, such as Winston Churchill, as warmongers. Many across Europe came to hope that appeasement would find a way to accommodate Hitler's Germany within the world community and secure a sustainable and lasting peace.

However, Chamberlain and his supporters were not to know that even as Hitler was entertaining his international guests at his retreat in the Bavarian mountains, he was secretly preparing for war. Central to his ambitions had always been the establishment of a large German empire in the East, and his plan of eastward expansion had always revolved around a war against the USSR that would give *Lebensraum*, or living space, to the German people. It was a plan of ethnic expansion about which Hitler had first written in *Mein Kampf* in 1923, and was to be prosecuted at the expense of the Slavic peoples of Eastern Europe.

These plans for war were confirmed at a meeting between Hitler and his senior military advisers in November 1937. The minutes of this meeting were recorded by one of Hitler's military aides, Colonel Friedrich Hossbach, and so have come to be known as the Hossbach Memorandum. The memorandum clearly confirms how important a war of expansion into the East was to Hitler's planning and, further, that he was well aware that Germany's rearmament programme would not allow this to happen until 1940 at the earliest. The minutes then go on to show that he intended to embark on an aggressive diplomatic campaign to bully as many of Germany's neighbours as possible into submission to Nazi domination. In this way, he hoped to gain as much territory in central Europe as possible without provoking a full-scale European war for which Germany was unprepared. This was the goal Hitler set himself in 1937, and so the conviction held by Chamberlain and many others that Hitler was a reasonable international statesman who merely wished to return Germany to its rightful place in the European political order proved wholly incorrect.

War in the Far East and the Anschluss between Austria and Germany
In Europe, the end of 1937 came and went quietly with some hope for a more peaceful future. The same cannot be said for the Far East where tension between

China and Japan in Manchuria finally exploded into full-scale war. This began when the Japanese claimed that soldiers of the Nationalist army of Chiang Kai-shek had fired upon their troops on the Manchurian border and China was promptly invaded. With the Japanese army quickly sweeping southwards, the people of China, who had already endured nearly three decades of internal strife and civil war, were again to suffer.

This was nowhere more the case than in Nanjing, the old imperial capital, which suffered terribly in a six-week reign of terror following its capture by the invading Japanese army in December 1938. This so-called 'Rape of Nanjing' led to the massacre of between 200,000 and 300,000 of its occupants. The response of the League of Nations, which by this time had become nearly powerless and was desperately trying to reinvent itself as a humanitarian, non-political body, was practically non-existent. It merely called upon members to apply sanctions against Japan unilaterally.

Those European nations who still belonged to the League were more concerned with curbing the aggression of Hitler nearer to home, with the early months of 1938 dominated by the *Anschluss*, the union between Austria and Germany. For a long time, this had been an important element in Hitler's political agenda and, as an Austrian himself, it was one close to his heart. Hitler had used Germany's political and geographical presence to put pressure on successive Austrian governments since his arrival at the German Chancellery in 1933, and there can be little doubt that he was aware of the coup attempt by Austrian Nazis in July 1934 that resulted in the assassination of Engelbert Dollfuss, the Austrian chancellor. Dollfuss himself had run a right-wing, authoritarian regime since 1932, but had made it clear that his government had no intention of allowing any union with Germany.

Further diplomatic pressure followed and in 1936 the new chancellor, Kurt von Schuschnigg, was forced into an agreement that aligned the foreign policy of Austria to that of its larger neighbour. This coincided with a period when Hitler got rid of a number of his most senior generals, including General Ludwig Beck, the leader of the army since 1935, and replaced them with men who were much more aggressive, ruthless and pro-Nazi, and, as a result, much more willing to fall in with Hitler's plans for eastward expansion.

Hitler clearly hoped that this unceasing pressure would result in the Austrian government capitulating to the Nazis. Indeed, pressure did mount on Schuschnigg's government to such an extent that, after a tense meeting with Hitler in Berlin in February 1938, he was forced to accept Nazi representation in his cabinet that included Arthur Seyss-Inquart, a vociferous supporter of the

Nazis who became minister of the interior. Seyss-Inquart was to go on to run Austria as a province of Greater Germany after the *Anschluss*, before being transferred to the Netherlands after its fall to the Nazi *Blitzkrieg* in May 1940. He was later executed at Nuremberg.

However, Schuschnigg was not willing to accept this Nazi infiltration without a fight and announced that a plebiscite would be held to decide the question of the *Anschluss*. He was confident that the majority of Austrians would vote to retain their independence from Nazi Germany. But Schuschnigg's brave attempt to call Hitler's bluff and so preserve Austrian sovereignty in fact led to its early demise. Hitler could not be certain that a plebiscite would vote for the *Anschluss*, and so he ordered the invasion before the people of Austria had the opportunity to vote.

This invasion was carried out on 12 March 1938 and caught the Austrian government by surprise. Hitler had been very wary in the days running up to this, but was left staggered by the positive reaction of the Austrian people who took to the streets to welcome his invading troops. A plebiscite held under the strict control of the new Nazi regime run by Seyss-Inquart was hastily organised, with 99% voting in favour of the union. Despite opposition to the *Anschluss* from abroad, Hitler in March 1938 contemptuously tossed aside a crucial element of the Treaty of Versailles.

France historically had most to lose from such a union and was forthright in its protests. But it was caught at a time of internal paralysis and little was done to co-ordinate the country's response. Britain objected to this violation of the 1919 Treaty, but Chamberlain's government was increasingly concerned about provoking a war in Europe when relations with Japan in the Far East were at such a low ebb. The idea of a war in Europe and the Far East was enough to convince Chamberlain that more dialogue was needed. Only the Nationalists in Spain and Italy, which had fallen out with its Stresa allies over Abyssinia, offered their support to the newly enlarged German empire.

German Claims in Czechoslovakia and the Munich Conference

With the Axis alliance made stronger by the *Anschluss*, Europe plunged further into crisis. Chamberlain's response was to try to drive a wedge between Hitler and Mussolini, and negotiations were opened that eventually saw Britain accept Italian sovereignty in Abyssinia in return for the Italian withdrawal from the fighting in Spain. But these negotiations led to the resignation of Anthony Eden, the foreign secretary, who bitterly opposed his prime minister's continuing adherence to appeasement. Winston Churchill, who had long opposed the government's foreign policy from the backbenches of the House of Commons, also shared this view. As the crisis deepened, support for Churchill increased.

The British and French governments hoped that the negotiations with Italy would leave Mussolini more inclined to take their side in the negotiations soon to take place over German claims in Czechoslovakia. The state of Czechoslovakia, which was now surrounded on three sides by the new Greater Germany created by the *Anschluss,* was a creation of the Treaty of Versailles and its destruction was central to Hitler's plan for *Lebensraum* and the eastward expansion of the German empire.

But Czechoslovakia had developed into a well-organised, democratic nation state that enjoyed the security of treaties with both France and the USSR that guaranteed its borders. It was going to be more difficult to take over than Austria. However, Nazi supporters in the Sudetenland, the region of Czechoslovakia bordering Austria and Germany in which most of the three and a half million ethnic Germans lived, had for a number of years been agitating for closer links with Germany.

In the months following the *Anschluss,* Hitler was able to use the disciplined organisation of the Sudeten Nazis to whip up unrest there against the government of President Eduard Beneš in Prague. The Czechoslovakian government was portrayed as a tyranny, and local Nazi leaders claimed that the right of self-determination was being denied to the Sudeten Germans. Countless anti-Beneš demonstrations were orchestrated all over the Sudetenland as Nazi demands for concessions intensified through the summer of 1938.

Beneš was fearful that further intransigence would lead to the invasion of the whole of Czechoslovakia and eventually, giving way to British and French pressure to compromise, he accepted Nazi autonomy in the Sudetenland. When Hitler ordered the Sudeten Nazis to reject this offer in early September, Chamberlain made his most public commitment to appeasement thus far when he flew to Germany and met with Hitler at the latter's mountain retreat. Hitler made it clear at the meeting that autonomy was not enough, and that it was Germany's intention to annex the Sudetenland directly to the Third Reich.

Further frenzied negotiations took place during the following week, with Britain and France working hard to persuade Beneš to sign an agreement to hand over any area of Czechoslovakian territory in which over half the population was ethnically German. On 21 September 1938, Beneš very reluctantly accepted this Anglo-French proposal. However, at a further meeting at Godesberg in the Rhineland on 22 September, Hitler told Chamberlain that his demands had increased and that it was his intention to invade the whole of Sudetenland the following week. He did not intend to hold a plebiscite and there would be no compensation given for any loss of land or property.

This was too much for the Czechoslovakian government that rejected it out of hand and ordered the full mobilisation of its armed forces. France made it clear that it would reluctantly honour its treaty agreements with Czechoslovakia and go to war in its defence. The USSR let it be known that it intended to support the French lead. In Britain, the navy was put on full alert as both the British and French governments warned Hitler that force would be used against him if he did not return to the negotiating table.

For a few days after the Godesberg meeting, it seemed as though war was inevitable. But Chamberlain, in a last ditch effort to prevent an outbreak of fighting, persuaded Mussolini, who he knew was unprepared for a general European war, to make one final intervention with Hitler. As a result, Hitler agreed to postpone the invasion and meet with the Italian leader, Chamberlain and Daladier in Munich on 29 September 1938. Czechoslovakia itself and the USSR, Czechoslovakia's other major ally, were not invited.

The Munich Conference did little more than give some sort of international respectability to Germany's invasion plans. The Sudetenland was ceded to Germany and territorial demands by Poland and Hungary for areas of Czechoslovakia containing ethnic Poles and Hungarians were also met. In return, Hitler agreed to accept the borders of the rump Czechoslovakia, which were guaranteed in an international treaty signed by the four powers. As a result of the changes forced upon it at Munich, Czechoslovakia lost one third of its population, 70% of its industry and important military defences in the Sudetenland. Germany, on the other hand, had increased its population by ten million as a result of the *Anschluss* and the annexation of the Sudetenland.

On the morning after the conference, Chamberlain met with Hitler privately and signed an agreement that stated that their two countries would never settle disputes with each other through war. On his return home, Chamberlain waved the piece of paper on which this agreement was signed and claimed that the Munich Agreement had brought 'peace in our time'. Public acclaim for both Chamberlain and Daladier seemed to suggest that the price of peace, in the shape of the sacrifice of Czechoslovakia, was considered a price worth paying. However, critics such as Winston Churchill and Anthony Eden argued that Czechoslovakia would not survive for long and predicted that Nazi expansion in central Europe would not stop with the Sudetenland.

War did not come in September 1938 and Hitler was allowed to add another piece to his central European empire. Certainly, the governments of Britain and France used the year between the Munich Conference and the invasion of Poland to step up their rearmament programmes and were, as a result, better prepared for war when it eventually did come a year later. But Chamberlain and the appeasers did not give in to Hitler at Munich in order to buy more time in order to prepare for war. They believed that the Munich Conference had delivered peace and that Hitler's appetite for conquest in central Europe had been satiated.

They were proved wrong when on 15 March 1939 the predictions of Churchill and the other critics of the Munich Agreement came true. On the pretext of restoring order to a country that had endured ceaseless Nazi interference and intimidation during the previous winter, German tanks rolled over the border and the rest of Czechoslovakia was incorporated into the German Reich. Finally, attitudes against Hitler in Britain and France hardened for there could be no possible justification for the invasion of the rump Czechoslovakia that had been left after Munich. Prague, after all, was not a German city. Belatedly, appeasement was abandoned.

Nazi Pressure on Poland and the Coming of War

After the incorporation of Austria, the Sudetenland and rump Czechoslovakia into the Third Reich, Hitler turned his attention eastwards and in particular looked towards the city of Danzig on the Baltic Sea that had been taken away from Germany in 1919. This had become a free city governed by a commissioner appointed by the League of Nations and an elected senate, which since 1933 had been dominated by the Nazis. Under the terms of the Treaty of Versailles, Danzig was separated from the rest of Germany by a narrow strip of land a hundred miles wide, known as the Polish Corridor, that had been created in order to give Poland free access to the sea.

In April 1939, Hitler ordered an increase in Nazi activity in Danzig and on the German-Polish border. He demanded the return of the city to German sovereignty, and also access to road and rail links for Germans across the Polish Corridor. Having observed what had happened to Czechoslovakia in 1938, the Poles refused to bow to early British pressure and negotiate. After a period of uncertainty, which was finally broken by Hitler's withdrawal from the Treaty of Non-Aggression of 1934 that he had signed with Poland, both Britain and France committed themselves to the defence of Poland.

The rift between Britain and France and the fascist states widened when Mussolini ordered the invasion of Albania in April 1939. This brought fascist Italy to the border of Greece whose legitimacy was guaranteed by Britain. In May 1939, the fascist states made efforts to strengthen their alliance system, with Franco's Spain joining the Anti-Comintern Pact and Hitler and Mussolini signing the Pact of Steel that declared a ten-year alliance.

By this time, the USA, which in the interwar period had remained a reluctant participant in the affairs of the Old World, had officially requested assurances from Germany and Italy that they would not attack thirty-one named countries. In Britain, the government announced limited military conscription. This, in turn, led to the German denunciation of the 1935 Anglo-German Naval Agreement.

As international relations in Europe deteriorated through the early summer of 1939, negotiations opened between the governments of the USSR, Britain and France. Soviet support was essential if any stand against Hitler over Poland was to be effective, but Chamberlain's dislike and fear of communism matched those he felt towards fascism. Negotiations were further complicated by Poland's historical fears of an invasion from Russia.

Talks continued fruitlessly into August when Stalin finally lost patience with the powers that had snubbed him at Munich and he ordered Molotov, his new foreign minister, to open talks with Germany. Molotov, as a result, invited Joachim von Ribbentrop, his Nazi opposite number, to Moscow and the outcome of their meeting was the Nazi-Soviet Pact, which was signed on 24 August 1939. This pact included a secret clause that mapped out an agreement concerning Soviet and Nazi spheres of influence in Eastern Europe. In essence, the two foreign ministers agreed that Poland would be split between their two countries.

Hitler hoped that the public announcement of the Nazi-Soviet Pact, as well as a marked increase of pro-Nazi activity in Danzig, would lead to another climbdown by Britain and France and allow him to add one more piece of territory without war. However, Chamberlain responded with a personal letter to the Führer stating that the pact made no difference to Britain's commitment to Poland. But despite this clear statement of British intent and further warnings from Mussolini that Italy was not yet ready for war, Hitler ordered the final preparations for the full-scale invasion of Poland.

On 1 September 1939, six heavily armed Panzer tank divisions, supported from the air by the Luftwaffe, rolled into Poland. Two days later, having received no response to his ultimatum demanding the withdrawal of all German forces from Polish territory, Chamberlain spoke to the nation. In a radio broadcast on 3 September 1939, he announced that he had received no undertaking from the German government that its forces would be withdrawn and so, as a result, a state of war existed between Britain and Germany. A similar announcement was made in Paris a few hours later.

There can be no doubt that the blame for starting the war that was to engulf the world until 1945 must rest firmly with Adolf Hitler. He showed throughout the 1930s a resolution and a determination to achieve the goal of an extended German empire that he had first described in *Mein Kampf*. War was declared in 1939 because Hitler wanted land and raw materials in central and eastern Europe to which he had no right.

The actions of those who chose to appease him between 1935 and 1939 certainly helped him by allowing Germany to take so much territory in central Europe and by allowing the German economy to prepare for war. They were certainly guilty of being tricked by Hitler. They saw certain injustices in the Treaty of Versailles and in many ways, especially up to 1938, they admired the way in which Hitler had transformed and energised Germany since 1933. They came from countries that looked tired and worn out in comparison to the Third Reich, countries that were deeply affected by self-doubt brought on by the Great Depression.

They were also perhaps willing to ignore the political reality of the Nazi state. The Nuremberg Laws in 1935 had taken away the right of citizenship from 600,000 German Jews, and it was clear from then on that a government-authorised programme of Jewish persecution had begun. Jews were submitted to public humiliation, and Jewish shops and businesses were picketed, boycotted and vandalised.

The world had been left with no illusions about this anti-Semitism after the night of 9-10 November 1938. This was the Night of Broken Glass, the *Kristallnacht,* when Jewish shops, businesses and synagogues all over Germany were smashed and burnt in a pogrom that was to take around 400 lives and lead to the imprisonment, in the concentration camps, of about 25,000 German Jews. And the Jews were not the only group persecuted. Members of many other religious, ethnic, social and political groups increasingly faced long terms of incarceration in the new concentration camps that were being built all over the Nazi empire.

Perhaps the appeasers chose to ignore all this because they wanted to believe that a peaceful settlement could be found. Despite all these failings, however, the men who faced Hitler and chose to appease him in the 1930s were not guilty of starting the war. It was a megalomaniac's dream of world domination that started the war that was to bring so much death and destruction to the world over the next six years and that megalomaniac was Adolf Hitler.

War, Peace and War Again
The 1940s

September 1939
(The *Blitzkrieg* on Poland)
to
June 1950
(The Outbreak of the Korean War)

The *Blitzkrieg* on Poland, Auschwitz-Birkenau and the War in the East

The Phoney War and the Elevation of Winston Churchill

The *Blitzkrieg* on France and the Evacuation of Dunkirk

The Fall of France and the Battle of Britain

Britain Alone: September 1940 to December 1941

The Globalisation of War: Barbarossa and the Attack on Pearl Harbour

The Turning Tide: The Battles of Midway, El Alamein and Stalingrad

The Battle for Asia, the Bombing of Europe and the Invasion of Italy

Operation Overlord, D-Day and the Normandy Landings

The Defeat of Germany and the Atrocities of the Concentration Camps

The End of War in the Far East, the Potsdam Conference and the A-Bomb

The Aftermath of War and the Emergence of Two New Superpowers

Retreat from Empire: Post-War Britain and France

The Potsdam Conference, the UN and the Nuremberg Trials

The Origins of the Cold War

The Berlin Blockade and Airlift, and the Cold War Divide

The *Blitzkrieg* on Poland, Auschwitz-Birkenau and the War in the East

As Hitler had long planned, the German attack on Poland in September 1939 was to be a *Blitzkrieg*, a lightning attack, the tactics and strategy for which had been meticulously planned well in advance. These demanded a bombing and dive-bombing campaign by the Luftwaffe along clearly designated corridors of enemy territory followed by an assault by tanks driving in behind this initial aerial assault. The attack was then to be finished off with the deployment of highly specialised and ruthless infantry units that were to come in behind the tanks in order to mop up any last remnants of resistance that might remain.

In early September 1939, these military plans were followed to the letter, with the onslaught by the Luftwaffe followed by six Panzer tank divisions sweeping in from the west in a three-pronged attack. One of these soon took Danzig, with the Polish army quickly brushed aside. In the wake of this initial aerial and tank offensive came the infantry with the quick and decisive victory that Hitler had promised soon duly delivered.

On 28 September 1939, Warsaw surrendered just over four weeks after the initial invasion. Hitler had refused to allow his commanders to besiege the city, but instead insisted that it be reduced to rubble. The speed and ferocity of the Nazi attack took the world by surprise, with the subjugation of Poland taking a mere thirty-six days. Once again, the will of the Führer had prevailed and in Germany his popular acclaim reached new heights.

In Poland, things were very different, with the *Blitzkrieg* ushering in a reign of terror that was to affect the entire population. On 17 October 1939, the Nazi leadership met in Berlin and agreed that Nazi-occupied Poland would be split into three administrative regions. Ominously for the Polish people, responsibility for these was given to the SS that soon began applying the central theme of orders issued by Himmler and the Führer. They were ordered to destroy the historical, racial and cultural notion of Poland.

As a result, small specialised death squads, the *Einsatzgruppen*, recruited primarily from the SS, and with members chosen due to the strength and depth of their devotion to Nazi racist doctrine, were unleashed on Poland, launching an appalling regime of terror on the people of Poland that was to last for the next five years. The *Einsatzgruppen* began their reign of brutality in occupied Poland, but later were to push eastwards after Operation Barbarossa in the summer of 1941 and were responsible for the deaths of some two million people before the end of the war in 1945.

Poland was to be statistically the worst-affected country involved in the war, losing over six million people, which constituted over 15% of its population. The Nazis in Poland were willing to dominate, terrorise and even exterminate the Polish population in search of *Lebensraum*, new living space for the German Reich. In this way, the SS army of occupation that followed behind the tanks in September 1939 made sure that life for those Poles who survived the invasion was very grim indeed, with disease, starvation and summary justice all endured throughout the years of occupation.

In order to carry out the Führer's wishes, Himmler ordered the employment of the most inhumane methods imaginable, with labour camps springing up all over the country as the ferocity of the Nazi regime took effect. Over two million Poles were forced to work in these labour camps during the war in order to supply the needs of the Third Reich, and Poland's large Jewish population was particularly badly treated.

In October 1939, as if as a symbol of the new regime, the concentration camp at Auschwitz-Birkenau was opened. Situated ten miles from the medieval town of Krakow near the border of the former Czechoslovakia, it was initially used as a detention centre for Polish political prisoners. But its location near a good railway network and its discrete position in the countryside away from any large town soon led to its change of purpose.

By July 1941, it had been converted into the Third Reich's largest camp of mass extermination after Himmler had responded to Hitler's order that the implementation of the Final Solution, the plan for the extermination of the Jewish race in Europe, be stepped up. This was formally explained to senior Nazi officials at a conference held in the Berlin suburb of Wannsee in January 1942, chaired by SS General Reinhard Heydrich. At the Wannsee Conference, Heydrich stressed the importance of this new policy, and made it clear that a network of camps, primarily located in Poland, were being set up where the Jewish population of Nazi-occupied Europe was to be sent. It was made clear that none would return.

Such was the success of the logistical organisation that came after Wannsee that over four million of the six million Jews who were to die in the Holocaust were to lose their lives after January 1942. Extra crematoria were built to dispose of the gassed bodies, and Himmler was so intent on his task that the railway track at the Birkenau camp was extended to the doors of the gas chambers themselves. This new efficiency meant that at the height of its destructive capability, Auschwitz-Birkenau could gas and dispose of, through cremation, the bodies of thousands of inmates every day. In time, Jews and other enemies of the Nazi state from all over occupied Europe were sent to the death camp at

Auschwitz-Birkenau, with an estimated figure of around a million of the six million Jews who perished in the Holocaust dying there. To this number can be added a further five million who also lost their lives in the various concentration camps set up across the Nazi Empire.

Much of the experimentation, both organisational and scientific, that culminated in the gas chambers of Auschwitz-Birkenau and the other death camps built for the Final Solution took place during the mass, but secret, euthanasia programme that the Nazi state had set up in 1939. This programme concerned itself with what was euphemistically called the 'racial hygiene' of the German people, the cleansing of the Reich, but which in reality was no more than a programme of state-sponsored murder. In turn, this followed on from an earlier sterilisation programme that was set up immediately after the Nazis came to power in 1933.

The state-sponsored euthanasia programme of 1939 aimed to eliminate a number of different groups of 'undesirables', and these most especially included all of the Reich's physically and mentally handicapped. The programme began with the euthanasia of about 5,000 children, with the parents involved told that their hospitalised child had died from disease or from complications following surgery. Later, six specially set up extermination centres across Germany were used to murder a further 80,000 handicapped adults. Most of these were killed by lethal injection, but experiments during the euthanasia campaign were also conducted into the use of poison gas that was so effectively used later in the Death Camps.

Poles fleeing from the Nazis in the West were to find no sympathy in the East. In accordance with the recently signed Nazi-Soviet Pact, Stalin ordered the Red Army over the border into eastern Poland where it met the advancing German army at Brest-Litovsk, the location of the surrender of the Bolsheviks to Germany in 1917. After further consultation with Berlin, the USSR attacked and soon took over the Baltic states of Latvia, Estonia and Lithuania.

So it was clear that the USSR was now an active ally of the Nazis in Eastern Europe in the winter campaign of 1939-40, and there were some in the British cabinet, led by Churchill, who wanted to consider war against Stalin's colluding regime. But this was opposed by Chamberlain who remained committed to keeping British troops as far away from any conflict as possible. The rationale for this was that Britain had neither the trained men nor the armaments needed to help make any difference. This inaction in defence of Poland, where it was quite clear that British and French help would be needed to stave off Nazi conquest, was bitterly resented there.

Soviet expansion was temporarily halted by a fierce guerrilla war in Finland where the Finnish army used its experience of Arctic conditions to hold off the advancing Red Army through that first winter of the war. One makeshift weapon invented by the Finns during this campaign was the Molotov Cocktail, a crude petrol bomb named after the Soviet foreign minister. It was Molotov who was orchestrating the fight against Finland.

But, eventually the sheer size of the Red Army took its toll, and a peace treaty was signed in March 1940 that ceded large tracts of eastern Finland to the USSR. However, the inadequacy of the Red Army in dealing with the Finns was the confirmation many Nazi observers close to Hitler needed that the Stalinist purges of the 1930s had decimated the Soviet military hierarchy and so the Red Army's ability to prosecute war. Many came to the conclusion that any future expansion eastwards into Soviet territory would be easier than had first been thought.

The Phoney War and the Elevation of Winston Churchill

In the West, the declaration of war had brought few changes and, as 1939 turned into 1940, no bombs fell on Britain or France. As Hitler concentrated on the war in the East, he hoped his show of strength would force Britain and France into a peace treaty that would end the war in the West. This would allow him to concentrate on his central war aim, the establishment of a German empire in the East. But his overtures in October 1939 were rejected by both the British and French governments and, in anticipation of a German attack, France ordered the mobilisation of six million men.

Most of these new French conscripts were sent to reinforce the Maginot Line, the eighty-seven-mile-long series of armed forts along France's common border with Germany that had been built in the 1930s to counter Nazi rearmament. Two hundred thousand British soldiers were sent to France to support this force, and were stationed along the much shorter border with Belgium. But the anticipated attack from Germany never came, and an uneasy stand-off was maintained through the bitterly cold winter of 1939-40, with the French, British and German armies nervously facing each other across the same ground over which their fathers and grandfathers had fought between 1914 and 1918.

As this uneasy stalemate in the West continued through the winter, little was done to come to the defence of Poland on whose behalf Britain and France had gone to war in September. Indeed, the Western Allies could do little more than look on impotently as Germany and the USSR carved up Eastern Europe, the Baltic States and Scandinavia for themselves.

In Britain, the cabinet was still dominated by the appeasers who had tried to negotiate with Hitler in the mid-1930s although Winston Churchill, as First Lord of the Admiralty, and Anthony Eden, as minister for the dominions, had been recalled to government. Chamberlain's major objective in those early months of the war had been to keep the epicentre of any military action as far away from Britain as possible to allow British factories to hurriedly increase military output.

Fear of a bombing campaign by the Luftwaffe had initially led to the mass evacuation of nearly two million children from British cities across the country. But when this threat never materialised, many families brought their children back home and life returned to an uneasy normality. The nightly blackout, however, remained a permanent reminder of the war, and Anderson Shelters were built in gardens all over the country in preparation for the air raids ahead.

Life through the winter of 1939-40 settled into a struggle against the ration book and the freezing cold, although national morale received a boost in December 1939 when the German battleship, the *Graf Spee,* was hunted down in the South Atlantic and sunk near Montevideo. However, such successes were few and far between as Hitler continued to control the pace and direction of the war. This period of inactivity came to be known as the Phoney War when the armies of France and Britain manned the Western Front through the bitter winter while war raged on in Finland and Poland.

The war was going very much the way Hitler had planned and by the spring of 1940 it had become clear to the British cabinet that some positive action was needed not only to wrest the initiative from the Nazis but also to restore flagging national confidence. As a result, military leaders highlighted three areas of possible Nazi vulnerability. These included an attack from the south on Axis positions in North Africa, the launching of a bombing campaign of German cities by the RAF and the stepping up of activity in Scandinavia to cut off the supply of Swedish iron ore crucial to the German war machine.

In April 1940, it was decided to use the strength of the British navy to attempt the third of these options and Churchill, in his new position as leader of the navy, ordered the mining of the sea lanes in the Baltic Sea that carried Swedish iron ore to Germany. Hitler's response to this first aggressive British move of the war was quick and decisive. He could not risk the loss of these supply routes from the north and so ordered the invasion of Denmark and Norway, as a protection for Sweden.

As a result, a British force was sent to Norway to help resistance there, but its intervention soon proved a fiasco and ended in evacuation only a month later in early June with the loss of upwards of 5,000 men. It also clearly showed the superiority of both German military strategy and firepower. The Norwegian campaign ended with the Royal Navy evacuating as many men as it could before it was chased back across the North Sea by the Luftwaffe. A crucial lesson learnt by the British military command from the Norwegian campaign was the importance of air superiority in modern warfare. This was proved once again a few months later in the Battle of Britain.

The most senior casualty of the Norwegian fiasco was the prime minister, Neville Chamberlain, who resigned on 10 May 1940. So as Hitler turned his attention to Western Europe and ordered the attack on the Low Countries, Churchill was called to Buckingham Palace and asked to form a coalition government that embraced all parties. The irony of this, perhaps not lost on the new prime minister, was that his predecessor had lost his job because of mistakes in planning and strategy in Norway that were the responsibility, at least in part, of Churchill himself. Chamberlain was to die soon after from cancer in November 1940.

Churchill's government of National Unity included Clement Attlee who was leader of the Labour Party and who in May 1940 became Lord Privy Seal, before becoming deputy prime minister in 1942. Attlee was to become responsible for administering domestic affairs during the war while Churchill himself oversaw the various committees that were more directly involved in prosecuting the war, a division of responsibility that suited both men.

The *Blitzkrieg* on France and the Evacuation of Dunkirk

After the bombing of Rotterdam on 14 May 1940, when civilian districts were specifically targeted for the first time, the Netherlands soon surrendered, allowing the Nazis to continue their *Blitzkrieg* attack into Belgium. Britain and France responded quickly by strengthening their defences along the Belgian border while further south France felt confident in the well-fortified protection of the Maginot Line on its common border with Germany.

However, between these two lines of defence lay a fifty-mile gap around the Ardennes Forest. This was protected only weakly, with men being rushed north to reinforce the defence of the Belgian border and south towards the Maginot Line. It was the conclusion of the Allied generals commanding the British and French armies that Hitler would not be foolhardy enough to order an attack through such difficult terrain as the Ardennes Forest. This was soon to prove very costly.

After ordering the destruction of as much of the air force capacity of the enemy as possible in pre-emptive air strikes against Allied airfields across France, it was through the Ardennes Forest that Hitler launched his *Blitzkrieg* on France. Punching a hole through the weakened Allied defences, division after division of Panzers, 1,200 in total, poured through the forest, over the River Meuse and into north-eastern France. It was now the turn of the Western Allies to be surprised by the speed and efficiency of the German attack as France experienced the Nazi war machine in May 1940 as Poland had done ten months earlier.

The French army, whose discipline and efficiency had been damaged by the cold winter of the Phoney War, was largely impotent against the power and strength of this Panzer attack that sped through the Ardennes before swinging north in order to trap the predominantly British Allied forces that had been deployed on the Belgian border. This split the Allied armies in half, with the speed of the initial Allied collapse leading to political panic in France. In response to the deepening crisis and in an attempt to shore up fast-evaporating confidence, Marshal Philippe Pétain, the eighty-four-year-old hero of Verdun, was recalled from Madrid, where he was ambassador to Franco's government, and appointed deputy prime minister.

But even his reputation could not halt the Nazi assault, and soon a sense of defeatism began to pervade both the French military and its political command. In the meantime, some eight million refugees were fleeing westwards, choking the road systems and hampering any meaningful Allied defence still further. French military commanders ordered that the defence of Paris be given priority, with French units deployed on the Maginot Line falling back eastwards towards the capital. Consequently, it became much easier for the Nazis to gain control of the east of the country and, as France plunged deeper into crisis, the Channel coast was reached at Noyelles-sur-Mer on the Somme estuary on 20 May 1940.

Amid this chaos, Lord Gort, the general in command of the British Expeditionary Force, found himself leading a force that had been encircled by two German armies that were quickly closing in on him. So, acting unilaterally, as he was still officially under the command of the French High Command, Gort gave orders to make for the coast in preparation for mass evacuation. His sole aim soon became to save as many British and Allied troops as possible, and between 29 May and 3 June 1940 around 320,000 men were evacuated from the beaches of Dunkirk.

These men were rescued not only by the Royal and Merchant Navies but also by hundreds of other boats and ships, large and small, that had responded to the urgent appeal made by the government in London. All this was done under incessant bombing, with many of those whose rearguard action saved so many others soon finding themselves either killed or captured, and marched off to spend the war as prisoners of war.

The Dunkirk evacuation had saved about 200,000 British soldiers and about 120,000 from France, many of whom went on to join de Gaulle's Free French Army. But most of their equipment and armour was abandoned, and the air forces of both nations were severely weakened. These substantial losses could have been even worse if kind seas and the tremendous courage and effort of all those connected with the evacuation had not intervened. The Allies were also helped when Hitler inexplicably gave orders for the attack on Dunkirk to be halted on the city's outskirts for four days, a delay that allowed many to get away. But the evacuation seemed to be no more than a postponement of the inevitable.

It seemed that the rest of France, and then Britain, would succumb to the Nazis, just as so many other countries had done since 1936. Dunkirk has subsequently been portrayed in Britain as a great triumph of national spirit in the face of adversity. In reality, it was a brave but desperate rearguard action that came at the end of a military campaign in which the German army had shown enormous superiority in every sphere of combat. In May 1940, the future seemed bleak for Churchill and the people of Britain.

The Fall of France and the Battle of Britain

After forcing the Allied armies off continental Europe at Dunkirk, the German commanders turned their attention to the conquest of Paris and, after a quick campaign against the rump French army, took the French capital on 14 June 1940. Marshal Pétain had by then replaced Paul Reynaud as prime minister and he now sued for peace.

Hitler ordered his generals to offer terms that humiliated France as Germany had been humiliated in 1918, and he was very specific about how the French surrender should be accepted. He ordered that the same railway carriage used by the French to accept Germany's surrender after World War One should be used for the French surrender. This carriage had belonged to Marshal Foch himself, and had in the 1920s been turned into a museum on the very spot in the Forest of Compiègne where the armistice of 1918 had been signed. Hitler and an entourage that included Goering, Speer, Hess and Ribbentrop arrived at the site on 22 June 1940 in order to accept the surrender, with Hitler himself sitting in the seat where Foch had sat in 1918. However, he disdainfully left proceedings early, just as Foch had done twenty-one years earlier, before French negotiators were forced to sign the Armistice agreement that ceded two-thirds of their country to their Nazi conquerors.

Northern and eastern France would remain under German occupation, but the cost of administering this would be met by the satellite regime that was to be based at Vichy in the south. With the French humiliation complete and happy that the German defeat of 1918 had at last been avenged, Hitler made a fleeting three-hour early morning trip to the French capital on 23 June in order to see the sites of Paris that included Garnier's nineteenth-century baroque opera house, which he had always much admired, the Eiffel Tower and the tomb of Napoleon.

By July 1940, Pétain had established himself as the autocratic leader of Vichy France, with his willingness to liaise and co-operate with Berlin confirmed immediately when he handed over Reynaud to the German authorities. The former prime minister was to remain a prisoner of war until 1945. Meanwhile, General Charles de Gaulle, who had commanded an armoured division in the May campaign against the Nazi *Blitzkrieg*, had escaped to London where he set up the Committee of National Liberation. This, in time, was to form the rallying point for those committed to the liberation of France.

When it became clear that the government in Vichy intended to work closely with the Nazis, the British government ordered the destruction of the French navy off the Algerian coast with the loss of 1,300 French lives. As a result, Pétain immediately broke off relations with Britain whose isolation was now complete. Poland, Denmark, Norway, the Netherlands, Belgium, Luxembourg and France had all fallen to the Nazi *Blitzkrieg*. With only the English Channel standing between it and the power of the Nazi war machine, it seemed only a matter of time before Britain would join them.

After the fall of France, Hitler had assumed that Britain would follow the French example and sue for peace. This would conclude his war in the West and allow him once again to concentrate on the establishment of a German empire in the East. Therefore, it was only reluctantly that he accepted that it was Churchill's intention to fight on, and that he needed to turn his attention to Operation Sea Lion, the plan for the invasion of Britain.

Hitler was informed that it would take two months to assemble the amount of naval transport in the Channel that was needed for the invasion. He also knew that the establishment of air superiority had been the key to Germany's success in the battle for France, and that dominance of the skies over the

Channel would be crucial if British naval strength was to be successfully countered. So as a prelude to the invasion, which was planned for early September, he agreed to let Goering's Luftwaffe use the time to destroy the already depleted RAF that had been tasked with protecting the Royal Navy, which was primarily occupied defending the English Channel.

In the summer of 1940, Britain faced a situation of the utmost gravity. Its forces had experienced a terrible defeat in France where thousands of men, nearly all of its heavy artillery and over 500 aircraft had been lost. In addition to this, Britain was now facing an enemy that dominated the whole of western and central Europe. However, Churchill's oratory and constant public appearances did much to maintain national morale in the face of such bleak circumstances, and in one of his most famous speeches during the battle for France, he had promised that 'We shall never surrender.' Now he galvanised the British public into working against the common enemy.

In May 1940, he announced the formation of the Local Defence Volunteers, which was soon renamed the Home Guard, with a million men answering his call and joining up. Its formation allowed the limited resources of the regular army to be deployed more efficiently and, as a result, a number of mobile units ready to respond to the German invasion were established at bases along the south coast. The Home Guard, especially up until 1942, was massively important to the morale of the nation and performed an important social as well as military role before it was disbanded in December 1944.

But it was in the air that Churchill knew that Britain was at its weakest, and experience in Norway and France had shown that air superiority was vital if the invasion of Britain was not to become inevitable. After the loss of so many aircraft in France in April 1940, the RAF was able to put in the air just over 250 aeroplanes, and so he brought Lord Beaverbrook into his cabinet as minister for aircraft production. Beaverbrook, a dynamic entrepreneur and newspaper magnate, now worked closely with the trade unions and the munition workers, and soon managed to double production of aircraft such as the Spitfire. In the early summer of 1940, Britain was not ready for the battle to come, but it was at least beginning to get ready.

Towards the end of July 1940, Hitler ordered the Luftwaffe to attack and the Battle of Britain began. In an attempt to wear down British Fighter Command, Goering first targeted British shipping in the English Channel and the southern coastal ports. However, he soon found that this led to heavy losses for his own air force, and so in August he ordered his pilots to switch their attacks to concentrate on the RAF airfields and aerodromes dotted across southern England and on the radar stations that had been built to protect them.

In response to Goering's orders, wave after wave of German bombers flew over the Channel from their bases in northern France and Belgium in order to try and destroy the air installations that held the key to the protection of Britain. Radar, newly invented in the 1930s, alerted British fighters of the positions of these attacks and they scrambled to intercept them. British radar stations could predict these German movements in terms of distance, numbers of aircraft and altitude, and this meant that the stretched forces of the RAF could be used to maximum efficiency at all times. Radar, more than any other single factor, saved Britain from invasion because, without it, the bravery of the airmen would have been for nothing. Later in the war, the use of radar was also crucial in seeking out and destroying many German submarines, and so also helped to win the war in the Atlantic.

In simple terms, the British fighters needed to destroy the German bombers before they could drop their ordnance on their targets. At the same time, the German fighters flying with the bombers needed to stop them. The dogfights between the rival fighters, which resulted from these confrontations, defined the nature of the Battle of Britain that raged through the summer of 1940.

The liberty of Britain now rested with the skill of the few hundred men who piloted the Spitfires and Hurricanes that flew high over the fields of Surrey, Sussex, Kent and Hampshire. In terms of aircraft and pilots available, the Luftwaffe held a very great advantage over the RAF, and Goering was confident that his men would quickly win the victory he had promised his Führer. But they flew from bases across the Channel and this meant that fuel limitations restricted the length of their combat time, and it soon became clear that the quick victory that Goering had promised was not going to happen.

However, the supply rate of machines from the German factories seemed to suggest that it was only a matter of time before Goering achieved his primary objective and succeeded in destroying Britain's southern airfields and radar stations. During the twelve weeks of the Battle of Britain, the RAF and Allied pilots who flew with them were outnumbered by a factor of three to one and, in all, over 1,000 Allied aircraft were shot down. In response, around 1,700 enemy aircraft were destroyed. Also, despite the efforts of Lord Beaverbrook and the munition workers, Britain was simply running out of aircraft and, more importantly, the trained pilots that were needed to fly them. It seemed that an invasion before the weather deteriorated in the autumn was inevitable.

However, British commanders did not know that the success of the RAF and Allied pilots in July and August had deeply affected morale within the Luftwaffe. They also didn't know that the RAF counter-attack against the German invasion flotilla being assembled in the ports of northern France and Belgium had sown seeds of doubt in the German High Command. Senior commanders in the Nazi hierarchy began to question whether the Luftwaffe was ever going to be able to guarantee the air superiority needed to protect this invasion force.

Hitler himself had never been keen on the idea of the invasion of Britain. He saw Britain as his natural ally in northern Europe and considered the war against Britain as a distraction from his main concerns in the East. On 17 September 1940, he concluded that the Luftwaffe would not be able to guarantee the aerial domination needed for the invasion and Operation Sea Lion was postponed until the following spring.

The campaign against the RAF was called off and Hitler ordered his Luftwaffe commanders to cease their attacks on the airfields and the radar stations. The Battle of Britain had been won and Churchill praised the pilots who had won the Battle of Britain saying that 'Never in the field of human conflict was so much owed by so many to so few.'

Britain Alone: September 1940 to December 1941

At least in the short term, Britain had been saved from invasion. However, the victory did not save Britain entirely as Hitler ordered the Luftwaffe to redirect its efforts and begin a night-time bombing campaign that targeted London. In an attempt to weaken British national spirit and destroy essential industrial and commercial facilities, the *Blitz*, as this bombing came to be known, was soon extended to include attacks on many other British cities, towns and industrial centres.

In nine months of bombing between September 1940 and May 1941, night-time Luftwaffe raids dropped thousands of tonnes of high-explosive and incendiary bombs on British cities and towns as far apart as Glasgow and Plymouth. Over 40,000 people lost their lives in these raids, and huge damage was done to the industrial, commercial and social fabric of the cities that were bombed. London itself was to endure fifty-seven consecutive nights of bombing and, in total, was bombed on seventy-one separate occasions.

In the summer of 1940, Britain had been saved from invasion by the courage and resourcefulness of a few thousand airmen. Through its second winter of the war, Britain now survived through the courage, resourcefulness and spirit of its people. Inspired by the leadership of Winston Churchill, the nation united against the common enemy and worked hard to put out the fires and rescue the injured from the rubble of the nightly raids. The *Blitz* brought the British nation together in a way that was to have the most profound impact in the immediate post-war years, with the state accepting responsibility for its people in a way that had never been imagined in the 1930s.

On the other side of the Atlantic, the images of Britain holding out through the *Blitz* had an important effect on US public opinion. President Roosevelt was a keen supporter of Britain and had done as much as he could to supply Britain since the beginning of the war. Many in the USA had been shocked by the success of the Nazis and were pleased to see their progress halted by the Battle of Britain.

Isolationism had dominated US foreign policy since Versailles in 1919, but by the end of the 1930s there was evidence that a more aggressive policy towards the dictators was gaining support. As a consequence, President Roosevelt was able to add to the measures that he had already taken in support of Britain, and by the end of 1940 talked about the USA becoming 'the arsenal of democracy'. One major result of this was the Lend-Lease agreement that allowed Britain to receive military supplies from the USA in exchange for deferred payment or payment in kind. This followed an initial agreement in September 1940 that had granted the use of a number of British military bases in the Caribbean and Newfoundland in return for the immediate delivery of fifty old US destroyers. Churchill had originally asked for the destroyers as a gift, but Roosevelt knew that this would be opposed by US public opinion, which showed a three-quarter majority still in favour of isolationism, and by the US Congress. Drawn-out negotiations over Lend-Lease also in the end forced an abandonment of Britain's long-term adherence to imperial preference.

The Lend-Lease programme gained the approval of Congress in March 1941 and proved to be vitally important to Britain's continued survival, allowing it to maintain its solitary fight against Germany and pay for the naval war in the Atlantic. Both Churchill and Roosevelt knew that if Britain lost in this theatre of war, a German blockade would starve it out of the war within a matter of months. Indeed, the sea lanes across the North Atlantic remained Britain's lifeline throughout the war.

With the threat of invasion removed only until the following spring, Churchill and his cabinet realised that the key to their country's survival lay in shifting the focus of the war away from British shores. Senior military advisers were asked to suggest areas in which the Axis powers might prove vulnerable and, as a result, Allied offensives were launched in the Atlantic and in North Africa.

In the Atlantic, the Royal Navy remained a potent weapon, with its large presence bolstered by money and ships that arrived as a result of Lend-Lease. This presence was increasingly used to try to blockade Germany. The Germans for their part realised the importance of imports, and especially the imports of foodstuffs, to the British war effort, and strove to halt the passage of the merchant ships that plied across the North Atlantic shipping lanes. In this quest, they were particularly successful in the first half of 1942. Ships carrying supplies to the northern Russian ports, which included tanks that were to be used in the defence of Stalingrad, had to run the gauntlet of the German navy and U-boats, as well as the Luftwaffe flying from bases in occupied Norway, and were also to suffer huge casualties.

So the war in the Atlantic was very much a war of attrition in which, until 1943 at least, neither side was able to get the upper hand. Later in the war, Allied ships sailed in convoys that were heavily protected by US navy and Royal Navy destroyers, and eventually more sophisticated radar systems were developed that meant that the Allies could seek out and destroy more U-boats than the Germans could afford to lose.

The success of the convoy system was coupled with massively important developments made at Bletchley Park, the British military's main encryption centre that had been set up in 1938. These centred on the breaking of the Enigma code, the code employed by the German military in order to send its messages. The first breakthrough in reading Enigma wartime codes came, with Polish assistance, in January 1940 and further advances were made sporadically over the next few years. These were most especially helped by the capture of an intact machine from a U-Boat on 9 May 1941 by the crew of the HMS *Bulldog*. Churchill himself took a close interest in the work being done at Bletchley Park and was central in sanctioning finance that allowed its expansion.

This led to the recruitment of various mathematical and engineering geniuses, eventually culminating in the construction of a code-breaking machine, designed primarily by Alan Turing, which in essence speeded up the process of reading the German messages by reducing hugely the number of different permutations that had to be calculated. As a result of this success in breaking the German codes, which meant that the U-Boats could be located and destroyed more easily, shortening the war considerably, the war in the Atlantic was to all intents and purposes over by the early summer of 1943. However, this was not before thousands of sailors from both sides had given their lives in some of the fiercest fighting of the war.

In North Africa, General Sir Archibald Wavell, the commander of the combined British and Commonwealth forces, was ordered to prepare plans to counter Italian advances into Egypt. As a result, initial Italian successes won in 1940 were overturned, with a series of attacks launched in February 1941 driving the Allied army 800 miles into Italian-held Libya. The Allied advance also led to the capture of 100,000 Italian troops.

These successes against the Italian army were to bring some sense of hope to millions in Britain who were enduring the hardship of rations, the blackout and the constant bombing of the *Blitz* through the winter of 1940-41. The successes of Wavell's Desert Army received saturation reporting in the British press, but the initial advance could not be maintained. Early in spring 1941, an Italian attack in the Balkans threatened Greece, and Wavell was ordered to suspend his successful Libyan campaign. Instead, he was ordered to send reinforcements across the Mediterranean to aid the defence of Greece where heavy losses had already been inflicted on the Italian army.

These Italian losses persuaded Hitler that Mussolini could not be trusted to guarantee Axis security in the Balkans and southern Europe. Domination of the region, sitting as it did on Germany's right flank, was essential before Hitler could embark on the campaign against the USSR planned for June 1941. In preparation for this, Hitler had already moved into Romania and Bulgaria, having forced agreements from the governments there. Among other things, this had secured the vast resources of the Romanian oilfields, which in time were to provide about a third of Germany's fuel needs. Pressure was also applied on Yugoslavia to accept Nazi domination, but when a coup d'état resulted in the installation of a government hostile to the Nazis, negotiations were ended and Hitler ordered a full-scale invasion.

Despite ferocious rearguard resistance from partisans operating from the mountains, Yugoslavia soon fell, and the German army moved quickly southwards into Greece. This was bravely defended by troops from Australia, New Zealand and Greece itself in particular, with their rearguard action resulting in many Allied troops being able to retreat successfully and escape capture. However, this only slowed up the Nazi takeover of the country, which was finally evacuated by the Allies at the end of April 1941. The Allied armies retreated to the island of Crete, which itself was captured by the Germans at the end of May in the first-ever military campaign won principally by means of an airborne paratroop offensive.

The German *Blitzkrieg* that swept through the Balkans, Greece and Crete in the early months of 1941 was proving to be just as successful as the one that had destroyed resistance in Western Europe at the beginning of the war. The vulnerability of the Axis powers in North Africa, which Churchill and his military advisers had detected at the end of 1940, had proved short-lived as once again the Allies stared defeat in the face.

After the capture of Crete and with much of Europe now under his control, Hitler sent General Erwin Rommel, a commander who had distinguished himself by leading the Panzer offensive through the Ardennes in May 1940, to Tripoli to deal with the last Allied resistance in North Africa. His mission was to reclaim land lost by Italian forces earlier in the year, and victories at Benghazi and Tobruk, where 25,000 British and Commonwealth troops were captured in June 1942, allowed his Afrika Corps to push eastwards across Libya and into British-held Egypt.

Rommel, who came to be known as the *Desert Fox* by his troops, pushed on 200 miles into Egypt before finally reaching the coastal town of El Alamein, only seventy miles from the strategically crucial port of Alexandria. Increasingly, Allied commanders began to contemplate the threat that this German offensive would have on vital communications routes through the Suez Canal, with an Allied evacuation from North Africa becoming a very real possibility.

But Hitler crucially chose this moment to intensify his campaign against the USSR, and Rommel received neither the men nor the arms needed to finish off Allied resistance in Egypt. As a result, the German advance ground to a halt, and was finally stopped for the first time in a year by the Eighth Army, under the command of Field Marshal Bernard Montgomery. This was at the first Battle of El Alamein in July 1942.

The war in North Africa was not lost and the Allies were able to cling onto Egypt. Montgomery was ably supported by the Royal Navy that managed to maintain a supply route through important Mediterranean bases such as Gibraltar and Malta. For the bravery and courage of its people during these years, the island of Malta had been awarded the George Cross in April 1942.

The Globalisation of War: Barbarossa and the Attack on Pearl Harbour
By the early summer of 1941, Hitler's popularity and confidence was at its peak and he felt ready to embark on the principal war aim that had preoccupied him for most of his adult life. On 30 June 1941, seventy-nine armoured divisions, comprising over four million troops and supported by the full firepower of the Luftwaffe, poured over the border into the USSR, beginning what was to become the bloodiest military campaign in the history of warfare.

Operation Barbarossa consisted of a three-pronged attack that struck north-eastwards towards Leningrad, eastwards towards Moscow and south-eastwards into the Ukraine and the Don industrial basin. A six-week *Blitzkrieg* campaign was to destroy the country that Hitler had described as 'that rotten edifice'. Initially, Hitler's bold strike into the heart of the Soviet empire was staggeringly successful and within a week half the industrial and agricultural capacity of the USSR had been captured. This initial advance averaged seventy miles a day and soon took the German army to within a hundred miles of Moscow. The USSR, as Hitler had predicted, seemed to be collapsing in the most spectacular style.

In the wake of these early German successes, Hitler gave Himmler full authority to set up an SS-run police state. As in Poland in 1939 and 1940, the full terror of this was soon unleashed as by August 1941 all three advances had achieved most of their pre-set military objectives. But the crucial premise upon which Operation Barbarossa was based was that total victory would be achieved within six weeks and now, with victory in his grasp, Hitler made a fatal mistake. Rather than maintaining the attack on Moscow and the Soviet seat of government, he ordered the armoured divisions that were approaching it to sweep south and help capture the industrial areas around Kiev in the Ukraine. It was only when this had been achieved that he ordered these divisions back to the north to complete their primary objective.

However, as with Napoleon's March on Moscow in 1812, the Nazi High Command did not pay enough attention to the Russian winter and Moscow was never captured. Early in October, the snows came, leaving the German army massively exposed, sitting at the end of a supply line that stretched across hundreds of miles of occupied Eastern Europe. But they had been so confident that Operation Barbarossa would lead to a decisive and speedy victory within their six-week window that no provisions had been made to counter its extremes, with many German soldiers so badly supplied that they were even left without basic winter clothing.

As this crisis in the East grew, Hitler steadfastly refused to sanction any tactical retreat for the winter, which his generals continuously implored, and continued instead to demand nothing less than total victory. Hampered by the weather and by the intransigence of the Führer, the German military machine that had succeeded with such ease in Poland, France, the Balkans and North Africa now ground to a halt.

This was sensed in Moscow where encouraging news was being received from the Far East. In July 1941, General Tojo, Japan's new militarist prime minister who had overseen the Japanese invasion of China in the 1930s, had secured an agreement with the Vichy government that allowed the Japanese army to move into French Indochina, thus directly threatening British and US interests in Malaya and the Philippines respectively. It was this Japanese interest in South East Asia that finally persuaded Stalin that the threat of Japanese aggression against the USSR further north in Siberia was unlikely. This allowed Red Army commanders to transfer men from the Siberian army to help with the more pressing problem of the defence of the West. This force could be used there in a counter-attack that Stalin and his generals now planned against the overstretched and badly supplied Germany army.

On 6 December 1941, a day before Pearl Harbour was attacked, this counter-attack was launched, with Soviet successes quick and decisive. The Siberian army was well accustomed and well equipped to cope with the rigours of the Russian winter, and soon over 300,000 German soldiers had been either killed or captured. The Red Army pushed westwards and, as it did so, the full extent of the horror of the SS-run Nazi occupation became apparent. The inhabitants of whole villages were found massacred and whole towns were discovered burnt to the ground. The USSR lost twenty million citizens in World War Two and many of these were killed by retreating Nazi forces in the winter campaigns of 1941 and 1942.

After two years of war, the retreat from Moscow was the first major setback for the German army and led Hitler to take full military control of his armies in the East. He was obsessed with the campaign for *Lebensraum,* and for the rest of the war he was to spend much of his time directing the war against the USSR from his headquarters, the Wolf's Lair, deep in the forests of East Prussia. As a result of this obsession, some 80% of all those German soldiers serving on the Eastern Front were to lose their lives.

News of the Soviet counter-attack on the Eastern Front was overshadowed by events on 7 December 1941 when Japanese forces attacked the US Pacific Fleet while it was at anchor at the Pearl Harbour naval base, just to the west of Honolulu on the Hawaiian island of Oahu. Japan's colonial ambitions in Asia had been clear since its invasion of Manchuria in 1931, but it was not until the Japanese occupation of French Indochina in June 1941 that the interests of Britain and the USA had become directly threatened. Pearl Harbour proved to be the culmination of six months of tension that had long threatened war.

With Allied, British and, importantly, US interests in the region now increasingly under threat, relations between the two sides quickly deteriorated, with Churchill and Roosevelt ordering an embargo on oil and other raw materials that aimed to cut off vital supplies to Japanese industry. Both had hoped that this would force Japan to look for a negotiated settlement, and protracted negotiations between the protagonists were held through the autumn of 1941.

During these negotiations, it became clear to Tojo and his cabinet that Japan was left with only two options to consider. Firstly, it could agree to a humiliating climbdown, bow to US and Allied pressure and order a full withdrawal. This would ensure the lifting of the embargo and the restoration of oil supplies so crucial to the Japanese military machine.

On the other hand, Japan could choose a second course of action that would secure an alternative oil supply from the Dutch East Indies, which in all likeliness would provoke a war with Britain and the USA. This second choice, therefore, would have to coincide with a pre-emptive strike against the US Pacific Fleet at anchor in Hawaii that, strategists in Tokyo argued, would give the Japanese navy about a year to take over and dominate the Pacific theatre of operations before any possibility of a serious US response. It was this second option that Tojo and his military advisers decided to follow.

Negotiations were still continuing in Washington when Japanese aircraft carriers stole to within 200 miles of Hawaii and the 400 or so aircraft that attacked Pearl Harbour took to the air. In the surprise dawn raid, this attack sank a major part of the US Pacific Fleet with the loss of nearly 2,500 sailors and marines, including over 1,100 who perished when USS *Arizona* was hit. Crucially, however, no aircraft carriers, which were soon to prove so important in the naval war that followed, were in port on the morning of the attack, and so the damage to US naval strength was less dramatic than it might have been. In addition, the Japanese attack also failed to blow up the huge oil supply dumps that were situated at the naval base.

Hitler and Mussolini were suitably impressed and four days later joined Japan by declaring war on the USA. The attack on Pearl Harbour gave Japan the clear naval superiority in the Pacific region and in South East Asia that its military planners had wanted, and this was now used to great effect. By the end of January 1942, they had taken Guam, Hong Kong and Borneo in the Dutch East Indies, and forced US forces in the Philippines back onto the Bataan Peninsula in the south. In April 1942, this force was to be one of the last Allied forces in the South East Asian theatre of operations to surrender, with the Japanese victory completed with the capture of the southern islands of the Dutch East Indies, Java and Sumatra. By this time, Japanese forces had also attacked and captured Burma, cutting off any land supply route to China.

On 15 February 1942, the island fortress of Singapore, which the British had thought impregnable, had fallen, with over 120,000 British and Commonwealth troops marched into captivity. The fall of Singapore represented the worst military defeat in British history and deeply affected national morale. To the Japanese, it represented an extremely important naval base from which their future campaigns could be directed.

All these territories were added to the Japanese empire that now threatened Allied territory as far apart as India and the northern coast of Australia. This, in essence, fulfilled the primary objective of the campaign conceived by Tojo and his advisers, which had precipitated the attack on Pearl Harbour. Japan had secured the supply of raw materials for its war machine by creating a band of strategic defences across the region that would be very difficult to attack.

By the early summer of 1942, the success of the Japanese in the Pacific and in South East Asia, of Rommel in North Africa and of the renewed Nazi advance against the USSR had stretched the territorial possessions of the aggressor states to the greatest they were ever to be. This, among other things, was to put a huge strain on the leadership of Churchill who in 1942 was challenged twice with votes of no confidence in the House of Commons. While acknowledging his magnificent grit of 1940 and 1941, detractors criticised him for a certain amount of dithering and clouded thinking, and questioned whether he possessed the ability to strategically plan the best way forward.

As it turned out, Churchill was to remain at Downing Street and a major reason for this was that, even at this time when the Axis powers were at their geographically strongest, there were early signs that the Allies were beginning to turn the tide in the war. In April 1942, US bombers had managed for the first time to hit targets in Japan, including Tokyo, while in Europe a co-ordinated bombing campaign against industrial and military facilities vital to the German war effort, which had been launched at the end of 1941, was intensified.

Axis military successes up until 1942 had been won in regionalised theatres of war, and the military advisers who planned these presumed that these *Blitzkrieg* attacks would knock each individual enemy out of the war. When this did not happen, it became clear that in the long term their continued success was unsustainable. In short, the Japanese attack on Pearl Harbour and the German declaration of war on the USA meant that the Axis powers would have to fight against both the USA and the USSR.

The Turning Tide: The Battles of Midway, El Alamein and Stalingrad

In 1942, an Allied victory was certainly not a foregone conclusion. However, decisions made in Tokyo and Berlin to open up hostilities into a truly global world war against both the USA and the USSR made it far more likely, and it was during 1942 that the Soviet, British, Commonwealth and US alliance began to bring its economic and logistical superiority to bear.

For the Allies, the war at this stage became about the organisation and coordination of the vast resources now available, and ordering the supply routes needed for their distribution. Once this was done, and this was to take at least two years, the victory over Nazism and the aggressor states was to become almost an inevitability. This new situation led to a series of decisive victories in various different theatres of war around the world that eventually led to an Allied victory in 1945.

The first of these victories took place at sea in the northern Pacific in June 1942 near the island of Midway, 1,300 miles to the north-east of Hawaii, and brought to an end the series of victories that Japan had enjoyed since Pearl Harbour. These victories before the Battle of Midway had included the Battle of the Coral Sea, which had been fought over two days in early May 1942 and which had led to the loss of one US carrier, so technically ending in a Japanese victory. However, it more importantly also resulted in damage to two Japanese aircraft carriers and this in turn led to the cancellation of Japanese plans to take New Guinea. This had always been seen as crucial in the essentially defensive war plans that had been drawn up before Pearl Harbour. This was to have dire strategic consequences in the years ahead.

After the Battle of the Coral Sea, the US navy used intercepted radio messages, decoded at Bletchley Park, to surprise the Japanese fleet that was converging on Midway. The ensuing battle led to the loss of four Japanese aircraft carriers while the USA was to lose only one. By the time of Midway, the war had already shown that the aircraft carrier was the principal weapon of offence in modern naval warfare using, as it did, the speed and flexibility of the fighters on board. The Battle of Midway stopped Japanese expansion westwards although Japan continued to dominate the Pacific further south for another two years.

To the west, Japanese forces had driven deep into Burma and soon came to threaten the borders of India. In order to do this and aware of the limitations of their naval capabilities, Japanese commanders had ordered plans to be drawn up for the construction of a railway across Thailand to supply its army in Burma. This was built between June 1942 and October 1943 and claimed the lives of some 12,000 Allied prisoners of war who, in contravention of the Geneva Convention, were forced to build it. In addition, the railway also cost the lives of some 80,000 indentured workers from South East Asia, brought in mainly from Java. The story of the construction of the 300-mile-long Death Railway, with its famous bridge over the River Kwai, in time came to symbolise the barbaric nature of the war that Japan waged in the Far East.

In July 1942, a month after Midway, the beginning of a second decisive victory for the Allies took place in North Africa where Rommel's offensive was finally stopped at the first Battle of El Alamein. After this, the two armies separated and spent the summer and early autumn facing each other across a thirty-five-mile front in the desert near the Mediterranean Sea. However, Allied commanders kept themselves busy and by October had formulated a plan for a winter campaign, code-named Operation Torch, which aimed to break the German stranglehold in North Africa.

The result was a two-pronged attack in which the Eighth Army would try to break out from Egypt while the US army would attack from the west. In twelve days of fighting during the last week of October and the first week of November 1942, Allied troops of the Eighth Army, the Desert Rats, supplied with the new and powerful US Sherman tank through the Lend-Lease programme, succeeded in the first of these objectives, routing the Afrika Corps in the second Battle of El Alamein. Over half of Rommel's army was destroyed and over the next two months, the tanks of the Eighth Army rolled westwards across the Libyan desert.

From the west, the US offensive, led by General Dwight Eisenhower, advanced from Algeria in the second part of the pincer movement, which by May 1943 had trapped the Axis armies in Tunis. By this point, Operation Torch had secured the capture of 250,000 Axis troops. The war in North Africa, which nine months before had threatened to cut off the vital Allied oilfields of Persia and the Middle East and important communications links with the Commonwealth through the Suez Canal, was over. Importantly, the Allies had gained a base from which they could launch an attack on Italy only one hundred or so miles across the Mediterranean Sea.

The importance and priority of the invasion of Italy had been agreed to by Churchill and Roosevelt when they met at the Casablanca Conference in January 1943. This meant that an invasion of France would be put off until at least 1944. The two leaders were again to meet in Africa nine months later, this time in Cairo, where they met with Chiang Kai-shek to discuss the future of the Far East after the defeat of Japan.

One crucial effect that the end of the war in North Africa brought was the release of many ships from duty in the Mediterranean Sea. Many of these were subsequently redeployed to the Atlantic for the war against the German U-boats. In 1940 and 1941, these had been enormously successful against Allied shipping, but the arrival of so many new Allied destroyers, as well as the development of more sophisticated aerial radar systems, now began to tip the balance at a crucial stage in the war. In fact, the German navy lost so many submarines in 1943 that they were forced to withdraw their fleet from the Atlantic theatre of operations altogether, preferring to concentrate their attacks on the convoys supplying the Soviet ports to the north of the Arctic Circle.

The victories at the Battle of Midway and the Battles of El Alamein, and the various positive ramifications that these brought, were of vital importance and were warmly received by Allied forces across the world. But a third Allied success was needed in the USSR if the back of the Nazi war machine was to be broken, and this eventually came with perhaps the most decisive battle of the war. This raged between September 1942 and January 1943 in the southern Soviet city of Stalingrad.

The prelude to the battle was the Nazi spring offensive through the Balkans the previous year that had driven the Allies across the Mediterranean and back into North Africa. This had secured Hitler's right flank and it was his intention to use this added security in a new offensive in the East. In a deviation from Operation Barbarossa, which had attacked on three fronts but which had ultimately cost a million German lives, he ordered a concentration of his armies in the south. His aim was to drive eastwards towards Stalingrad, in the process devastating the Soviet war effort by cutting off the oil-rich Caucasus region from the rest of the USSR.

Initially, Hitler's revised plans for the summer campaign of 1942 worked well, and quick initial territorial gains were made against Soviet army units that were ordered to fall back. As a consequence, the city of Rostov, which held the key to the Caucasus to the south, soon fell. But Hitler now changed his original plan and ordered the main body of his army to head south to secure the oilfields rather than merely cutting them off. The remainder of his forces were ordered to push north-eastwards towards Stalingrad, 250 miles away. Crucially, Hitler had split his army in two.

Stalin knew that keeping control of Stalingrad was central to the survival of the USSR. As a result, he ordered the strengthening of its air defences and drafted in extra troops to defend the city. A deep fear of the Nazis in general and of the SS in particular, coupled with a sense of true patriotic zeal, led to the city quickly responding to Stalin's appeals although this was also helped by the deployment of large numbers of the NKVD, Stalin's secret police, who lurked behind the front lines ready to deal with any deserters. As a result, workers' militias were formed and these forces fought bravely side by side with the Red Army. However, despite these efforts, over 80% of the city had been lost by the end of October 1942.

But the Germans were once again at the end of a very long supply line, and Hitler's generals again asked for a tactical withdrawal so as not to expose a weakened German army to a second Russian winter. But again Hitler refused to listen to the advice of his generals in the field and would countenance nothing other than total victory. Meanwhile, the Soviet leadership ordered the build-up of Soviet tank divisions north and south of the River Volga, far to the west of the city.

In November 1942, when this build-up was complete, the Soviet tanks struck in a *Blitzkrieg* of their own and, after four days of fighting, the northern and southern armies joined up. The 250,000-strong German army besieging Stalingrad to the east was now trapped deep inside enemy territory, with the only link with Germany now through the Luftwaffe, which soon began airlifting upwards of 500 tonnes of supplies daily in the most atrocious weather.

However, the Soviet army did not now turn eastwards towards Stalingrad but rather drove westwards, pursuing the German army that had attacked the Caucasus but which was now in full retreat. As this happened and as the Russian winter took hold, the army of General von Paulus in Stalingrad became more and more isolated, with its supply by air becoming more and more irregular.

Finally, on 24 January 1943 in the depths of the Russian winter, General von Paulus disobeyed the direct orders of his Führer and surrendered. This was despite the fact that only two days before Hitler had promoted him to the rank of field marshal making it clear that no commanding German officer of that rank had ever been captured alive before. But von Paulus refused to commit suicide, and was held by the Red Army after his surrender before eventually joining, in the aftermath of the Stauffenberg Bomb Plot, a Soviet-backed anti-Nazi German committee in exile. He died in East Germany in 1957.

The German death toll at Stalingrad stood at 150,000, with a further 90,000 marched into captivity. Of these, some 50,000 men perished almost immediately in the terrible conditions they were to encounter on their way to prisoner of war camps in Siberia. The siege of Stalingrad was to be Hitler's last chance of creating *Lebensraum* for the German people about which he had first written in *Mein Kampf* twenty years before. The Stalingrad campaign broke the back of the German army in central Europe, destroying the power base of the Axis alliance that had been central to its success for the first three years of the war.

The Battle for Asia, the Bombing of Europe and the Invasion of Italy

The Soviet victory at Stalingrad was mirrored in Asia by other Allied successes and by the end of 1942 Allied troops, under the command of General Douglas MacArthur, had begun the fight back against Japan. This had begun in August 1942 in the Solomon Islands, just to the east of New Guinea, with the Battle of Guadalcanal. This eventually led to the capture of the military air base there, but fanatical fighting by Japanese troops defending it meant that this did not happen until February 1943.

After Guadalcanal, MacArthur and his commanders developed the strategy of island-hopping that saw the Allies slowly battling their way north-westwards across the top of New Guinea and the islands of the western Pacific towards the Philippines, often circumventing Japanese strongholds along the way, which were then in turn blockaded. But Japanese defence was brave and determined and, in the jungle environment, MacArthur's troops were prone to ambush. But despite this, the Allies by the end of 1943 had won back much of the land lost in the earlier Japanese offensives. However, the Philippines, which MacArthur saw as the launch pad for the attack on Japan itself, was not liberated in October 1944.

Meanwhile, the British, Indian and Gurkha troops who made up the Fourteenth Army had begun their own offensive campaign in Burma. For two years, they had defended the Indian border against a Japanese force that dominated the sea, land and air. These men had called themselves 'the forgotten army', but in March 1944 they were able to repulse Japanese advances at the Battles of Imphal and Kohima.

These battles again showed the importance of aerial power in modern warfare and, with the Japanese falling back in disarray, Lord Mountbatten, the Supreme Allied Commander of South East Asia, took the decision to pursue the enemy through the monsoon summer months. During this campaign, Major General Wingate and his Chindits, troops trained to operate as a guerrilla force deep behind enemy lines, destroyed the myth of Japanese invincibility in jungle warfare, and by early 1945, despite high casualty rates caused mostly by tropical disease, the last Japanese units had been chased out of Burma.

The Allied war effort in Europe had concentrated on an enormous bombing campaign against German cities and industry, and this too was beginning to pay dividends. In May 1942, Cologne was targeted and largely destroyed while in March 1943 the Dambusters, in their Lancaster bombers, had succeeded in breaking the dams of the Ruhr valley using Barnes Wallis' revolutionary bouncing bomb, massively hampering German industry in its very heartland. This ferocious campaign was maintained against many German cities in an attempt to break German civilian morale.

Towards the end of the war in 1944 and early 1945, the bombing campaign had been intensified to such an extent that four times the tonnage of bombs was dropped than had been in 1942. In particular, Hamburg, Berlin and Dresden were singled out. In February 1945, a two-day campaign ripped out the heart of Dresden, with tens of thousands dying in the firestorms that the massive use of incendiary bombs brought. In total, about half a million German civilians were to lose their lives in this sustained bombing campaign, which increasingly included area bombing sorties that specifically targeted civilian population centres. As a deliberate and explicit policy, this strategy of area bombing was sanctioned by Churchill and the war cabinet at the beginning of 1942, and was carried out by Britain and the USA until the very end of the war in April 1945.

In June 1943, the battle for Italy began. Sicily was quickly quelled and progress northwards from the toe of the Italian mainland against the dispirited and badly led Italian forces initially progressed well. Allied plans were further boosted a month later when Mussolini was arrested, imprisoned and replaced by General Pietro Badaglio, who had been in charge of the Italian invasion of Abyssinia in 1935. Soon after, Badaglio signed an armistice with the Allies and declared war on Germany.

However, Hitler was not willing to give in to the Allied advance so easily and, despite heavy logistical commitments on the Eastern Front, ordered extra troops and resources to Italy. These new forces were ordered to maintain a line of defence just north of Naples. He also sent a squad of German paratroopers to rescue Mussolini from prison in the Apennine Mountains, and in September 1943 re-established his old ally as the leader of German-held Italy in the north.

Churchill had hoped that the Allies had exposed a weakness in the Axis defences and that the initial offensive on Sicily and southern Italy would lead to a much-needed and speedy victory. However, the soft underbelly of Europe that the Allies had hoped for in fact proved to be, in Churchill's phrase, 'a tough old gut', with further advances slow and casualties high. In January 1944, the Allied beachhead at Anzio, forty miles south of Rome, faced strong and concerted German opposition and the battle for the strategically important town of Monte Cassino was to last until May. Rome did eventually fall in June 1944, but not before many more Allied troops had lost their lives.

The war in Italy dragged on into the early months of 1945 when Hitler was finally forced to withdraw his troops because of the dual threat that came from the invasion from the West following D-Day and the Soviet offensive in the East. Mussolini attempted to escape to safety with his Nazi comrades, but was captured near Lake Como in April 1945 by soldiers of the Italian resistance. Soon after, his mutilated body was brought to Milan where it was strung up by the feet on a meat hook for display on a metal hoarding outside a petrol station. He was displayed there alongside the bodies of his mistress and twelve other Fascists with whom he had been captured.

Operation Overlord, D-Day and the Normandy Landings

The success of the Western Allies from 1942 in the Far East, in North Africa and then, eventually, in Italy led Stalin to demand the relief of his Red Army, which had suffered the brunt of German aggression since 1941. This had included the heaviest fighting of 1943 that included the Battle of Kursk in July and August, the largest tank battle in history.

Stalin made this clear at the first of the Great Power conferences, which was held in Teheran at the end of 1943, when he told Roosevelt and Churchill that he wanted to see the opening up of a new front in the West as soon as possible. Churchill's suspicion of communism led him to fear Soviet expansion into the Balkans, and so he let Roosevelt and Eisenhower know that his government wanted to see this second front opened there.

But he was unable to gain US support for this plan and it was finally agreed that the invasion of Europe would start in northern France no later than May 1944. This date was later postponed by a month because of bad weather. In preparation, thousands of US troops and millions of tonnes of supplies were transported to Britain across the increasingly safe North Atlantic sea lanes through the spring of 1944.

Hitler knew that an invasion of northern France was coming, and he informed his generals fighting the Red Army that they would receive no further reinforcements in their bitter struggle there until he had dealt with this new threat. This struggle in the East had in January 1944 seen the liberation of Leningrad, which had endured a siege that lasted nearly 900 days and killed a million people. A successful Soviet offensive had then driven south-westwards towards Poland. A second Soviet offensive in the south was launched in April 1944 with troops pouring into southern Europe.

With the German army tied down in the East through the spring of 1944, planning for Operation Overlord, the code name for the invasion of France, began in earnest. For two months preceding the invasion, Allied bombing sorties concentrated their attacks on the railway lines, ports, bridges and industrial complexes of German-occupied northern France. These attacks were co-ordinated with the massive bombing campaigns that were destroying so many cities and industrial centres in Germany, but, most importantly, the plans for and location of the invasion itself were kept secret.

These intricate plans included the diversionary massing of troops and equipment in Scotland and in south-east England, on the Kent and Sussex coasts, in order to fool German intelligence that the invasion would be launched somewhere other than Normandy. These forces included fake inflatable tanks, aircraft, ships and landing craft and the effectiveness of other diversionary tactics to spread disinformation were monitored through broken codes. All this meant that the German High Command could not prepare with any certainty or with any real sense of purpose in the months that preceded the invasion. This was despite the construction between 1942 and 1944 of the Atlantic Wall, a series of bunkers and minefields that stretched from Norway to the French Atlantic coast.

At low tide on the morning of 6 June 1944, D-Day began, with the Allied armies under the leadership of the Supreme Allied Commander, General Dwight D. Eisenhower, landing on the beaches of Normandy. Allied paratroopers had been dropped behind enemy lines near the landing beaches the night before in order to disrupt Nazi communications already hampered by the incessant aerial bombardment of the previous few weeks.

British and Canadian forces landed on the beaches to the east of the landing ground, code-named Sword, Juno and Gold. US troops took the two beaches, code-named Omaha and Utah, further west. In all, 150,000 Allied troops were landed on D-Day, protected by some 11,000 aircraft and 5,000 ships.

However, despite the surprise location of the landings, Nazi resistance was fierce and US forces at Omaha in particular were badly hit. They were met there by experienced German veterans who used the sand dunes that dominated the beach to devastating effect. Over 2,000 US troops were killed in the first few hours of fighting, with many never even making it out of the sea and onto the beach.

But Eisenhower and Montgomery, his field commander, were aided in the first few days of the invasion by the enormous Allied naval and aerial firepower available to them, and by Hitler's unwillingness to commit troops so far west. He believed that the Normandy landings were merely a bluff and was still expecting the real Allied invasion to come further east near Calais.

By 12 June 1944, the five beachheads had been joined up into a single bridgehead, and by the end of the month 850,000 troops had been landed.

The US forces then drove west, cutting off the Cotentin peninsula and taking Cherbourg whose port had been badly damaged by the retreating German army. British and Canadian forces pushed south, finally taking Caen on 9 July 1944.

During this breakout from the beaches of Normandy in the first few weeks of July 1944, delegates from forty-four Allied countries met in New Hampshire to discuss and formulate a new set of rules and institutions that would govern, and give security and calm, to post-war international finance and banking. This Bretton Woods Conference established the World Bank and the International Monetary Fund, and it was agreed that each government would implement a monetary policy that tied their currency to a set exchange rate with the US dollar. This new, highly regulated and international system was agreed upon in order to fight against the vagaries and fluctuations that many felt were the reason for the growth of the aggressor states in the interwar period, especially after the Wall Street Crash of 1929. The agreement at Bretton Woods was also seen as a clear indication that the USA was serious about being at the centre of world trade, banking and finance in the soon-anticipated post-war world.

In the weeks that followed D-Day, German operations suffered a major blow when Rommel, Germany's most successful general, was seriously injured when his car was machine-gunned by Allied aircraft. He was subsequently taken back to Berlin where he was implicated in the Stauffenberg Bomb Plot, the conspiracy to assassinate Hitler that was carried out by senior army officers on 20 July 1944. In October 1944, perhaps under duress from the Gestapo, Rommel took his own life.

Colonel Claus von Stauffenberg was also to lose his life. He and the other co-conspirators, who had so nearly succeeded in assassinating the Führer with the briefcase bomb that they had planted in the conference room at the Wolf's Lair, Hitler's headquarters in the forests of eastern Prussia, were tortured and then killed, along with around 5,000 others, including the families of the conspirators, in the recriminations that followed.

The capture of Cherbourg and Caen had taken longer than had been expected, but with victory at the Battle of Falaise the Allies were able to begin a general advance across northern France. General Patton led the US Third Army first south-eastwards before turning north again in an attempt to encircle the enemy. At the beginning of August, information about a German counter-attack had been decoded at Bletchley Park and Montgomery rushed troops to the point of attack, stopping the Germans in their tracks.

The German army was now in full retreat and suffering terrible casualties from the Allied air forces that dominated the skies. Through the Normandy campaign, the German casualty rate was to be ten times as great as that of the Allies. The Allies were also helped greatly by the development of penicillin, which by D-Day had been in industrial production for about three years. With an average wait for the wounded before field surgery estimated at about twelve hours and with the 1945 form of the drug being some twenty times more powerful than the one initially produced in 1940, it was vital in staving off infection, and especially gangrene, during the long fight across northern France and into the German Reich. On 24 August 1944, Free French and US troops entered Paris while ten days later Brussels was also liberated.

In the East, further Soviet advances matched those in the West, with the Red Army liberating the Baltic States before moving into Poland. By August 1944, it had reached the outskirts of Warsaw where the Polish resistance had risen up to surprise the Nazi army of occupation. By the beginning of October, this Warsaw Uprising had taken over two-thirds of the city, but, despite pleas from both Britain and the USA to support the uprising, Stalin ordered his armies to halt on the outskirts of the city in order to wait for supplies. This allowed Germany to send extra reinforcements to Warsaw and the resistance was slowly brought to its knees. The Warsaw Uprising, which lasted for sixty-three days and which saw the destruction of huge swathes of the city, claimed the lives of over 150,000 Poles. Many more were to die in the subsequent SS reprisals. The Red Army finally entered the city three months later in January 1945.

The Defeat of Germany and the Atrocities of the Concentration Camps
In the West, Patton's forces had swept southwards and linked up with the Free French and US forces that had invaded from the Mediterranean port of Marseilles. By November 1944, these forces had captured the important industrial area of the Saarland, a blow that was to have the most profound effect on the German war machine. Its capture came at a time when the supply of oil to the German army had already reached critically low levels.

This push eastwards coincided with the second Quebec Conference in September 1944 where Roosevelt and Churchill agreed to the vindictive Morgenthau Plan. This harsh plan for the occupation and administration of Germany after the Nazis envisaged the reduction of Germany, and Austria, to a state of agricultural and pastoral primitiveness with its entire means of industrial capability and production taken away. The plan, which was similar in spirit and purpose to the German army's plan for France that was vetoed by Bismarck in 1871, was in time rejected in favour of a more positive approach.

Meanwhile, Montgomery was sent north-eastwards into the Low Countries to capture the bridges over the various important river systems there that would give the best base from which to attack Germany. Airborne assaults soon led to the capture of important bridges over the Meuse and Waal rivers, but Montgomery was increasingly hampered by the single-lane roads, which meant that his army could only move slowly through the Belgian countryside.

In late September 1944, 10,000 paratroopers of the British First Airborne Division, supported by Polish volunteers, were dropped behind enemy lines to secure the bridge over the Rhine at Arnhem, so as to allow the advance of the British Second Army. But they were surprised near the bridge by a strong and unexpected German force that was regrouping after the retreat from Normandy, and ten days of vicious fighting left 1,000 Allied soldiers dead, with a further 6,500 finally being forced to surrender. The loss of the bridge over the Rhine at Arnhem, a bridge too far, meant that the Allied offensive, which had aimed to end the war in Europe by the end of 1944, ground to a halt.

The major casualties of this were the people of the Netherlands who for another winter had to endure the German army of occupation. However, these did not include Anne Frank, a Jewish girl from a German family who had escaped to the Netherlands with her family at the age of four when Hitler had come to power in 1933. From 1942 until their capture in August 1944, the Franks, along with two other Jewish families, had lived in hiding in a secret annexe in the back rooms of the Amsterdam offices of Anne Frank's father.

Anne Frank and her sister were both sent to Auschwitz-Birkenau in September 1944 before being transferred to the concentration camp at Bergen-Belsen a month later. They died there in the last weeks of the war from typhus. Their mother had also been sent to Auschwitz-Birkenau and died there in January 1945. The diary that Anne Frank wrote during her years of hiding was published posthumously by her father, the only member of the Frank family to survive the Holocaust.

After the rout that had followed the invasion of Normandy, the victory at Arnhem gave the German army a chance to regroup. In the East, too, it was able to slow down the Soviet advance as the supply lines between Germany and the front became shorter. Hitler was not going to give up without a fight and he still retained the loyalty and devotion of the German people. As the Allied commanders were planning their next move, he took them by surprise by ordering a counter-attack.

On 16 December 1944, an army of 250,000 broke through Allied lines in Belgium and drove westwards into the Ardennes Forest. This drove a wedge between the Allied armies of Montgomery and Patton, and for a month the hopes of Hitler and the German people were revived. But the Battle of the Bulge, as the offensive came to be known, was ultimately doomed to failure, with German industry no longer able to provide the resources needed to sustain such a bold plan, and soon Allied aerial bombardments, which bad weather had cancelled at the beginning of the German offensive, hit back hard at the German tanks that had breached Allied lines in December.

By early January 1945, this last great Nazi *Blitzkrieg* had been contained and by the time Stalin, Churchill and Roosevelt met for their second Great Power conference at the beginning of February, the Allies once again had control of the West. This second conference was held in the Crimean city of Yalta and agreed, among other things, that the USSR would enter the war in the Far East against Japan as soon as the war in Europe had ended. Final Soviet approval for the formation of the United Nations Organisation was also gained.

For Hitler and his Thousand-Year Reich, the end was near. The bombing campaign that had devastated Germany since 1943 may not have broken the spirit of the German people, but it had broken German industry, which no longer could service the German army. This was confirmed on 23 February 1945 when Patton's forces finally crossed into the industrial Ruhr, just after part of it had been deliberately flooded by the last retreating German units that had defended it. This finally cut off Hitler's last means of supplying his army.

The final Soviet offensive on Berlin was launched on 16 April 1945. This was bitterly opposed by the last German soldiers remaining in the city who were desperate not to be taken prisoner and marched off to Siberia. By this stage, Eisenhower had decided that the German capital was not his prime military objective, and had instead ordered the bulk of his armies to swing south and concentrate their attack on the Bavarian mountains where he expected the final Nazi diehards to collect. On 21 April 1945, US and Soviet troops met up at Torgau on the River Elbe, seventy miles to the west of Berlin, and within a week, all organised Nazi resistance had disintegrated.

By this time, Hitler had become a sick, broken and deranged man. He had chosen to stay in Berlin where from his bunker near the Reich Chancellery he commanded the last few loyal members of his personal staff. Many others, however, had already fled. On 30 April 1945, having handed over command to Admiral Karl Doenitz and with the Red Army only a few hundred yards away, he watched his new bride, Eva Braun, kill herself by biting into a cyanide capsule before killing himself with a gunshot to the head. Hitler, the demagogue who had started a war that had killed upwards of sixty million people, was dead. The next day Josef Goebbels, Hitler's propaganda chief and most loyal lieutenant, ordered an SS doctor to administer a lethal dose of poison to each of his six children, before shooting himself and his wife.

With Hitler gone, it was left to others to sign the final official acts of surrender that took place during the following week. As a result, President Harry Truman, who had succeeded Roosevelt on the latter's death in April, and Winston Churchill declared 8 May 1945 as Victory in Europe Day. After six long years, VE Day brought an end to the war in Europe.

As the war was ending, the true extent of the horror of Hitler's rule was becoming clear to advancing Allied armies all over occupied Europe. The liberation of concentration camp after concentration camp bore testimony to the millions who had died to serve his demonic vision. Rumours of a 'Final Solution' had been circling since 1941 and more concrete evidence was forthcoming from 1944, but the scale of the genocide uncovered during the liberation of Europe was utterly shocking.

In January 1945, the Red Army had come across the camp at Auschwitz-Birkenau, near Krakow in occupied Poland, and uncovered the remains of the crematoria that the SS had hurriedly tried to destroy. They also found the notes of Dr Josef Mengele, the 'Angel of Death', who served at Auschwitz for twenty-one months from 1943 and whose brutal experiments, especially on twins, had sent thousands to their deaths.

In April 1945, the concentration camp of Bergen-Belsen was liberated by British troops who found 40,000 prisoners barely alive, surrounded by the bodies of some 10,000 unburied and rotting corpses. In the weeks and months that followed, haunting images and stories from many other concentration camps were to shock the world already hardened by the destruction and agony of years of war. They catalogued crimes unprecedented in human history.

The End of War in the Far East, the Potsdam Conference and the A-Bomb
By April 1945, the war in Europe against the German Nazis and the Italian fascists had been won. But the war against the Japanese militarists still continued although successes in the Philippines, Burma and a spring offensive

by Chiang Kai-shek in China had shown that the defeat of Japan was ultimately inevitable.

The Allies were also helped, as they drew closer to Japan, by the capture of air bases that were quickly used to launch a massive bombing campaign against Japanese cities, ports and industrial centres. Three such bases were on the island of Iwo Jima, the battle for which lasted over a month in February and March 1945 and which led to over 25,000 US casualties including nearly 7,000 dead. The battle was also the site of one the war's most iconic images, a photograph of six US troops, five marines and one sailor, raising the Stars and Stripes on Mount Suribachi. Later, a bronze statue of this was erected in Washington as a memorial to those in the US Marine Corps who had fought in the Far East campaign.

The Battle of Iwo Jima also cost the lives of the vast majority of Japanese soldiers who defended the island, with only just over 200 captured and taken as prisoners of war. This was out of a total garrison that numbered over 18,000 men. This fanaticism was primarily due to an adherence to the creed of *bushido*, an old and originally Samurai doctrine that demanded total allegiance to the emperor and that saw honour in military sacrifice and death.

So an early end to the war in the Far East did not seem likely, despite all these Allied successes. The Allied armies faced a fanatical enemy that did not consider the possibility of surrender and, although much of Japan's navy and air force had been destroyed, its army still occupied large areas of China and many small islands in the Pacific. In addition to the fanatical defence by the Japanese army, the Allied forces had to contend with new *kamikaze* units, whose pilots began to fly their fighters, packed with high explosives, into Allied shipping from the end of 1944.

This was particularly the case at the Battle of Okinawa, a large and populated island, sixty miles long and eighteen miles wide, and only 340 miles from the Japanese mainland. This raged for eighty-two days between April and June 1945 and was to be the last great battle of World War Two. During the battle, which has been referred to as the 'typhoon of steel', 1,500 *kamikaze* attacks were launched on the US navy. The battle was to be the last in the series of island hops that had started in Guadalcanal in 1942 and was to be the bloodiest of them all.

Over 12,000 US personnel were killed in the battle alongside over 70,000 Japanese soldiers and sailors who fought a relentless rearguard action throughout the whole campaign. In addition, around 140,000 of the island's civilian population of about 300,000 were also to die, the second greatest loss of civilian life in the war after Stalingrad three years before. As a result of the ferocity of the fighting on Okinawa, Allied military commanders in the Far East became convinced that any conventional victory that demanded an invasion of mainland Japan would be slow and that Allied casualties would be extremely high.

The realities concerning the nature of war in the Far East were clear to President Truman when he arrived to meet with Stalin and Churchill for the third Great Power conference in the German town of Potsdam on 17 July 1945. Churchill was accompanied by Clement Attlee who replaced him as the leader of the British delegation after the declaration of the Labour Party's landslide victory in the general election.

As the leaders settled down to tense discussions about the division of Germany and questions surrounding German reparations and the borders of Eastern Europe, Truman contemplated a series of top-secret messages from Washington that kept him informed of vital breakthroughs that had been made by the team of scientists working on the Manhattan Project, a research programme set up in 1942 charged with developing an atomic bomb. The chief scientist in charge, Robert Oppenheimer, had earlier in July reported that his team was now in possession of three fully operative atomic bombs, and Truman had taken the decision to sanction the testing of the first of these in the New Mexico desert on 16 July 1945.

When he received confirmation from Oppenheimer's team that this test had been successful, Truman informed the other leaders at Potsdam that he had given the order to drop the second bomb on Japan. He hoped that this would force a Japanese surrender and save the lives of the thousands of US and Allied servicemen still fighting in Asia.

On 6 August 1945, this bomb, which possessed the destructive capability of 20,000 tonnes of TNT, was dropped on the Japanese city of Hiroshima. The effects were staggering, with some 75,000 people dying instantly from the blast that destroyed most of the city. Thousands more were soon to die from the after-effects of the radioactive fallout. Three days later, the final bomb in the US arsenal was dropped on the city of Nagasaki, instantly killing a further 40,000.

The Japanese government did not know that this third bomb was the last in the US stockpile and, fearing further attack, sued for peace. The one condition that they requested was that Emperor Hirohito should be allowed to retain his imperial position. The US occupying force conducting negotiations accepted this condition, and on 15 August 1945 General MacArthur and representatives of the Japanese government met on board the US aircraft carrier,

USS *Missouri*, at anchor in Tokyo Harbour. It was there that the surrender documents ending the bloodiest war in history were signed.

The Aftermath of War and the Emergence of Two Superpowers

As the leaders of the Grand Alliance in Potsdam learnt of the Japanese surrender, they surveyed a world in ruin. Six years or more of Nazi rule had turned Europe into a political and economic wasteland, and even after the death of Hitler, millions still faced the threat of starvation, civil war and further persecution. This suffering and hardship was to be found particularly in the East where many now faced the new threat of life under Soviet occupation. A similar pattern of disaster had also emerged in Asia where large areas of the continent had been destroyed by the Japanese armies of occupation.

The war had cost around sixty million lives and, of this number, more than twenty-five million had come from the USSR. Much of the Great Patriotic War, as Stalin had called the war against Germany, had been fought deep inside Soviet territory and many of Hitler's best-trained units had been stationed there. China had also suffered enormously and its losses in the war against Japan and the fighting between the rival factions within the country numbered upwards of fourteen million. In addition, the war had also created eighty million refugees in China and soon its people were to experience even more agony when a civil war between the Communists and the Nationalists broke out in the middle of 1946.

Germany had suffered huge military casualties of between seven and nine million while the lives of as many as half a million German civilians had also been lost. Many of these had died during the sustained Allied bombing campaign that had started in 1941. The British civilian death toll stood at about 65,000, while countless military graveyards around the world still pay tribute to the British and Commonwealth soldiers, sailors and airmen who gave their lives in the war. British military losses numbered just under 400,000.

Only the USA of the main belligerents was to emerge from the war in a relatively strong position and its military casualties of 400,000 were relatively low, considering that it had a force of around twelve million deployed in Europe alone by the end of the war. Its mainland territory was never threatened and its civilian casualties remained negligible.

Importantly, this had also resulted, in stark contrast to the experiences of many other countries, in little physical damage to US industry that had expanded massively throughout the war. The US economy had become, as Roosevelt had said, 'the arsenal for democracy', and it emerged from the war in excellent health. Indeed, it dominated the world economy in a way, with the possible exception of Britain during the years of conflict in Europe and North America in the 1860s, that had never been seen before.

The political and economic strength of the USA and the passionate defence of the USSR by the Red Army had made it clear long before the end of the war that a new political reality had emerged in international relations. Furthermore, it had also become clear, from about the end of 1942, that the Axis powers were going to be defeated as a result of the combined might of these two new superpowers. Consequently, it was apparent that it was going to be these powers, and not Britain and France, who would play the leading roles in reshaping the post-war world.

Retreat from Empire: Post-War Britain and France

In the immediate aftermath of the war, Britain and the other European liberal democracies that had struggled to maintain their positions of pre-eminence between the wars simply no longer had the economic base from which to compete. Britain was never invaded and its forces had remained in the foreground of the military action against the Axis powers in Europe, North Africa and the Far East. But this had been paid for with Lend-Lease dollars and Britain emerged from the war triumphant, but economically exhausted, propped up by a new and hastily arranged $3.75 billion loan from the USA.

Its empire in Asia had been savaged by Japan during five long years of war and Churchill had been forced to open negotiations on independence for the Indian subcontinent in exchange for support for the war in Burma. After the war, Attlee's Labour government had increased momentum towards independence there, seeing it more and more as an expensive liability that Britain could ill afford. As a result, Lord Louis Mountbatten, who had led Allied forces in South East Asia from 1943, was sent to oversee this transfer of power as the last British Viceroy, and Attlee was keen that this should happen no later than 1948.

However, two years of careful planning could not stop a series of violent riots between rival Hindu, Muslim and Sikh groups that saw the loss of around half a million lives. In an attempt to stop the killing, Mountbatten brought forward the date for independence by a year, hoping that this would force the leaders of the warring factions to work together. However, his efforts were in vain and the peaceful transfer of power that Gandhi and his supporters had worked towards for thirty years never took place.

Britain finally withdrew from the Indian subcontinent in August 1947 when the new nation states of India and Pakistan were brought into existence. Pakistan, the area of Muslim majority, was itself cut in two, with East Pakistan going on to become Bangladesh in 1971. In February 1948, independence was also granted to Ceylon, which became Sri Lanka, and Burma. This finally ended 190 years of British colonial involvement on the Indian subcontinent.

Another problem that continued to sap British energy was Palestine, which Britain had ruled as a mandate of the League of Nations since 1919. Pre-war anti-semitism in Europe had resulted in the emigration of some half a million Zionist Jews to Palestine by 1939, creating an incendiary political and social problem between the two rival populations. This had been confirmed by a Royal Commission report that concluded as early as 1936 that the Jewish and Palestinian Arab populations could not live peacefully together. This influx of Jewish settlers continued to grow throughout the war with many fleeing the Holocaust in Europe.

After the war, relations between the two peoples worsened and by 1946 Palestine was in ferment. As a result, Britain increasingly was left with a situation that it could not, and more importantly, did not want to police. This feeling was compounded in July 1946 when Jewish militants from the right-wing Zionist paramilitary group, *Irgun*, killed over ninety people in a bomb attack on the British Mandate headquarters at the King David Hotel in Jerusalem, and in July 1947 when various ships from Europe illegally carrying Jewish passengers, many of whom were survivors from the concentration camps, began arriving in Palestinian ports. These included those on board the overcrowded *Exodus 1947* that carried over 4,000 who were refused entry into Palestine at the port of Haifa. This was in accordance with earlier agreements, with those detained being returned to internment camps in Europe by the Royal Navy.

Increased Jewish militancy, as well as political pressure from US public opinion, especially after the *Exodus* incident, weakened Attlee's resolve to deal with the problem of Palestine, and led to the announcement that it was Britain's intention to hand back the administration of the mandate to the UN. As a result, plans for the partition of Palestine were hastily drawn in 1948 by UNSCOP, the United Nations Special Committee on Palestine, which had been set up the previous year, and these proposed the creation of both a Jewish and a Palestinian state. But these proposals were rejected by both sides and, when Britain finally pulled out in May 1948, David Ben Gurion unilaterally declared the creation of the state of Israel. This new state was immediately attacked by five neighbouring Arab countries.

This first Arab-Israeli war was to last for eight months before a UN-brokered truce confirmed a convincing Israeli victory. However, the truce brought no real peace and the Arab-Israeli problem continued to create tension in the region throughout the remainder of the century. Problems surrounding the creation of a Jewish nation state on land claimed by Palestinian Arabs were not helped by the importance that both the superpowers attached to the region. As the century progressed, Israel was generally able to count on the support of the USA while the USSR was often willing to support the claims of its Arab enemies.

Britain's gradual withdrawal from empire during the late 1940s allowed Attlee's administration to concentrate on reconstruction at home. The war had united the country in a way that had seemed impossible in 1939, and it was clear from the landslide victory of 1945 that the people of Britain believed that the Labour Party was best placed to build on this unity.

The Labour manifesto had emphasised its commitment to the Welfare State and democratic socialism, with the government accepting responsibility for the health and social security of the whole nation. This was very much in line with the findings of the Beveridge Report that had been published in 1942. This had identified 'five great evils' – squalor, ignorance, want, idleness and disease – that were to be challenged by the Welfare State and this was to be funded by taxation and a national insurance programme. After the war, the British people wanted a government committed to this improvement of society, a commitment to social welfare, 'from the cradle to the grave'.

Central to this pledge was the Labour Party's support for the National Health Service. The NHS came into being in July 1948 and offered free and comprehensive health care throughout the country. Initial opposition from some medical bodies was soon overcome and the NHS, despite its ever-increasing costs, was to go on to become a model copied in many other countries. The war had changed the role of the state within British society immeasurably and this was reflected in the nationalisation of key elements of the industrial economy that included steel, coal, gas and the railways. This process had begun in March 1946 when the Bank of England, after 252 years, had lost its independence. This created a culture of state control over industry and commerce that lasted until the privatisation revolution carried out by Margaret Thatcher in the 1980s.

France emerged from the war both politically and economically fragile. Five years of Nazi domination had left very deep scars that were to take a long time to heal, and its people tended to look inwards in an attempt to make some sense of their terrible war experience. Negotiations about a constitution to replace the discredited Third Republic took over a year to conclude and finally rejected de Gaulle's demands for a strong presidency. Furthermore, much of the territory in the Far East lost to the Japanese during the Vichy period was never recovered, despite a long war against the newly proclaimed republic of Vietnam that began in 1946.

Although France returned to become a leader in world affairs and a permanent member of the UN Security Council, it was never able to recapture the position of pre-eminence that it had held before the war. Like Britain, it had to learn to play an increasingly subordinate role to the USA in the new post-war world order. Unlike Britain, however, it was a position, particularly under de Gaulle in the 1960s, that it was loath to adopt.

The Potsdam Conference, the UN and the Nuremberg Trials

The decline in influence of Britain and France and the new importance in international affairs of the USA and the USSR had become clear before delegates met at Potsdam to discuss the same two issues that had dominated proceedings at Versailles twenty-six years earlier. Firstly, there was the question of how to deal with Germany and its allies and, secondly, leaders discussed how to make sure that the world never went to war again.

The question of how to deal with the defeated Germany had first been discussed at Yalta. These discussions continued at Potsdam where it was decided that Germany should have no central government but that it should be split into four administrative zones. These zones would be run by Britain, the USA, the USSR and France. A similar arrangement would cover the government of Berlin, despite the fact that the German capital was located well within the Soviet zone.

The border between Poland and Germany was also agreed and it was decided to send those Germans living in Poland, Hungary and Czechoslovakia back to Germany to avoid future ethnic problems such as those that had inflamed the Sudetenland in the 1930s. It was also agreed that Germany should remain a single economic unit.

No peace treaties were signed at Potsdam and a Council of Foreign Ministers, which included representatives from China, was convened to work out details for these. Increasingly, however, agreement between various Council members became more and more difficult to find as fundamental ideological differences between East and West, which had defined the interwar period, once again resurfaced. It was these renewed differences that were to dominate the nature of international relations for the next four decades.

However, the euphoria and general sense of goodwill that followed the defeat of Germany and the fascist right meant that, initially at least, the Grand Alliance was more successful in dealing with the second great question of 1945. Despite the increasing tension and suspicion over the political future of Europe, the Allies were successful in setting up a replacement for the discredited League of Nations.

In January 1942, Britain, the USA, the USSR and twenty-three other nations who were fighting the Axis powers met in Washington and pledged themselves to a post-war organisation dedicated to guaranteeing basic human rights. This came five months after a similar declaration, the Atlantic Charter, had been signed in August 1941 by Churchill and Roosevelt at a meeting on board HMS *Prince of Wales*, 'somewhere at sea' in the same North Atlantic that was being fought over so viciously at the time. At their meeting, the Allied leaders agreed a set of principles for international partnership and government that would form the basis of the United Nations Organisation.

Further negotiations continued through the war until delegates from fifty nations met at San Francisco between April and June 1945 to write a draft charter for the UN. As with the League of Nations, the UN was dominated by three main administrative sections: the General Assembly, the Security Council and the Secretariat. This was ratified in London at the first session of the General Assembly in October 1945.

The General Assembly was to meet annually to discuss general policy and every member state received one vote. The Security Council originally consisted of eleven members and was empowered to deal with crises as they occurred. Six of the members were elected from the General Assembly on two-year terms of office while Britain, France, the USA, the USSR and China, the major belligerents in the war against the Axis powers, became permanent members. Finally, a Secretary General was appointed to control the Secretariat, whose function was to make sure that the decisions of the Security Council and the General Assembly were carried out.

It was hoped that the UN would prove to be more effective as a body of international authority than the League had been. In order to do this, delegates knew that the new organisation needed more authority and power than the League had had and for this the charter made provision. Importantly, this was given the backing of both the USSR and the USA. Finally, it aimed to guarantee human rights and to make sure that the horrors of the Nazi era were never again repeated.

Post-war Allied co-operation also led to the successful prosecution of many leading Nazis. In October 1945, the new governments in Norway and France executed the Nazi collaborators, Quisling and Laval, who had led their countries during the war, while Pétain had his death penalty commuted to life imprisonment by General de Gaulle.

Meanwhile, judges from Britain, France, the USA and the USSR met in November 1945 at Nuremberg, the city of the great Nazi rallies of the 1930s, to hear evidence against over 170 alleged Nazi leaders including Ribbentrop, Goering and Hess. The Nuremberg Trials lasted until the end of 1946 and sifted through evidence collected from all over the Nazi empire. Allied prosecution lawyers were helped in their task by the meticulous record keeping of the Nazi state and many of those on trial were convicted for their crimes.

On 15 October 1946, Goering took his own life only a few hours before he was due to be executed. A few hours later, Ribbentrop and nine other leading Nazis were hanged in the Nuremberg prison gymnasium. Albert Speer, Hitler's favourite architect and a man who had become increasingly close to Hitler during the war, was sentenced to twenty years in prison. Rudolf Hess, Hitler's second in command for much of the 1920s and 1930s who had flown to Scotland in 1941 on his own initiative in a vain attempt to secure peace with Britain, was sentenced to life imprisonment. He died forty-one years later in 1987 while still in captivity in Spandau Prison in West Berlin where he had been the sole inmate since 1966. Immediately following his death, the prison was torn down and demolished so that it would not become a neo-Nazi shrine.

It is certain that many Nazis escaped punishment and continued to evade justice for the rest of their lives, with many, including Mengele and perhaps Martin Bormann, escaping to South America. But the Nuremberg trials did allow the world to see justice being done, and they also served to illustrate clearly the barbarity and awfulness of the Nazi regime. In particular, the trials were successful in highlighting the horrors of the concentration camps, and the true enormity and scale of the Holocaust against the Jews, the Gypsies and the Slavic peoples was made public.

The Origins of the Cold War

Despite the success that surrounded the foundation of the UN and the prosecutions at Nuremberg, it was perhaps inevitable that the ideological split between the communist and capitalist worlds would once again re-emerge after the war against Nazism had been won. In essence, the wartime Grand Alliance had never been any more than a liaison of necessity and, with the defeat of Germany, Italy and Japan, it was no longer either needed or desired. Soon, the friendly co-operation between East and West that had symbolised relations at the end of the war was replaced by suspicion, animosity and intrigue.

The first illustration that the communist and capitalist worlds were returning to their pre-war state of animosity came over the question of who should govern Poland after liberation. The Western Allies had lent their support from 1943 to the London Poles with whom Stalin had broken off diplomatic relations in 1941. This was after allegations made by the London Poles that the Red Army had massacred upwards of 22,000 Polish soldiers, policemen and officers in the Katyn Forest during the Soviet invasion. The London Poles wanted to create a Western-style liberal democracy and were deeply suspicious of Soviet intentions. However, Stalin gave his support to the Polish Committee of National Liberation, a communist group that had been established in the city of Lublin after its liberation by the Red Army in July 1944.

By the time of the conference at Yalta, Britain and the USA were faced with the political reality that the Red Army had overrun much of Eastern Europe and were in effect the only real authority in the region. Therefore, Roosevelt and Churchill had seen little option but to accept Stalin's demand that the communist-dominated Lublin Poles form the bulk of the new Polish government.

In return, they did manage to secure the concession from Stalin that free and democratic elections would be held at the earliest possible opportunity and that some representation in the new government would be offered to the London Poles. However, it soon became clear to Truman and Attlee in the months that followed VE Day that these promises were hollow ones, and that a compliant, Soviet-backed communist government was being established firmly under Moscow's control. A similar pattern soon emerged in Hungary, Romania and Bulgaria.

In this way, Stalin had managed by 1947 to implement the most important element of his post-war foreign policy. By creating a series of satellite states in Eastern Europe strongly aligned to Moscow, he managed to construct a strong military and geographical buffer zone between the USSR and Germany. Only in Yugoslavia did Stalin come across a communist government that refused to accept Soviet hegemony. General Tito, the leader of Yugoslavia from 1945 until his death in 1980, had led the communist partisans against the Nazis and he was unwilling to give up the freedom and independence that he and his supporters had worked so hard for five years to gain.

The countries in Western Europe that had been liberated by the Western Allies in general adopted liberal democratic models of government. In Italy, this followed a plebiscite that voted in 1946 to abolish the monarchy and replace it with a republic. As in France, the economic mess in Italy that followed the war saw support for the communists grow although it was the Christian Democrats that featured most strongly in the new government. Western-style liberal democracy and free elections also returned to France where the Fourth Republic replaced the Third in December 1946. But this inherited many of the faults of its predecessor and was finally replaced with the Fifth Republic in 1958. The Netherlands, Belgium, Luxembourg and the countries of Scandinavia also soon returned to liberal democratic models of government.

Free elections were arranged in many other liberated countries of Western Europe and a number of different political parties were elected to government. However, one common factor, not surprisingly, linked all of these. They all showed a clear commitment to fight any resurgence of the radical right that had caused ruin of Europe during the previous two decades.

At Yalta and Potsdam, post-war geographical spheres of influence had been discussed and an uneasy status quo in Europe had been reached by 1946. This saw a new balance of power in Europe, with the USSR dominating Eastern Europe while the USA continued to influence political, economic and social issues in the West.

But there were areas on the periphery where both sides wished to exert and extend their influence, and in these areas tension increased as relations between Moscow and Washington deteriorated. As a result, the focus of the stress and discord between East and West shifted in 1946 and 1947 from Poland, Eastern Europe and Germany to the Middle East, the eastern Mediterranean and the Balkans. Iran, Turkey and Greece in particular were countries on this periphery in regions where the two new superpowers squared off.

Problems first began in 1946 when massive British and US military and political pressure, and perhaps the implied threat of US nuclear capability, had been needed to persuade Stalin to withdraw the Red Army from Iran by the date set at Yalta. Meanwhile, Stalin continued to exert pressure on the government in Turkey, arguing that a strong Soviet presence was needed there to protect the USSR's southern borders. Truman rejected these arguments and, in one of the first sorties of the Cold War, immediately showed his continuing commitment to Turkey by increasing US naval presence in the eastern Mediterranean.

However, the incident that finally brought Washington and Moscow into open conflict was the Greek Civil War, which had broken out in October 1946. This followed a complicated sequence of events that had threatened war for over a year. After the Nazis had been driven out at the end of the war, the monarchists with British help had returned to power. But the communist partisans, who had fought the Nazis throughout the war and whose support base was strong throughout the country, also claimed the right to govern.

When Britain refused Stalin's demands at the UN to withdraw its troops, the Greek communists went into open revolt, and it soon became clear that they would take over the country if British support for the monarchists was withdrawn. However, six long years of war had nearly bankrupted Britain and so Attlee was forced to inform Truman that he intended to withdraw British troops from Greece by the summer of 1947.

Thereafter, it seemed likely that a Soviet-backed regime would be installed in Greece, directly threatening vital Western interests in the eastern Mediterranean. These mostly concerned the increasingly important supply routes through the Suez Canal to the oilfields of the Middle East. Truman was not willing to jeopardise these vital interests, and so, as a result, set about formulating a foreign policy that would successfully counter this communist threat in southern Europe.

This policy came to be known as the Truman Doctrine and was announced in a speech to Congress in March 1947. By this time, there had been a massive shift in American public opinion against Stalin, and this allowed Truman to pledge US support to any peoples resisting 'attempted subjugation', in practice offering to help any nation on the periphery of the Soviet Bloc wishing to remain independent of it. The Truman Doctrine aimed to limit the influence and spread of communism either through economic aid and assistance or through armed intervention, and it formed the basis of US foreign policy for the next forty years.

Truman soon showed his commitment to the doctrine when he secured Congressional support for a $US400 million grant to aid the pro-Western governments in Greece and Turkey. This signalled an important shift in post-war US foreign policy, and it coincided with the setting up of the House Un-American Committee, which in the early 1950s was dominated by Senator Joseph McCarthy. The fear of and revulsion for communism, which to a certain extent had been suspended during the war, was once again returning to US politics and public consciousness. The perceived threat of Soviet expansion in post-war Europe, the Middle East and elsewhere also led to the creation in September 1947 of the CIA, with Truman taking a highly aggressive attitude towards the gathering of intelligence. The CIA was to be at the forefront of the fight against communism for the next forty years.

As the opening salvos of the Cold War were being shot, it soon became clear to Truman that his doctrine would not work unless a full and lasting economic recovery was accomplished throughout the whole of Europe, and that the kind of economic destitution that still faced most European countries in 1947 would only lead to an increase in popularity for communism, which had already been seen in, especially, Italy and France. Truman concluded that a strong and prosperous Europe was needed to deter the spread of communism that had already moved into Eastern Europe.

The job of finding the solution to these problems was given to Truman's secretary of state, General George Marshall, who in June 1947 put forward plans for the recovery of Europe in a speech at Harvard University. The European Recovery Programme, or Marshall Plan, planned to invest heavily in Europe and help set up an integrated and co-operative economic unit that would lead to renewed prosperity for the whole of the war-torn continent. It was also hoped that a rejuvenated European economy would create a vibrant market for goods being churned out by the buoyant US industrial sector. Britain was to be the largest recipient of Marshall Aid and, in all, sixteen countries were to be helped.

Marshall Aid was offered on the condition that Europe itself made the first steps towards collaboration and, as a consequence, the Organisation for European Economic Co-operation was set up in April 1948. This was the precursor to the Common Market, the EEC, the European Community and the European Union. Recovery in Europe from the hardships of the war had not been helped by the exceptionally harsh winter of 1946-47, and so Marshall Aid was warmly welcomed by Britain, France and the other recipients across Western Europe. However, after lengthy negotiations at a specially convened conference in Paris, it was rejected by the USSR and its satellites.

Stalin's major objective in 1945 had been to ensure the USSR's own security and he believed that this was best preserved by destroying Germany's economic base. He was worried that German military power might one day unite with the strength of the US economy and turn on the USSR, and he feared that Marshall Aid was the first step in this process. The tense situation was not helped early in 1948 when Czechoslovakia, the only country overrun by the Red Army in 1945 to have held free elections, fell to a Soviet-backed communist takeover.

In the USA and across Western Europe, this was seen as evidence of Stalin's increasingly aggressive foreign policy and consequently support for the Marshall Plan, especially in the US Congress, increased. Marshall Aid lasted from 1947 to 1952 and its benefit to recipient countries was enormous. Cities were rebuilt, jobs were created and a huge amount of effort was put in to the re-establishment of food supplies.

As such, it was crucial in the redevelopment of a continent that had been ruined by six years of unprecedented destruction although, due to Stalin, not all of Europe's people were to benefit. This created an economic gulf between East and West that was to widen as the century continued. This condemned the people of Eastern Europe to a living standard far below the one enjoyed in the West, and this situation was to change very little, even after the collapse of communism in the early 1990s.

The Marshall Plan was stimulated by Western fears of the spread of communism and these were not confined to Europe. In China, civil war between the communists under Mao Tse-tung and the Nationalists under Chiang Kai-shek once again broke out in the middle of 1946, with Mao returning to the guerrilla tactics that had been so successful since the Long March in 1934.

Paramount importance was attached to gaining peasant support, and slowly the Red Army was able to push north-eastwards against a Nationalist army racked by corruption and internal power struggles, eventually seizing Beijing in January 1949. Mao then ordered his generals to push south, forcing the rump of Chiang Kai-shek's army to abandon mainland China and take refuge on the island of Taiwan. It was at this time that the Cold War became hot for Britain for the first time. This was when the frigate, HMS *Amethyst*, was fired on by communist forces on 20 April 1949 as it sailed up the Yangtze River, along international waterways, to deliver supplies to the British community stranded at Nanking. This resulted in a 14-week stand-off with this new enemy in the Far East that was only ended when the ship made a dash for the sea over 100-miles away.

As a result of Chiang's flight to Taiwan, Mao was able to proclaim the establishment of the People's Republic of China from the steps of the Imperial Forbidden City in Beijing in October 1949. He then quickly took steps to secure the revolution by implementing a series of land reforms that not only centralised power but also granted increased rights to the peasants whose support had been so important in the communist victory.

So by the end of 1949, the Western Allies faced the political reality of having to face major communist rivals on two fronts. In a speech in Fulton, Missouri, in March 1946 Winston Churchill had coined the term 'Iron Curtain' to describe the barrier that had come down and divided Europe between the worlds of communism and liberal democracy. Now it was said that a 'Bamboo Curtain' divided Asia in a similar way.

The Berlin Blockade and Airlift, and the Cold War Divide

By the beginning of 1948, a Cold War was being waged between two new superpowers, with the clash between the rival political ideologies that each supported defining international affairs for the rest of the century. This had begun with tension over the future of Poland and Germany, intensified with events in Turkey and Greece and increased over negotiations concerning Marshall Aid. This constant state of aggression and non-co-operation between East and West was further deepened by the communist revolution in China.

But it was over the question of the administration of Germany that it really was to find its focus. It had been agreed at Yalta and Potsdam that Germany should be split into four administrative zones, with each run by one of the four victorious Allies. It was also agreed that the richer spoils should go to the USSR and France because of their wartime losses. As a result, these two zones between 1945 and 1947 were largely stripped of their plant machinery, currency and raw materials as reparation for the damage done by the Nazi regime.

However, Britain and the USA had been forced to import food and emergency provisions into their poorer zones to forestall a human tragedy during a similar period, and by 1947 this was a situation that was becoming more and more intolerable to authorities in both Washington and London. As a result, and in an attempt to make their sectors more economically viable, a joint decision was therefore taken to amalgamate the US and British zones into one economic unit. This decision was soon justified, with an improved economic performance taking the strain off the two occupying powers, and the French zone was soon also incorporated into this Western entity. At the same time, a similar arrangement was being made in West Berlin.

All this was met with severe protest from the USSR, which claimed that the new arrangements between the Western Allies went against the agreements made at Potsdam, and diplomats from both sides of the Iron Curtain could see that the tense compromise that had been worked out for the administration of Germany was breaking down. However, it was not until June 1948 that this deterioration in relations erupted into open hostility.

The merging of the Western zones had been followed by discussions about how best to secure its future. These had focused on how to improve the economic performance of the new entity as well as how to counter what were increasingly seen as threats from the communist East. As a consequence, it was decided that a new currency, the Deutschmark, should be created as a replacement for the discredited Reichsmark and that, at the same time, the newly constituted Western zone would be eligible to apply for Marshall Aid.

Stalin's response was swift and decisive, with a new rival currency set up in the Soviet zone within a week. When the Western Allies refused to allow the use of this new Soviet-backed currency in their zone in Berlin, Stalin ordered the blockade of all road and rail links to the city from the west. His intention was to isolate the newly amalgamated Western zone of the city and force the Western Allies out of Berlin.

Truman's response to the Berlin Blockade was equally swift and robust, with round-the-clock supply flights quickly organised from bases in the Western sector to feed and service West Berlin's population of two million. The Berlin Airlift was to last for eleven months and, in total, over 200,000 flights made the 300-mile-round journey to West Berlin as the stand-off between East and West intensified.

In retaliation to the Soviet blockade, the Western powers stopped the delivery of essential supplies to communist regimes in Eastern Europe, hugely damaging ailing economies there, and in April 1949 they collectively supported the creation of the Federal Republic of Germany, or West Germany. Finally, Stalin saw that the West was not going to give up West Berlin and the blockade was called off in May 1949. The split that was to divide Germany for a generation was finalised in October 1949 when the formation of the German Democratic Republic, or East Germany, was announced.

In September 1939, the world had gone to war, with the worlds of communism and capitalism uniting in 1941 and 1942 in an alliance of necessity in order to defeat the combined forces of Nazi Germany, fascist Italy and militarist Japan. Victory had come in 1945, but still war was to rage on as the ideological split between East and West re-emerged once again. This Cold War, fought across the world in any number of proxy wars and threatening the world with destruction through nuclear annihilation on more than one occasion, was to dominate international affairs for the next forty years.

This had begun slowly, but by the time of the Berlin Blockade and Airlift in 1948 and 1949 any semblance of alliance or friendship that might have lingered since 1945 had gone. It showed, on the one hand, that Stalin was serious about his commitment to a strong, communist Eastern Bloc that he intended to dominate and, on the other, that the USA intended to stand firm by its commitment to the Truman Doctrine.

Before the end of the crisis, the nations of Western Europe and North America had drawn together into an alliance of common protection against the threat of communism. This was NATO, the North Atlantic Treaty Organisation, which twelve countries including Britain, France and the USA joined in April 1949. In 1955, West Germany also joined NATO. On the other side of the ideological divide, China soon joined the USSR and the satellite nations of communist Eastern Europe in a series of treaties of mutual protection.

The two superpowers had nearly come to blows in 1948 and 1949 over the crisis in Berlin, and it seemed more likely than not that an armed confrontation of sorts would soon turn the Cold War hot. This analysis proved correct within a year when the two sides did go to war. However, this was to be not in Germany or in Europe, but instead was to take place on the other side of the world, thousands of miles from Berlin.

The Cold War Peace
The 1950s

June 1950
(The Outbreak of the Korean War)
to
May 1960
(The Paris Summit Conference)

The Korean War

The Rise of McCarthyism

Stalin's Last Years and the New Approach of Nikita Khushchev

The Suez Crisis and European Decolonisation

The Origins of the European Community

The Non-Aligned Movement and the People's Republic of China

The USA in the 1950s: the Boom Years and the Civil Rights Movement

Apartheid in South Africa

The Escalation of the Arms Race and the Return of Cold War Hostility

The Korean War

Europe had provided the focus for the initial confrontations of the Cold War, but it was in Asia that these sparks of animosity turned into full-scale war. Tension in the region had been increasing since before the proclamation of the People's Republic of China in October 1949, and conflict of sorts had long seemed likely. This finally erupted in June 1950 when 130,000 troops from communist North Korea attacked the US-backed republic in the South. It was not long before President Truman confirmed that his doctrine aimed to protect countries not only in Europe, and contingency plans to send US troops to South Korea were quickly put into operation.

But this immediate show of US support could not stop the initial communist advance, with the North Korean army quickly capturing Seoul, the South Korean capital. However, the North Korean attack coincided with a period when the USSR was boycotting meetings of the UN Security Council in protest at the US refusal to accept the legitimacy of the new communist regime in China. Truman now used this Soviet absence to force through emergency resolutions that, firstly, condemned the communist attack and, secondly, committed UN troops to the defence of South Korea.

Many nations pledged their support in principle to these resolutions, but by September 1950 only a small British force from Hong Kong had actually arrived on the Korean peninsula to share the fighting with the South Korean army and the US troops that were to dominate the UN force. The commander of the US army of occupation in Japan, General Douglas MacArthur, was put in charge of these UN forces.

As the USA was working at the UN in New York to secure backing for the military operation, North Korean forces continued their progress southwards, eventually forcing the South Korean-UN armies back to the port of Pusan in the very south of the Korean peninsula. But as the situation became more and more grave and UN military commanders began to make preparations for evacuation, MacArthur showed his vision and genius as a military commander.

Rather than attack the North Koreans with a conventional frontal assault, he planned to cut across the communist supply lines with an audacious marine-based campaign that would strike in the north, 200 miles behind enemy lines. This would relieve Seoul and force the communists to organise a general withdrawal. In early September 1950, this attack was launched at the port of Inchon, just a few miles to the west of Seoul.

As a result, the South Korean capital was recaptured within a week as the South Korean-UN alliance pushed eastwards across the Korean peninsula. This cut off a large part of the North Korean army that remained around Pusan to the south. Such was the success of MacArthur's Inchon strategy that within a month the last North Korean troops around Pusan had either been captured or chased back across the thirty-eighth parallel that marked the border between the two belligerents. South Korean integrity had once again been restored.

China had already warned the USA that it would interpret any incursion into North Korea across the thirty-eighth parallel as an act of war. But Truman and MacArthur, boosted by Congressional approval for a massive defence budget increase, were not to be deterred, and still hoped that the threat of nuclear retaliation would keep communist China out of the war. Both men remained determined to reunify Korea and end the spread of communism in Asia.

But Mao took little notice of this implied threat of US nuclear retaliation and in November 1950 the Red Army attacked the UN force as it approached the Yalu River. This was close to the Sino-North Korean border and threatened vital Chinese industrial concerns in the region. The Chinese Red Army was an experienced and well-organised military unit, having only just ended fighting for the first time since 1928, and it now used this experience to great effect, soon forcing MacArthur's troops back across the thirty-eighth parallel. Seoul was taken for a second time before the communist advance was finally stopped in February 1951, one hundred miles further south. It was along this new front line that the forces of capitalism and communism in Asia were to face each other in a bitter war of attrition over the next two years.

Truman soon came to believe that containment, the policy that had been used so successfully in Eastern Europe, should be adopted in the fight against the communists in Korea. This drew fierce criticism from MacArthur who not only wanted to see the defeat of communism in North Korea but also advocated renewed support for the Nationalist army of Chiang Kai-shek based in Taiwan. Truman, as a result, increasingly came to consider MacArthur a liability and had him sacked in April 1951 for refusing to follow orders. However, MacArthur's words of defiance had caught the mood of public opinion during the McCarthy years of the early 1950s, and he was to return home a hero, enjoying a ticker-tape parade in New York held in his honour.

While MacArthur returned to the USA after nearly ten years of active service in the Far East, the war in Korea dragged on through 1952 and into 1953. In this increasingly brutal war of attrition, artillery power was to play an increasingly important role and both sides were to suffer huge casualties. A number of attempts were made to negotiate a peace settlement, but for two years talks brought little progress.

Finally, the election of President Eisenhower in the USA, the death of Stalin in the USSR and the renewed threat of nuclear war at last created a climate in which peace could be made, and a ceasefire that ended the fighting was signed in July 1953. The three-year struggle had claimed the lives of over three million people. After the end of hostilities, North Korea remained under communist rule and an autocratic and repressive regime developed there that survived the century. In the south, South Korea continued to be allied to the West with a strong capitalist economy that soon made it one of the leading industrial manufacturers in eastern Asia.

However, the ceasefire did not actually end the war itself, which was still officially being waged forty-seven years later at the end of the century, because the North Koreans refused to sign a peace accord. As a result, relations remained fraught throughout the Cold War and beyond as armed units from both sides took up positions facing against each other across the demilitarised zone that had been agreed upon in 1953.

The Rise of McCarthyism

In the USA, the deterioration of relations with the USSR in the last years of Stalin's long dictatorship, the loss of China to Mao in 1949 and the continuing spread of communism through Asia led to an anti-communist phobia that was expressed in the witch-hunts of McCarthyism. These were led by Senator Joseph McCarthy who had announced in February 1950 to a shocked nation that he was in possession of evidence that proved that 205 named employees of the State Department, which was responsible for foreign affairs and so dealt with the USSR, were communist sympathisers.

His revelation closely followed the conviction for perjury of Alger Hiss, a former senior State Department official who had accompanied Roosevelt to Yalta. Hiss, who had left government service in 1947, had been accused of giving secrets to the USSR. The clamour against Hiss was led by, among others, an ambitious young right-wing lawyer from California called Richard Nixon who during the trial was a first-term Republican Congressman.

The conviction of Hiss was used by McCarthy as evidence for his claim and, as he shot to national prominence, he was to use his position in Washington to smear and discredit all those who refused to co-operate with his investigations. Among his most important victims were such leading Democrats as the secretary of state, Dean Acheson, and his predecessor, General George

Marshall. His sustained campaign against the record of the Democrat government led in part to the Republican landslide victory in the presidential election of 1952.

After the inauguration of President Eisenhower, with Nixon as his vice president, McCarthy widened the scope of his offensive to challenge liberals and intellectuals from many walks of life. Among others, scientists, actors, journalists and writers were investigated and a blacklist was drawn up of those who refused to give evidence. Their number included Charlie Chaplin, who was hounded out of the country in 1952, Arthur Miller, whose play, *The Crucible*, used the setting of the Salem witch-hunts in seventeenth-century Massachusetts to discredit the McCarthy witch-hunts of the 1950s, Orson Welles, the film director, and Robert Oppenheimer, the chief scientist of the Manhattan Project. The anti-communist vitriol of McCarthyism also played its part in the trial, conviction and execution in June 1953 of Julius and Ethel Rosenberg on charges of selling secrets to the USSR during the war.

In time, McCarthy's tactics and procedures were exposed, and televised proceedings of McCarthy's attack on the army in 1954 showed him as a vicious and vindictive bully who used his position to extract testimony at any cost. This came at a time when many US families had loved ones in Korea, with many others having lost fathers and sons in World War Two. McCarthy's attack included slurs against such decorated World War Two heroes as General Marshall and even President Eisenhower himself, and the insinuation that the army was an institution that harboured communism soon turned public opinion against him. His methods and behaviour were heavily criticised by a Senate committee soon after, and he was to disappear from public life as quickly as he had entered it. He died in relative obscurity in 1956.

Despite his personal fall from power, his investigations had articulated a fear of and revulsion for communism that was widespread in the USA. This was to last long after McCarthy had passed from the Washington committee rooms that he dominated with such ferocity in the early 1950s. The early years of the Cold War had created a deep-seated loathing of the communist world that was to remain ever-present in the USA, even during the years of détente in the 1970s.

This anti-communist stance was widely supported in Britain where a majority Conservative government was returned for the first time in a generation after the general election of October 1951. This was led by the ageing Winston Churchill who within four months was advising a new monarch after the accession of Elizabeth II to the throne in February 1952.

Churchill was to be the first of ten prime ministers who would serve the queen before the end of the century. He was also in charge of the country when Tenzing Norgay, a Nepalese, and Edmund Hillary, a New Zealander, conquered Mount Everest on 29 May 1953 as members of a British-led expedition.

Stalin's Last Years and the New Approach of Nikita Khrushchev

As the McCarthy witch-hunts gathered momentum in the USA, the Soviet people were enduring the last years of Stalin's tyranny. Stalin had maintained a strong grip on power after World War Two, and those who had hoped that the euphoria of the Soviet victory in 1945 would lead to a brighter future were soon disappointed. He had soon returned to the oppressive policies of the 1930s, and made it clear to those closest to him that victory over Germany was to be used to increase his control of the country.

He had ordered a massive programme of reconstruction that by 1950 had returned Soviet industrial output to pre-war levels, seen the explosion of the first Soviet atomic bomb on the steppes of remote Kazakhstan and expanded Soviet influence deep into Eastern Europe. But the success of this reconstruction was borne by the ordinary Soviet people who were expected to make every possible sacrifice to rebuild the country in order to challenge the capitalist West. Taxes were increased, work shifts lengthened and prices raised.

As the Cold War intensified during the early 1950s, Stalin became more and more adamant that the influence and expression of Western ideas should be banned from Soviet society. Any dissent was crushed as ruthlessly as it had been in the purges of the 1930s, with more and more Soviet citizens sent to the labour camps or exiled to one of the industrial towns that had sprung up in the Urals and all over Siberia. A taste of this future policy had been experienced in 1945 when many Soviet soldiers liberated from German POW camps were transported straight to labour camps in Siberia. This was done to stop them spreading counter-revolutionary ideas that they may have encountered in the West.

This paranoia and delusion had always been present in Stalin's behaviour and it surfaced for a last time during the Doctors' Plot of 1953. Anti-Jewish sentiment within the country had been growing for some time before nine Jewish doctors were arrested in Moscow and accused of conspiring to murder the party leadership. They were linked with the death in 1947 of Andrei Zhdanov, the party leader in Leningrad, and a sustained campaign in the government press was instigated against them. There were many who feared that this would be the start of one final Stalinist purge. But the nine doctors, and perhaps many more who might have come after them, were saved from execution when it was announced in March 1953 that Stalin had suffered a massive stroke and died.

With the demise of McCarthy in the USA and the death of Stalin in the USSR, the world was able to enjoy a period of relative thaw in the Cold War. For a time, this had seemed unlikely, with Lavrenti Beria, the head of the Soviet secret police and the architect of Stalin's terror, poised to take the place of his benefactor. But fearing that they would be the first victims of the new regime, Beria's colleagues closed ranks and had him arrested. He was executed as a British spy in December 1953.

With Beria gone, the two men who had masterminded his demise, Georgy Malenkov and Nikita Khrushchev, brokered a collective leadership deal. However, it was not long before Khrushchev was able to use his position as general secretary of the Communist Party, as Stalin had done in the 1920s, to secure support from crucial elements in the army, industry and the party itself and, in the first of a series of power struggles that brought Khrushchev to power alone, Malenkov was out-manoeuvred and forced to resign in February 1955.

However, this power struggle within the collective leadership between 1953 and 1958 was not accompanied by the terror and repression that had characterised Stalin's time, and Beria was only one of very few who lost their lives to the new regime. Malenkov, for example, was appointed minister of energy although he was disgraced two years later as a member of the 'Anti-Party Group'. He was then sent to Siberia where he became a director of a power station. Molotov, Stalin's foreign minister, was also denounced and was expelled from government in early 1957 before being sent to Mongolia as ambassador. Later, he was expelled from the party itself and was not readmitted until just before his death in the mid-1980s.

In the wake of Stalin's death, the new administration began to relax some of the worst constraints of his long reign. Prisoners were set free from the labour camps, a concentrated effort was made to increase the production of consumer goods to improve living standards, and artists, musicians, authors and other cultural figures were to enjoy more freedom from the strictures of state control.

By February 1956, Khrushchev felt strong enough to risk criticising the excesses of Stalinism and in his Secret Speech at the Twentieth Party Congress of the Communist Party, he attacked Stalin personally for the purges of the 1930s, for his war-time record and for the development of a cult of personality. It became known as the 'Secret' Speech because its details should have remained private to the Congress, but were leaked to the Soviet and international press beforehand.

In practice, the process of de-Stalinisation that began in 1953, and that culminated with the Secret Speech, did little to change the party and state structures that had grown up in the 1930s and 1940s. The most important consequence of this was that, by and large, the improvements to living standards promised by Khrushchev never materialised. However, it did bring about a respite from the terror that had been endured for a generation, and the majority of Soviet citizens welcomed the new reforms implemented by their new and more enlightened leaders. It also led to the release of many from the Gulag and these included Alexander Solzhenitsyn who returned from internal exile in Siberia in 1957.

Khrushchev also presided over a change in Soviet foreign policy that saw the adoption of a far less aggressive attitude towards the West. He called this policy peaceful coexistence, having become convinced that Eisenhower was serious in his commitment to fight communist expansion. He concluded that Soviet influence outside the area occupied by the Red Army at the end of the war would not be easily gained through military conflict.

Khrushchev argued that it was necessary for communism to find other ways of competing with the capitalist world, and that the class struggle would have to take on a different character. Peaceful coexistence would show the outside world the benefits of communist society, and this, Khrushchev argued, would lead to the slow but inevitable destruction of capitalism. To support his new foreign policy, Khrushchev embarked on a number of high-profile foreign visits and ordered the encouragement of cultural, trade and social links with the West.

However, many of these backfired, with it clear to many in the USSR just how far the communist world had fallen behind the West. This was particularly the case during the Kitchen Debate, a spontaneous but fierce exchange of views between Vice President Nixon and Khrushchev during their joint visit to a model kitchen at the American National Exhibition being held in Moscow in July 1959. Khruchshev made fun of the gadgets in the kitchen, and suggested that the communist world would soon pass the capitalist West and wave contemptuously at it as it did so. Nixon pointed to the kitchen on show and retorted that it was workers under capitalism, not communism, who were better off. He made it clear that he thought that that was a situation that was not going to change in the foreseeable future.

Khrushchev also found problems in China where peaceful coexistence was seen as a betrayal. This led to a split between the two communist giants that was never fully mended for thirty years, and consequently thousands of advisers, engineers and technicians, who had been sent to China by Stalin, were brought home.

In the West, the changes after the death of Stalin were greeted with reserved enthusiasm. Stalin had been a difficult figure to deal with and the last years of his life had produced an angry stalemate in East-West relations. Khrushchev's new commitment to peaceful coexistence offered a chance to normalise relations after a decade of post-war rancour. Conciliatory stances on Vietnam, Korea and Austria suggested that the new Soviet leadership wanted a thaw in the Cold War, and the first chance to put this to the test came in 1955 at the Geneva Summit Conference.

Eisenhower, Khrushchev and the British and French leaders, Anthony Eden and Edgar Faure, attended the conference, with negotiations concentrating on arms reductions and on how best to ease tensions in the Far East in the aftermath of the Korean War. The Geneva Summit Conference was important to both sides as a symbol of goodwill. At the same time, Khrushchev co-operated with the Western Allies in finally signing a peace treaty with Austria, and worked with Tito to bring about a *rapprochement* with Yugoslavia.

However, the West soon found that a change of leader and a change of foreign policy did not stop Soviet aggression in Eastern Europe. In June 1956, riots in Poland in protest against high prices and the Soviet military presence there were put down with the cost of some fifty lives, but it was to be in Hungary that an even greater threat to Soviet authority was to emerge.

By the summer of 1956, reports of Khrushchev's anti-Stalin Secret Speech had reached Hungary, which was in the clutches of a crisis caused by a series of bad harvests. Encouraged by the liberal tone of the speech, a nationalist uprising, led by Imre Nagy and Janos Kadar, replaced the old Stalinist rule of Matyas Rakosi. For a while, it seemed that Khrushchev would accept this new more liberal regime and allow the satellite nations of Eastern Europe more freedom to direct their own affairs.

But when Nagy announced that he intended to withdraw from the Warsaw Pact and join Austria and Switzerland in becoming neutral countries at the heart of Europe, Khrushchev and Kadar had had enough, with the latter breaking away to form his own government in eastern Hungary. This allied itself closely to Moscow, and Red Army troops and tanks were soon sent to retake Budapest. As a result, nearly a quarter of a million Hungarians sought refuge in the West.

Resistance to the tanks of the Red Army was short-lived, and Nagy and many of his supporters were soon captured. Many were then executed in what was seen in the West as a return to the worst excesses of Stalinism. Kadar was installed as Hungary's new leader and he led his country as a receptive and compliant satellite within the Warsaw Pact until 1988. Peaceful coexistence may have brought the Bolshoi Ballet to London, but it did not save the Poles or the Hungarians in their struggles against Khrushchev's new regime in the USSR.

The Suez Crisis and European Decolonisation

Western reaction to Soviet aggression in Hungary remained somewhat muted because of a new crisis developing in the Middle East that for a time divided the USA from its major European allies, Britain and France. Since its completion in 1869, the Suez Canal had always been a vital link between the empire in India and Britain itself, and when this link had been threatened in the early 1880s, Britain had acted unilaterally and colonised the whole of Egypt. As a result, the canal remained a possession of crucial importance at the centre of the British Empire for fifty years and, with the development of the oilfields of Iran and the Arabian Peninsula, it was to become even more vital.

This importance was recognised in a treaty of 1936 that had negotiated the British withdrawal from Egypt. Under its provisions, Britain retained the right to station troops in the Canal Zone. The implementation of this treaty was delayed by World War Two and by the uncertainty in the region caused by the proclamation of the state of Israel in 1948. However, Britain had pulled its troops out of Egypt by the early 1950s, and a further treaty in October 1954 agreed that Britain would withdraw the remaining troops from the Canal Zone within twenty months.

But this agreement was put in doubt a month later when a coup d'état in Egypt brought to power Gamal Nasser, a charismatic thirty-six-year-old colonel in the Egyptian army. Nasser quickly made it clear that his long-term goals included the creation of a pan-Arabic state that stretched across North Africa and the Middle East. He also made it very clear that his primary short-term goals included the annihilation of the state of Israel and the expulsion of the colonial influence of Britain and France from the region. In particular, this saw him concentrate his attacks on the French in Algeria where his willingness to grant asylum in Egypt to leaders of the nationalist movement there had led to tense relations with both colonial powers.

However, despite these strained relations, the last British troops remaining in the Canal Zone were withdrawn on schedule in June 1956, thus ending three-quarters of a century of British rule in Egypt. Indeed, despite his anti-colonial rhetoric, Nasser had a keen eye on what was best for Egypt and during the two years following his coup had opened negotiations with both East and West.

Both saw the Middle East as an important strategic and economic region in which Nasser and Egypt played a key role, and the new Egyptian leader was successful in skilfully playing each off against the other. From the East, he secured pledges from the USSR and Czechoslovakia for military hardware that could be used in his fight against Israel. From the West, he won funds from the USA and Britain that could be used to finance the construction of a new dam on the Nile at Aswan. Nasser saw this project at Aswan as crucial to Egypt's economic development, providing hydroelectric power for Egyptian industry and controlling the floodwaters of the Nile for Egyptian agriculture. The economic progress that this would bring would pay for the war against Israel and the funding of the pan-Arab super state to which Nasser was so deeply committed.

By the time of the British withdrawal from the Canal Zone in June 1956, Nasser's anti-Western rhetoric and his dealings with the Eastern Bloc were making him powerful enemies in the USA, and this had led to Eisenhower suspending US support for the Aswan Dam project. Eisenhower knew that it was election year and he hoped that his stance in the Middle East would not only force Nasser to become more co-operative with the West but would also boost his ratings at home.

However, Nasser remained less than compliant and his position was soon strengthened when the USSR offered to fund the project. But Nasser rejected this Soviet offer and decided instead to take another tack. He announced that he intended to finance the Aswan Dam project through the nationalisation of the Suez Canal Company, which would bring in an annual profit of some £35 million sterling. The only problem with this was that the company was almost completely owned by British and French banking and business interests.

Nasser's standing among his people, and among the peoples of the whole Arab world, grew immeasurably, but the British and French governments were furious, warning Nasser that they would not accept his decision without a fight. Three months of fruitless negotiations followed, with the USA, despite Eisenhower's earlier position, quick to warn Britain and France that they should act with caution.

But British and French representatives made it clear that the compensation being offered was not acceptable, and they were further frustrated by the success of the new Egyptian administrators of the canal. They confounded predictions and kept the canal open and functioning properly. This gave Nasser the finance he needed for the dam, and it slowly became apparent in London and Paris that only armed intervention would restore British and French control.

This was the situation that faced Sir Anthony Eden who had finally replaced the eighty-year-old Winston Churchill as British prime minister in April 1955. In the 1930s, Eden had resigned as a minister in Chamberlain's government in protest against appeasement, and so towards the end of 1956 he was quick to draw parallels between Hitler's aggression and Nasser's nationalisation of the Suez Canal Company. Eden was resolved not to let another dictator bully and coerce his way into a position of power.

In short, Eden looked to depose Nasser before he was able to build Egypt into the centre of a pan-Arab state. Nasser's support for the nationalists in Algeria and his opposition to the creation of a Jewish state meant that Eden could rely on the support of France and Israel, and consequently secret negotiations were opened between the three governments. In October 1956, these talks culminated in a plan that would restore the Canal Zone to British and French control. It was hoped that it would also bring about the downfall of Nasser.

Under this plan, Israeli tanks invaded the Sinai Desert, thus provoking a response from the Egyptian army that moved eastwards to meet them. Britain and France, as a result, issued an ultimatum to both sides, demanding a secession of fighting. When Nasser refused, a combined British and French bombardment, in defiance of a UN resolution, was ordered on Port Said, the Egyptian port on the Mediterranean Sea at the entrance of the Suez Canal. Within five days, British and French control of the Canal Zone had been restored.

Eden now expected the downfall of Nasser and the gratitude of the USA and the Western world. Instead, his part in the Suez invasion was greeted with universal condemnation, which came not only from the Arab world but also from around the Commonwealth, from large sections of British domestic public opinion and, most importantly, from the USA. Britain and France were widely condemned in the UN where they were criticised for old-style colonial conquest. This, in turn, provoked an economic crisis in both Britain and France.

As a military venture, the invasion had been a complete success. But in diplomatic and economic terms, it was a complete disaster. Sustained criticism from John Foster Dulles, Eisenhower's secretary of state, made it clear that the

USA did not support the Anglo-French action, and that it would not come to the rescue of either the French franc or the pound sterling. As the relationship between Eden and Dulles became more and more strained, it became clear that without US support Britain and France would soon descend to a state of near bankruptcy. The governments of Britain and France were forced quickly to accept this new political reality and the humiliating withdrawal of their troops was ordered in December 1956.

The Suez Crisis ended British and French claims to an imperial role in the Middle East, and their impotence in the face of US opposition was keenly noted in those parts of the world that still endured European colonial rule. Soon, a new generation of politicians emerged in both Britain and France who accepted the changing global roles that their countries were to play. In Britain, ill-health brought on by the pressures of the Suez Crisis soon forced Eden's resignation in January 1957. He was replaced by Harold Macmillan who over the next six years presided over a Conservative government that oversaw the final stage of British decolonisation.

In Egypt, the crisis led to the exaltation of Nasser who throughout the decolonisation period became a figure of extreme admiration and popular esteem not only in Egypt but also across the world. Nasser had always envisaged that Egypt would lead a unified pan-Arab empire and the start of this was launched in 1958 when Egypt united with Syria to form the ill-fated United Arab Republic. This fell apart three years later with Syria's withdrawal although pan-Arabism was taken up later by figures such as Gaddafi in Libya. Nasser's death of a heart attack in September 1970 brought the Arab world to a standstill, with his funeral procession in Cairo being followed by some five million supporters.

The war had ruined the economies of all those countries in Europe that had colonial possessions, and any attempt in the decade after 1945 to reclaim these was to a certain extent a reaction to this. The drive for empire in the nineteenth century had been primarily stimulated by the search for new markets and the drive to reclaim empire after World War Two shared this same motive. But these colonies after 1945 had generally not made money, and after the Suez Crisis it became clear very quickly that the era of European colonial rule across the world was coming to an end. In the early 1960s, apart from in peculiar cases such as Portugal that held onto its colonies into the 1970s, this was generally accepted by both sides of the colonial divide. In the wider geopolitics of the Cold War, this decolonisation process was encouraged by both the USA and the USSR.

France had spent nearly a decade trying to regain the empire in Indochina that had been lost to Japan during the war. After 1945, a republic had been set up in Vietnam under the leadership of Ho Chi Minh and, although the French were able to restore their authority around Saigon in the south, any attempt to move further north had ended in military defeat. Guerrilla forces had been active throughout the country in the war against the Japanese and these forces had earned the support of the local population.

This guerrilla force, and its support among the peasants, was used after the war to hamper French efforts to retake Indochina and, in a scenario similar to the one faced by the USA in Vietnam twenty years later, more and more money spent resulted in more and more lives lost. A final confrontation around the strategically important village of Dien Bien Phu between March and May 1954 led to the loss of over 10,000 French troops, and an agreement was soon, as a result, signed that ceded sovereignty to independent governments in Laos, Cambodia and Vietnam. The withdrawal of France from South East Asia, and also the Dutch from Indonesia earlier in 1948, led to the destabilisation of the region, and encouraged the USA, China and the USSR to increase their political presence there. This eventually led to the Vietnam War ten years later.

The defeat at Dien Bien Phu and France's withdrawal from Indochina, as well as its climbdown over Suez, also weakened the political legitimacy of the Fourth Republic that had struggled to reassert France's sense of nationhood after the experience of Vichy. However, these problems were nothing compared to those connected with the struggle for independence in Algeria, which polarised French public opinion, threatened civil war and eventually led to the break up of the Fourth Republic itself.

Algeria had been formally colonised in 1882 and had gradually acquired a large white settler population, which in the 1950s existed alongside an increasingly nationalist majority Arab population. The Allies in World War Two had secured Arab support against Vichy French occupation with promises of independence at a later date, and these were formalised in 1947 when an agreement was signed that promised a gradual handover of authority to the local Arab population. However, this agreement was largely ignored by the French military commanders in Algiers who increasingly sided with the many white settlers bitterly opposed to any move towards independence.

By 1954, Arab nationalists had become frustrated by both the impasse in the political handover of power and the increasing levels of violence used against them by the French army. As a result, they went into open revolt, setting up a guerrilla force to fight for complete Algerian independence. At the same time, the white settlers responded by setting up their own guerrilla group, the OAS, that had the tacit support of many French military commanders in Algeria. When a resolution supporting Algerian independence was passed in the UN at the same time as military commanders in Algeria were censured for the brutality of their repression, the army, in league with the OAS, went into open revolt. France was convulsed in panic, with many fearing a military coup similar to the one that started the Spanish Civil War in 1936.

In this time of crisis, France turned once again to de Gaulle who quickly took control and suspended the constitution. It was replaced four months later with one that greatly increased the authority of the president. This was exactly the type of constitution that de Gaulle had wanted in 1945. It allowed him to dominate French politics for the next decade after becoming the first president of the new Fifth Republic.

It was obvious to de Gaulle that France could not carve out a new role for itself in world affairs while still shouldering the burden of empire and he, as a consequence, made it clear that it was his intention not only to withdraw from Algeria but also to grant independence to all of France's remaining African colonies. His policy in Algeria made him the subject of a bitter campaign of violence with repeated assassination attempts on his life made by the OAS. After two further army-OAS insurrections in 1960 and 1961, Algerian independence finally came in July 1962. At around the same time, French Togoland, Senegal, Tunisia, Côte d'Ivoire, Congo, Cameroon and Chad all gained their independence. However, independence did not come before Algeria helped France become the fourth member of the nuclear club. Its first atomic bomb was exploded in the Algerian desert in February 1960.

Britain had also lost some imperial possessions between the end of the war and the Suez Crisis, but at the same time had managed to retain its status as a world power. This was primarily due to the part it played in the victory over Nazism but was also as a result of the large overseas empire that it still retained and the legacy that this had given. Britain was a permanent member of the Security Council of the UN, had been a major belligerent in the Korean War and had developed its own nuclear capability.

But despite all of these accomplishments, its status had been tarnished by the Suez Crisis and this led to a radical re-evaluation of its future role in world affairs. This resulted in many in Britain taking the view that developing positive relations with the British Commonwealth, the USA and the evolving European Community was the best way of retaining national prestige and status.

It was difficult for these relationships to be fostered while Britain still retained a formal empire, and so one major repercussion of the Suez Crisis was a radical change in policy towards decolonisation that was brought in by the Conservative government under Macmillan. This brought about the swift process of African decolonisation, which began in 1957 when the colonial possession of the Gold Coast became the independent state of Ghana.

British resolve to retain a large colonial presence in Africa had also been weakened by the Mau Mau uprising in Kenya. The Mau Mau was a secret society set up within the Kikuyu tribe who lived in the highlands to the north of Nairobi. In 1952, Mau Mau guerrillas had gone into revolt, trying to drive out the white settlers who farmed the rich agricultural pastures that once had been their tribal land. The British authorities moved quickly against them, declaring a state of emergency and arresting the leader most closely associated with the uprising and the movement for Kenyan independence, Jomo Kenyatta. He was to spend most of the 1950s in prison. Over 10,000 Mau Mau supporters were killed, often brutally, during the state of emergency that lasted until 1960. But the guerrilla attacks on the secluded settler farms around the Rift Valley were never stamped out, and the expensive campaign against the Mau Mau eventually sapped the will of the British government in London and of the colonial administration in Nairobi. Kenyatta was released from prison in August 1961 and Kenya was granted independence in December 1963.

At around the same time, independence was granted to Tanganyika, which became Tanzania, Malawi, Zambia and Uganda in the east and south of the continent and to the West African nations of Nigeria, Sierra Leone and the Gambia. Similar nationalist movements and uprisings also led to independence in Aden and in Malaysia at a similar time.

The Origins of the European Community

The decision taken by Britain in the late 1950s to retain close ties with the Commonwealth and restore the special relationship with the USA in the aftermath of the Suez Crisis was in part why it was excluded from the European Community for the next decade or so. The first moves towards Europe-wide integration had begun with the European Recovery Programme in the 1940s, and this had been followed in 1952 with the formation of the European Coal and Steel Community.

France, the entity that was to become West Germany, Italy, Belgium, the Netherlands and Luxembourg had all joined the ECSC, whose purpose was to stimulate trade and aid post-war recovery. Indeed, one of the stipulations that

Marshall had laid down in 1947 was that Europe itself must make efforts to develop an integrated economy so as to avoid the problems of the interwar period. The ECSC created a free trade area between the six member countries that looked to stimulate growth in the essential industries of steel, iron and coal.

Within the booming economies of Western Europe in the early 1950s, the ECSC was a huge success, and European integration was extended in 1957 when the same six countries signed the Treaty of Rome. This created the European Economic Community, or Common Market. The EEC was an important departure from the ECSC. The Treaty of Rome guaranteed the development of free trade, the free movement of capital and labour, and the adoption of co-ordinated and collective social and economic policies. Eventually, closer political integration was envisaged with the creation of a European parliament, a council of ministers and an integrated and supranational legal system.

Macmillan's government decided that this was too close a liaison for Britain to make with Europe and distanced itself from negotiations. This early aloofness, along with Britain's close alliance with the USA, the Commonwealth and its insistence on maintaining an independent nuclear capability, was enough to persuade France under de Gaulle that Britain should be barred from the EEC, and twice in the 1960s he was to use the French veto to block Britain's application for membership, a move that increasingly frustrated other members of the EEC.

As moves towards European integration gathered pace through the EEC, a rival organisation was set up by those countries that felt less inclined towards the more political elements implied in the Treaty of Rome. Seven such countries met in Stockholm in 1959 and agreed to set up the European Free Trade Association. The original members of EFTA were Britain, Switzerland, Norway, Denmark, Austria, Portugal and Sweden. EFTA was never able to rival the EEC in size, but its contribution to the development of trade, industry and commerce within Europe was important, allowing these countries a chance to work in Europe despite exclusion from the EEC. After all, even at the height of the British Empire in the late nineteenth century, Europe had always been the vital market for British manufactured goods. This was even more the case in the 1950s after the retreat from empire.

The success of the various bodies constituted through the 1950s to develop European integration and restore and rebuild shattered wartime economies illustrated the foresight of the authors of the European Recovery Plan. Marshall

Aid had given Europe the enormous injection of capital that had been essential to begin recovery in Europe after World War Two. But the responsibility for this recovery was soon assumed by the leaders of Europe itself who oversaw not only the recovery but also the massive expansion of Europe's national economies. This, in time, led to improved standards of living and a better quality of life for millions of people across the continent, with trade between members of the EEC quadrupling within ten years.

Of all the successful economies of Western Europe, West Germany's stood out, and this was especially the case when compared with its East German neighbour. This early success was directed by Konrad Adenauer who was chancellor between 1949 and 1963. This economic success, in hand with the real and lasting friendship that was built up between West Germany and France, was the key reason behind the success of the EEC. By the end of the decade, Western Europe could look forward to a prosperous and stable future when only fifteen years before it had been in ruins.

The Non-Aligned Movement and the People's Republic of China

The end of European colonialism created a void that both the USA and the USSR were keen to fill. The USA had already strengthened its military bases in the Philippines, and Khrushchev had visited South East Asia in 1955 to denounce European imperialism there. However, their intrusions were not always welcomed and in 1955 a group of newly independent states and interested parties had met in the Indonesian city of Bandung to discuss ways of diminishing superpower influence within the developing world.

The Bandung Conference was convened at the instigation of President Sukarno who had led Indonesia to independence in 1950. Delegates agreed to create a commonwealth of emerging nations, which aimed to protect mutual interests when they were threatened by superpower interference. There were some that hoped that this group might one day grow in stature and authority and come to rival the world's other superpowers. Key figures in this Non-Aligned Movement included such diverse leaders as Tito from Yugoslavia, Nasser from Egypt and Nehru from India.

The Non-Aligned Movement was never able to achieve the goals set by its founders and the different needs of such a disparate group never allowed any lasting agreement. With the retreat from empire by Europe and with the emergence of China as a third global superpower, it is perhaps inevitable that emerging countries in Africa, Asia and the Middle East would be dragged into the Cold War.

Many were inevitably lured by promises of aid, investment or military assistance, and many members became adept at playing one superpower off against the other. By the mid-1960s, the Non-Aligned Movement had ceased to exist in any meaningful form, but had been important at a crucial time in the history of the developing world. Most importantly, it had given a focus to nationalist movements in many parts of the world that were still struggling for independence.

The struggle for independence in southern Asia had largely been won by the middle of the 1950s and as Britain, France and the Netherlands left, it was China that was to cast its shadow across the region. Mao governed the world's most populous nation and he soon set about transforming it into what he considered to be the model of a modern communist state.

His first moves had been to reward the peasant class, which made up over 95% of the population and whose loyalty during the long years of struggle had been so important to the communist success. Initially, this took the form of People's Courts, which were set up in villages all over the country and which cleansed Chinese society over the next five years or so. Several million landlords and opponents of the new regime were condemned to death in these courts for their part in what were seen as the atrocities of the past.

Having rid China of the landlord class, Mao organised a series of land reforms that, brushing away 1,000 years of feudal rule, transferred responsibility for most of China's agricultural land to the peasants. They were encouraged to group together into co-operatives in order to maximise their productive capacity and by the middle of the 1950s most of China's agriculture had been collectivised. The changes that these early reforms brought cemented Mao's position as the champion of the people, and even after his death he was to remain a figure of the most enormous importance in communities, and especially rural communities, all over China.

Land reform and the reorganisation of China's agriculture had been Mao's priority in the first years after the revolution and this had been continued into the 1950s, despite the distraction caused by the war in Korea. However, he knew that China needed to develop an industrial infrastructure if it was to modernise successfully and so in 1950 he signed the Treaty of Friendship, Alliance and Mutual Assistance with the USSR. This secured long-term loans for Chinese industry with initial investment concentrating on heavy industry, mining and the development of a transport infrastructure.

As a result, Mao asked his chief economic planner, Deng Xiaoping, to launch the first Five-Year Plan, extending to industry the policy of centralisation that had begun immediately after the communist takeover. This began in 1953 and before it had been completed, Mao had also launched the Hundred Flowers Campaign, the first of his great radical, theoretical campaigns on behalf of the people. Mao believed in permanent revolution and that party officials and administrators needed to stay closely in contact with the feelings and opinions of the people in order to ward off complacency and bourgeois tendencies.

The Hundred Flowers Campaign in 1956 encouraged criticism of the party and its officials in order to ensure the health of the 1949 Revolution. This criticism, Mao said, would allow China to bloom like a hundred flowers. However, the Five-Year Plan and the collectivisation programmes of the early 1950s had been neither popular nor successful, and the party, as a consequence, came in for severe and sustained criticism. The campaign was consequently soon quickly abandoned in 1957, with China returning to a state of repressive censorship and centralised control.

The abandonment of the Hundred Flowers Campaign also coincided with the deterioration of relations with the USSR. Mao was distrustful of Khrushchev's policy of peaceful coexistence towards the West, and increasingly came to the conclusion that the USSR had given up its right to call itself the leader of the communist world. The Sino-Soviet split lasted, on and off, for the next thirty years and was at times skilfully used in the West, especially by Nixon and Kissinger in the early 1970s.

The initial result of this split was the second Five-Year Plan, which came to be known as the Great Leap Forward. As a result, it was to take on far greater political importance, with Mao determined to show that China, in stark contrast to the USSR, had not lost sight of the goals of the communist revolution. The central edifice of the Great Leap Forward was the commune, around which industry and agriculture would develop and through which Chinese society would evolve.

Communes of some 20,000 people were organised by combining upwards of thirty villages, and peasants and industrial workers dressed in the same uniform, the blue Mao suit, to emphasise the collective revolutionary spirit of commune life. However, the withdrawal of Soviet technical assistance, bad management of many communes and three years of failed harvests meant that the Great Leap Forward was an unmitigated disaster, with perhaps over thirty million people losing their lives in the famine that it caused.

The failure of the Great Leap Forward to solve the problems of China's relative backwardness forced Mao to give up some of the powers he had held since 1949. However, he did retain his position as party chairman and it was through this position a few years later that he was to launch his final and most notorious ideological assault on Chinese society, the Cultural Revolution.

One other great consequence of the dire situation in China was open rebellion in Tibet, with the Dalai Lama being forced into exile in March 1959 after the Red Army had restored order and annexed the country. Thousands were to die in the repression that followed, with thousands more escaping over the Himalayas to relative safety in northern India and Nepal.

The USA in the 1950s: the Boom Years and the Civil Rights Movement

In the USA, both the Truman and Eisenhower administrations had continued to support the claims of Chiang Kai-shek long after he and the remnants of his Nationalist army had been forced off the Chinese mainland and onto the island of Taiwan in the late 1940s. This was despite the obvious strength of the communist grip on power that had been shown most clearly in the Korean War. Indeed, the very existence of communist China was not acknowledged by the USA until 1971.

In the early years of the Eisenhower administration, the Korean War, the growing strength of communist China and the threat of the growing Soviet nuclear capability had all contributed towards persuading US public opinion that a new aggressive foreign policy was needed. McCarthyism had also played an important role in this, as had a new self-confidence brought about by the dominant US economy.

For all these reasons, John Foster Dulles made it clear at the beginning of his long tenure at the State Department that he intended to strengthen US and NATO defences against the communist world. As a result, he and his president committed the USA to building up security in Western Europe while concluding a series of anti-Soviet treaties throughout Asia and the Middle East. The Eisenhower administration also pledged itself to massively expanding the strength and range of its nuclear capability. This all combined to provoke the communist bloc to sign the Friendship, Co-operation and Mutual Assistance Treaty, commonly known as the Warsaw Pact, in May 1955.

Dulles could adopt such strident policies abroad because the USA had emerged from the war with the world's most powerful economy, with no country coming close to threatening its grip on world trade. In this new age of plenty, the USA came to fascinate the whole world. Hollywood made films that were watched globally and US industry dominated global markets, producing bigger and better goods than their European and Japanese competitors. By the middle of the decade, Rock'n'Roll music had burst onto the scene, with millions of teenagers across the world soon trying to emulate their US counterparts. At the centre of this new phenomenon was Elvis Presley who became the first global teen idol after his debut hit, 'Heartbreak Hotel', in March 1956.

In 1950, the Diners' Club Card, given out initially to only about 200 people and accepted in only fourteen restaurants, became the world's first credit card when it was launched in New York, while in July 1955 Disneyland opened its doors for the first time. At around the same time and in various early guises, the first McDonald's restaurants opened, bringing in the era of American fast food. By the end of the century, McDonalds had spread to 119 countries. By 1960, nearly every US household owned a television and nearly every US homeowner drove a car.

Increased mechanisation in agriculture had brought down the price of food and the average family could now boast a standard of living and quality of life that was the envy not only of the communist world but also of Western Europe. Supermarkets overflowed with food and new suburban housing estates grew up around cities and towns all over the USA. At the same time, research at various American institutions in the immediate post-war period led to the discovery of a polio vaccine in 1952, with further developments through the decade allowing for its near eradication over the next twenty years or so. All these various changes and improvements seemed to suggest that the aftermath of World War Two had brought the fulfilment of the American Dream.

However, there were elements within US society who were not sharing in this age of plenty. Agricultural mechanisation may have driven down the price of food, but it also drove many smaller farmers out of business. Rural poverty in many areas, especially in many eastern states, increased rapidly, with many forced to find work in the alien world of the city. Little or no social welfare was provided for them there and for this underclass of urban poor the American Dream was no more than a myth.

It also proved a myth for the millions of black people who still lived under the injustice of segregation. The Civil War in the 1860s had won the fight against slavery, but a series of laws, the so-called Jim Crow laws, had been passed in various state assemblies all over the South to circumvent any notion of equality. These laws used such devices as literary tests, property qualifications and poll taxes to exclude the black population from the political process.

They remained excluded and segregated, and any black person who challenged the system could expect to experience the vigilante justice of groups such as the Ku Klux Clan. As a consequence, as many as five million African

Americans from the South chose instead to leave and join the second Great Migration, a movement that lasted from the end of the war until the late 1960s that took them to the cities of the North and to California in search of their part in the American Dream. But these many migrants were to find that other parts of the USA were also full of prejudice, and they were often forced to work for low pay and live in ghettos with low standards of housing.

The first signs of change had come in 1948 when Truman had succeeded in ending segregation in the armed services although in practice this did not occur until the outbreak of the Korean War. However, the first great civil rights success did not occur until 1954 when the Brown family from Kansas took their local school board to court after its refusal to end school segregation and allow their daughter to enrol in an all-white school. The Supreme Court found for the family and unanimously voted that segregation in schools was unconstitutional.

The legal ramifications of the Brown judgement were enormous, and soon legal challenges to segregation were filed all over the country. However, it was one thing to win a legal decision in Washington and quite another to have this acted upon. Many Southern states refused to change their segregation laws after the Brown judgement and it took two further incidents to force these changes through.

The first took place in December 1955 when Rosa Parks, a black resident of Montgomery, Alabama, was fined for refusing to give up her seat to a white passenger on a city bus. Rosa Parks was a member of the NAACP, the National Association for the Advancement of Colored People, a leading civil rights organisation that had been founded in 1909. In support of Mrs Parks, the NAACP organised a boycott of the city's buses and for a year most of Montgomery's buses ran empty. The Montgomery Bus Boycott attracted huge media attention and focused the nation's mind on the whole question of segregation.

It also threw up a new leader of the civil rights movement. Dr Martin Luther King was then a twenty-six-year-old Baptist minister with a doctorate in theology and ethics who had lived in Montgomery for less than a year. He took a prominent role in the boycott during which he began to develop his ideas about non-violent opposition that he learnt from Mahatma Gandhi. Martin Luther King was to dominate the civil rights movement for the next ten years. Eventually, in November 1956, the boycott came to an end when the Supreme Court ruled that segregation on the Montgomery buses was unconstitutional.

The second incident that put the civil rights issue on the political agenda took place in Arkansas in 1957 when nine black children were enrolled in a whites-only high school in the state capital of Little Rock. On their first day at school, they were met by state troopers who refused to let them onto the school premises. According to the authorities in charge, this was done because the presence of the children at the high school made it impossible to maintain order or guarantee their safety. In reality, it was done to preserve the segregated school system that had been challenged by the Brown family in Kansas three years earlier.

Two weeks later, the Supreme Court found in favour of the nine children and ruled that the actions of those in Little Rock who were fighting desegregation had been unconstitutional. The nine once again tried to attend, but found that an angry white mob had collected at the school gates. Once again, the children were unable to attend school and were hastily rushed away for their own safety. These scenes were shown on live television all across the USA and forced Eisenhower to act. He sent federal troops to Little Rock to ensure that the constitution was upheld and that the children could attend school. An armed federal presence eventually enabled the nine to enrol and these soldiers remained in Little Rock for the next year, patrolling the grounds and classrooms of the high school in order to protect the children. The USA may have been the envy of the world in terms of its economic success, but for many it remained a centre of bigotry and prejudice.

Apartheid in South Africa

The segregationist policies that were clung to in the Southern states of the USA were similar to those followed by the National Party in South Africa, which in 1948 had won a decisive election victory under the leadership of Daniel Malan. This had followed growing fears within the white minority population about changing attitudes spreading throughout the British Empire. These had already led to independence in India and Pakistan, and other indigenous peoples elsewhere were also clamouring for change.

The policies the National Party adopted through the 1950s came to be known as apartheid, the Afrikaans word for apartness, which was exactly what Malan and his colleagues wanted. They aimed to separate the different ethnic groups that made up South Africa and, in theory at least, land was to be put aside for each group. Inevitably, however, white dominance was maintained, with the white minority receiving the best land, the best resources and the best mineral rights. In this way, apartheid was to bolster white supremacy in South

Africa, just as the Jim Crow laws had reinforced white dominance in the USA. The black majority remained repressed and without rights while white South Africans continued to reap the benefits of their social, economic and political dominance.

Through the 1950s and into the 1960s, a series of acts were passed through parliament that reinforced this white supremacy. Black workers were denied the right to strike or vote and mixed marriages were banned. Education became segregated while other acts forced segregation on buses and beaches, and in public toilets and post offices. Even park benches and water fountains were designated racially. But the most hated of all the apartheid laws was the Pass Law of 1952, which forced all non-whites living away from their homelands to carry a passbook at all times. Imprisonment would face those found without their books or outside the areas designated in the book. The Pass Law was used ruthlessly by the South African police to monitor and control the majority black population.

In the forefront of the opposition to apartheid was the African National Congress, which Nelson Mandela led to victory in the first post-apartheid elections thirty-five years later. In March 1960, the ANC was banned and its leaders began to be imprisoned. This came ten days after the Sharpeville massacre when sixty-nine demonstrators were shot dead while demonstrating outside a police station in the Sharpeville township just outside Johannesburg. Television images of Sharpeville stiffened opposition to apartheid across the outside world.

Nelson Mandela himself was sentenced to life imprisonment in June 1964 and was to spend the next twenty-seven years in prison, eighteen of these on Robben Island. The clampdown on the ANC leadership in the late 1950s and early 1960s forced it underground or abroad and greatly weakened internal opposition to the apartheid regime. Such was the severity of these repressive policies that this opposition was not to resurface with any great success until the late 1970s.

The Escalation of the Arms Race and the Return of Cold War Hostility

As apartheid began to flourish in South Africa, international relations at the end of the decade were becoming increasingly complicated, with a series of developments taxing policy makers on both sides of the political divide. European decolonisation had created vacuums in the Middle East, South East Asia and the Far East, and both sides soon showed that they were keen to fill the void that was left. Despite its commitment to peaceful coexistence, the USSR increased its support for Nasser in Egypt and threatened to intervene in other parts of the Middle East. Khrushchev had also visited South East Asia in 1955 and made it clear that he intended to develop Soviet links there.

At about this time, US strategists began talking about the Domino Theory, warning that one emerging nation after another would fall to communism if left unprotected. In response to this, the USA sponsored a series of anti-communist treaties and alliances that aimed to give protection to those countries with common borders with the communist world that seemed vulnerable. In 1949, NATO had been formed to protect Western Europe, and South East Asia was similarly protected by SEATO in 1954. This was followed a year later when the Middle East and the subcontinent were drawn together by the Baghdad Treaty, later extended into CENTO, the Central Treaty Organisation. All these treaties and pacts were to form a belt around the USSR, from Europe to the Far East, in order to contain the communist threat. This policy of containment was to form the basis of US foreign policy until the 1980s.

In theory, both sides talked of peaceful coexistence and committed themselves to improving superpower relations. In practice, however, both sides were committed to expanding their political, economic and strategic boundaries and, in order to do so, were willing to massively extend their military budgets. The foreign policy of the USA for much of the 1950s had been based on the assumption that if the USSR or its allies tried to break out of the areas protected by these treaties, Washington would have the nuclear capability to launch a massive retaliatory counter-offensive. This was bolstered in 1952 with the launching of USS *Nautilus*, the world's first nuclear-powered submarine, which later in 1958 was to be the first to pass under the North Pole.

However, the premise on which this policy was based had to be torn up in August 1957 when the USSR announced that it had successfully tested its first intercontinental ballistic missile, or ICBM. Soviet missile superiority was further confirmed two months later, in October 1957, with the launch of Sputnik, an aluminium sphere weighing less than two hundred pounds with a diameter of just less than two feet and the world's first satellite. By the end of 1957, the Soviet lead was further underlined when Sputnik II, a much heavier body weighing half a tonne, sent a dog into space. In the USA, it became clear, not only to the scientists and the politicians but also to the general public, that a nation that could launch a satellite capable of orbiting the earth would soon be able to launch an ICBM that was capable of delivering a nuclear warhead. As a result, confidence in US nuclear and technological superiority, which had been taken for granted since Hiroshima and Nagasaki in 1945, was shattered.

201

The Sputnik and Soviet ICBM programmes shocked the USA into action and by the end of the decade the technological gap between the superpowers had been made up. This was primarily through the work of NASA, which came into being at the end of 1958, with millions of dollars being spent on the development of the Atlas ICBM project. It also worked hard to perfect a series of delivery systems and by 1960 had a fleet of long-range nuclear bombers and the capability to launch ballistic missiles from submarines. In this regard, their capacity to strike at the heart of the enemy greatly outmatched that of the USSR.

The technological developments of the late 1950s began an arms race that was to dominate East-West relations for the next thirty years. The nuclear weapon programmes of the 1950s and 1960s meant that the two superpowers were soon able to deliver a nuclear attack some 5,000 times more powerful than the ones launched on Hiroshima or Nagasaki.

Khrushchev knew that the Soviet technological breakthroughs had seriously damaged US confidence, and in 1958 he tried to use them to reintroduce the question of Berlin into the Cold War debate. He had become increasingly frustrated by the success of capitalist West Berlin and the defections from East Germany that this had caused. He was also acutely aware of the stinging criticism that his policy of peaceful coexistence was receiving in China, and he needed to show his resolve in order to retain the leadership of the communist world.

Therefore, he demanded a total troop withdrawal from Berlin and insisted that the East German authorities should be left unhindered to work out a relationship with West Berlin. To the West and to the people of West Berlin, this seemed tantamount to giving the city to East Germany, and all three of the Western Allies quickly rejected the proposition. Khrushchev's demand had been a crude attempt to force the Western Allies out of Berlin, but it only served to increase resolve in the West to support the city. Within a year, it had led to an increase in the deployment of US conventional and nuclear weaponry within Europe, and Khrushchev was forced to back down. Eisenhower had won the first battle in this new Cold War dominated by the threat of nuclear war.

By the spring of 1959, the confrontation over troop withdrawals from Berlin had been resolved. This coincided with the death of Dulles in May 1959 that resulted in Eisenhower adopting a far more conciliatory stance in his relations with the USSR. It was also the year before the presidential election, and the Republicans, especially Vice President Nixon, the Republican candidate, were keen for good international publicity to boost early campaigning. As a result, a preliminary meeting in Geneva between representatives from the two sides agreed to a series of three summit meetings between Khrushchev and Eisenhower. It was agreed that the two leaders would first meet in the USA, then attend a summit in Paris, before finally concluding their talks in Moscow.

Khrushchev arrived in Washington in September 1959 on a whistle-stop tour that lasted eleven days and that included meeting, among others, Frank Sinatra in Hollywood. Large and friendly crowds greeted him warmly throughout his trip. At the end of his time in the USA at a series of friendly meetings with Eisenhower, the two leaders agreed to leave any negotiations over Berlin until the meeting in Paris. Most importantly, in a speech to the General Assembly of the UN in New York, Khrushchev proposed a total ban of nuclear weapons within four years.

To observers in the West, his visit seemed to confirm the commitment to peaceful coexistence that so many had doubted during the Berlin crisis earlier in the year. Many hoped that a new era of honesty and friendship had arrived, and that the threat to world peace that had been faced since the beginning of the decade had lifted. Khrushchev's visit to the USA was a great success for both sides, and the world eagerly awaited the Paris Summit Conference, which the British prime minister, Harold Macmillan, and the French president, Charles de Gaulle, were also due to attend. It was hoped that the goodwill from the first meeting could be maintained.

However, any hopes of progress were dashed only a few days before the conference when a US U2 reconnaissance aeroplane, flying over the USSR, was shot down. The pilot was able to bail out, but was arrested by Soviet officials and put on trial for spying. Khrushchev demanded a public apology and a guarantee from Eisenhower that the incident would not be repeated. However, President Eisenhower knew that he could not suffer the humiliation of issuing an international public apology, and it was equally clear that he could not be seen to be having US foreign policy dictated to him by his Soviet opposite number. Not least because it was only six months until the presidential election, he quickly rejected Khrushchev's two demands, which met with a swift response from the Soviet leader.

Khrushchev denounced the USA and its partners and stormed out of the conference. After all the optimism that had preceded it, the Paris Summit Conference had met for only one day. Meanwhile, the pilot, Gary Powers, was put on trial and was sentenced to three years of hard labour. He was, however, released early in exchange for a Soviet spy and returned to the USA in February 1962.

The Soviet delegation soon left Paris for Moscow and the invitation to Eisenhower to visit the USSR was cancelled. The *rapprochement* between capitalism and communism was over as the world once again returned to the rhetoric of the Cold War. Thus, the new decade began, just as the old one had done ten years before, with an ideological and political crisis splitting the worlds of East and West. But now each had the capability to annihilate the other 1,000 times over, and it would not be long before that apocalyptic scenario was nearly carried out.

The Years of Transition
The 1960s

May 1960
(The End of the Paris Summit Conference)
to
July 1969
(The First Man on the Moon)

Cold War Confrontation and the Berlin Wall
The USA in the Early 1960s and the Cuban Missile Crisis
France and Britain in the Early 1960s
The Assassination of John F. Kennedy
The Fall of Khrushchev and the Rise of Brezhnev
Britain under the Labour Government of Harold Wilson
The USA and the Vietnam War
Chairman Mao and the Cultural Revolution
The Arab-Israeli Conflict and the Six-Day War
The Prague Spring, *Ostpolitik* and Détente
The First Man on the Moon

Cold War Confrontation and the Berlin Wall

The decision by Khrushchev to walk out of the Paris Peace Conference ended a period of limited friendship and co-operation between the two post-war superpowers that had lasted on and off since the death of Stalin. It also precipitated an international crisis that not only restarted the Cold War but also nearly ended in nuclear disaster two years later with the Cuban Missile Crisis.

It is not difficult to see why Khrushchev chose to follow such a precipitous path. Criticism of peaceful co-existence had always existed within important elements of the Soviet hierarchy, but this had remained muted during the years in which Khrushchev's star was in the ascendancy. However, when important reforms to agriculture and industry began to fail at the end of the 1950s, Khrushchev's grip on power was loosened. This had allowed hardliners in the USSR and powerful critics abroad, most notably in China, to clamour for, among other things, a tougher stance towards the West. Knowing that his future rested on his ability to placate these elements by forcing concessions from his capitalist adversaries, Khrushchev entered the new decade fighting for his political life.

The withdrawal of the Soviet delegation from talks in France came just months before the US presidential election in which John F. Kennedy, at the age of forty-three, had become his country's youngest-ever elected president. Kennedy had only narrowly won the election, defeating Richard Nixon by a tiny nationwide margin of only just over 100,000 votes. The Kennedy-Nixon election was also distinguished by being the first in which television played a central role.

Kennedy had campaigned on an ambitious programme of civil rights and social reform legislation, but also used his campaign and his inaugural speech to warn his enemies and assure his allies that his administration would continue to follow the strong foreign policy of his predecessor. Kennedy intended to match the tough stance in international affairs that Khrushchev had adopted at Paris.

However, Kennedy's foreign policy credibility and the very image of the new president himself were soon badly damaged by the Bay of Pigs fiasco in Cuba, only months after he and his young family had moved into the White House. This disaster for Kennedy came three years after Cuba, which had long been a compliant US ally in the Caribbean, had been taken over by a left-leaning guerrilla army led by Fidel Castro. This army had defeated the US-backed military dictatorship of General Batista who himself had come to power in a coup in 1952.

Castro's government in Havana had taken an increasingly hostile stance towards the West, and many US companies, which had invested heavily in Cuba during the Batista years, soon found their assets nationalised. At the same time, Castro began to initiate trade and commercial links with the USSR, which meant that the economic slump predicted by the USA never came. These links were confirmed when Khrushchev and Castro signed a huge deal in 1960 concerning Cuba's vital sugar harvest.

Castro was encouraged in this by the Argentine Marxist revolutionary, Che Guevara, who had been Castro's right-hand man during the years of struggle. Guevara continued to be a leading member of Castro's inner circle for four years until his revolutionary spirit took him to Africa and then on to Bolivia where he was killed by government troops in 1967.

In response to this communist threat not a hundred miles from the Florida Keys, Eisenhower had, in one of the last acts of his presidency, cut off diplomatic relations with Castro's government. He had then sanctioned the secret training of an army of Cuban Exiles that by early 1961 was ready for action.

But the new president was far from happy with the way in which information about the invasion force had been kept from him by the CIA during his first months in Washington and when he finally agreed to the military operation to invade Cuba, he refused to sanction US air support for the mission. As a result, the Cuban Exile troops who landed at the Bay of Pigs on the south of the island in April 1961 were soon cut off from their supplies, with the invasion ending in catastrophe after only three days. Consequently, most of the 1,500 Cuban Exile soldiers involved in the invasion were either captured or killed.

So this early attempt to expel communism from the Western hemisphere ended in a disaster that dealt a severe blow to the credibility of the new Kennedy administration. In many quarters, the Bay of Pigs fiasco was seen as evidence of the new president's lack of diplomatic and political guile, and Kennedy was still dealing with its repercussions when he travelled to Vienna for his first meeting with Khrushchev in June 1961. In Austria, he was to find the Soviet leader keen to press home the advantage that the Bay of Pigs incident had given.

The ebullient and abrasive mood of Khrushchev and the Soviet delegation had been further buoyed by news on 12 April 1961 that a Soviet cosmonaut, Yuri Gagarin, had become the first man in space, successfully completing a 108-minute journey into orbit. Just over three weeks later, Gagarin was followed by Alan Shepard, but the NASA astronaut's fifteen-minute suborbital journey was much less spectacular.

Khrushchev chose Vienna to return to the thorny question of Germany and, in particular, Berlin, reiterating the demand first made in 1958 that all Allied troops should be withdrawn from the city as quickly as possible. Kennedy restated the continued commitment of his country to the long-term security of Western Europe, including West Berlin, and immediately rejected the Soviet proposal. Neither leader was in a mood for compromise and both left the Austrian capital knowing that their meeting had done little to bring about a thaw in East-West relations.

A major long-term objective of Soviet foreign policy in Europe had always been to force the withdrawal of Western troops from West Berlin. However, by the early 1960s, a far more pressing short-term problem was facing the Soviet and East German authorities. This concerned the migration of thousands of East Germans westwards in search of a better life, a problem that had increased through the 1950s as the yawning gap in living standards between West and East Germany had become wider and wider.

However, this had grown into a torrent in the early 1960s after the resumption of Cold War tension, and this massive haemorrhage of East Germany's skilled work force was threatening the very future of the entire East German economy. The migration was especially pronounced through the porous checkpoints that separated East and West Berlin and so, in order to stop this, orders were given to build a wall to divide the city. Despite angry protests from the West, this was completed by the summer of 1961. The Berlin Wall, which in the communist world was referred to as the Anti-Fascist Protection Rampart, was to be nearly a hundred miles in length and was to become a permanent reminder of the ideological split between communism and capitalism. For a generation and a half, it was to remain the most potent symbol of the Cold War divide.

Another reminder of the ideological split between the two sides was the escalation of the arms race. Soviet developments such as the Sputnik and ICBM programmes in the late 1950s had shocked many observers in the USA who had assumed that US nuclear supremacy would last forever. As a result, both Eisenhower and Kennedy worked hard to close this gap and this had been done, and indeed reversed, by 1961.

However, the announcement of the first Soviet H-Bomb in the same year prompted Kennedy to press Congress for more funds, and by 1962 these seemed to have bought the USA the military superiority that its people demanded. Kennedy also knew that the US economy was three times the size of its Soviet rival and that Khrushchev was dealing with a number of difficult economic problems. As a result, he was confident that if the high levels of military spending were maintained, and there was strong support for this from within Congress, he could guarantee US military superiority for the foreseeable future. Indeed, the strength of the US economy would guarantee that the size of this superiority would slowly grow larger and larger.

The USA in the Early 1960s and the Cuban Missile Crisis

The USA had experienced massive socio-economic change since victory in 1945, with the most obvious manifestation of this being a massive improvement in living standards. Across the country better food, better housing and better wages had all come together to mark the 1950s as a decade of prosperity and plenty, and many Americans, as a result, were much better off in 1960 than they had been in the aftermath of war in the late 1940s. This theme of improvement was picked up by Kennedy in his election campaign, proclaiming that the USA stood on the edge of a 'New Frontier'.

However, there were huge swathes of society that had not been a part of this success and Kennedy looked to address this imbalance in the years before his assassination. This included programmes of improvement to do with housing, fairer taxes, education and equal rights for women, and it was particularly to concentrate on civil rights for the 12-15% of the population who were non-white. This minority had continued to suffer after early successes in the late 1950s and so came together in August 1963 for the Great March on Washington. This was supported by a crowd of over 200,000 who gathered at the Lincoln Memorial to listen to Martin Luther King give his 'I have a dream' speech.

However, at the same time as thousands were listening to King, thousands more had turned their backs on the non-violent message of the mainstream civil rights groups and increasingly were choosing to follow Malcolm X, one of the most prominent leaders of the Nation of Islam. This group argued for the separation of the races and for the setting up of a black homeland for the African-American people left in the USA by slavery. Malcolm X was eventually to renounce these beliefs in 1964 before being gunned down the following year by radical Nation of Islam members motivated by what they saw as his treachery.

The campaign for civil rights was continued by President Johnson after the assassination of Kennedy, and it formed a central platform of his 'Great Society' crusade, which compared with the New Deal in its size and breadth. At its core was a commitment to the elimination of poverty and racial and social injustice from US society, with Johnson using his considerable power and prestige on Capital Hill, which had been earned as a leading senator in the 1950s, to force through the various changes needed to allow the passing of the Civil Rights Act in July 1964.

This aimed to legislate against all forms of discrimination in all of its many guises. In reality, however, it initially did little to change the lives of many who consequently continued to follow Martin Luther King in his new cause. This increasingly saw him become involved in the fight against social injustice and, in particular, he campaigned on the issue of unfair housing policies in the years prior to his assassination.

But the civil rights movement was resisted, especially across the Southern states where George Wallace had become the governor of Alabama in 1963. Later, Wallace, with his running mate Curtis LeMay, was to run a popular presidential campaign in 1968 against Nixon and Humphrey in which he was to win nearly ten million votes. This was in the same year that riots ripped through over a hundred US cities following the assassination of Dr King, and two African-American athletes at the Mexico Olympics, Tommie Smith and John Carlos, gave a black-gloved clenched fist sign in support of Black Power during the US national anthem at their medal ceremony. It was also the year in which Bobby Kennedy was assassinated in Los Angeles, with all these events following the deterioration of the war in Vietnam following the psychological blow caused by the Tet Offensive in February.

In the USSR, Khrushchev was acutely aware that the failure of his economic reforms, as well as the military implications of the USA's ever-increasing economic superiority, threatened his political survival. So in a bold move that aimed to silence his critics at home while at the same time contesting US military superiority abroad, he decided to challenge the USA not a hundred miles from its own shores.

By the early summer of 1962, secret preparations for this plan were completed when he secured an agreement with Castro to station Soviet nuclear missiles on Cuban soil. These would be maintained at a fraction of the cost of any large-scale ICBM force in the USSR. The secret construction of the missile bases that would house this new nuclear capability continued through the summer of 1962.

Evidence of increased Soviet activity on Cuba was collected through the summer and into the autumn of 1962, and US suspicions were confirmed on 15 October with the analysis of surveillance photographs taken on a U2 spy mission flying over Cuba the day before. These photographs clearly showed that medium-range and intermediate-range ballistic nuclear missiles were being deployed at various new and camouflaged missile sites, and so began the thirteen-day hiatus that came to be known as the Cuban Missile Crisis.

As the crisis deepened, Kennedy ordered his defence experts to advise him on the best way to proceed, and he was consequently given three options to consider. Firstly, there was the possibility of launching an air strike against the bases before they became operational. However, these would undoubtedly kill some of the Soviet military personnel, technicians and scientists working there and thus provoke the threat of a Soviet response. Secondly, Kennedy looked at authorising an invasion of Cuba in order to topple the Castro regime. However, the Bay of Pigs fiasco had shown that Castro had strong support from the Cuban people and so the chances of a successful invasion were far from certain. In addition, an invasion would probably also provoke a strong response from the USSR. Finally, Kennedy was asked to consider the imposition of a naval blockade on Cuba while at the same time issuing a statement demanding the removal of any missiles already there. It was this last plan that Kennedy decided to choose.

Kennedy ordered a general alert within the whole US navy and sent a hundred ships to the seas around the Caribbean to implement the blockade. All member countries of the UN, including the USSR, were informed that the blockade would begin on 24 October, and two days earlier Kennedy spoke to the nation. He stated his intention to blockade Cuba and told the listening world that a formal communiqué had demanded the removal of the missiles.

He concluded that if the USSR landed any more missiles on Cuba, it would be considered as an act of war. The nuclear holocaust that had for so long seemed just the threat of warring politicians now seemed a distinct possibility. On 23 October 1962, as the Soviet ships carrying the missiles continued on their way across the Atlantic getting closer and closer to the 800-mile exclusion zone, no word was received from either Moscow or Havana.

In the meantime, the USA was busy gaining support for the blockade from its allies in both NATO and the Organisation of American States, and Kennedy was fortunate that the crisis came at a time when a rift between the USSR and China weakened the response of the communist world. On 24 October, the Soviet ambassador to Washington was summoned and informed that it was the intention of the US government to send back any Soviet ship that entered the exclusion zone. As the crisis continued, rumours spread that staff at the Soviet embassy were burning documents in preparation for war. Meanwhile, in order to give the USSR more time to think, the exclusion zone was reduced from 800 miles to 500 miles. In response, the Soviet ships continued on course for Cuba, but reduced their speed.

On 25 October 1962, Khrushchev broke his silence and issued a statement claiming that the USA was breaking international law. But he was embarrassed at the UN in New York when the US ambassador, Adlai Stevenson, published photographs of the missile sites, and a day later he sent a note to Kennedy offering to turn back the ships if Kennedy promised not to invade Cuba. After rejecting a second note that tried to link the withdrawal of the missiles in Cuba to the removal of NATO missiles in Turkey, Kennedy issued his own ultimatum.

He informed Khrushchev that the entire nuclear arsenal of the USA was pointed at the USSR and that he would order the invasion of Cuba on Monday 29 October if the ships carrying the missiles were not turned back and the missiles already in Cuba removed. This coincided with secret talks between Bobby Kennedy and the Soviet ambassador, who was an old ally of Khrushchev, and on Sunday 28 October the news that the waiting world had been praying for eventually came.

The USSR would withdraw the missiles from Cuba if the USA undertook to call off its threat of invasion. Kennedy quickly agreed to this and the Soviet ships in the Atlantic carrying the missiles turned around. By the middle of November, the missiles already on Cuban soil had been removed. The Cuban Missile Crisis, which for a fortnight had threatened nuclear Armageddon, was over.

The Cuban Missile Crisis had brought the world to the brink of nuclear war and in its aftermath came a new urgency in international affairs. The first evidence of this was the installation of a hotline between Washington and Moscow so that direct talks between the leaders of the superpowers could be held in times of crisis. In the meantime, Kennedy responded to Khrushchev's efforts at conciliation by signalling a willingness to withdraw some US missiles stationed in Turkey, which, in any case, had become obsolete. This was completed six months later.

However, the real legacy of the Cuban Missile Crisis was the Partial Nuclear Test Ban Treaty, the first-ever nuclear control agreement, which was signed by the USA, USSR and Britain in August 1963. However, the leaders of France and China, the other nuclear powers in the early 1960s, refused to sign. France under de Gaulle was wary of giving away its rights as an international nuclear power and China, bitterly disappointed with the conciliatory stance that Khrushchev had taken over the crisis, was withdrawing further and further from the international community in the years preceding the Cultural Revolution.

In the USA, Kennedy emerged from the crisis with his reputation greatly enhanced, with earlier mistakes such as the Bay of Pigs fiasco quickly forgotten. Khrushchev, on the other hand, had failed in his bid to neutralise the US nuclear threat by placing his own deterrent in Kennedy's backyard. He claimed victory, saying that the crisis had forced the USA to withdraw NATO missiles from Turkey, but in reality the Soviet hierarchy knew that the crisis had underlined the military superiority of the West. It was not long before Khrushchev was relieved of his duties in a bloodless coup, led by a Soviet elite that had grown tired of his extravagant behaviour and failing policies.

France and Britain in the Early 1960s

The Cuban Missile Crisis had reaffirmed the USA as the world's predominant world power, a fact readily acknowledged in London where the Macmillan government was trying to fashion a role for Britain in the newly emerging post-colonial world. Governments in London throughout the century had always been keen to emphasise the special relationship between Britain and the USA, and Macmillan's was no different.

In December 1962, Macmillan met Kennedy at Nassau in the Bahamas to discuss Britain's role in the Western alliance through the 1960s. Both knew that the fleet of British bombers, which since the early 1950s had carried the British nuclear arsenal, needed upgrading and that US finance and technology would be needed to do this. At Nassau, Kennedy offered to equip British submarines with the new Polaris missile system so long as Britain agreed to operate as part of NATO's Multinational Nuclear Force. Despite objections from de Gaulle, Macmillan agreed, and signed the agreement that gave Polaris to Britain.

De Gaulle opposed the Polaris deal, which on Macmillan's insistence was also offered to France, because he opposed linking the European and US deterrents, arguing that this would necessarily increase the likelihood of Europe being used as the battlefield of any future nuclear conflict. Future US generals, he reasoned, would be far more likely to recommend a pre-emptive strike against the USSR if they knew that European cities, and not US ones, were going to bear the brunt of any Soviet retaliation.

Throughout the 1960s, de Gaulle remained committed to a strong and independent French nuclear deterrent and refused to be drawn into a US-dominated nuclear alliance. De Gaulle continued to favour direct negotiations with the USSR and its allies, and travelled extensively behind the Iron Curtain in pursuit of this aim. Arguments with France within the Western alliance rumbled on through the 1960s until French forces were withdrawn from NATO in 1966.

Macmillan's agreement with Kennedy at Nassau, which guaranteed Britain's membership in the nuclear club for another generation, came near the end of

214

his long tenure as prime minister. He had taken over after ill health and the Suez Crisis had forced Eden out of office, and he had presided over some of the most profound changes that his country was to experience in the second half of the century.

The Suez Crisis had confirmed what many both in Britain and abroad had suspected since the end of World War Two. Britain could no longer make the pretence of being a world power without the support of the USA and Macmillan had been quick to accept this. Under his leadership, Britain instead began to work towards creating a new post-imperial sense of national identity based on a partnership with the USA, the emerging Commonwealth and Europe.

In Africa, his government presided over the withdrawal from empire, ending a post-war decolonisation process that had begun with independence for the subcontinent in the late 1940s. Macmillan visited Africa in February 1960 and warned supporters of apartheid in South Africa, in a speech to parliamentarians in Cape Town, that the 'wind of change' was blowing and that the sun was setting on the European imperial era. New nations across Africa soon claimed their independence, ending a colonial relationship with Britain that had begun four centuries before.

But the white minority in South Africa did not heed Macmillan's advice and, by a small majority, voted to cede from the Commonwealth in order to retain the privileges it enjoyed under apartheid. Similar policies were adopted in Rhodesia, which eventually declared independence from Britain unilaterally in November 1965. Under this Unilateral Declaration of Independence, or UDI, Rhodesia remained under the rule of a white minority government until civil war swept Robert Mugabe to power as president of newly named Zimbabwe in 1979. The people of South Africa had to wait another eleven years to see the first in a series of developments that would eventually lead to the end of apartheid and fully democratic elections in 1994. This began with the release of Nelson Mandela from prison on Robben Island in February 1990.

However, emergence from European colonial rule guaranteed neither political freedom nor economic improvement. For example, civil war broke out in Nigeria in 1967 when the eastern region of the country broke away to form the Republic of Biafra. After three bloody years of fighting, the government finally won and the Biafran republic was crushed. In the meantime, millions of Biafrans died of the malnutrition and starvation that plagued the country as a result of the war.

The Biafran War was only one of many bloody internal battles fought throughout the continent in the aftermath of independence. And the Biafran famine that followed was the first of many African famines reported in the Western media over the next thirty years. This led to a number of massive charity campaigns, with the most famous appeal coming with the *Band Aid* appeal for Ethiopian famine relief in 1985. The power of television and the work of the many Western charity relief organisations active throughout Africa, however, had by the end of the century done little to improve the lives of the vast majority of Africans across the continent who continued to struggle to survive under often corrupt and wasteful governments. They remained some of the poorest people on earth.

Macmillan also had some success in modernising Britain at home, famously claiming that his fellow Britons 'had never had it so good'. With the economy finally showing signs of recovering from the war, he also introduced legislation that modernised the House of Lords, which had not been touched since the beginning of the century. By introducing the life peerage system, he enabled the country to draw upon the knowledge and experience of a great many experts from all walks of life whose voices otherwise would not have been heard in national politics.

In his last year in office, Macmillan was himself dogged by ill health and his administration was attacked over the political controversy surrounding the Profumo affair. John Profumo, a minister at the War Office, was accused of having a relationship with a London society call girl who was also known to have had relations with a Soviet military attaché. The minister denied any involvement in the affair, but later admitted that he had misled the House of Commons and he was forced to resign.

A government inquiry subsequently found that the minister's relationship had not compromised the defence of the realm, but it was a body blow to a government already accused of complacency and mismanagement. Macmillan himself faced criticism in the press over his aloofness and patrician bearing as well as for his lack of control over his party, and soon retired from office in October 1963. Macmillan was replaced by Alec Douglas-Home who, having renounced his peerage, led the country from the House of Commons for a little less than a year before losing the 1964 general election to Harold Wilson.

The Assassination of John F. Kennedy

On 22 November 1963, Douglas-Home's first month in office was tragically disturbed with the news from the other side of the Atlantic that President Kennedy had been shot in Dallas. Kennedy had arrived in Texas that morning on a campaign tour organised to bolster his popularity in advance of the 1964 presidential election. He had already visited Fort Worth during the morning, and was travelling in an open-top limousine on his way to a lunch appointment where he was to address members of the local business community. Towards the end of the journey, at about 12.30pm local time, the president's cavalcade swung into Dealey Plaza on the outskirts of Dallas.

It was at this point that shots rang out and Kennedy was hit by two bullets, one hitting him in the neck while the other blew away the top right side of his head. John Connally, the governor of Texas who was sitting immediately in front of him, was also hit and received wounds to his back, chest, wrist and leg. The other occupants of the car were Mrs Kennedy and Mrs Connally, who were sitting next to their husbands, and a Secret Service driver and his partner in the front of the car. All four were unharmed.

Immediately after the shooting, the limousine sped away to nearby Parkland Memorial Hospital where both Kennedy and Connally received emergency medical treatment. Connally had received serious wounds, but was to recover fully in the weeks and months ahead. However, the president's condition was far more serious, and at just past 1pm local time efforts to revive him ended unsuccessfully. The president received the last rights of the Roman Catholic Church and soon after was pronounced dead.

Argument immediately broke out concerning who had jurisdiction for the president's body. This was quickly won by the Secret Service, and the president's body was whisked away from the hospital and taken to the airport. Accompanied by Mrs Kennedy and Vice President Lyndon Johnson, who had been with the president during his visit to Texas, the body was then flown back to Washington on Air Force One. During the flight, Johnson took the oath of office, becoming his country's thirty-sixth president.

On arrival in Washington, the body was taken to the Bethesda Naval Hospital where a post mortem was performed. It later became apparent that at this time many standard procedures were either ignored or carried out incorrectly. Consequently, it is not surprising that events surrounding the post mortem have always given focus to those who have argued that Kennedy's death was ordered by those closely connected with organising his personal safety.

By the time of the argument concerning jurisdiction of the body at Parkland, police in Texas had already picked up a suspect. Lee Harvey Oswald was arrested at about 3pm at a cinema theatre in the suburbs of Dallas. He was initially charged with the murder of a Dallas police officer who had been shot a little after Kennedy, but less than twelve hours later Oswald was also charged with the assassination of the president.

Oswald was an ex-US marine and something of a social misfit who had lived in the USSR for two years in the early 1960s. During his time there, he had met a Russian girl and their subsequent marriage was to produce two daughters, the second being born just a month before the assassination. In 1962, when he returned to the USA with his young family, Oswald had joined several left-wing pressure groups that supported the Soviet presence in Cuba. In October 1963, Oswald had followed his wife to Dallas where a friend of hers was able to help him find work at the Texas School Book Depository, which overlooked Dealey Plaza. On the day of Kennedy's assassination, Oswald had been working at the Depository.

Investigations in the immediate aftermath of the assassination uncovered a cheap Italian-made, mail-order rifle hidden on the sixth floor of the Depository. The rifle was checked and it was found to belong to Oswald. During the hysteria of the next few days, Oswald's guilt was quickly presumed as the myth of the mad lone assassin began to take shape. However, Oswald always protested his innocence during the two days that he spent in custody being interviewed by the Dallas police, claiming to have been set up for both the assassination of Kennedy and the murder of the policeman.

On 24 November 1963, as he was being led through the basement car park of the Dallas police headquarters on his way to transfer to county jail, Lee Harvey Oswald was shot by Jack Ruby, a Dallas nightclub owner who was subsequently discovered to have had close ties to the Mafia. Oswald was rushed to the same hospital that had treated Kennedy two days earlier, but again doctors could not save the life of a man ripped apart by an assassin's bullet.

The following day a world television audience of millions watched as Kennedy's young widow and her two children led mourners at the president's funeral from Arlington National Cemetery. Kennedy had changed the face of modern politics with his vision, youth and vigour and the weight of his loss was felt across the world. While Jackie Kennedy and her family mourned at Arlington, a very different service was being carried out in Dallas where Oswald's wife, Marina, and other members of his family came together to bury the alleged assassin. On the same day, friends and family of murdered Dallas police officer J. D. Tippit also gathered for a funeral caused by the fateful events of 22 November 1963. Meanwhile, Jack Ruby was remanded into custody.

Immediately after the assassination, a commission of inquiry headed by Earl Warren, the Chief Justice of the Supreme Court, was set up by President Johnson. Warren was joined by six other senior dignitaries who included a future president, Gerald Ford. For nearly a year, the Warren Commission investigated the events surrounding the assassination, interviewing over 500 witnesses and producing a massive report, thousands of pages long. At the core of their findings were three central conclusions.

Firstly, they were of the opinion that Lee Harvey Oswald had acted alone and that there was no evidence of a conspiracy between him and any other agencies. Oswald was portrayed as a social misfit and a loner who had had no coherent motive for his actions. Secondly, they concluded that Oswald fired three shots from his Italian-made, mail-order rifle and that these shots were fired from the sixth floor of the Texas School Book Depository. The first shot missed the president, grazing a bystander who was standing by the underpass at the end of Dealey Plaza. The second bullet, which proved to be so controversial later on, was said to have hit Kennedy in the back of the neck before wounding Connally, who was sitting in front of him, in the back, chest, wrist and leg. The third bullet, which the Commission concluded killed the president, hit him on the top right side of the back of his head, blowing away a large portion of his brain. The third significant conclusion that the Warren Commission made was that Ruby had killed Oswald out of compassion, wishing to spare Jackie Kennedy from the anguish of a public trial. Little comment was made of Ruby's links with the Mafia, and the Commission was happy that Ruby also had acted alone.

Almost immediately after it was published in September 1964, the accuracy of the Warren Commission Report was called into question. But the government of Lyndon Johnson quickly accepted the veracity of its findings and officially refuted the accusations of those who thought there had been a cover-up. It was not until the mid-1970s that the most telling piece of evidence contradicting the Warren Commission's lone assassin theory came to light. This was the release of cine-camera footage of the assassination itself taken in Dealey Plaza by Abraham Zapruder, an amateur cameraman and local businessmen who had come out of his office with his secretary to watch the presidential cavalcade drive past. Analysis of Zapruder's eight-millimetre film of the seconds surrounding the assassination showed the president's head being forced to the back and to the left.

This seemed to indicate that the fatal shot that killed the president had come from in front and to the right, suggesting an assassin on the grassy knoll in front of the presidential limousine rather than in the Texas School Book Depository behind it. This evidence supported the testimonies of around fifty eyewitnesses who had been ignored by the Warren Commission. All had said that they heard shots from the grassy knoll.

The Zapruder Film also raised serious questions about the second bullet. The Commission had concluded that it had passed through Kennedy's neck, before piercing Connally's back, chest and wrist and ending up lodged in his leg. However, the evidence of the Zapruder Film suggested that Connally was still holding his white Stetson cowboy hat at the time that Kennedy was reaching for his neck.

It is therefore claimed by some that if the bullet that hit the president's neck was the same one as hit Connally's wrist, as the Commission had claimed, then Connally's injury would not allow him to hold his hat in such a manner. It was the mystery surrounding this second bullet, which came to be known as the 'Magic Bullet' because of the path and speed it was supposed to have taken, that soon became the focal point for those who aimed to show that the conclusions of the Commission were incorrect.

Over the years, many organisations have been implicated in the many conspiracy theories that have been put forward to explain the assassination, and certainly there were many who gained from the president's death. Kennedy and his brother Robert had made powerful enemies with their pledge to fight organised crime, and the Mafia has been constantly linked with his death. The Mafia had also lost vast sums in Cuba when Castro had taken over in 1959, and Mafia bosses were less than pleased that Kennedy had not done more to back the Cuban Exiles. The Mafia has sometimes been linked with Cuban Exile groups who had their own grievances against Kennedy and felt bitterly let down by his weak stance against Castro.

Those connected with the military-industrial complex, that group of men from business, politics and the military that ran the arms race who President Eisenhower had warned against in 1959 in the speech he made on leaving office, have also come under suspicion. Certainly their profits would have been hit if Kennedy's policy of slowing the military build-up in Vietnam had continued.

Rogue elements from within the various government security services serving the president have also come under suspicion, and certainly these contained important and influential groups that were strongly protective of the autonomy that the Kennedy brothers had tried to curb. There are some who have argued that the chain of events surrounding the assassination, especially between the time immediately after the shooting and the post mortem in Washington, suggested the presence and participation of those who had the authority of an official government agency.

Despite the intense interest that Kennedy's assassination has provoked since

1963 and the multitude of different conspiracy theories that this has given rise to, his real assassins will probably never be known. It seems likely that they were the hired guns of one or more of the above groups who worked secretly on their plan until their masters became convinced that their aims and interests, whether economic, military, social or otherwise, were best served by Kennedy's assassination.

The Fall of Khrushchev and the Rise of Brezhnev

As Johnson assumed presidential duties in the USA, Khrushchev's grip on power in the USSR was weakening. His handling of the economy and foreign affairs had increasingly drawn criticism from within the Presidium, which took the place of the Politburo between 1952 and the mid-1960s, and in October 1964 it made its move to oust him. Khrushchev was on holiday in the Crimea when he received a message from his colleagues that he was needed in Moscow. On his return, he was informed that he was being retired due to old age and ill health. Khrushchev had been outmanoeuvred and there was nothing for him to do but to disappear into retirement in the Moscow suburbs.

Khrushchev was replaced as general secretary of the Communist Party by Leonid Brezhnev who Khrushchev himself had promoted into the Presidium in 1957. Brezhnev came to power as the leader of a collective leadership, but soon came to dominate Soviet politics and remained in control of the USSR until his death in 1982. Brezhnev was a technocrat whose first aim was to stabilise the USSR economy. But he and his colleagues also worked hard to transform the USSR from a land-based power dominating Eastern Europe into a global nuclear superpower that could negotiate with the West from a position of equality.

Under Brezhnev's leadership, the USSR successfully made this transformation although its concentration on the military sector resulted in many other areas of the Soviet economy being ignored. This was to have the most profound effect on the future of the republics that made up the USSR in the 1980s and 1990s.

Khrushchev had tried to retain his country's superpower status by leapfrogging the US security cordon and placing missiles in Cuba. This had badly backfired and led to his eventual downfall. The Cuban Missile Crisis had confirmed US nuclear superiority, and Brezhnev in 1964 was left with no immediate alternative but to return to a policy of friendship, co-operation and compromise with both the USA and NATO. A series of treaties that aimed to stop the proliferation and testing of nuclear weapons were agreed, and cordial relations with the West became even more necessary when relations with China deteriorated during the Cultural Revolution.

However, Soviet strategists in the aftermath of the Cuban Missile Crisis soon identified two areas in which the USSR could develop in order to become a true global superpower, and it was on these that Brezhnev and his colleagues concentrated their energy. Firstly, they looked at strengthening the defence of the Soviet border with Western Europe and from 1965 hundreds of nuclear warheads were deployed to sites in Eastern Europe, targeting cities and military bases in NATO countries to the west. The second identified the need for a modern nuclear submarine fleet capable of moving secretly around the world's seas and oceans as a deterrent against an attack from the West. By 1970, Brezhnev had successfully implemented these two major changes in Soviet foreign policy, masterminding the transformation of the USSR into a truly global superpower with a conventional and nuclear arsenal that could challenge the USA and its Western allies.

However, the West was also keeping abreast of developments in the arms race and the USA was spending billions of dollars every year to keep ahead of its communist rivals. Despite attempts to improve relations in the aftermath of the Cuban Missile Crisis, Washington remained wary of the USSR and viewed the Soviet nuclear build-up with huge concern. So despite the superficial improvement in relations between East and West following the missile crisis, the tricky subjects of weapon limitation and the technology of delivery systems were not addressed.

This meant that towards the end of the decade both sides had stockpiled huge arsenals of nuclear warheads. As a result, a situation of MAD, or mutually assured destruction, had been reached so that, despite the thaw in the Cold War, the world was a much more dangerous place than it had been in 1962. This was highlighted when tension increased in the summer of 1968 when Soviet tanks rolled over the border into Czechoslovakia to stop the reforms being carried there by the government of Alexander Dubček. Once again, relations between East and West cooled.

Britain under the Labour Government of Harold Wilson

While the two superpowers developed under the new leaderships of Johnson and Brezhnev, Britain elected its first Labour government since 1945. Harold Wilson took up the reins of power from a Conservative administration that had looked increasingly tired and vulnerable, and used his formidable intelligence to try to modernise Britain during an era of the most profound social change. Wilson's first government coincided with the onset of the permissive society while popular culture became focused on Britain after the arrival of The Beatles in 1962. They were to become a worldwide phenomenon when Beatlemania hit the rest of the world following their sell-out US tour in 1964. But it was also to be a time of great scientific and technological change, and Wilson had called for Britain to be at the heart of this in his 'white heat' of technology speech to party conference in October 1963.

However, during this time of enormous social change, the nation also had the chance to reflect on its immediate past, with the country mourning the death of Winston Churchill in January 1965. Churchill was among only a small number of ordinary British subjects ever to be honoured with a state funeral, and was the first prime minister to be so honoured since Gladstone in 1898.

Due to its relations with the USA and the Commonwealth, Britain had chosen to exclude itself from the first movement towards European co-operation made in the 1950s. But Macmillan had tried to join the European Economic Community in 1961 and Wilson followed suit in 1967. Once again, however, Britain's membership application was vetoed by France, a stance that angered many of de Gaulle's European colleagues. They saw Britain's entry as an important development, but de Gaulle accused Britain of being openly hostile to the European project, insisting that Britain could not be committed to the EEC while continuing to have such close links with both the Commonwealth and the USA. French objections to British membership were not lifted until after his resignation in 1969.

Another key issue that surfaced during Wilson's first government was the renewed outbreak of sectarian violence in Northern Ireland. This had begun in 1968 after a campaign by a number of Roman Catholic pressure groups to secure civil rights improvements had led to trouble. They were demonstrating against what they saw as partisan rule by the Protestant majority in the Northern Irish assembly at Stormont and, taking their cue from the civil rights movement in the USA, they organised a series of marches and rallies in support of their cause. They looked in particular at stopping discrimination against Roman Catholics in housing, schools, the police force and in wage bargaining.

These demonstrations brought about a violent reaction from some members of the loyalist majority and, with Northern Ireland teetering towards sectarian civil war, Wilson decided that he had no other option than to send in detachments of the British Army to maintain order. At first, these soldiers were welcomed by the beleaguered Roman Catholic community, but, as tension grew, the army became increasingly seen as working with the Protestant-dominated police force, the Royal Ulster Constabulary.

The rampage of violence continued through 1969, with the summer being marred by a series of riots and petrol bombings. Unemployment and social deprivation in the large sectarian urban housing estates fanned the violence and prejudice still further, with terrorist groups finding no problem recruiting in this atmosphere of hate. As violence grew on the streets of Northern Ireland, gangs of extremists armed themselves for the struggles ahead. Para-military groups on both sides of the sectarian divide sprang up, with the IRA in particular growing in strength.

In 1971, the Provisional IRA, taking their name from the Provisional Government that had been set up after the Easter Rising in 1916, broke away from the Official IRA over disagreements about how to carry on the struggle for an independent Ireland. From 1971 until the series of ceasefires in the late 1990s, the struggle between the British Army and the Provisional IRA increasingly defined the character of the troubles in Northern Ireland.

The USA and the Vietnam War

As events in Northern Ireland became more violent, the USA was becoming increasingly embroiled in events in South East Asia. US influence in the region had grown after the defeat of the French at Dien Bien Phu in 1954, and Dulles, Eisenhower's aggressively anti-communist secretary of state, had little time for the Paris Agreement that had split Vietnam between the communists in the North and the republicans in the South. His adherence to the Domino Theory demanded an increased US military presence in South Vietnam to counter the threat from the North. This was a policy that was continued by the Kennedy administration so that by 1962 over 10,000 US military personnel were stationed in South Vietnam advising the government of President Ngo Dinh Diem.

This increase was necessary primarily because of the growth in support for the Viet Cong, a communist South Vietnamese guerrilla force committed to the overthrow of President Diem's regime. The Viet Cong was particularly strong in rural areas where the terror and oppression of Diem's forces had been particularly brutal. The Viet Cong soon gained the support of the government of Ho Chi Minh in North Vietnam, which in turn was supplied by the communist regimes in China and the USSR. The Viet Cong, as the USA was soon to find out, was fast becoming a formidable fighting force.

By the time of Diem's assassination in 1963, the indiscipline and corruption of his government had led South Vietnam to the brink of ruin. The Viet Cong had increased its hold over large tracts of land throughout the country, and Kennedy had become so unhappy with his South Vietnamese allies that he had ordered a complete re-evaluation of US military strategy in the region.

It seemed to him and many of his closest advisers that the Viet Cong in South Vietnam were managing to emulate the feats of Mao's Red Army in the 1930s and 1940s. They were winning the battle for the hearts and minds of the peasants who made up such a large percentage of the population, and the battle was being made easier for the enemy by the continued brutality, violence and incompetence of the South Vietnamese government forces.

Diem was assassinated three weeks before Kennedy in November 1963 and was replaced by a military dictatorship led by General Nguyen Van Thieu who immediately redoubled efforts to rid South Vietnam of the Viet Cong. He found support for this from Johnson's new administration and again the number of US military personnel serving in South Vietnam was increased.

Supporters of the theory that Kennedy was assassinated because of his opposition to the military build-up in Vietnam point to this speedy reversal of policy by the new administration. The military-industrial complex, which Eisenhower had warned against in 1959, certainly seemed to have had a more useful ally in Johnson than Kennedy. However, these renewed efforts did little to stem the growing influence of the Viet Cong, with every atrocity by the South's army, the Army of the Republic of Vietnam, the ARVN, further strengthening its grassroots support. This was to be very important a few years later.

Throughout the early months of 1964, Johnson knew that he faced the same problem that had troubled Kennedy a year earlier. However, where Kennedy had looked maybe to loosen US ties in South Vietnam, Johnson looked to do the opposite. Consequently, he increased the number of US personnel in the region to over 20,000 while at the same time authorising a covert intelligence operation by the CIA against the government in the North. He warned Ho Chi Minh of the consequences of further support for the Viet Cong and he started to prepare US public opinion for a further escalation of the conflict.

In August 1964, reports reached Washington that the North Vietnamese navy had torpedoed a US destroyer operating in the Gulf of Tonkin near North Vietnamese territorial waters. The same ship was allegedly attacked a second time a week later although the seriousness and indeed the authenticity of these attacks were later called into question by a Congressional investigation.

However, these attacks were skilfully used by Johnson to secure support for war in Washington, and soon Congress was to pass the Tonkin Gulf Resolution. This gave huge new powers to the president to raise finance for a war whose military aims soon came to include all-out war against North Vietnam. However, this did not begin until after a US garrison at Pleiku was attacked and destroyed by the North Vietnamese army and the Viet Cong in February 1965. Johnson promptly used his new powers to reinforce US positions near the border, and initiate a two-pronged military strategy that was to remain at the heart of US policy for the rest of the war.

Firstly, he ordered the implementation of Operation Rolling Thunder, a large-scale bombing campaign against the North, which he was sure would soon bring Hanoi to heel. With the exception of a few weeks during a series of abortive peace talks during Nixon's time at the White House, this bombing was to continue for the next eight years. Although it destroyed a vast amount of North Vietnam's infrastructure, Soviet anti-aircraft defence systems, hastily supplied by Moscow, went some way towards saving Hanoi from complete destruction, and the North was not forced out of the war as Johnson had hoped.

Johnson's second strategy was to order a full-scale war of attrition in the South to seek out and destroy the Viet Cong and their sympathisers. As a result, US ground forces were massively increased until they reached a figure approaching half a million men in 1967. Supported by the ARVN, which grew massively in 1965 and 1966, the generals were sure that this force would soon exhaust the enemy. However, both strategies were ultimately doomed because of the tremendous strength and resolve of the Viet Cong, the communists in the North and the people of South Vietnam, who in large numbers supported the fight against what they saw as the elite regime of Thieu. The use of both these strategies was to cause the most enormous physical and environmental damage in Vietnam, but ultimately neither were to have any long-term impact on the outcome of the war.

The lack of success of the US-South Vietnamese forces and the success of the guerrilla tactics of the Viet Cong throughout the war led at times to a terrible sense of frustration that often ended in bloodshed and the use of summary justice. The victims of these acts were more often than not innocent villagers who came under constant suspicion of collaboration by both sides. As in all civil wars, levels of inhumanity by both sides were high, but it was the soldiers of the ARVN who in particular were to earn an unenvied reputation for savagery, even among their allies. However, the most infamous illustration of this habitual brutality was carried out by a patrolling US infantry unit that in March 1968 was responsible for a massacre of just over 500 South Vietnamese peasants at the small village of My Lai. The massacre at My Lai did much to sway US public opinion against the war when it became public at the end of 1969.

As the lack of success of the war in the South became of increasing concern to the US military leadership, more and more extreme methods were sought to halt the success of the guerrilla tactics that were being used by the Viet Cong in the jungles of South Vietnam. Orders were issued that the jungle, which hid the enemy, was to be strategically cleared and so thousands upon thousands of tonnes of napalm, an incendiary liquid that burst into flames on impact, were dropped across the country to flush out the Viet Cong. Also, a massive programme of chemical spraying was ordered, with defoliants such as Agent Orange being used in order to kill the camouflage that the jungle gave. Efforts were also increased to cut off the Viet Cong's main supply route along the Ho Chi Minh Trail, the 700-mile-long jungle trail through Cambodia and Laos from North Vietnam that kept the Viet Cong soldiers fed and armed.

The stalemate in the war was not broken until the beginning of 1968 when the Viet Cong and the North Vietnamese army launched an organised and sustained offensive against the South that coincided with Tet, the lunar New Year holiday, being celebrated at the time. The Tet Offensive struck deep inside and all over South Vietnam, with over a hundred cities and towns, which were believed to be safely in the hands of the South Vietnamese army and their US backers, attacked with impunity. These included the loss of the US base at Khe Sanh, which resulted in massive US casualties in a six-month battle, an assault by communist forces on the holy city of Hue, which was only retaken after a month-long battle, and attacks on the very heart of Saigon itself where stunned journalists reported live accounts of the assault on the US embassy and many other key facilities.

Both sides suffered heavy losses during the offensive and ultimately the territorial gains of the Viet Cong were small. However, the real success of the Tet Offensive was psychological, with it clearly showing the strength of the communists throughout the whole of South Vietnam. This more than any other single factor persuaded many in the US military that their country was involved in a war that ultimately could not be won. The Tet Offensive also had a profound effect on US public opinion, with nightly television reports of US losses from places like Khe Sanh and Hue beamed back into living rooms throughout the country. Many watching soon came to the conclusion that US soldiers were fighting and dying for no good reason. The Tet Offensive soon claimed a major political casualty, with President Johnson announcing that he would not be seeking re-election for a second term of office. Three years of war had broken his spirit for the political fight.

He and his advisers had not paid enough attention to the resolve of Ho Chi Minh's government in the North, to the Viet Cong soldiers fighting in the jungles and paddy fields of South Vietnam or to the peasants who supported them so loyally. The Tet Offensive had shown clearly the dilemma that he faced and this was inherited by his successor, Richard Nixon. Either the USA could withdraw from the war and abandon South Vietnam to communism or it could remain enmeshed in the conflict indefinitely, using its economic might to maintain a military presence but knowing that it was fighting a war that was ultimately unwinnable.

The election of 1968 and Nixon's landslide victory clearly showed the depth of feeling against the war, and Nixon's pledge to end US involvement as quickly as possible was a major reason for his triumph. After his election, Nixon speeded up the process of 'Vietnamisation' that had started under Johnson and increased pressure on the South to take a more central role in its own defence. However, US commitment remained substantial and, despite occasional peace talks in Paris, the bombing of the North continued. In this way, and despite the death of Ho Chi Minh in September 1969, the war in Vietnam dragged on long into the 1970s.

Chairman Mao and the Cultural Revolution

As the world's attention remained very much focused on the war in Vietnam, another event in the communist world was destroying the lives of millions. Mao's concept of a radical peasant-based communist society had failed in the 1950s to make the developments needed to challenge the capitalist world, and a series of failed campaigns led to Mao losing some of his power in 1959. However, few real economic improvements had been made by those who replaced him, and so in 1966 Mao rounded on his critics, using his position and prestige within the party to launch the Cultural Revolution.

This was to be used to restore the revolutionary energy that had characterised the years of struggle between 1934 and 1949. The essence of his argument was that the communist revolution had been brought about through the struggle of the peasants, but that this struggle had been forgotten by reforming liberal elements who had come to dominate China. Chinese society, including the Communist Party itself, needed to return to the revolutionary principles of the peasant armies of the 1930s and 1940s that had brought about this revolution.

The Cultural Revolution concentrated on gaining the support of the young, with huge rallies of students organised at which the writings of Mao were read out. These writings were set down in Mao's *Little Red Book*, which was carried by millions of young Chinese zealots and which in time was to become the third-highest-selling book ever. Soon Mao's personality had been elevated to cult status, very much like Stalin's had been in the USSR a generation earlier. Much of the organisation of the Cultural Revolution was handled by Jiang Qing, a former actress and Mao's fourth wife. She wholeheartedly shared her husband's revolutionary zeal.

Young students and idealists were organised into units of Red Guards that were sent out to expose the enemies of the people. Doctors, teachers, industrialists and intellectuals were all rounded up and sent to the countryside for re-education. The most famous victim of the Cultural Revolution was Deng Xiaoping who had been in charge of economic planning during the 1950s. He was also a survivor of the Long March and had been with Mao all through the struggle against the Nationalists and the Japanese.

However, Deng was only one of many who suffered during the Cultural Revolution. Many were executed by the cadres of Red Guards sent into the countryside, and hundreds of thousands more lost their lives in the famine that Mao's agricultural reforms brought. In their zeal to deliver Mao's message, rival Red Guard units clashed with each other and by 1968 the country was close to civil war.

As a result, Mao was forced to disband the Red Guards, and the Red Army had to be sent into the factories, collective farms and co-operatives to restore order. The revolution that Mao had called for in 1966 had nearly led to the country's destruction, and in 1969 it was finally abandoned although many of the excesses endured since 1966 were to continue. For many in the Western world, the terrible brutality of the Cultural Revolution confirmed their fears about Chinese communism. Despite the improvement in relations following Nixon's visit to China in the early 1970s, these fears continued long after Mao's death in 1976.

The Arab-Israeli Conflict and the Six-Day War

Another area of the world in turmoil was the Middle East where an uneasy truce between Israel and the Arab states it bordered was broken in June 1967. This came after a period when Israeli leaders had become increasingly concerned about their country's security, following a number of border incidents involving Egypt, Jordan and Syria that had culminated in Nasser ordering the withdrawal of UN troops patrolling the Sinai Desert. These troops had patrolled the desert since 1956 in accordance with the treaty that had ended the previous Arab-Israeli war.

Interpreting this as an act of aggression, Israel launched a pre-emptive strike against its Arab neighbours on 5 June 1967 that was to last for one day less than a week. As its name suggests, the Six-Day War was a war that Israel won with stunning ease. In a strike similar in nature to the German attack on Allied airfields in northern France in 1940, Israel was able to destroy the bulk of the Arab air forces of Egypt, Jordan, Syria and Iraq as they stood on the ground. Having won the battle for the sky, Israeli commanders were able to move their troops quickly through the Sinai Desert, routing the Egyptian army within four days.

Meanwhile, simultaneous attacks were launched against Jordan, and the West Bank of the Jordan River and East Jerusalem were soon captured. Having defeated Egypt and Jordan, Israel turned its attention to Syria, which had been shelling Israel from positions in the Golan Heights, the mountains to the north of Israel. The Golan Heights were finally taken on 10 June 1967, but not until after both Israeli and Syrian forces had experienced heavy casualties.

The UN-sponsored truce that ended the Six-Day War left Israel occupying huge tracts of land surrounding its border. Israel did not lay official claim to most of this land, but was determined to hold them as a buffer against any future Arab attack. These Occupied Territories comprised the Gaza Strip, the Sinai Desert, the West Bank and the Golan Heights. However, East Jerusalem contained the Wailing Wall, the only remaining part of the Second Temple destroyed in Roman times, and this had always been considered as part of Israel. This was quickly brought into the Jewish state.

The spoils of the Six-Day War created the problem of controlling over half a million displaced Arabs in the Occupied Territories, and it was here that many Palestinian groups opposing Israel were to grow. Of these, the Palestine Liberation Organisation, the PLO, under the leadership of Yasser Arafat, an engineer who had grown up in Cairo, was to become the most powerful.

The Prague Spring, *Ostpolitik* and Détente

In Europe, relations between East and West since the Cuban Missile Crisis had taken on a far calmer nature. Both superpowers had been frightened by how close to nuclear war the world had come in 1962 and both had committed themselves to far more open dialogue. However, this had not stopped both sides stockpiling huge arsenals of nuclear warheads that made the world potentially a far more dangerous place in the late 1960s than it had been when Kennedy and Khrushchev had locked horns at the beginning of the decade.

Any doubts that the huge divide between East and West still existed were banished in August 1968 when Soviet tanks rolled over the border into Czechoslovakia, ending the liberal reforms of Alexander Dubček. During the so-called Prague Spring that preceded the tanks, Dubček had tried to develop a more liberal style of communism that, while remaining loyal to the Warsaw Pact, also sought to expand political and economic links with the West. But as support for Dubček grew, Brezhnev acted decisively, unwilling as he was to allow the amount of autonomy being sought by the reformers.

As far as Brezhnev was concerned, Czechoslovakia was to remain very much within the Soviet-dominated Eastern Bloc of Warsaw Pact countries that since 1945 had formed a buffer zone with the West. The USSR's increasingly strong global presence meant that the USA, embroiled as it was in Vietnam, could do little in defence of Czechoslovakia. In deference to the spheres of influence in central Europe worked out at Potsdam a generation before, the occupation of Czechoslovakia was grudgingly accepted in the West.

Despite the political realities of events such as the Vietnam War and the Soviet invasion of Czechoslovakia, the constantly escalating dangers inherent in the spiralling arms race were becoming increasingly apparent to politicians on both sides of the ideological divide as the decade closed. The Cuban Missile Crisis had led to a number of measures designed to make the world a safer place, but these would be, in essence, useless if some restraints were not put on the amount of nuclear warheads stockpiled by each side. As a result, both Washington and Moscow began adopting a more friendly and co-operative stance towards each other that resulted in a decade of talks, treaties and agreements that are collectively known as détente.

Initially, however, cordial relations had been hampered by the perennial question of Germany, which had remained at the heart of Cold War conflict since 1947. In an effort to resolve this question, Willy Brandt, the former mayor of West Berlin who had become the West German foreign minister in 1966, adopted a far more friendly and co-operative approach to relations with East Germany and his eastern neighbours. Brandt's *Ostpolitik*, his policy towards the East, gathered momentum once he had become chancellor of West Germany in 1969, and improvements in relations between the two Germanys did much to create an atmosphere in which arms limitation talks could go ahead. These talks eventually began in November 1969 and, after three years of painstaking negotiations, culminated with the signing of the Strategic Arms

Limitation Talks Treaty. SALT I was eventually signed in Moscow in May 1972.

The First Man on the Moon

In May 1961 in a speech to a joint session of Congress, Kennedy had challenged NASA and the wider scientific community to send a man to the moon, and return him safely to earth, by the end of the decade. Throughout the 1960s, this challenge had been eagerly followed by successive White House administrations, with much of the technology that had been developed in the arms race called upon to create a machine capable of completing the round trip of nearly half a million miles.

However, tragedy struck in January 1967 on the very first Apollo mission when an electrical fault ignited a fire in the oxygen-rich atmosphere of the rocket capsule cockpit. Tragically, this killed the three astronauts who were making their final preparations for lift-off. However, lessons were quickly learnt from the Apollo 1 tragedy and within two years NASA was ready for its ultimate challenge.

On 16 July 1969, Apollo 11 was launched, with the moon landing as its prime objective, and for four days the world waited as Neil Armstrong, Buzz Aldrin and Michael Collins sped away on their 250,000-mile journey. Once safely in the moon's orbit, Armstrong and Aldrin took their positions in the lunar module, *Eagle,* and separated from the main spacecraft, *Columbia*. As Collins continued to orbit the moon, Armstrong took control of *Eagle* and prepared for the descent to the moon's surface. Soon, *Eagle* landed softly on the dusty surface of the Sea of Tranquility although it later emerged that, in trying to find a safe place to land, Armstrong had nearly run out of fuel. As the world watched and waited, Armstrong and Aldrin made their final preparations for the first moon walk.

Six hours later on 21 July 1969, the door of the module opened and Neil Armstrong slowly came down the steps. As he stepped onto the moon's powdery surface, he said, 'That's one small step for man, one giant leap for mankind.' He was soon joined by Aldrin, and they began collecting rock and soil samples and carrying out some other scientific experiments.

Armstrong spent a little over two hours on the moon's surface before joining Aldrin back in *Eagle*. Having successfully rejoined Collins in *Columbia* after their twenty-one-and-a-half-hour lunar mission, all three spoke to the waiting world and were congratulated by President Nixon. The rockets were then boosted to allow the escape from the moon's gravitational pull and the three astronauts began the long journey back to earth. Three days later, they safely splashed down in the Pacific Ocean.

The Apollo 11 mission was the first of six successful US lunar missions that in total allowed twelve astronauts to stand on the moon before the Apollo programme was cancelled after the successful return of Apollo 17 in December 1972. These men, however, were not joined by the astronauts of Apollo 13 whose landing in April 1970 had to be aborted a day away from the moon after a small explosion crippled their rocket. Their long struggle home, and their ultimate survival against all odds, was to take a further four days of ingenuity and high skill.

As détente increased into the early 1970s, US astronauts were also to carry out a series of joint ventures with Soviet cosmonauts and these included a joint flight in 1975. These often focused on scientific work carried out on Skylab, which was launched by NASA in 1973 and which orbited earth for the next six years, and later NASA's work became dominated by the Space Shuttle programme, which was begun in 1981 and was to run into the next century. However, none of these new projects were to capture the imagination of the world as much as that first flight of fantasy in July 1969, which had answered Kennedy's challenge so successfully.

Détente – The Uneasy Peace
The 1970s

April 1970
(The Invasion of Cambodia and Laos)
to
November 1980
(The Invasion of Afghanistan)

The Vietnam War and the Invasion of Cambodia and Laos

The End of the Vietnam War and its Consequences

International Relations and the Significance of SALT I

Britain: Northern Ireland, Immigration, the Economy and Europe

The Yom Kippur War and the Oil Crisis of 1973

The Watergate Scandal

China in the 1970s

The Independence of Zimbabwe and Apartheid in South Africa

Jimmy Carter, Leonid Brezhnev and the Second Cold War

The Government of James Callaghan and the Election of Margaret Thatcher

The Iranian Revolution and the Invasion of Afghanistan

The Vietnam War and the Invasion of Laos and Cambodia

As the attention of the world focused on the crew of Apollo 11 and their historic mission a quarter of a million miles away, the war in Vietnam continued to claim the lives of thousands of soldiers and civilians on both sides of the conflict. This was despite Nixon's pledge in 1968 for the quick withdrawal of US troops, the 'peace with honour' that he had talked about throughout the election campaign, which had been a major factor in his success over his Democratic opponent Hubert Humphrey, Johnson's pro-war vice president. However, at the turn of the decade and a year or so into his presidency, there were still no signs that Nixon's commitment to the war was diminishing, with the USA remaining as deeply embroiled in the conflict as ever.

On arriving at the White House, Nixon had adopted a two-pronged strategy that he hoped would allow the USA to leave Vietnam with its credibility intact. On the one hand, he continued the massive bombing campaign against North Vietnam that was designed to keep up pressure on Ho Chi Minh to negotiate a settlement. On the other, he encouraged a process of 'Vietnamisation' within South Vietnam that aimed to increase both the political and economic self-sufficiency of the Thieu regime.

This process reduced the number of US troops in Vietnam from over 500,000 in 1968 to around 100,000 in 1971. At the same time, the South Vietnamese army, which Nixon remained committed to train and supply, had swelled to over half a million. Nixon and his advisers hoped that this two-pronged attack would bring the communists to the negotiating table, thereby guaranteeing the security, and indeed the very existence, of a pro-Western government in the South.

However, neither strategy had forced North Vietnam or the Viet Cong to negotiate seriously at peace talks held intermittently in Paris since 1968, and by 1970 Nixon was clear that a new direction in policy was needed. His main war aim was the preservation of a pro-Western republic in the South and he and his advisers increasingly came to believe that this could only be achieved if the military ascendancy lost after the Tet Offensive in 1968 was once again regained.

As a result, Nixon announced in early 1970 that a joint US-South Vietnamese offensive was to be launched against the Viet Cong in Cambodia. This aimed to hit at the very heart of the enemy by cutting off its supply route along the Ho Chi Minh Trail and by destroying the secret command headquarters of the North Vietnamese army that had been located by U2 reconnaissance missions over the Cambodian jungle. Nixon hoped that this massive show of firepower in Cambodia would preserve South Vietnam and allow the USA to disengage from the war with its honour and credibility intact.

But the escalation of the war into Cambodia was greeted with widespread condemnation from both within the USA and around the world. These protests came not only from the student population that had been at the heart of the anti-war protests of 1968 but also from many other respectable elements of Western and US society. Several senior US government officials resigned over the issue, and many ordinary citizens, responding to the growing inflation in the national economy caused by the deficit financing of the war, joined in spirit the thousands of demonstrators who marched on Washington in a series of protests against the invasion in particular and the war in general. Opinion against the war had hardened when news of the massacre at My Lai became public in various magazine articles around November 1969, and this was added to in May 1970 when six students were shot dead by National Guards during campus protests at Kent State and Jackson Universities.

In Cambodia itself, the legacy of the invasion was a steady growth in support for the Khmer Rouge, the peasant-based, communist guerrilla force that eventually took power in 1975. This began a programme of social re-education, under the leadership of Pol Pot, that was even more extreme and violent than the Cultural Revolution in neighbouring China a decade earlier.

The invasion of Cambodia was not the military success that Nixon had hoped for and it did little to change the widely held view that the USA was fighting a war that it could not win. Slowly, Nixon also came to the same conclusion and began belatedly to look elsewhere for help in extricating the USA from the war. Having failed to persuade North Vietnam and the Viet Cong to negotiate, he turned his attention back to superpower politics where détente had arrived tentatively in the last years of the 1960s.

This had led to arms limitation talks in Helsinki that had suggested the adoption of a more conciliatory approach to international relations by politicians on both sides of the Iron Curtain. Nixon now hoped to use this political and diplomatic thaw to persuade both Moscow and Beijing to put pressure on Ho Chi Minh and negotiate a settlement that allowed the pro-Western government to remain in power in South Vietnam. However, these hopes had not been helped in June 1969 when the USSR recognised the Viet Cong as the legitimate government of South Vietnam, and they were further hindered through 1970 and 1971 by President Thieu's stubborn insistence that his army would soon win an outright military victory.

The stalemate in the war continued through 1970 and was only finally broken in February 1971 when US-supported South Vietnamese army units invaded Laos, North Vietnam's western neighbour. The invasion was supposed to show the success of the 'Vietnamisation' process, but proved a major disaster, with the South Vietnamese army soon badly beaten. US troops did not directly take part in the invasion because of a law, passed by Congress in 1970 after the incursion into Cambodia, that had put limitations on the president's powers to wage war.

However, the importance of US intelligence and US supplies was still huge, and nightly news programmes across the USA showing pictures of the pitiful retreat of the South Vietnamese army were clearly an embarrassment to the Nixon administration. As a result, calls for an end to US involvement in the war in Vietnam again increased. Meanwhile, morale among US troops in Vietnam remained desperately low, with no US soldier wanting to fill the last body bag sent home. Matters were made worse by unfair drafting procedures that saw the exploitation of the poor and of various ethnic minorities, and widespread drug use was also reported.

The End of the Vietnam War and its Consequences
Nixon replied to the military failure in Laos by ordering an increase to the bombing sorties over North Vietnam. This prompted a series of meetings in Paris between Henry Kissinger, the president's special adviser, and North Vietnamese representatives, and these talks nearly brought peace. However, hopes were again scuppered by Nixon's belated backing for President Thieu's demands that no communist forces should be allowed to remain in the South.

With negotiations once again stalled and with Kissinger and Nixon beginning to argue over policy, the initiative was wrested by the communists. Improved US relations with both the USSR and China had never stopped the continued supply of weapons to the communists, and these were successfully used in a new offensive that was launched in March 1972. The main objective of this spring offensive was to destabilise the Nixon administration in the run-up to the November election.

In this, the Viet Cong were singularly unsuccessful, with other foreign policy victories carrying Nixon to a landslide victory. However, militarily the offensive was a huge success and this was especially the case around the Mekong Delta near Saigon. Ominously for the Thieu government, this clearly showed that the 'Vietnamisation' process, which had been so spectacularly unsuccessful

239

so recently in Laos and which had been at the centre of Nixon's policy in Vietnam for four years, had again failed to deal with the communist threat.

Nixon responded to this new communist offensive by ordering a renewed intensification of bombing raids over North Vietnam. These non-stop sorties were the heaviest of the war and forced the Northern Vietnamese back to the negotiating table in Paris where it was agreed that a National Council of Reconciliation would be set up. Crucially, US negotiators in Paris accepted that the Viet Cong would be represented on this council. However, this agreement was vetoed by Nixon at the eleventh hour, again after last-minute consultations with President Thieu.

Following the breakdown of talks in Paris and the re-election of Nixon, bombing sorties over the North were again increased in a twelve-day reign of terror in December 1972. Nixon had employed this tactic since 1968 and it finally paid off on 31 January 1973 when an accord was signed that ended direct US involvement in the Vietnam War. The accord differed little from the one thrashed out in October, and Thieu had once again raised objections over Viet Cong involvement.

But Nixon was by this time increasingly compromised by the Watergate scandal and he told his South Vietnamese counterpart that US air force protection of the South would be withdrawn if South Vietnam refused to sign. Only grudgingly, therefore, did Thieu sign the ceasefire agreement, taking some solace from the fact that he could still rely on US aerial protection. But with Nixon fighting for his political life and with public opinion increasingly opposed to any US involvement in Vietnam, this protection was in fact withdrawn relatively soon after the ceasefire, forcing South Vietnam to face the communists alone for the first time since 1965.

As a result, communist forces flooded down the increasingly well-developed Ho Chi Minh Trail in preparation for a final assault on the Mekong Delta and Saigon itself. In essence, the war had become a matter of supply, with the South having lost its superpower backer. North Vietnam and the Viet Cong still retained the support of the USSR and China, and it now seemed only a matter of time before the reunification of Vietnam under communist rule.

In early 1974, Thieu made one final effort to counter this communist stranglehold, breaking the ceasefire and attacking the communists with all the limited force left at his disposal. However, early victories were soon reversed and within a year the Viet Cong and the North Vietnamese had closed in on Saigon. President Ford made one last effort to rally support for South Vietnam, but his pleas to Congress were quickly and firmly rejected. The end finally came in April 1975 when communist forces attacked and captured Saigon. The South's capital was soon renamed Ho Chi Minh City as the two Vietnams were united once again. Within a month, both Laos and Cambodia had also fallen to communism.

The main war aim that had persuaded President Eisenhower to extend US influence into South East Asia almost twenty years earlier had clearly not been achieved, with the longest and most costly war in US history failing to rid Vietnam of communism. Indeed, only the closest and fondest of Nixon's critics could claim that the USA had in 1973 achieved the 'peace with honour' that he had talked of in the election of 1968. In the USA, the wounds of the war were to heal only slowly, and it was not until 1982 that a memorial in Washington was set up for Vietnam veterans who so often felt rejected after returning home.

For the people of Cambodia, the end of the war marked the beginning of three years of hell on earth with the defeat of the US-backed government in April 1975 bringing to power the Khmer Rouge. The leader of the Khmer Rouge was Pol Pot, a revolutionary communist who immediately renamed the country Democratic Kampuchea. He soon gave notice of his intentions by resetting the date in Kampuchea to the Year Zero, and emptying all the towns of their inhabitants. Within a few months, the capital of Phnom Penh lay deserted.

Pol Pot's style of revolutionary peasant-based communism was derived from Ho Chi Minh and Mao Tse-tung, and his expulsion of thousands of townspeople into the countryside and the persecution of the educated middle classes echoed Mao's Cultural Revolution a decade earlier. Whole towns were destroyed, with millions reorganised into agrarian cadres and set to work in the fields.

Malnutrition and physical exhaustion were important causes of death, but the terrible Stalinist-style purges ordered by Pol Pot himself were also to claim the lives of countless thousands. In the main, these purges were carried out by the black-uniformed teenage fanatics of the Khmer Rouge, where even the wearing of spectacles, indicating, as it did, that the owner had received an education, or the speaking of English or French, the language of the colonial past, was enough to condemn a person to death.

Pol Pot's rule was not to take him past Year Three in his new calendar, but his fall did not come before the extermination of some two million Cambodians, a fifth of the country's population. Pol Pot's terror was finally stopped in 1979 when Vietnamese forces took Phnom Penh after a series of border disputes had ended in war. After 1979, the Khmer Rouge retreated to well-guarded hideouts in the hills in the north-east bordering Thailand where it waged a guerrilla war against the new regime until well into the 1990s. Pol Pot eventually died in this jungle exile in 1998.

International Relations and the Significance of SALT I

The major reason for Nixon's landslide election victory over Senator George McGovern in 1972 was the success, despite Vietnam, that he and Kissinger had enjoyed in international superpower politics during his first term in office. At the heart of this success were negotiations held in Helsinki and Vienna between 1969 and 1972 that resulted in the signing of the first Strategic Arms Limitation Treaty. SALT I was negotiated during a period of relative co-operation and friendship between East and West and was the world's first nuclear arms limitation treaty.

The establishment of diplomatic relations with communist China, which had been frozen since Mao's revolution in 1949, also added to Nixon's stature both at home and abroad. Importantly, this came at a time when Sino-Soviet relations remained frosty, and Nixon was given credit for driving a wedge between the two rival communist superpowers. As a result, it was felt that he had made the USA much safer in 1972 than it had been in 1968.

After the Cuban Missile Crisis in 1962, a greater effort at co-operation and friendship had been made by both the superpowers and this had initially led to the signing of the Nuclear Test Ban Treaty the following summer. This had been followed with the UN-sponsored Nuclear Non-Proliferation Treaty in 1968, but crucially neither treaty stopped the stockpiling of nuclear weapons. The SALT talks were so important because they attempted to do this for the first time, limiting and controlling the size of the nuclear arsenals held by each side.

The talks aimed to reverse the build-up that had continued after 1962, despite the various agreements hastily put in place following the Cuban Missile Crisis, and negotiations lasted for nearly three years. To the USA, an agreement was important to stop the massive growth of the Soviet nuclear arsenal that Brezhnev had ordered since 1964. To the USSR, an agreement was important to protect the military parity that had been achieved by this build-up. To the waiting world, an agreement was important to limit the possibility of a nuclear holocaust that had so nearly ended civilisation in October 1962.

From the very start, the US delegation let it be known that any progress at the SALT talks would be dependent on Moscow's willingness to bring pressure on the government in Hanoi to negotiate a settlement in Vietnam. For a year, this hampered progress, with the USSR either unwilling or unable to persuade Ho Chi Minh's government to join negotiations in Paris, and these problems were further compounded when Nixon ordered the invasion of Cambodia in 1970.

Early negotiations also foundered over a difference of opinion concerning definitions for ICBMs and these differences over offensive weapons continued to dog talks until the bitter end in 1972. The Soviet delegation wanted all the West's ICBMs counted while the USA insisted that only its own missiles were to be considered. With talks over offensive weapons stalled, delegates found that a little more headway could be made over negotiations concerning defensive anti-ballistic missiles. However, an agreement over ABMs was also put back when the US Senate voted to finance a new ABM system designed to protect the huge ICBM arsenals housed under the prairies of Montana and Dakota.

In addition to this new defensive ABM system, the US Senate also agreed to finance the development of the multiple independently targetable re-entry vehicle system. MIRV was a new offensive ICBM system designed to overcome any Soviet ABM system by launching more than one nuclear warhead from each missile fired. The development of this new generation of offensive weapons would cost billions of dollars, with the largest conceived MIRV missile carrying a destructive power that was over 200 times greater than that dropped on Hiroshima. This received the enthusiastic support of the president.

With talks on both offensive and defensive weapons deadlocked in Vienna, Nixon sent Kissinger to Moscow to open secret backchannel talks directly with the Soviet leadership. But these secret meetings, held through 1971, also made little headway, with the USSR frustrating Kissinger by introducing the whole question of submarine-launched ballistic missiles, the SLBMs. With progress now deadlocked at both the SALT negotiations and the secret talks, Kissinger and Nixon looked to apply pressure on Moscow from a new direction.

Since the end of the Cultural Revolution in 1969, and despite differences over the war in Vietnam, a few tentative steps had been made to improve Sino-US relations, and these were now used by Kissinger to draw Washington closer to the communist government in Beijing. Both Nixon and Kissinger knew that this came at a time of bitter conflict between the USSR and China, with both communist superpowers having just increased the size of their respective army detachments along their long common border. The culmination of Kissinger's 'triangular diplomacy' came in February 1972 with Nixon's state visit to Beijing.

Having reasserted pressure on the USSR through this *rapprochement* with China, Kissinger again opened negotiations directly with the Kremlin. On the matter of defensive systems, it was agreed that each side would be allowed to retain two ABM sites. One would protect each capital city while the other would be used to protect a designated ICBM site in each country. This was to guarantee the deterrent capability of each side. Common ground was far less easy to find concerning ICBMs, and negotiations were still going on as Nixon arrived in Moscow for the official signing of the treaty itself.

Eventually, a combination of negotiations at the SALT talks still taking place in Helsinki and backchannel work being conducted in Moscow resulted in an interim five-year accord, which still allowed each side to keep a staggeringly large number of weapons. Under the agreement, the USA retained 1,054 ICBMs and 710 SLBMs. The USSR kept 1,618 ICBMs and 950 SLBMs. The MIRV capability and the bomber strength of the USA were not included in the agreement and were the reason that Nixon, and eventually the US Senate, were willing to accept this disparity. After three long years of difficult negotiations, Nixon and Brezhnev met in the grandeur of the Kremlin and signed the SALT I treaty.

Britain: Northern Ireland, Immigration, the Economy and Europe

By the time Brezhnev and Nixon met in Moscow to sign SALT I, Britain had become a somewhat muted figure on the world stage. The adjustments that had been made during the period of decolonisation had led to a crisis of identity, and these problems were compounded by an ailing economy that neither Conservative nor Labour governments had been able to deal with satisfactorily. In addition, after 1968 both the Wilson administration and the government of Edward Heath that replaced it after the general election of 1970 were forced to deal with the increased sectarian violence that had engulfed Northern Ireland.

In particular, this had seen the growth of the IRA and its campaign against British rule in Northern Ireland, and its support within the nationalist community and that of the splinter Provisional IRA, which had been established in December 1969, was strengthened from 1970 when a new tough approach to the problem of terrorism was adopted by the government at Stormont. Using a new law passed by the Unionist-dominated assembly, the Royal Ulster Constabulary and the British Army stationed in Northern Ireland were given new powers to arrest and detain suspected terrorists in the interests of internal security. This policy of Internment was used almost exclusively against the Roman Catholic community and alienated even moderate Catholic opinion.

Relations between the divided communities within Northern Ireland deteriorated still further in January 1972 when thirteen Roman Catholic protesters were shot dead by members of the British Army during an anti-Internment march in Londonderry. Events surrounding the shootings on Bloody Sunday, as the day was soon called, remain a subject of intense controversy, but to the nationalist community, the dead protesters soon became martyrs. Partly as a result of the violence that escalated after Bloody Sunday and partly because of the record of the Stormont Assembly, Heath suspended the Northern Irish government in March 1972 and introduced direct rule from London for the first time since 1922. This was to last until 1999.

This period of increasing strife in Northern Ireland in the early 1970s was not helped by the performance of the British economy that showed few signs of recovery. Heath had inherited an economy in poor health, and he had hoped that a combination of lower taxes and stricter trade union laws would help stimulate business and enterprise. He hoped to develop an economy that kept inflation down while boosting British business competitiveness abroad. However, economic indicators throughout his tenure in office remained stubbornly negative, with unemployment and inflation continuing to rise. In addition, Heath's attempts to curb the power of the trade unions led to a series of crippling strikes.

The issue of race was also to dog his administration despite the distance that he had put between himself and Enoch Powell whose radical views on non-white immigration in the late 1960s had embarrassed many in the Conservative Party. However, continued relations with South Africa, and particularly the decision to continue the trade in arms with the apartheid regime, led to stiff opposition both from within Britain and from around the Commonwealth. In January 1971, his stance over South Africa was roundly condemned at a conference of Commonwealth leaders in Singapore.

The Heath government was also widely criticised over the crisis surrounding Ugandan immigration in 1972. The crisis had been precipitated by the decision by Idi Amin, who had seized power the previous year in a military coup, to expel all of Uganda's Asian community. Given only sixty days to leave the country, thousands had rushed over the border into neighbouring Kenya where many, as British passport holders, had applied for refuge in Britain. Heath's attempts to use legal loopholes to deny or slow down their entry into Britain was condemned by many both in Britain and around the world.

Eventually, many did arrive in Britain and time was to show that they were the lucky ones. Idi Amin remained dictator of Uganda, the country once described by Churchill as the pearl of Africa, until April 1979 and presided over a regime that tortured and murdered some half a million of his countrymen. Even on a continent renowned for its corruption, cruelty and injustice, and in one where most of the fifty or so countries that gained independence in the 1960s were soon taken over by some form of military dictatorship, Amin's particular brand of government stood out for its terror and barbarism.

The Heath government will be best remembered for taking Britain into the European Economic Community. The importance of closer ties with Europe had long been a central belief in his political philosophy, and he had been an important figure in the negotiating team that had nearly secured British membership during Macmillan's government in the early 1960s. Now negotiations were driven energetically by the prime minister himself who saw membership as the key to Britain's future prosperity. Negotiations with the EEC began soon after Heath's 1970 general election victory and were greatly helped by the departure of President de Gaulle in 1969.

De Gaulle had long opposed British membership of the EEC, but his successor, Georges Pompidou, had fewer reservations and made it clear that he would not use the French veto to block Britain's application. So having fulfilled the various criteria for membership set down by the other members of the Community, Britain, along with the Republic of Ireland and Denmark, joined the original six members in January 1973.

British enthusiasm for membership was not universal and the Wilson government, which replaced Heath's in February 1974, was split over the issue to such an extent that a national referendum was called to decide the matter of continued membership. In the referendum, the people of Britain voted two-to-one in favour of remaining in the EEC although the question of Britain's relationship with the rest of Europe continued to cause deep divisions within both main political parties that were to rumble on into the next century.

Heath had hoped that membership of the EEC would help improve Britain's economic performance, but this was not to happen. Matters were made considerably worse in October 1973 when an oil crisis, precipitated by the Yom Kippur War, resulted in the quadrupling of oil prices in Britain. In November 1973, Heath was forced to call a state of emergency, and by January 1974 the rationing of electricity to industry, homes and schools had been ordered.

The Three-Day Week that this brought about led to one of the lowest points in British economic history. It also led to the threat of strike action from, among others, the railwaymen, the electricity workers and, especially, the miners. With the crisis worsening, Heath decided to take on the unions by appealing to the electorate directly. But his decision backfired a month later when the Labour Party unexpectedly won most seats in a hung parliament at the snap general election, with Harold Wilson once again returning to Downing Street.

The Yom Kippur War and the Oil Crisis of 1973

Heath's defeat in February 1974 was largely brought about by the industrial unrest caused by the international oil crisis precipitated by the Yom Kippur War. This was the fourth Arab-Israeli conflict in a generation, and largely arose from problems left over from the Six-Day War that had left large tracts of Arab land under Israeli control. These Occupied Territories included the Sinai Desert, the Golan Heights, the West Bank and the Gaza Strip.

After the war in 1967, control of this land had passed to Moshe Dayan, the eye-patched general who had led the Israeli armed forces with so much success in the war itself. Dayan was constrained by UN Resolution 242, which had been passed during the ceasefire negotiations in 1967, and which stipulated that the Occupied Territories should eventually be given back. But the resolution had also stated that no land would be returned until Israel's internal security was guaranteed. Dayan's first priority was to protect Israel from any future Arab attack, and so he decided to administer the Occupied Territories as a military buffer zone.

But political and economic pressure from within Israel soon after 1967 had demanded Jewish settlement in the Occupied Territories, with many Arabs, as a result, driven from their homes. Many flocked to the already overcrowded refugee camps in Lebanon, Syria and Jordan where deep resentment against Israel festered. It was here that Yasser Arafat, the leader of the PLO, was to build up his forces between 1968 and 1970, and during this time the PLO used its power base in Jordan to launch a series of increasingly radical campaigns against Israel. However, the growth of the PLO within Jordan increasingly brought it into conflict with the Jordanian leader, King Hussein, who, following a series of airline hijacks, eventually expelled Arafat and his organisation from his country in September 1970.

But the PLO's expulsion from Jordan did not stop the campaign of terror against Israel and its allies, with the amount of terrorist activity around the world in the early 1970s increasing dramatically. Many of these attacks were carried out by Black September, a radical Palestinian group whose name was inspired by the expulsion of the PLO from Jordan. Black September went on to become one of the most infamous of the many terrorist organisations that emerged at this time that included the Baader-Meinhof group in Germany, the Red Brigade in Italy and the Provisional IRA in Britain.

Activists from these groups carried out a series of atrocities including hijackings, bombings and assassinations that aimed to bring revolutionary change through terror. The most spectacular example of the power of terrorism came in September 1972 when members of Black September burst into the Israeli quarters at the Munich Olympic Village, killing two athletes and taking nine more hostage. After a tense stand-off with the West German police that captivated world attention for a week, the terrorists were escorted with their hostages to the airport where a rescue attempt resulted in the deaths of all the remaining hostages and five terrorists.

With the internal security of Israel already threatened by continuous terrorist activity, events in Munich further hardened Israeli resolve to retain the Arab land taken in 1967. This created a dilemma not only for Arafat and the Palestinian people, but also for the leaders of the other Arab countries who had had land taken. This was particularly true of Egypt where Gamal Nasser's death in 1970 had led to the succession of Anwar Sadat. Sadat had hoped that economic, political and military pressure would bring the Israelis to the negotiating table, but had become convinced by 1973 that Israel had no intention of agreeing to a settlement that would give back Egyptian land in Sinai.

So working closely with President Assad of Syria, he began organising secret plans for war. This was launched on 6 October 1973, a date that coincided with the holy festival of Yom Kippur, the Jewish Day of Atonement. This was a Jewish religious holiday when many Israeli soldiers were expected to be on leave and away from their posts. Initial successes by both Syrian and Egyptian forces were quick and decisive, with Israel losing many aircraft, tanks and soldiers in the first few hours of battle.

However, Israeli forces were quick to regroup and, initially concentrating their efforts on the strategically important Golan Heights, they were able to reclaim much of the land lost within the next few days. By 10 October 1973, the Golan Heights had been retaken and Israeli military commanders gave the order to march on Damascus. With the Syrian capital under increasing pressure, Assad asked for and received further shipments of arms from the USSR. With the stakes rising daily in what was becoming a crucial battle in the Cold War as well as a local struggle between Israel and its Arab neighbours, the USA retaliated by sending extra supplies to Israel.

With Damascus under threat, Sadat ordered a counter-attack across the

Sinai Desert. However, the Egyptian army was defeated and driven back, as it had been in 1967, and the Suez Canal once again taken, with further Israeli advances only stopped by a ceasefire brokered in Moscow by Kissinger and Andrei Gromyko, the Soviet foreign minister. Fearing that an escalation of the war would bring them further into the conflict, both men had used their considerable political and economic authority over their respective allies and, after one abortive ceasefire, an agreement to stop the war was signed on 24 October 1973. Yet another attempt to solve the Arab-Israeli conflict through force had failed. Israel was once again the military victor, but remained diplomatically and geopolitically as isolated as ever. One notable political casualty from the war was Golda Meir who had been Israeli prime minister since 1969. She was forced to resign in early 1974 as a consequence of her government's perceived unpreparedness in this fourth Arab-Israeli war.

The war in the Middle East added one more element to the already complicated web that made up international relations in the early 1970s. This had been dominated since 1945 by the East-West rivalry between the USA and the USSR although China in the 1970s was also beginning to emerge as a superpower in its own right. India was also increasingly keen to make its mark upon world politics and this was particularly the case after December 1971 when it entered the war between East and West Pakistan that had begun six months earlier. This intervention by the government of Indira Gandhi, who was to lead her country from 1966 to 1977 and then again from 1980 until her assassination by her own bodyguards in 1984, was decisive, with India's subsequent victory in the war resulting in independence for East Pakistan, which went on to become Bangladesh. It also led to India becoming the leading political power in the region.

After the Yom Kippur War, the influence and opinions of the oil-rich Arab nations that dominated OPEC, the Organisation of Petroleum-Exporting Countries, had increasingly to be taken into consideration within this complicated web. These countries supplied over 60% of the world's oil and many objected to US support for Israel in 1973. OPEC's influence on world oil supply meant that the Middle East remained a focal point of international importance throughout the last years of the Cold War.

The Watergate Scandal

As the Middle East crisis rumbled on through 1973, Nixon was increasingly drawn into the Watergate affair that plunged the USA into its worst constitutional crisis since the Civil War. For two years, the scandal rocked the country, with evidence from the various inquiries into the affair uncovering a series of illegal activities connected with the Nixon White House. Most damaging of these was the revelation that an illegal team of spies, accountable only to the White House, had been set up in 1970. These men for two years had carried out a series of illegal phone taps, buggings and other surveillance operations that targeted Nixon's opponents, and inquiries into Watergate eventually came to focus on just how much Nixon knew about these affairs.

The crisis began in June 1972 when five men were arrested during an attempted break-in at the Watergate Building in Washington. The arrested men had been trying to break into offices rented by the Democratic Party, and the suspicion of the arresting officers was initially raised by the amount of surveillance and camera equipment found at the scene of the crime. Police became even more concerned when it was discovered that the burglars had connections with the CIA and that one of the arrested could be connected to the White House through a telephone number in his address book. The FBI carried out their own inquiry during the summer of 1972, and it was interference into this investigation that was eventually to prove Nixon's role in a cover-up.

However, the first signs of trouble for Nixon did not surface until the late spring of 1973, some months after his landslide re-election and the successful negotiations that had ended US involvement in Vietnam. At this time, he was still riding high in the opinion polls after a series of international successes in China, the USSR and Vietnam, but tricky questions about Watergate were beginning to surface. Increasingly, the focus of these fell on the five Watergate burglars who were still awaiting trial, and from the very beginning Nixon and his aides knew that their political futures relied on the silence of these five men. They hoped that this silence would allow the break-in to be treated as a simple case of burglary, and it was to this end that Nixon authorised the setting up of a million-dollar slush fund to buy the five men's co-operation.

This strategy presupposed that all the men were willing to stay silent, but, more importantly, that the affair would stay out of the limelight. However, as Watergate slowly began to unravel and gain momentum through the spring and into the summer of 1973, it was clear that neither of these things were going to happen, with the investigative journalism of the *Washington Post* in particular keeping the story in the public eye. So with Nixon continuing to deny the existence of any connection between the White House and the Watergate burglars, but with the noose slowly tightening around the necks of those in the White House involved in the scandal, talk of a White House cover-up grew more and more widespread until finally the Senate itself announced that it was going to look into the affair.

With evidence against the Nixon White House mounting daily, the president moved to isolate himself from the crisis by finding a scapegoat from within his own staff. As a result, John Dean III, the president's counsel who had been running the covert operation since 1970, was blamed for the bungled break-in while other senior officials were also forced to resign. However, Dean was not willing to sacrifice himself without a fight, and so agreed to testify before the Senate Committee in exchange for immunity from prosecution. In the meantime, the scandal remained in the public eye as the five Watergate burglars went on trial in Washington.

Dean eventually testified on live television in front of millions of viewers across the nation that Nixon was involved in the cover-up and that it had been Nixon who had authorised the million-dollar slush fund that was to be used to pay off the Watergate burglars. This was strenuously denied by Nixon and his aides who used all their power to discredit Dean's account of events.

However, it was then sensationally discovered, during a routine interview with a member of the White House staff, that Nixon had ordered the installation of a secret tape recorder in the Oval Office of the White House in 1971. Unknown to Dean and many other senior aides, all conversations since then had been studiously taped, catalogued and stored. The president had originally wanted the tapes to help him write his memoirs. These tapes could now be used to substantiate or discredit Dean's testimony and they soon became the focus of the Senate's inquiry.

But Nixon once again showed his appetite for the political fight and refused to give up the tapes. Using the power of his international standing and the support that he still retained in Congress, he claimed that the tapes contained matters of national security and that executive presidential privilege meant that he was not legally bound to hand them over. However, this stubborn rearguard action only further inflamed public opinion, and he was finally ordered to hand them over by the Supreme Court in April 1974 on the grounds that they might uncover criminal activity.

Nixon was forced grudgingly to comply and when their contents were published and became an instant bestseller, they shocked a waiting public. Full of racist comment and foul language, they painted a shocking picture of conspiracy and intrigue in the Nixon White House. However, little was revealed about the Watergate cover-up itself until technicians found gaps in the tapes where eighteen minutes of conversation, crucial to Dean's testimony concerning the million-dollar slush fund, had been erased.

Nixon's aides blamed this on a clerical error made by Nixon's White House secretary, but Congress chose to believe neither Nixon's aides nor his secretary and moves were made to impeach him. In early August, Nixon was finally forced to hand over the incriminating tapes that clearly confirmed his complicity in the affair and finally substantiated Dean's story of the previous year. As a result, and having finally lost his last supporters in Congress, Nixon resigned his presidency in disgrace on 9 August 1974.

He was replaced by Vice President Gerald Ford who served uniquely as both vice president and president without having been elected to either office. He had succeeded Spiro Agnew as vice president a year earlier after Agnew had been forced to resign following corruption charges. One of Ford's first decisions was to grant his predecessor a pardon for his role in Watergate leaving Nixon free to contemplate his mistakes during a long retirement in California.

China in the 1970s

One of Nixon's most important contributions as president had been the *rapprochement* with China that culminated in his visit to Beijing in February 1972. In China, Mao had justified these closer links with the capitalist West with a new analysis of international relations that saw China, now with its seat as a permanent member of the Security Council of the UN, as the natural leader of the developing world. In reality, however, it had more to do with the deterioration of relations with the USSR, with Sino-Soviet relations remaining fractious for much of the decade. Within China itself, Mao's hold on power remained unchallenged, but his deteriorating health meant that he took an increasingly less active role in everyday politics.

This precipitated a power struggle beneath him that took the form of a split between right and left. However, between the end of the Cultural Revolution and Mao's death in 1976, neither of these factions were able to gain any obvious advantage in the race for the succession. The right was led by the prime minister, the influential Zhou Enlai, who was the mastermind behind the *rapprochement* with the West in the early 1970s. His deputy was Deng Xiaoping who was to have such an influence on China in the 1980s, but who had been banished during the Cultural Revolution and forced to work as an ordinary shop floor worker in a tractor factory.

Both men wanted to adopt a more pragmatic approach to government, especially with regard to the domestic economy, but they were opposed by the equally influential Jiang Qing, Mao's wife, whose leftist faction wanted to return to the revolutionary zeal of the Cultural Revolution. As Mao's health deteriorated, this power struggle intensified, with the political, economic and philosophical differences between the two sides becoming more and more marked.

Tension further increased in January 1976 when a political vacuum at the centre of government was created by the death of Zhou Enlai. Zhou was replaced by Hua Guofeng, a compromise candidate favoured by Mao himself, and neither faction seemed to benefit directly from his appointment. However, when Mao eventually died in September 1976 at the age of eighty-three, Hua quickly made his move to secure power. Fearing a return to the excesses of the Cultural Revolution, he teamed up with the generals, whose support was vital in any power struggle, and ordered the arrests of Jiang and her three closest colleagues. In a series of show trials that followed, these leaders of the left, the so-called 'Gang of Four', were blamed for almost every conceivable mishap to affect China since the Revolution, and Hua used the 1977 Party Congress to round on them. Jiang was eventually sentenced to death in 1980 although this was later commuted to life imprisonment. She died in 1991.

After thirty years of radical reforms and great idealistic plans, the people of China were more concerned with stability and economic progress than with the revolutionary zeal of the 'Gang of Four'. So in order to help this drive forward, Deng, who had built a reputation as an architect of economic planning as far back as the 1940s, was recalled to office after a year in the political wilderness, and slowly came to mould a policy that was to fuse communist political organisation with capitalist economic theory. Mao still remained a hugely important icon within China, with his role in leading the Long March, the war against Japan and final victory over Chiang Kai-shek in 1949 guaranteeing this. But criticism of his later policies, and especially the Cultural Revolution, slowly surfaced as a new political and economic openness began to take shape in the 1980s when Deng took over the reins of power.

The Independence of Zimbabwe and Apartheid in South Africa

As China emerged as a third superpower in the early 1970s, pressure on the last white minority regimes in Africa mounted. Portuguese influence over Mozambique and Angola stretched back to the Voyages of Discovery in the fifteenth century, but it finally succumbed to this pressure in 1975, leaving only the white minority governments in South Africa and Rhodesia stubbornly holding onto power. In South Africa, the majority black population would have to wait until the early 1990s before the dismantlement of apartheid, but in Rhodesia independence was to come much earlier. This was not, however, until after a fierce and protracted civil war that began in 1976.

In November 1965, the government of Ian Smith had unilaterally declared its independence from Britain in an attempt to maintain the status of the white minority population. Smith's government had been condemned in the UN for this and was punished with a series of sanctions. But between 1965 and 1976, these had had little effect on Smith's Rhodesia due to both the aid it received from South Africa and the disunity of the black nationalist opposition.

However, this opposition eventually came together as the Patriotic Front in 1976 and united under the leadership of Robert Mugabe. His forces concentrated their attacks on outlying white farms and settlements, and aimed to disrupt the economy and the confidence that white Rhodesians had in their government. By March 1978, these tactics had begun to pay off and Smith agreed to a power-sharing deal with some moderate black leaders. However, the Patriotic Front still remained outside this negotiated settlement, and Mugabe and his fellow rebel leader, Joshua Nkomo, as a result ordered an escalation of the war. Meanwhile, sanctions remained in place.

By September 1979, it was clear that the Patriotic Front could not be ignored any longer, and a British-sponsored conference in London was organised to which all sides, including the Patriotic Front, were invited. Following an agreement at the London Conference, Rhodesia-Zimbabwe, as the country had become in 1979, returned to British rule in preparation for multicultural elections. In April 1980, the last British governor general left Harare, the newly named capital, and handed over power to Mugabe who in free elections had been elected president of the independent nation of Zimbabwe.

The majority population of South Africa was much less successful at forcing an end to apartheid. South Africa was unique in that it had a large and well-organised white settler population that was able to function independently of any colonial power. Indeed, a major element within this settler population, the Boer Afrikaners, were actively hostile to British colonial influence and South Africa's departure from the Commonwealth in the early 1960s did little to dent the country's confidence.

Under Boer control, the South African government organised itself in an increasingly belligerent manner in order to preserve its own power and authority. The collapse of the Portuguese empire in Angola and Mozambique and the collapse of white minority rule in Rhodesia did little to lessen this belligerence as the government in Pretoria worked hard to preserve the racial and social injustice and inequalities of apartheid through the 1970s and 1980s.

This government belligerence was shown most graphically with the policing of the riots that raged in Soweto in 1976. Soweto was a shanty town on the outskirts of Johannesburg where thousands of immigrant workers from the homelands crowded in search of work. The homelands were designated areas where certain ethnic groups were forced to live, and permission and special passes were needed to move out of them. The catalyst for the riots in 1976 was a government order making the teaching of Afrikaans compulsory in schools throughout South Africa. To the black community, the Afrikaans language symbolised hundreds of years of white oppression and its compulsory teaching was an outrage.

A boycott in schools across the country was widely supported, and in June 1976 a crowd of about 10,000, dominated by schoolchildren, marched through Soweto on their way to an open-air rally. But they were met by the South African police and army who opened fire on them, setting off the Soweto Uprising that was to last for a month and claim the lives of hundreds. Many of these deaths were attributed to the heavy-handed tactics of the South African security forces, with thousands beaten or imprisoned before being returned to their respective homelands. In early July, the minister in charge of education announced that plans to force the instruction of black students in Afrikaans had been dropped.

The most striking example of the institutionalised violence of the apartheid state was the murder in police custody of Steve Biko, the leader of the Black Conscience Movement. Biko had founded the movement in the early 1970s as an attempt to help build confidence in the black majority population after years of persecution and belittlement through apartheid. In August 1977, Biko was travelling on his way to an illegal meeting when he was caught by police outside Port Elizabeth. He was taken into custody and held in solitary confinement for nearly three weeks.

While in custody, he was beaten and tortured with such severity that he suffered head injuries that eventually led to his death. He was denied any proper medical provision in Port Elizabeth, but was instead taken to a secure prison hospital in Pretoria. Medical clearance for this journey was received from doctors who themselves worked for the state, and Biko was transported the 600 miles to Pretoria unconscious in the back of a police vehicle. Once in Pretoria, he soon died of his injuries. Biko's death at the age of thirty stole from the anti-apartheid movement a leader of great presence and dignity whose death soon became a symbol in South Africa and around the world of all that was wrong with apartheid. But he was only one of many thousands who had their lives taken prematurely by a government and a system that hung onto power until the early 1990s.

Jimmy Carter, Leonid Brezhnev and the Second Cold War

The issue of human rights dominating the politics of South Africa was also to dominate international relations between the superpowers during the last years of the decade. Détente had helped improve the working relations between the USA and the USSR and had led to the first arms control agreement in 1972. However, the ideological divide between the two remained as wide as ever and towards the end of the 1970s this increasingly became focused on the issue of human rights. Eventually, this led to the breakdown of détente and the restoration of hostilities as the world returned to a state of aggressive Cold War in the early 1980s. This did not officially end until George Bush and Mikhail Gorbachev declared the Cold War over in 1991.

However, this deterioration of relations did not begin until after the Helsinki Conference in 1975, which is often regarded as the high point of détente. At this conference, delegates agreed upon three main principles for future co-operation. Firstly, it was agreed to implement strategies to stop accidental nuclear war. Secondly, agreement was made to increase industrial and commercial co-operation and collaboration. And thirdly, a number of agreements concerning human rights were signed. It was on this third issue that differences between the superpowers soon emerged.

President Jimmy Carter had been elected in 1976 and committed himself to running a more open and accountable administration after the years of corruption and secrecy surrounding Watergate and the Vietnam War. In his election campaign, he had made much of his relative distance from Washington politics, but this soon began working against him once he assumed office. He was seen as aloof by many in Congress and was never able to gain the support there that he needed to implement many of his most important policies. At the heart of these were the control of the increasingly frail US economy and the implementation of the Helsinki Accords.

His inability to improve the domestic economy meant that unemployment remained stubbornly high throughout his presidency, and this was especially in areas of severe poverty where he had particularly pledged his support. This inability to tame the economy, as well as his constant confrontations with

Congress, led in part to his defeat by Reagan in 1980. But although these domestic issues were important, a series of foreign policy failures were far more damaging. Therefore, it is ironic that Carter will always be remembered for a new peace process in the Middle East that culminated with the Camp David Agreement in 1978. Under this agreement, peace was restored between Israel and Egypt, with the former agreeing to the withdrawal of its forces from the Sinai Desert, which became demilitarised under UN control.

Carter's success in the Middle East was soon overshadowed by a deterioration in relations with the USSR. Brezhnev was never as severe or dictatorial as Stalin had been, but he nonetheless maintained an iron grip of control over the country and his ruthlessness ensured that the prisons of Siberia remained full. This continued despite the agreement in Helsinki concerning human rights. Meanwhile, the Soviet economy was failing, with the country increasingly prone to corruption, inefficiency and wastefulness. As a result, the standard of living of the Soviet people fell further and further behind that enjoyed in the West. The USSR was literally grinding to an economic halt and Brezhnev, handicapped as he was by deteriorating health caused by heart problems, had few new ideas. As in South Africa in the last years of apartheid, the Brezhnev regime increasingly came to rely on force and violence as an instrument of state control.

Carter's answer to this Soviet stance was to try and link the issue of human rights with the SALT II talks taking place in Vienna. These talks dragged on through his presidency, with both sides increasingly unwilling to give up their nuclear firepower in light of their deteriorating relationship. Finally, agreement was made and the SALT II treaty was signed in Vienna in June 1979. But this did not stop the arms race, with both sides quickly moving to develop technology not covered by the treaty. So despite years of negotiations, SALT II did little to make the world a safer place, and the new Cold War environment of the early years of the 1980s meant that the number of nuclear weapons in existence was to grow alarmingly.

The Government of James Callaghan and the Election of Margaret Thatcher

Carter's efforts to reinvigorate the US economy were mirrored in Britain where James Callaghan had replaced Harold Wilson as prime minister in 1976. Wilson's resignation had shocked many close to him, but after eight years at Downing Street and a lifetime in government that stretched back to the post-war Attlee administration, he had tired of politics.

Callaghan inherited a country increasingly at odds with itself. British national pride and self-confidence, which had been so high in 1945 after the victory over fascism but which had been increasingly challenged through the 1950s and 1960s, had reached its lowest ebb in the late 1970s, with Britain's lost status symbolised most demonstrably by the loss of the third, and most fractious, Cod War against Iceland in June 1976. This, however, followed one cause of national celebration, at the beginning of the year, when Concorde made its inaugural commercial flight.

This British malaise was especially clear after December 1976 when Callaghan's government was forced to apply for an extension to the nation's loan from the International Monetary Fund in order to stave off national bankruptcy. However, this was only granted on condition that the government adhered to a number of austerity measures connected with public spending, which primarily were put in place to tackle the problem of soaring inflation. By 1978, these measures had managed to bring inflation down to single figures, but this was not achieved without the pain of continued high unemployment and the maintenance of a freeze on pay. The malaise caused by the weakening economy, however, was momentarily lifted in July 1978 when news came of the birth in Oldham of Louise Brown, the world's first 'test-tube' baby.

With the economy in recession and with the benefits of EEC membership still not altogether clear, there was little cheer for Callaghan during 1977 and 1978. His task was made even more difficult by the growing confidence of the opposition under Margaret Thatcher, who had become leader of the Conservative Party in 1975, and Callaghan was further handicapped by the constraints of the Lib-Lab Pact, which was agreed with the Liberal Party in October 1977. As the government continued to fight its battles with the economy, opinion polls increasingly suggested that the people of Britain were ready for more radical change. This was eventually to come with the Conservative victory in May 1979.

Trade union power had been used to topple Heath in 1974 and it was now used to turn out Callaghan. Throughout 1978, union leaders were keen to negotiate higher pay deals after three years of austerity, but Denis Healey, Callaghan's chancellor of the exchequer, was still restrained by the IMF deal and refused to give in to their demands. As a result, industry after industry through the winter of 1978-79, the 'Winter of Discontent', was rocked by strike action over pay.

In March 1979, Callaghan, whose administration had struggled on through the winter as a minority government after the pact with the Liberals had been ended the previous September, was defeated in a House of Commons vote over devolution. In the wake of this loss, the Conservative opposition forced a vote of no confidence, which the government also lost, and a general election was called for early May. In the election, the Conservatives were returned, with Margaret Thatcher, winning a forty-four-seat majority, becoming Britain's first female prime minister. Before being forced out of office at the end of 1990, she served at Downing Street for eleven years, winning three consecutive elections and becoming Britain's longest-serving prime minister in a single stint since the 1820s.

At the 1979 general election, Britain overwhelmingly rejected not only the Labour Party but also the consensus politics that both political parties had adopted in the 1950s. In its place, a new right-wing radicalism was chosen, with Thatcher looking to diminish the role of the state while creating a free enterprise economy run by privatised industry. At the heart of this was to be enterprise, choice and entrepreneurship and, if this was to happen, the Conservatives believed that the trade unions would have to be tamed. As a result, much of her first term in office was spent doing this. However, Thatcher's radical new Britain did not benefit everybody, with economic recession and unemployment, especially in the old industrial areas where she remained extremely unpopular, plaguing Britain well into the new decade.

The Iranian Revolution and the Invasion of Afghanistan

Thatcher's right-wing conservatism in Britain soon found a natural ally across the Atlantic where Ronald Reagan defeated Carter in the 1980 presidential election. At sixty-nine years old, Reagan became the oldest president ever elected for a first term in office. Carter's inability to deal with the economy and Congress were two important contributory factors in Reagan's success, but it was two crises abroad that finally destroyed any hopes for his re-election.

The first of these crises took place in Iran where an Islamic Revolution had brought Ayatollah Khomeini to power in February 1979. Khomeini returned to Teheran after twenty years in exile in France, and quickly established a strict, fundamentalist Shiite regime throughout the country as Carter watched this once staunch ally in the sensitive Gulf region now develop into a centre of anti-US and anti-Western rhetoric.

In November 1979, events in Iran took a new twist that was to directly affect the result of the US presidential election a year later. Since the Ayatollah's return, Iranian diplomatic efforts had tried to force the extradition of the Shah from the USA where he was receiving medical treatment. The failure of these efforts eventually became too much for a number of fundamentalist students who showed their commitment to the Ayatollah's Revolution by bursting into the US embassy in Teheran and taking hostage fifty-two US nationals.

Demands for the Shah's extradition were intensified and for six months the hostages were kept captive in the embassy grounds, with Khomeini and his Revolutionary Guards doing little to secure their release. When in March 1980 the Ayatollah came out and publicly supported the hostage-takers, Carter decided to act, sanctioning a controversial rescue attempt launched from an aircraft carrier in the Indian Ocean. An elite anti-terrorist force was to be flown into the embassy grounds by helicopter where they would free the hostages and return safely to the waiting aircraft carrier.

However, when the mission suffered mechanical problems at a desert rendezvous far to the south of Teheran, it was decided to abort the mission. But as this decision was being made, disaster struck, with one helicopter crashing into another while manoeuvring to refuel. As a result, six servicemen lost their lives, with Carter going on national television to report the tragedy and assume full responsibility.

By the time that Carter ordered the abortive rescue attempt of the hostages in Iran, a second equally explosive crisis was well under way in neighbouring Afghanistan. In April 1978, a pro-Soviet regime had seized power in Kabul, but its grip on power was far from secure and it faced stiff opposition from a guerrilla force organised by the Mujahideen. By the end of 1979, this force threatened to topple the government and Brezhnev was forced to order the full-scale invasion of Afghanistan to shore up the faltering pro-Soviet regime there. In December 1979, Soviet tanks rolled over the border into Afghanistan, and by January 1980 nearly 100,000 Soviet troops had taken up positions in what was the first act of Soviet territorial aggression outside Eastern Europe since 1945.

The Soviet invasion of Afghanistan drew condemnation from the West and, with attention firmly focused on Iran and Afghanistan, Carter ordered a series of sanctions against the USSR that intensified an already deteriorating Cold War situation. Ratification of SALT II by Congress was postponed, the export of grain and high-tech equipment needed primarily in the computer and oil sectors was suspended, and Carter organised a US boycott of the Olympic Games in Moscow.

The threat of Soviet expansion into the Persian Gulf and Indian Ocean region was overtly challenged, with Carter ordering the build-up of US military strength in Kenya, Oman and Pakistan as well as in the Gulf itself. However,

Carter's political reputation was soon further damaged when it emerged that his brother had received money from the anti-US regime in Libya led by Colonel Gaddafi and that the president had suppressed this information in a Watergate-style cover-up of his own.

As the US election campaign began to gain momentum through 1980, Reagan's strategists and speech-writers focused their attacks on Carter's economic record at home and his foreign policy failures abroad. They successfully were able to depict the president as vacillating, misguided and weak, and Reagan was returned to the White House by a landslide.

The Triumph of the West
The 1980s

November 1980
(The Election of Ronald Reagan)

to

December 1989
(The Death of Ceaușescu)

The Presidency of Ronald Reagan

The Iran-Iraq War, the Middle East and the Israeli Invasion of Lebanon

Solidarity, the USSR and the Emergence of Mikhail Gorbachev

The Government of Margaret Thatcher and the Falklands War of 1982

The Governments of Mitterrand and Kohl

Gorbachev and the Implementation of *Perestroika* and *Glasnost*

The End of the Cold War

Reagan and Libya, Iran and the Contras

The Middle East at the End of the Decade

China under Deng Xiaoping and the Tiananmen Square Massacre

The Collapse of Communism in Eastern Europe

The Presidency of Ronald Reagan

Reagan's age did not seem to have diminished his energy or commitment, and he soon showed how determined he was to bring about a new revival in his country's fortunes. Following the turmoil and corruption of the 1970s, Reagan's government promised new hope and new ambition, and his cause was helped early in his presidency by two unrelated events that together helped boost his popularity.

The first took place only hours after his inaugural speech when the fifty-two Iranian Embassy hostages in Teheran, who had been held in captivity for fifteen months, were released. This brought to an end an incident that had severely handicapped Carter and had threatened to create similar problems for the new president. The second event occurred soon after when Reagan was perversely to benefit from an assassination attempt on his life in March 1981 that left him in hospital with gunshot wounds. The sympathy he received during his successful recuperation in hospital helped bolster his popularity, and his speedy recovery and cheerful outlook confirmed for many the toughness of character and sense of purpose that they had hoped to find in the new president. This attempt on Reagan's life took place two months before a similar shooting critically wounded Pope John Paul in May 1981, with the pontiff, like the president, eventually making a full recovery.

At the heart of Reagan's campaign for national revival were two policies that in time were to define his presidency. The first of these rejected the foreign policy initiatives surrounding détente that had been followed by Nixon, Ford and Carter through the late 1960s and into the 1970s. Instead, Reagan adopted a far more abrasive foreign policy that challenged the USSR in almost every sphere of influence. The second involved the rejection of fifty years of Keynesian-dominated economic policy that had been followed by successive US presidents since Roosevelt's New Deal in the 1930s. The global repercussions of these two key departures in US policy were to reverberate around the world as the decade took shape.

Carter had begun to change US policy towards détente after the Soviet invasion of Afghanistan a year earlier. But Reagan in his election campaign signalled that he intended to go much further. He made it clear that he believed in the inherent evil of the communist political philosophy, and saw détente and the arms limitation treaties of the 1970s as no more than a means of perpetuating its existence. Reagan also reaffirmed US determination to keep communism out of the Western Hemisphere, a policy that was to cause him so much trouble in the years to come over his dealings in Nicaragua.

In relation to the USSR, Reagan made it quite clear that during his presidency the USA would seek to reassert the nuclear superiority that had been given up in the 1960s, and which had been challenged so obviously by the Soviet build-up of SS-20s on the border of the Iron Curtain in the late 1970s. This led to the massive stockpiling of nuclear weapons, especially during his first term, and these included the new cruise and Pershing II missile systems later deployed in Europe in 1982 and 1983. The Tomahawk cruise missiles were a guided system deployed predominently in Britain and Italy, while Pershing II missiles were ballistic rockets that were sent to West Germany.

Reagan's aggressive policy of escalating the Cold War through nuclear build-up in Europe was challenged in Moscow by Brezhnev and then by his successors, Yuri Andropov and Konstantin Chernenko. All increased the Soviet commitment to the defence of the communist world and huge forces were deployed in Eastern Europe along the Iron Curtain. With the world returning once again to a state of Cold War alert, few diplomats or politicians in the early 1980s from either side of the political divide would have predicted the Bush-Gorbachev *rapprochement* that formally ended the Cold War only a few years later.

On the domestic front, Reagan was determined to use new and radical economic policies to drag the USA out of recession. Reagan's belief in and commitment to capitalism were as deep as his hatred for communism, and he surrounded himself with right-leaning monetarist advisers who helped shape an economic revolution, which was similar to the one being orchestrated by the Thatcher government in Britain. He believed that the entrepreneurial spirit that had been strangled since the 1960s should be once again allowed to flourish.

So at the heart of his new domestic economic policy, Reagan placed a series of tax cuts and government deregulations that aimed at stimulating enterprise and entrepreneurship in the business and industrial sectors. As in Britain under Thatcher, the price paid for this unerring commitment to deregulated market-driven economics was a rise in unemployment to record levels. There were many losers in the harsh economic world of Reaganomics, and the poor and the needy at the bottom of society were often those most harshly hit. Millions of dollars in subsidies and payments were cut from the welfare budget while Reagan continued to cut the taxes of high earners. This was particularly the case early in his presidency when unemployment remained stubbornly high.

The economic picture brightened in 1983 with a resurgent stock market, a decrease in inflation and unemployment, and several months of rising industrial output helping lift the gloom. The recovery continued through 1984, and it was during this period of increased prosperity that a new class of workers, the Yuppies, became a popular social phenomenon. These young urban professionals, whose status and worth in society were defined by their materialism, single-mindedness and economic productivity, began to make their mark on the decade not only in the USA but throughout the developed world.

Despite the hardships some were to feel, many voters liked the benefits of the Reagan presidency and he was once again returned to the Oval Office in 1984. He defeated the Democratic candidate, former Vice President Walter Mondale, whose running partner, Geraldine Ferraro, was the first-ever woman involved in a presidential election campaign. Despite her presence, however, Reagan won by a landslide.

Reagan will always be remembered as the president who won the Cold War. However, this victory came late in the decade, and it was not won until after a series of events in many different parts of the world had challenged his presidency to the limit. These challenges often involved ideological, military or commercial rivalry with the USSR, and some felt that his approach to these was too aggressive. But Reagan, like Mrs Thatcher, his closest ally, was a conviction politician who felt deeply that the USSR should be challenged in the most exacting way possible. Ultimately, this was exactly what happened, with the USA's ability to spend more on the arms race eventually bankrupting its communist adversary.

The first place in which superpower tension had erupted at the beginning of this new phase of the Cold War was Afghanistan. Carter's response to the Soviet invasion had been swift and severe, and Reagan continued to follow a similar policy. Sanctions were maintained although some observers, especially within Western Europe, came to believe that they were, at best, ineffectual and, at worst, harmful. Similar arguments were soon used with regard to sanctions on Poland following the declaration of martial law by the Warsaw government of General Jaruzelski in 1981.

In Afghanistan, the invasion led to a civil war that lasted for much of the decade. With Soviet assistance, the government for the most part remained in control of the main towns and cities, and of the country's transport network. These joint Afghan-Soviet forces were opposed by an army of national resistance led by the Mujahideen who in time came to control much of rural Afghanistan.

So over the years, a pattern of a guerrilla warfare developed, with the Mujahideen waging a fierce campaign against government forces that controlled the towns and the roads that supplied them. The Mujahideen aimed to frustrate and sap the morale of the Soviet soldiers conscripted to serve in Afghanistan and to many it seemed that the USSR had embarked on its own Vietnam. Vietnam had its jungles and Afghanistan had its mountain passes, and both proved to be wars that the superpowers could not win.

The Iran-Iraq War, the Middle East and the Israeli Invasion of Lebanon

A second destabilising conflict in the region that further added to the political tension between the superpowers was the Iran-Iraq War. This had erupted in September 1980, with its origins lying in the deep religious and territorial rivalry in the oil-rich northern Persian Gulf. The war itself had started when Iraq invaded Iranian territory on the Gulf coast in an attempt to become the dominant power in the region. It tried to do this by destroying the infrastructure of the Iranian oil industry.

It was also provoked by the threat that Iraq felt from the Shiite-dominated government of Ayatollah Khomeini after the overthrow of the Shah. Saddam Hussein, who had become president of Iraq in 1979, presided over a Sunni-minority government and feared that Shiite fundamentalism, imported from Iran, would spread to Iraq's majority Shia population, especially around the Gulf region in the south. A similar fear in 1991 led to the crushing of a Shiite uprising in southern Iraq after the Gulf War had liberated Kuwait.

For several years, Iraqi forces were able to occupy large areas of this important strategic and commercial territory. However, Iran launched a counter-offensive in 1982 and gradually claimed back much of the land lost earlier in the war. During the next six years, a stalemate followed with a bloody and costly war of attrition developing between two conscript armies fighting in trenches that differed little from those of World War One. About a million young soldiers lost their lives in the war before hostilities finally ceased in August 1988.

Another region that remained a focus for superpower rivalry into the 1980s was the Middle East where the USSR continued to maintain its support for many Arab countries in their struggle against Israel. Israel, in turn, continued to find an invaluable ally in the USA. Tension had been lifted slightly by the Camp David Agreement in September 1978 but this did little to quell Israeli fears concerning the threat of attack from Syria, Jordan or the PLO, which since its expulsion from Jordan in 1970 had been operating its guerrilla raids into Israel from the hills of southern Lebanon. Despite these fears, Israel did fulfil one important commitment to the Camp David Agreement when it completed its withdrawal from the Sinai Peninsula in April 1982.

But increased PLO activity in southern Lebanon meant that the second stage of the agreement, the handover of the West Bank and Gaza Strip to Palestinian control, was suspended indefinitely and, with tension once again increasing in the Middle East, Menachem Begin, the Israeli prime minister, decided to strike. Initially, Begin's aim was to create a twenty-mile security cordon inside Lebanon along Israel's northern border. But early Israeli successes led Begin to become far more ambitious and a full-scale invasion of Lebanon was launched in June 1982. Israeli tank divisions made quick progress northwards in pursuit of the retreating PLO and soon took the important strategic city of Tyre. The Israeli advance continued and Beirut itself, which was in the grips of civil war between a number of competing factions, was put under siege.

The Israeli siege of Beirut was to last for nearly three months before a ceasefire allowed the withdrawal of the PLO to Cyprus. From there, Arafat and his council moved on to Tunisia where a government-in-exile was reconvened. During the siege of the city, the Israeli army was widely condemned for allowing a number of massacres in Palestinian refugee camps under its control, most notably at Sabra and Shatila. The victims of these atrocities, carried out by militias allied to Israel, included many women and children.

Eventually, Israeli forces withdrew from Beirut in 1983, leaving behind a city at war with itself. With Beirut bearing the brunt of the Lebanese civil war, French and US troops sent to the city as peacekeepers were also to suffer hugely before Syrian troops replaced them in 1987. It was these heavy US losses, blamed on extremist Iranian-backed groups such as the Hezbollah operating from eastern Lebanon, that persuaded Reagan to maintain his tough anti-terrorist stance throughout the decade. This eventually led to a series of highly charged incidents that rocked the region, and which included the 1986 US bombing of Tripoli and the kidnapping of several Westerners in Beirut later in the decade.

Solidarity, the USSR and the Emergence of Mikhail Gorbachev

With both Washington and Moscow following more belligerent foreign policies, the conflicts in Afghanistan, Iran-Iraq and the Middle East helped once again to reignite the Cold War. But superpower tension also returned to Europe, with Poland in particular becoming a focus for further conflict. In August 1980, striking shipyard workers at the Lenin Shipyard in Gdańsk had set up the Solidarity trade union that, under the energetic and charismatic leadership of Lech Walesa, an electrician at the shipyard, soon grew into a national body.

Working closely with the Roman Catholic Church, its campaign took on a political as well as social and economic dimension, and its huge membership and dynamic leadership soon won concessions at home and international standing abroad. However, further disagreements over food shortages through the autumn of 1981 led to a warning from Moscow that further concessions to Solidarity would not be tolerated. General Jaruzelski, Poland's new leader, was warned that the Red Army would be sent over the border to restore order if he proved too weak to do so himself.

As a result, Jaruzelski declared martial law in December 1981, with many Solidarity leaders, including Walesa himself, finding themselves imprisoned over the next few years. Importantly, however, none of Jaruzelski's policies during these years of military rule alleviated the country's terrible economic condition. Consequently, when the threat of terror and repression was eventually lifted at the end of the decade, the people of Poland increasingly looked to the West, rather than the East, for aid and assistance.

The Polish government's response to Solidarity was to a great extent directed from Moscow where Brezhnev, whose health had been deteriorating since the late 1970s, seemed an increasingly frail figure at the head of the Soviet government. This created an atmosphere of political paralysis within the USSR, just at the time when opposition from the West in general and from the Reagan administration in particular seemed so robust, confident and confrontational.

In November 1982, Brezhnev eventually died and was replaced by his chosen successor, Yuri Andropov, the leader of the KGB. But Andropov himself was also not a well man, needing constant medical attention for a kidney condition that was to kill him within fifteen months. During his short period of power, Andropov did try to shake up the Soviet political machinery, and particularly worked to stop the complacency, corruption and inefficiency endemic within the Soviet government. Andropov tacitly accepted that the USSR and the other communist countries of the Eastern bloc had fallen behind the West and that reforms were needed if they were to catch up. But these reforms were still very much envisaged within a Marxist-Leninist framework that eventually predicted the collapse of capitalism.

However, events seemed to suggest that it was communism, and not capitalism, that was about to collapse. Andropov and Gromyko, who remained an important figure in foreign affairs until the end of the decade, tried to stop the deployment of the Pershing II and cruise missile systems into Western Europe, and pulled out of talks in Geneva in protest at US-led NATO aggression. However, this did little to deter Reagan, with the final strengthening of NATO's European capability completed when the West German government confirmed that it would accept the stationing of Pershing II missiles on its soil at the end of 1983.

This blow to the USSR came just after the shooting down by Soviet fighters in September 1983 of a South Korean airliner en route to New York after it had strayed over Soviet airspace. Among the dead were a number of US citizens, including a member of Congress, and this further encouraged Reagan to ride roughshod over the 'evil empire' that he so clearly loathed. This helped create one of the most intense periods of the entire Cold War, with resentment and distrust increasing through the end of 1983 and into the opening months of 1984, the year in which Orwell's book about the evils of Stalinist totalitarianism was set.

Andropov died in February 1984 and it seemed that a new generation of party men would at last inherit the mantle of government. However, the old guard was not quite ready to relinquish its control of the Politburo and, still influenced by Gromyko, elected Konstantin Chernenko as general secretary. Chernenko was seventy-two years old and suffered from a lung disease that often left him short of breath and unable to do his duties.

These long periods of illness did in fact leave room for the new generation of Kremlin politicians to emerge, and it was Mikhail Gorbachev in particular who rose through the ranks. However, despite the emergence of this new generation of men like Gorbachev, who seemed aware of the problems faced by the USSR, the paralysis of government and the stagnation of the economy continued, with little being done to bridge the widening gap between East and West. Gorbachev did eventually try to address this by reducing the military budget later in the decade in an attempt to spend more on raising living standards. This policy, coupled with his reforms that led to the development of the market economy, eventually led to the abortive coup against him in August 1991.

The economic crisis faced by the USSR gradually began to affect the whole of the Eastern bloc. It also meant that Chernenko was forced to soften his tough stance towards both the Reagan administration and the missile deployments in Western Europe. As a result, negotiations were once again restarted in Geneva, with Mikhail Gorbachev given a leading role in forging a new relationship with the West.

One of the first Western politicians to meet Gorbachev during his swift rise to power was Mrs Thatcher. They met in London in November 1984, four months before the death of Chernenko, and their meeting was a vital episode in the chain of events that eventually led to the end of the Cold War. It also proved an early opportunity for the Western media to meet the new rising star of Soviet politics.

Both he and his wife, Raisa, were welcomed warmly by Mrs Thatcher in an atmosphere of informality far removed from that which had greeted previous leaders from behind the Iron Curtain. Mrs Thatcher later told reporters that she liked Gorbachev, and thought that he was a man with whom the West could 'do business'. Both in attitude and in appearance, he contrasted enormously with the grey faces of the Kremlin old guard who had preceded him.

He was soon promoted within the Politburo, chairing meetings when Chernenko's health forced his absence, and few were surprised when he was chosen as Chernenko's successor after the latter's death in March 1985. However, few of these commentators would have gone on to predict the enormous changes that he would preside over before relinquishing the reins of power six years later.

The Government of Margaret Thatcher and the Falklands War of 1982

Mrs Thatcher's contribution to the end of the Cold War was mainly in her role as Ronald Reagan's staunchest and most loyal ally. In particular, this took the form of a total commitment to the cruise and Pershing II deployments that formed the basis of NATO policy in Europe in the early 1980s. Thatcher was helped in this by the popular support that her government received from the British people. Indeed, one major reason why the Labour Party remained in opposition throughout the 1980s was the unpopularity of its commitment to unilateral nuclear disarmament. The Labour Party was clearly not trusted with the country's defence and this feeling lingered on into the 1990s.

The election loss in 1979 had soon led to the resignation of James Callaghan and his replacement by Michael Foot. Foot, a leading anti-nuclear campaigner since the 1950s, was the candidate of the political left, and his success in the leadership election soon opened up a divide that eventually split the party. It also led to seventeen years in opposition that were not to end until the mid-1990s when Tony Blair was once again able to regain the trust of the British electorate. However, this was not before the Labour Party had abandoned many of the fundamental beliefs on which the party's philosophy had been based for ninety years.

Despite the support of the electorate over the question of missile deployment and despite the political suicide of the Labour opposition for much of the 1980s, which included a 1983 election manifesto pledge to leave the

EEC, the government did face concerted and vocal opposition over the nuclear issue, and this in particular was to come from CND, the Campaign for Nuclear Disarmament. This enjoyed a national revival in the early 1980s as the threat of nuclear war seemed to increase, and it helped to organise a series of campaigns and demonstrations against the missile deployments. One particular protest that continued throughout most of the decade was the one led from the women's peace camp outside the US cruise missile base at Greenham Common in Berkshire.

The close alignment between Thatcher and Reagan renewed the 'special relationship' between Britain and the USA that had lasted for much of the century. Among other things, this was to cause a certain friction between Britain and its European colleagues, both within NATO and the European Community, with queries first aired by de Gaulle in the 1960s once again raised about Britain's commitment to Europe. Mrs Thatcher was never a committed pro-European like her predecessor, Edward Heath, but her government was committed to an economically integrated continent, with all nations within the community enjoying the benefits of the world's largest free trade area. This was confirmed in February 1986 when her government signed the Single European Act. This hugely important change in Britain's relationship with Europe resulted in the largest-ever transfer of power to Brussels, and in particular accepted the idea of majority voting in the Council of Ministers. All this was done in order to secure access to the single market that was to be in place by 1992.

But Mrs Thatcher never supported the notion of European political union, which she criticised in a speech in Bruges in September 1988, and was eventually to fall from power over, among other things, her opposition to the single currency that she saw as the first stage in this process. However, long before this was to happen in her third term in office, her tough approach to EU negotiations, and especially her success in reducing Britain's budgetary contribution in 1984, was to win her support not only in her own party but also more widely around the country.

Although not always popular in Europe, Mrs Thatcher's image as the 'Iron Lady' was one that won her much respect at home and abroad, and her leadership was an important factor in the return of national confidence. Under Mrs Thatcher's unique leadership, Britain also restored its international position at the centre of international world affairs. As an ardent believer in the benefits of capitalism and the free market, Mrs Thatcher proved to be one of the most enduring, confident, respected and well-known world leaders to emerge in the decade that saw the ultimate triumph of capitalist free market economics and liberal democracy.

Mrs Thatcher had inherited an economic malaise that dated back to the 1950s and which to a large extent surrounded the relative decline of the heavy industries that had been the backbone of British industrial dominance since the nineteenth century. No previous government had been able to deal with this situation with any measure of success and so, not surprisingly, a great deal of her first term in office was spent trying to deal with the economy.

At the heart of her economic policy lay a commitment to the radical transformation of the country from the state-dependent and state-dominated entity that it had been before 1979. But Mrs Thatcher aimed at more than just improving the economy. Her government also looked to redefine British national identity after the years of self-doubt and introspection that had followed the loss of empire and superpower status in the three decades that came after World War Two.

As such, the Conservative election success of 1979 marked a watershed in British post-war history appreciated by an electorate who in time were to re-elect her three times. This was the essence of Thatcherism and it was to keep her at Downing Street for eleven years, longer than any prime minister since Lord Liverpool in the 1820s.

At the heart of the government's economic programme was placed the fight against inflation, which remained stubbornly high until 1982, and so with unemployment also rising, pressure mounted on the prime minister and her ministers. As in the Great Depression of the 1930s, it was the industrial areas of northern England, Scotland and South Wales that were hardest hit by the recession, creating a north-south divide that was accentuated by the economic boom being enjoyed in London and the South East. But the prime minister remained firm in her belief that this economic hardship was needed to create a leaner and more competitive economy, and that the fight against inflation had to be won.

Another central component of the Thatcher revolution was the defeat of the trade unions that had brought down two governments during the previous decade. Overbearing and over-powerful trade unions were an anathema to the free enterprise economy to which Mrs Thatcher was committed and, as a result, her ministers were sent away to draft a series of laws aimed at reducing their powers. This process was accelerated after the promotion to the cabinet of Norman Tebbit, the ardent Thatcherite and anti-trade unionist. He was put in charge of employment policy in 1981.

A second election victory in 1983 led to further confrontation with the trade unions and, most especially, with the miners. The Miners' Strike in 1984-85 followed several long and bruising battles between the unions and the government in, among others, the steel, dock and print industries. Violence was to mar the long and vicious struggle of the Miners' Strike, which eventually ended in a comprehensive victory for the government and the mine operators.

With the defeat of the miners in 1985 came the final victory over the trade unions that had been fought for since 1979, and in its wake the Conservative government was able to introduce more anti-union legislation at Westminster. In particular, this curbed the practice of the closed shop where only union members could be employed in certain industries, and moves were also made to make the unions more accountable for losses incurred during strike action by their members.

Another foundation stone of the Thatcher economic revolution was the privatisation of the public utilities, a change that was later echoed in many other parts of the world. Therefore, Britain's early and revolutionary commitment to private rather than government ownership was of vital global significance. It was an ambitious and wide-reaching plan that in the government's opinion looked to save British industry through the vigour and enterprise of the private sector.

Opposition and trade union leaders accused the government of selling off the country's silver, and indeed this was a reference that was specifically used by Harold Macmillan when he criticised Thatcher over her privatisation policy in one of his last-ever speeches. But soon British Airways, Britoil (the government's holding in North Sea oil), British Steel and British Leyland, as well as many other government assets, were sold off to private enterprise.

Plans for the privatisation of British Telecom were later announced, capturing the imagination of the general public whose enthusiastic over-subscription for shares was used by ministers as evidence proving the popularity of their privatisation policies. Profits from the sale of nationalised industry allowed Mrs Thatcher to lower basic income tax to 25%, although criticism was later levelled against the directors of the utility companies for the huge bonuses that they paid themselves. Similarly popular had been the Right to Buy scheme, introduced in 1980, that gave tenants the legal right to purchase their council houses at a discount. Another privately-funded project that received the support of the British government was the Channel Tunnel. This resulted in an agreement with the French government, which was signed in February 1986. As a result, work began of the dual-rail twin-tunnel in the late

1980s, with the two sides meeting mid-Channel in December 1990. The first passenger-carrying train service was launched four years later in November 1994.

Generally, privatisation was well received by the British public and was seen as a means of liberating entrepreneurial skill and energy. As with Britain's independent nuclear deterrent, the success of the Conservative government's privatisation programme eventually forced the Labour Party to change its manifesto commitment to renationalisation.

Labour policy realignment over nuclear unilateralism or privatisation did not come until after two dreadful election losses in 1983 and 1987 had showed how distant it had become from the electorate that returned governments to Westminster every five years. This electorate remained deeply suspicious of the Labour Party throughout the 1980s, and remained fearful of the power exercised within it by the radical left. The power of these groups was graphically shown in a number of urban councils where they had won control and a predominantly pro-government press was more than willing to publicise their more radical and bizarre policy decisions.

At the heart of the argument that raged within the Labour Party through the 1980s, and which was only really resolved after the election of John Smith as leader in the early 1990s, was the commitment to Clause Four of the party's constitution. This stated that the nation's means of production, the factories and mines, the railways and the ports that produced the nation's industrial wealth, should be owned by the state. This clearly went against the privatisation policies of the Conservative government that were so popular with the general public.

In light of national and international reforms in the 1980s, this commitment seemed to the British electorate to be both regressive and outdated and, as such, was bound to lose votes. A nation of shareholders and homeowners had been created by the Thatcher government and although many soon cashed these in, especially in the case of British Telecom, many remained reluctant to support a party that still advocated renationalisation. In simple terms, the British people remained scared that a Labour government would return Britain to the policies of the 1960s and 1970s when government ownership and high taxes were used to subsidise ailing and antiquated British industries.

For some on the right of the Labour Party, the swing to the left after the election defeat in 1979 became too much. These politicians joined the so-called Gang of Four and split to form the Social Democrat Party in March 1981. Its leaders were David Owen, Bill Rodgers, Roy Jenkins and Shirley Williams who together aimed to breathe new life into the centre ground of British politics.

Initially, it seemed that they were going to do just that, with a number of by-election successes in 1981 and 1982 embarrassing the government. However, the SDP was never able to build on these early successes, and its split from the Labour Party served only to water down still further any meaningful opposition to the Thatcher government.

After the defection of the SDP, the Labour Party was to stumble through a decade of political disunity and in-fighting, with first Neil Kinnock and then John Smith trying to control the more radical elements on the extreme left. Eventually, this led to the victory of the right wing of the party and the formation of what became known under Tony Blair as New Labour. This consciously rejected many of the more socialist commitments of the past and, as the 1990s progressed, New Labour was to differ increasingly little in policy from its Conservative opponents. It did, however, differ enormously from the Labour Party that Foot had led in the early 1980s. In this new guise, the Labour Party eventually returned to government after its landslide victory in 1997.

The crisis within the Labour Party and the weakness of opposition to the Conservative government were important reasons for the re-election of Margaret Thatcher in 1983. But they were not as important as the intangible but very real benefit that victory in the Falklands War brought. The war began after South Georgia, the small British dependency in the South Atlantic, was invaded by soldiers of the military dictatorship that had ruled Argentina since 1976. Soon after in April 1982, the Falkland Islands, which had been held by Britain since 1833, were also invaded, with the British governor arrested at his residence in Port Stanley.

The Argentine action was quickly condemned at the UN, but President Leopoldo Galtieri, the general in charge of the Argentine Junta since 1981, refused to withdraw his forces. Galtieri had presided over the collapse of the Argentine economy and, with the country reeling under huge domestic inflation and massive foreign debts, he had pinned his reputation and his political survival on the reclamation of Las Malvinas, as the islands are known in Argentina.

As a result of the invasion, a British Task Force was hastily put together, with the first ships, many of which were fortuitously on manoeuvres near Gibraltar, leaving on the 8,000-mile journey to the South Atlantic in early April 1982. It was in the end to number over a hundred ships of the Royal and Merchant Navies, as well as some other requisitioned ships that were used to transport supplies and troops, and it was to carry some 11,000 men and women. During the month or so that it took to complete its journey south, exhaustive talks between the two sides were held through the mediation of General Alexander Haig, Reagan's secretary of state. Eventually, these talks were to break down, with both sides insisting that their claim to sovereignty over the islands was non-negotiable.

By the end of April, the British Task Force was approaching the Falkland Islands and orders were given to bomb the airfield at Port Stanley. Any hope of a negotiated settlement ended on 1 May 1982 when the War Cabinet in London gave orders to sink the Argentine cruiser, the *General Belgrano*. This was due to the threat that its Exocet missile capability posed to the approaching Task Force. The *General Belgrano* was attacked and sunk with the loss of 368 Argentine lives. Controversy over the sinking was to rage long after the last shots of the war had been fired, with some critics of the British action claiming that the cruiser had been sailing away from the islands when it was hit. Others contested that it was torpedoed while outside the exclusion zone stipulated by the British government itself.

The Argentine forces soon took their revenge by sinking HMS *Sheffield*. Meanwhile, aircraft from the carriers HMS *Hermes* and HMS *Invincible* kept up a fierce barrage on Argentine ground forces while naval commanders drew the ships of the Task Force nearer to Port San Carlos on the western side of East Falkland. This was the major island that made up the Falklands and was where most of the population lived. Port San Carlos was situated on San Carlos Water, the sound that separated the islands of East and West Falkland that was soon dubbed 'Bomb Alley'. This had been identified as the most sheltered and protected area from which to launch the infantry assault on Argentine positions.

On 21 and 22 May 1982, British ground troops were successfully landed at Port San Carlos despite the loss of two frigates, HMS *Antelope* and HMS *Ardent*. With a bridgehead established in the west of the island, preparations for the push south-eastwards towards the major concentration of Argentine troops around Port Stanley began. In the meantime, further Exocet attacks claimed firstly HMS *Coventry* and then the supply ship, *Atlantic Conveyor*.

However, these setbacks did not stop rapid infantry progress eastwards across East Falkland despite fierce, although somewhat sporadic, defence by Argentine ground forces. In particular, British forces faced heavy fighting and suffered substantial losses during the Battle of Goose Green, the Battle of Tumbledown and during the marine landing at Bluff Cove. British troops continued to pour into East Falkland, making secure the territory already captured and maintaining the essential supply lines that linked the ships of the

Task Force at anchor in San Carlos Bay and Port Stanley, seventy miles away. Eventually, after further fierce fighting around its approaches, Port Stanley was taken on 14 June 1982.

The most obvious result of the war was the swift fall of Galtieri and the military junta that had murdered upwards of 30,000 people, the so-called Disappeared, *Los Desaparecidos*, since its seizure of power in 1976. With Galtieri gone, Argentina began the difficult path back to democracy. For Britain, the war meant a massive increase in financial, as well as military, support for the 2,000 islanders, although geological surveys showing oil deposits nearby suggested that this might in the future prove a worthwhile investment.

The Governments of Mitterrand and Kohl

While Britain was coming to terms with the Conservative government of Margaret Thatcher, the peoples of West Germany and France were also learning to live under new leaders. In France, François Mitterrand became president in May 1981 while in West Germany Helmut Kohl took over as chancellor in October 1982. Both were to rule long into the 1990s, with both playing important roles in the events surrounding the end of the Cold War and the reconstruction of Europe after the fall of communism.

Mitterrand became the first socialist president of the Fifth Republic, but soon found that severe economic problems meant that he was unable to fulfil many of the more left-wing promises of his election manifesto. Faced with rising unemployment and spiralling inflation, he found himself forced to implement a series of austerity measures that cut benefits and welfare to those most in need. His problems were increased in 1986 when Jacques Chirac, the leader of the conservative Gaullist Party and mayor of Paris since the late 1970s, became prime minister of a right-leaning coalition government.

Despite the gap in their political beliefs, the two men were forced to work together for two years until Chirac resigned in 1988, having been defeated by Mitterrand in that year's presidential election. Mitterrand went on to serve a second seven-year term in office, despite the diagnosis of an incurable form of bone cancer early in his presidency in 1981, a fact that was kept secret from the French electorate until after his death.

In West Germany, the 1970s had been dominated by the governments of Willy Brandt and Helmut Schmidt. But when Schmidt's government fell in 1982 after an argument with coalition partners over economic policy, it was the leader of the conservative Christian Democrat Party, Helmut Kohl, who took over as chancellor. This status was confirmed a year later when his

Conservative coalition won a large majority at the polls. West Germany's economic performance steadily improved and, as the international trade slump of the 1980s slackened, Kohl's popularity increased.

Mirroring Conservative victories in the USA and Britain, Kohl won the election of 1987 and continued to rule Germany until 1998. Gaining an almost cult status for his role in German unification, Kohl's image was badly damaged at the end of the 1990s when evidence began surfacing of financial irregularities surrounding his party's finances. Investigations of widespread malpractice continued into the new century.

The 1980s also saw a huge growth in interest in the environment. This took place all over Western Europe, but found a focus in West Germany where the Green Party won widespread support. Reacting to the NATO nuclear build-up, to the growing problem of acid rain and the pollution that it caused, as well as a number of worldwide environmental disasters such as the Bhopal gas leak in India, the Exxon Valdez oil spill in Alaska and, most importantly, the Chernobyl nuclear leak in April 1986, the Greens were to become a considerable political force for change, winning seats not only in the national parliament but also at the European Parliament in Strasbourg. In other countries across Europe, environmentalists were less successful at securing direct political representation although public interest in looking after the environment remained high. This meant that Green issues remained at the centre of Europe's political agenda into the post-Cold War world of the 1990s.

Gorbachev and the Implementation of *Perestroika* and *Glasnost*

By the mid-1980s, the economic and political health of Western Europe and the USA was generally very good indeed. Significant improvements had been made since the difficult days of the 1970s and early 1980s, and the trade cycle was once again at its peak. This helped to cut unemployment and create an overall feeling of optimism and hope for the future.

It was also a period of confidence in the system of political and economic organisation that had allowed these improvements to happen. In Western Europe, North America and in many other parts of the world where it was practised, the success of capitalism, and to a lesser extent liberal democracy, had brought prosperity. This success was particularly glaring when contrasted with the appallingly woeful performance of the communist states behind the Iron Curtain.

Events in Poland in the early 1980s had shown that many ordinary people in the East who were experiencing these awful conditions looked towards the

West for help. But ordinary people were not the only ones looking westwards, with governments right across Eastern Europe coming to the same conclusion as the ten million Poles who had joined Solidarity. After forty years, politicians of a new generation were finally admitting the inefficiency, corruption and mismanagement that years of communism had brought, and this was nowhere more the case than in the USSR where the struggle for reform and modernisation was dominated by Mikhail Gorbachev.

Gorbachev was a lifelong Communist Party activist and had, like Khrushchev before him, risen in the party hierarchy as a specialist in agriculture. He was quick to stamp his authority on his new government, replacing four members of the Politburo only months after his election as party leader and promoting Gromyko away from power to the largely ceremonial position of State President. He worked hard to overcome the economic, social and political problems that he had inherited, but his courageous political leadership won him more friends in the West than at home in the USSR. Ultimately, this was because he was unable to deliver any significant improvement in the living standard of the Soviet people, the one thing that they craved above all else.

At the heart of Gorbachev's attempts at internal reform were the policies of *perestroika*, meaning the restructuring of the Soviet economy, and *glasnost*, meaning the beginning of a new openness concerning economic planning, performance and expectations. With the world emerging from the Cold War and with Gorbachev and Reagan embarking on a series of four superpower meetings, *perestroika* and *glasnost* came to symbolise in the West a new beginning in East-West relations.

This was because in the USSR Gorbachev insisted from the outset that the economic reforms of *perestroika* could not be achieved without the honesty and openness that *glasnost* demanded. Gorbachev envisaged that this openness would be directed towards the corruption and falsification of economic data that had been a fact of life within Soviet industry and agriculture since the time of Stalin. He hoped that this would bring about a new era of economic reality that in time would lead to an increase in production and efficiency. Gorbachev hoped that this would lead to an improved standard of living for all Soviet citizens, and his failure to deliver this eventually brought about his downfall.

This was because *glasnost* came to be used in a radically different way from the one that Gorbachev had initially proposed. Initially, dissidents used it to demand a new freedom and honesty in politics. But these dissidents were soon followed by thousands of ordinary citizens who came out to support demonstrations that demanded a new openness and accountability in many other areas of Soviet life. In particular, it was used to criticise the operation and administration of the Communist Party itself.

For some, *glasnost* was used to reaffirm ethnic and cultural loyalties that originated long before the 1917 Revolution and the expansion of the USSR under Stalin. This was particularly the case with the non-Russian people in the republics on the periphery of the Soviet empire. They used *glasnost* as a step towards fuller independence from Moscow and as the beginning of a process that would restore national identity. However, few in 1985 would have predicted the collapse of the USSR itself, or seen *glasnost* as the catalyst for the process that would end with full national independence for the fifteen republics of the USSR within seven years.

This new group of reformers that Gorbachev gathered around himself had hoped that *glasnost* would bring about a new and fresh approach to the relationship between the worker and the state. But, as in China in the 1950s during the Hundred Flowers Campaign when Mao for a short time had relaxed his grip on power, it produced an energy and venom against the Soviet system that shocked the state to its core.

Gorbachev never underestimated the enormity of the task on which he embarked and was well aware of the expectations placed on him by a people emerging from sixty years of totalitarian rule. However, unlike Mao, Gorbachev was never really able to control the forces that he had unleashed and, as the early enthusiasm and hope that *perestroika* and *glasnost* brought evaporated, he lost his way.

After suffering for so long under Stalin, Khrushchev, Brezhnev, Andropov and Chernenko, it is perhaps not surprising that these hopes and expectations should be so high. Gorbachev eventually failed to fulfil these because *glasnost* and *perestroika* were unable to bring about the higher standard of living that the Soviet people had been promised. In government, Gorbachev always remained a committed communist and hoped that his reforms would ultimately restore the Communist Party's fortunes. Therefore, the final irony of the Gorbachev era is that he was ultimately betrayed by the Communist Party itself. Worried that his reforms would threaten the privileges, status and prospects enjoyed as members of the ruling elite, Gorbachev's plans for *perestroika* and *glasnost* were strangled at source, leaving the corruption, inefficiency and mismanagement very much in place.

The End of the Cold War

Gorbachev's inability to bring about any real improvement to the lives of ordinary Soviet people meant that he was never as popular at home as he was in the West where his charisma and willingness to co-operate won him many friends. Gorbachev worked hard to cultivate this relationship because his domestic reforms demanded a reduction in defence spending that since the late 1970s had been bankrupting the USSR. He knew that this could only be done through substantial arms limitation and reduction agreements with the West, and it was this fresh attitude to East-West relations that made him such a popular figure there.

Gorbachev was quick to begin negotiations with the West and embarked on a series of talks that marked the final years of the Cold War. President Reagan, whose own presidency was beginning to falter under the accusations surrounding the weapons-for-hostages inquiries and the Iran-Contra scandal, was also keen to begin the process as quickly as possible.

The two superpower leaders met for the first time in Geneva in November 1985, just six months after Gorbachev had taken office. Both greeted each other warmly and although little headway was made in concrete terms at this first meeting other than agreeing to hold annual meetings, both went out of their way to stress the opening of a new era of friendship and co-operation between the two sides.

However, it seemed that this new era of Cold War thaw was destined to end as quickly as it had begun when the two men met a year later in Reykjavik, the Icelandic capital, in October 1986. At the heart of their disagreement was the US commitment to SDI, the Strategic Defence Initiative. SDI was a staggeringly expensive and almost science-fictional defence system announced by Reagan in 1983 that had been designed to replace the ABM system that had served the USA and NATO since the 1960s. The Reykjavik meeting also strained Reagan's relations with his European NATO partners who were largely excluded from negotiations. They felt that the bilateral US-USSR talks were ignoring key strategic issues particularly relevant to the security of Western Europe.

The SDI system was to be predominantly based in space and soon became known as the *Star Wars* programme. It comprised a series of satellites, lasers and heat sensors above the earth's atmosphere programmed to make sure that no enemy offensive nuclear missiles reached US or NATO targets. The SDI programme was both phenomenally expensive and extremely advanced technologically. The *Star Wars* programme was never developed to an operational standard and the programme was eventually cancelled by the first

President Bush. However, much of the technology developed in the programme was used later by the US military for conventional purposes, and these developments were to prove particularly important in the Gulf War of 1991.

Both the financial and technological gap between the USA and the USSR had been starkly illustrated earlier in the year at the Chernobyl nuclear power plant in the Ukraine. An explosion there had led to the world's worst-ever nuclear reactor disaster, spreading radioactive fall-out all over Western Asia and Eastern Europe. The contrast between the USA and its ability to fund and develop SDI and the USSR's inability to run Chernobyl properly was clear to many on both sides of the political divide.

Despite disagreements over SDI at Reykjavik, Gorbachev knew that he needed to continue arms negotiation talks with the USA and his perseverance was rewarded at the third annual meeting between the two leaders held in Washington in December 1987. By then, differences over SDI had been sorted out and the two men were able to sign a treaty that eliminated intermediate and short-range missiles in Europe. It was also agreed to continue reduction talks in 1988. This allowed Gorbachev to reduce the Soviet military budget and channel the money saved into essential modernisation programmes crucial to the development of *perestroika*.

Despite the problems that the Reagan presidency had created for itself domestically, Reagan himself remained extremely popular and the Washington Summit further confirmed his reputation as a strong and firm Cold War negotiator. At a final meeting between the two in May 1988, further reductions to intermediate arsenals were made at the first summit in the Soviet capital since Nixon's visit to sign SALT I in May 1972.

After George Bush Snr replaced Reagan at the beginning of 1989, the pace of disarmament was maintained, with both sides keen to capitalise on the Gorbachev-Reagan successes. For the USSR, these were particularly important because the cost of military spending was still holding back vital reforms at home. Further missile reductions were agreed in 1989 and a protocol was signed banning the use of chemical weapons.

These were followed by a unilateral Soviet decision to reduce its forces along the Iron Curtain, and soon after the total withdrawal of Soviet forces from Afghanistan was announced. Finally, the leaders of the two post-war superpowers met in the unusual setting of a Soviet warship at anchor off Malta. It was there in December 1989 that the protocol announcing the end of the Cold War was signed.

Reagan and Libya, Iran and the Contras

A crucial figure in the events that led to the end of the Cold War was Ronald Reagan. However, his presidency was not always without upset, and before he made way for Bush, his administration had to deal with a series of scandals and controversies. These at best tarnished his domestic and international reputation and at worst laid him open to charges of impeachment.

His administration's almost blinkered approach to certain matters of the most intricate diplomatic detail and international importance also led to criticism and even ridicule that in the end threatened to bring him and his presidency into disrepute. This approach was taken not only in regard to the Middle East, where most of the problems that he faced originated, but also in Central and South America where his work to ensure the maintenance of pro-Washington governments sometimes strained the boundaries of international law.

One of the most controversial decisions that Reagan made during his eight years at the White House was the bombing of Libya in April 1986. Libya had long been suspected of involvement in international terrorism, especially against US and Western targets within Europe, and when a bomb blast ripped through a discotheque frequented by US military personnel based in West Berlin killing two US soldiers, Reagan decided to act. Long-range bombers were dispatched from bases in Britain to bomb specific military installations and terrorist training centres in Libya that had been identified as targets before the mission.

The bombing soon became a diplomatic nightmare when the Western press and media were invited to film the damage to Tripoli that the bombing had brought. Pictures showed civilian and residential areas, including the partially destroyed French embassy, in ruin. Although Reagan may have had good reason for linking Libya with international terrorism, the bombing sanctioned by his administration was widely criticised not only in the Arab world and the Middle East but also elsewhere around the world.

One country that bitterly opposed the bombing of Libya was Iran, which Reagan had long suspected of financing the spate of kidnappings in Beirut in reprisal for the Israeli invasion of Lebanon in 1982. The response of the Reagan administration to this kidnapping crisis was to lead to the controversy that was to dog his presidency to the end. The crisis broke in 1986 when it was revealed that the USA had secretly sold arms to Iran in return for help in securing the release of US hostages held in Beirut. Amid scenes reminiscent of Watergate, information slowly leaked out over the next few years that implicated many of Reagan's senior officials in a series of illegal actions. All this seemed to suggest that the president, now very much in his dotage, was, at the very least, guilty of maintaining a shockingly lax grip on the management of his government.

Reagan admitted the sale, but was again overtaken by controversy when it was discovered that some of this money had been diverted to buy arms for the right-wing Contra rebels in Nicaragua fighting a bitter civil war against the communist Sandinista government. As interest in the Iran-Contra affair increased through the first half of 1987, more and more senior figures, including Oliver North and John Poindexter of the National Security Council, were drawn into the web of intrigue.

The Iran-Contra affair was to drag on into the presidency of Reagan's successor, with many questions still left unanswered, when a judicial decision in March 1990 ruled that Reagan was covered under executive privilege and would not have to produce his diaries for examination. The Iran-Contra affair tainted the last years of the Reagan administration and returned US politics once again to the corruption and illegality of the Watergate years.

However, it is remarkable that the affair had an almost negligible effect on Reagan himself, with his reputation as the *Teflon* president, to whom no dirt stuck, proving almost entirely accurate. Indeed, his popularity went a long way towards bringing about the election of his vice president, George Bush Snr, in 1988, with the electorate returning a Republican candidate for the third time in a row.

The Middle East at the End of the Decade

One of the regions that traditionally had been a centre of superpower rivalry was the Middle East, and the end of the Cold War did little to stop the strife ever-present in the region since before the creation of Israel in 1948. The 1980s had started encouragingly enough with optimism following the Camp David Agreement, but this was soon replaced with new levels of pessimism and diplomatic stagnation after the Israeli invasion of Lebanon in 1982. Although a military success, it was a diplomatic disaster for Israel, especially after the publicity that followed the massacre of Palestinian women and children at refugee camps under its control.

This laid Israel open to charges of misusing the military supplies and support it received from the USA, and never again would US support, which Israel relied on so heavily, be granted so readily by Washington. As a result, there slowly grew the feeling within Israel that the long-term security of the region in general and of Israel in particular would never be found without a negotiated settlement with the Palestinians. However, this fundamental change in attitude took a long time to take root, and it was not until the 1990s that direct talks between the two sides were to begin.

After the massacres at the Palestinian refugee camps in Beirut, Menachem Begin resigned as Israeli prime minister. He was the last of the triumvirate who had signed the peace agreement at Camp David remaining in office, with Carter having been replaced by Reagan in January 1981 and Sadat having lost his life to an assassin's bullet in October 1981. Sadat had been replaced by Hosni Mubarak, a former air force pilot and Sadat's deputy since 1975. Mubarak worked hard to mend relations with the rest of the Arab world still offended by the Camp David Agreement although he also managed to remain on cordial terms with Israel. Under the provisions signed by his predecessor at Camp David, Egypt took back control of the Sinai Desert on schedule in April 1982.

Israel finally withdrew its forces from Lebanon in 1985, having achieved its primary goal and chased out the PLO. It left behind a divided people who were to endure another decade of civil war between the various Christian and Muslim militias who had for centuries vied for power in the country. However, the expulsion of the PLO and the civil war in Lebanon did not make Israel any more secure after 1985 than it had been in 1982.

This was largely due to the emergence of another guerrilla force in the area that quickly took the place of the PLO and which continued to launch attacks across Israel's northern border. The new force was Hezbollah, a fundamentalist Shiite group that drew strength from the Iranian Revolution and whose ultimate aims were twofold. Firstly, it worked towards the creation of a pro-Iranian regime in Lebanon while secondly, but just as importantly, it looked to destroy Israel. It was the paramilitary wing of Hezbollah that was responsible for a number of kidnappings of US and other Western hostages, some of whom were held in solitary confinement in Beirut for up to five years.

The increased support for and activity of Hezbollah meant that Israel was very reluctant to enter into negotiations over the future of the Occupied Territories taken during the Arab-Israeli wars of 1967 and 1973. This was particularly the case after Begin's resignation brought to power a coalition government whose survival relied on the support of right-wing Zionist groups who not only opposed any agreements with the Arabs but also demanded the construction of further Jewish settlements in the Occupied Territories.

The political reality of Israel's military presence in the Occupied Territories was clearly seen by Arafat from his headquarters in North Africa. Arafat was also aware that the end of the Cold War had brought about a reduction in support for the Palestinian cause from the crumbling USSR. All these changes eventually led him to decide that a change of tactics was needed if his goal of a Palestinian state was to be achieved.

Using pressure brought on Israel by the *intifada*, a Palestinian uprising in the Occupied Territories that had began in December 1987, Arafat made arrangements to speak to a meeting of the UN General Assembly. This was to be in New York, but the venue had to be changed to Geneva when Arafat was refused a visa by US authorities. In his speech delivered in December 1988, Arafat renounced the further use of violence and accepted the right of the state of Israel to exist. This was the first of many steps taken before Arafat and his Israeli counterpart, Yitzhak Rabin, were able to sign a peace accord at the White House in September 1993.

China under Deng Xiaoping and the Tiananmen Square Massacre

While events surrounding the end of détente and the continuing crisis over the Middle East were preoccupying world attention, China under Deng Xiaoping was slowly emerging from the oppression of the Mao years. Deng had lived and suffered through the worst excesses of those years, and knew that changes were needed if China was to develop and modernise. By 1978, Deng, still officially Hua's deputy, felt confident enough to make some of these changes and announced a wide and comprehensive programme of economic planning based on the modernisation of four key areas. These were to be agriculture, industry, science and defence, and through the 1980s he used his considerable economic and organisational skills to make these work.

Deng eventually retired from frontline politics in 1987 at the age of eighty-three, leaving communist China much better off than at any time in its forty-year existence and well on the way to cementing its place as the world's third superpower. China's position of increasing geopolitical, cultural and economic importance was even more conspicuous given the problems that Gorbachev was experiencing in the USSR.

At the heart of this transformation under Deng was the success of combining capitalist economic planning and communist political structure. So while keeping political power and authority vigorously under the control of the Communist Party, Chinese economic planners were able to use the enormous amount of foreign capital that flowed into China to build the country into a modern industrial nation.

This capital was invested by numerous Western multinationals desperate to tap the huge new markets available in China, and this was used by the government to finance the internal development and economic expansion in the four key areas that Deng had identified in 1978. In order to facilitate this investment, Special Economic Zones were set up along China's coast from

Guangzhou, old Canton, in the south to Shanghai in the north, and concessions in these were granted to foreign companies. These SEZs proved very successful not only in encouraging foreign trade and investment central to Deng's plans for modernisation but also in helping raise the standard of living of ordinary people throughout China.

Deng was also successful in developing a new and more open foreign policy. In particular, he earned credit for the agreement over the future of Hong Kong that was signed with Britain in September 1984. He was also able to improve, particularly after the succession of Gorbachev, relations with the USSR that had been fraught for thirty years. Many observers came to believe that the great communist superpower of the Far East was determined on a new path of peaceful coexistence with both the USSR and the West. It seemed that the terror that dominated Mao's long rule had been replaced by a more conciliatory approach to politics both at home and abroad.

This popular perception of a new China was tragically exposed on the night of 3-4 June 1989 when hundreds, and perhaps thousands, of student protesters gathered in Tiananmen Square in Beijing were killed by soldiers of the People's Liberation Army. In the weeks that followed, thousands more were rounded up, imprisoned, tortured and killed for their opposition to the government.

The Tiananmen Square massacre had been preceded by a series of protests precipitated by the slow rate of democratic reform being taken by the Chinese government. This had contrasted with the enormous changes experienced in Eastern Europe, which the world had watched through the spring of 1989, and it had seemed inevitable that similar changes would also take place in China.

Tiananmen Square is a huge hundred-acre meeting place at the centre of Beijing bordered at one end by Mao's Mausoleum and at the other by the entrance to the Forbidden City, on which hung a huge portrait of Mao. It was from there that Mao had pronounced the People's Republic in 1949. Mao remained the founder of the nation, and Deng had been clever enough to retain him as an icon and a people's hero since his death in 1976. As a result, the square was of great symbolic importance as the heart of the People's Republic. Other demonstrations for reform and democracy were soon organised in cities across China, but it was in Tiananmen Square that the attention of the world remained focused. As the amount of foreign interest in the whole reform process grew, more and more film crews and journalists arrived in Beijing to document this popular uprising. Both the students and the government were to try to exploit this in the weeks that followed.

For a time at least, it seemed that the students, and not the police or the army who both kept a very low profile, were in charge of China's future. Confidence among the students remained high throughout May, and it seemed inevitable that concessions would be forced from the government as had been the case in the USSR. Indeed, so confident did the students become that they interrupted a high-level visit by Gorbachev to Beijing marking the end of thirty years of discord between the two countries. This left the Chinese government hierarchy hosting him highly embarrassed, and slowly their resolve to deal more decisively with the students strengthened.

Tension between the two sides was further heightened at the end of May when a thirty-foot-high likeness of the Statue of Liberty in New York, which the students called their 'Goddess to Democracy', was erected in the square. This proved too much for the autocratic leadership who had been willing to sanction economic liberalisation but who were not going to give up their political control.

As a consequence, final preparations were made for the clearing of the square and this began in the early hours of the morning on 4 June 1989. The students were primarily drawn from university campuses around Beijing and they had received some support from the army detachments garrisoned there. As a result, the PLA generals had decided to take no chances and had drafted in large numbers of troop reinforcements from outside Beijing in the days preceding the massacre.

Many of these came from Yenan, the north-western province where Mao had set up his headquarters after the Long March in 1934. The soldiers from Yenan were largely drawn from rural communities and had little in common with the urban students who now had taken over the square that represented the cradle of the communist revolution. The peasant soldiers from Yenan and other rural areas had always been absolute in their loyalty to the Communist Party and this loyalty was again expected and received. As a result, the students were cleared by the tanks and the guns of the PLA within a matter of hours.

So the changes to Chinese society that had seemed so inevitable a month earlier were never to take place, with the Chinese government in the aftermath of the massacre authorising a crackdown that systematically rooted out any opposition, dissent or criticism. The massacre drew condemnation from the West, but this was to last only a short time, with both Western governments and multinationals keen to maintain a presence in the huge emerging markets China had to offer. The economic as well as the political importance of China meant that the students were never to get the help and support from outside that, for instance, the trade unionists of Solidarity had received in Poland.

The Collapse of Communism in Eastern Europe

As the people of China were dealing with the political repercussions of the Tiananmen Square massacre, the people of Eastern Europe were living through the tumultuous and chaotic months that brought about the collapse of communism. In total contrast to the experiences of the students in Tiananmen Square, these people were to be a part of a disjointed, highly unpredictable but, nonetheless, markedly successful series of events that unfolded across the region during the second half of 1989.

For these people, this was to be the culmination of a series of reforms and changes that had begun in 1985 with the succession of Gorbachev. Eventually, they were to see the liberation of the whole of Eastern Europe from the communist repression under which they had suffered for so long. One of the first Soviet satellites to openly challenge the old system was Hungary, where the reformer, Karoly Grosz, had come to power in 1988. He soon posted his intentions by retiring many of the old-guard communists still in government before forcing through a series of far-reaching economic reforms that saw the communist, state-dominated command economy replaced with a new free-market model.

In October 1989, he dissolved the Communist Party before relaunching it as a left-leaning social democratic party. However, despite this repackaging his new party was roundly rejected in elections held at the beginning of 1990 and a right-centre coalition came to power in its place. This new government was increasingly inclined to look towards the West, and not the USSR, for help and assistance. Similar changes were also taking place in Poland where radical economic changes were soon matched by political ones, and in September 1989 Solidarity swept to power.

The people of Hungary and Poland were not the only peoples in Eastern Europe to force changes that in essence destroyed the communist governments that had ruled them for so long. They were joined by the people of East Germany who since 1971 had been ruled by the government of Erich Honecker. With news of the reforms in Poland and Hungary slowly reaching East Germany through a variety of underground sources, many East Germans became determined not to be caught in some authoritarian backlash.

So when the border with Czechoslovakia opened in the summer of 1989, they had responded in their thousands, escaping across the border before continuing their journey onwards through Austria into West Germany. Bemused border guards could do little under the crush of humanity, with some simply opening the gates at the border crossings that they guarded before often joining their departing countrymen in their flight to the West.

Honecker tried to enlist the support of the USSR against the sporadic demonstrations against his regime that were breaking out across East Germany. But Gorbachev refused to lend this support and instead strongly urged Honecker to implement the reforms that he himself was overseeing in the USSR. In October 1989, lack of support from Moscow and the weight of criticism from within East Germany forced Honecker to resign and, within a month, the Berlin Wall was being knocked down. Fittingly, this symbol of the Cold War that had divided the city for nearly three decades was torn down by the people who had spent their lives in its shadow. Pictures of ordinary people from both sides together hacking away at the concrete of the Berlin Wall were broadcast around the world.

Among the places where these pictures were seen was Czechoslovakia, which had endured one of the most oppressive regimes in Eastern Europe since Soviet tanks had rolled into Prague in 1968. Now inspired by the changes that had swept through Hungary, Poland and particularly East Germany, huge crowds gathered in Prague through November to demand similar changes and reform.

This time they felt confident that the communist government that was still trying to resist these changes would not get the support from Moscow that Brezhnev had given in 1968. As more and more people flocked to Prague and other major cities, Vaclav Havel led what became known as the 'Velvet Revolution', which within a month had swept away a generation and a half of communist repression. After free elections in December 1989, Havel was to become president.

In bleak contrast to the rest of Eastern Europe, little had changed through the autumn of 1989 for the people of Romania where the oppressive dictatorship of Nicolae Ceauşescu was still firmly in control. Ceauşescu had come to power in the 1960s, and had been for some time praised in the West for his criticism of the Brezhnev Doctrine and the intervention of the USSR in Eastern Europe.

However, his regime grew more and more despotic into the 1980s, with Ceauşescu criticised in particular for his ostentatious building schemes and his programme of racial and ethnic persecution, particularly against ethnic Hungarians in Transylvania. However, before December 1989 any criticism in

Romania itself was muted, with the increasingly harsh secret police ever-present and the power of the state unquestioned. Meanwhile, the Romanian people continued lives of poverty and persecution.

The extraordinary events that saw the end of this last Stalinist dictatorship began with the attempt to arrest an ethnically Hungarian political activist and priest in the Transylvanian town of Timisoara. This provoked an uprising in the town that was put down savagely by the army. But news of the massacre at Timisoara soon reached other cities, including Budapest, where similar riots, marches and demonstrations broke out.

Ceauşescu himself had been abroad on a state visit to China at the time, and he now raced back to restore order and punish the ringleaders. He had no intention of letting similar reforms to the ones that had spread through the USSR and Eastern Europe loosen the iron grip on power that he had held for over twenty years. But at a public rally set up in front of television cameras and beamed live across the country as a demonstration of his popularity, the crowd turned on him, shouting him down and forcing him to leave the podium. Importantly, he was beginning to lose the support of senior army officials and, as more and more Romanians joined the demonstrations and protests, Ceauşescu and his wife panicked and fled.

However, he was soon detained by the very forces of the state that he had run so ruthlessly for so long and, after a show trial before a military tribunal, was executed, along with his wife, by firing squad on Christmas Day, 1989. In the aftermath of the deaths, the full horrors of the Ceauşescu regime began to surface. In particular, harrowing television pictures of Romanian orphanages and mental hospitals touched the conscience of the watching world.

Many hoped that these events at the end of the decade would signal the beginning of a new era of world peace and prosperity. However, for millions across the USSR and Eastern Europe, it was to bring further hardship, hunger and, for some, especially in the Balkans and the Caucasus, years of civil war and the return to Europe of genocide. The promise of peace and prosperity that had been symbolised by the destruction of the Berlin Wall in November 1989 was soon broken as events not only in Europe but around the world began to unfold through the 1990s. These events were soon to prove that the collapse of communism and the end of the Cold War had made the world neither safer nor less violent.

The Information Age
The 1990s

February 1990
(The Release of Nelson Mandela)

to

December 1999
(The Last New Year's Eve of the Twentieth Century)

The End of Apartheid in South Africa

Gorbachev, Yeltsin and the Soviet Coup

The Invasion of Kuwait and Operation Desert Storm

An Increase of Tension in the Balkans and the Bosnian Civil War

The Rwandan Civil War of 1994

The Clinton Administration and the Middle East Peace Process

Russia under Boris Yeltsin and the War in Chechnya

The Impeachment of President Clinton

The Information Revolution and the Globalisation of Technology

The Governments of John Major and Tony Blair

The War in Kosovo

The Last New Year's Eve of the Twentieth Century

The End of Apartheid in South Africa

The new decade began with the world waiting expectantly to see the Soviet reaction to the political revolutions that had exploded throughout Eastern Europe at the end of 1989. But with the USSR both politically and economically weak and facing a myriad of its own problems, it was perhaps not surprising that little was heard from Moscow. Consequently, democratic rule, which would have been unimaginable just five years previously, quickly became political reality as Eastern Europe within a year threw off the shackles of forty-five years of communist dictatorship.

However, it was not long before the attention of the world shifted away from the emerging democracies of Eastern Europe to rest on South Africa where Nelson Mandela was released from prison in February 1990. He had been there for twenty-seven years. This came a week or so after the ban on the African National Congress had been lifted by President F. W. de Klerk, the last in a long line of apartheid presidents. Early in his presidency, de Klerk committed his government to the gradual abolition of apartheid, having come to the conclusion during the state of emergency between 1984 and 1987 that the time for reconciliation had come. However, although many in the mid-1980s looked at the moral arguments against apartheid as a reason for this reconciliation, there is no doubt that de Klerk was also motivated at this time by economic factors, with South Africa increasingly coming to suffer from UN sanctions.

Despite initial opposition from many within the white population, de Klerk pushed forward with his plans and embarked on a series of negotiations with prominent black leaders. By 1991, these negotiations had persuaded the world community that his government was serious about its commitment to end apartheid and sporting sanctions against South Africa were lifted. The authority of de Klerk was further confirmed by a referendum of the country's white population that voted decisively for his reform proposals.

By 1993, all economic sanctions had been lifted, and de Klerk and Mandela were jointly presented with the Nobel Peace Prize. Meanwhile, de Klerk continued to meet with leaders of the black community, the most important of which were Chief Mangosuthu Buthelezi of the Zulu-dominated Inkatha Freedom Party and Nelson Mandela himself. Mandela soon after his release from prison had been elected president of the ANC. As a result of these discussions, an agreement was reached to hold multicultural elections in April 1994.

However, the months leading up to these elections were marked by a series of violent massacres between rival Inkatha and ANC gangs in the black townships that surrounded South Africa's major cities. In addition to this violence, there was also the added threat of the Afrikaner Resistance Movement, an extreme right-wing group that borrowed the racial rhetoric, banners and uniforms of the Nazi era, and which pledged armed struggle in defence of apartheid and white majority rule. For a long time in the early 1990s, it seemed likely that the end of apartheid would bring about a long and bloody civil war between the ANC, the Inkatha Freedom Party and the Afrikaner Resistance Movement.

Eventually, however, this was not to be, with the election of 1994 returning an ANC-dominated government of national unity. Nelson Mandela took over as president and both Chief Buthelezi and de Klerk joined his cabinet. The civil war that the Afrikaner Resistance Movement had threatened never materialised, with it becoming over time increasingly marginalised on the extremes of South African politics.

The effect of the revolutions in Eastern Europe and the beginning of reform in South Africa was to galvanise opposition to totalitarian rule in many other parts of Africa, and riots and demonstrations demanding democratic change broke out across the continent throughout the early years of the decade. Fuelled both by anger at the economic inefficiencies that had led to declining standards of living since decolonisation in the early 1960s and by the arrogance and greed of a generation of post-colonial dictators, many hoped that new governments and a new sense of hope could be brought to the continent.

However, despite limited reform and democratisation, many Africans across the continent in general continued to live in economic poverty and under political tyranny. More than any other continent, Africa was to remain economically as well as politically backward, with the changes that many of its people had hoped would materialise in the aftermath of the collapse of communism never taking place. At the end of the century that had brought such improvement to the people of the developed world, the people of Africa continued to live in a world of malnutrition, poverty and subsistence, and suffer the tribulations of religious intolerance, tribal prejudice and political bondage.

Gorbachev, Yeltsin and the Soviet Coup

The decade had begun with the world anxiously awaiting the Soviet reaction to the revolutions in Eastern Europe. However, Gorbachev knew that Western investment would be jeopardised if he were to criticise the changes taking place in the former satellite states that Stalin had yoked to the USSR so effectively during the 1940s. As a result, Western fears were soon relieved, with both

Gorbachev and his foreign minister, Eduard Shevardnadze, going on to welcome the changes before calling for similar reforms for the USSR itself.

However, this reaction was not universally popular and Gorbachev faced criticism from many conservatives from within the Communist Party as well as from within the military. They argued that the whole future of the USSR itself had been placed in jeopardy by Gorbachev's weakness in relation to the fall of communism in Eastern Europe, and that his stance would encourage others to seek more independence from Moscow.

These hardliners believed that the legitimacy of the USSR would be placed at risk if any concessions were made to any of the fifteen separate states that made up the union. They were not persuaded otherwise when tanks were sent into Baku, the capital of the southern Caucasus republic of Azerbaijan, in January 1990, or when Gorbachev rejected the unilateral declaration of independence by the Baltic States three months later.

A month or so later, Gorbachev was also to face further problems during the traditional May Day march past in Red Square. This had once been a sacred day in the communist calendar, with the military parading its hardware beneath the Soviet leadership standing high up on the walls of the Kremlin. With *glasnost* and the end of the Cold War, a new and friendlier mood to the processions had been adopted in the late 1980s, but on May Day 1990 this turned to anger. Jeering and booing demonstrators poured past Gorbachev and other Politburo members who, in the eyes of thousands of Muscovites, had failed to deliver on the promises made to the Soviet people. In essence, they were still hungry and the shops were still empty after five years of *glasnost* and *perestroika*.

Later in the month, Boris Yeltsin was elected president of the Russian Federation, the largest and most powerful of the Soviet republics. Yeltsin had been the Moscow party chief until Gorbachev had dismissed him in 1987, and since then he had bided his time building up a huge support base. During his election campaign, he had been quick to criticise the slow rate of reform *perestroika* was bringing, and in July 1990 he stepped up his campaign against Gorbachev by resigning his membership of the Communist Party. By the end of the year, matters had gone from bad to worse for Gorbachev with the resignation of Shevardnadze.

This was a particularly harsh blow because Shevardnadze had become an essential ally in the fight against those conservative elements within his government who still opposed reform. The foreign secretary's resignation was doubly crippling when Shevardnadze made it clear that he had resigned over fears concerning new powers being given to Gorbachev to force through *perestroika.* These gave Gorbachev more power than any other Soviet leader since Stalin, and Shevardnadze openly worried about the possibility of a return to dictatorship.

As the focus of world attention moved to Desert Storm in February 1991, the crisis within the USSR continued. Opinion polarised between conservatives concerned that the rate of reform would bring about the disintegration of the USSR and the collapse of communism, and the supporters of Yeltsin who campaigned for an increase, not a decrease, in the rate of this reform. The conservatives looked on warily at the disintegration of the Warsaw Pact and the strengthening of ties with the West while Yeltsin talked about stripping even more power from the Party and the military.

During the summer of 1991, Gorbachev tried to negotiate a new relationship between the republics and the central Union in order to satisfy growing criticism. This loosened Moscow's traditional grip on power over the republics, but it did not go far enough for Yeltsin who wanted even more devolved power for his Russian Federation. These demands included total control over the Russian currency and its armed forces.

Eventually, however, a new treaty was agreed by all the republics except the three Baltic States and Georgia, which during the negotiations had unilaterally declared independence. For the conservatives who opposed Gorbachev, this was just too much and on 19 August 1991, during the weekend before the new agreement was due to be signed, they decided to act. The coup d'état was led by General Gennady Yanayev who claimed that Gorbachev was leading the USSR into ruin and that he and his co-conspirators were acting on behalf of the Soviet people. They ordered the arrest of Gorbachev at his holiday *dasha* in the Crimea and had him placed under house arrest. Meanwhile, tanks were sent onto the streets of Moscow.

However, the people themselves moved quickly against the coup and, galvanised particularly by the brave and robust leadership of Boris Yeltsin, also took to the streets. Doubts over the purpose and resolve of the coup leaders were soon raised and the spirits of all those who opposed the coup grew. Within days, it seemed that the growing optimism of Yeltsin's supporters was not misplaced when it remained less than clear whether the coup had the support of the police and the army.

At this point, the coup leaders also made the crucial mistake of allowing Yeltsin to escape to the building that housed the Russian parliament, the White House, and from here he was able to communicate with the outside world. Most importantly, Yeltsin was able to gain the public support of President Bush and

John Major. He then came out of the parliament building that had been surrounded not only by the army but also by a large group of his own supporters.

Before the cameras of the world's media that were following every move of the uprising, he stood on one of the tanks that had been sent to the White House and declared that the coup was illegal and that its leaders would be arrested. He soon dispatched a delegation from the Russian Federation to visit Gorbachev in the Crimea and, before the end of the day, reports surfaced of troops under the control of the coup leaders abandoning their posts. The resolve of Yanayev and his group buckled the following day and, after a skirmish on the outskirts of Moscow in which three Muscovites lost their lives, the tanks were sent back to their barracks.

Gorbachev was set free from his Crimean house arrest and returned to his office in the Kremlin. But the coup had destroyed his credibility, with many of its leaders owing their positions to Gorbachev himself. Yeltsin now used his newly found strategic and popular ascendancy to full advantage and on Friday 23 August had Gorbachev brought to the Russian parliament where he was forced by a goading Yeltsin, in the full and humiliating glare of live television, to read out the names of all those involved in the coup.

Yeltsin pushed home his advantage over his old rival by forcing him to sign a decree there and then banning the Communist Party within the Russian Federation. The decree also closed all of its offices and froze all of its assets. As a result of the coup and the week that followed, Gorbachev was never again to wield any significant power in Soviet or Russian politics and spent the next few months presiding over the disintegration of the USSR.

In September 1991, the Commonwealth of Independent States was formed and this belatedly aimed to bind together those republics that had not already claimed independence. But by this stage, the drive towards independent nation status had grown too strong and the CIS was never able to develop into any sort of meaningful political entity. It did no more than postpone the inevitable disintegration of the USSR that was formally completed in December 1991. The country created by Lenin, Trotsky and Stalin that had given so much to bring about the destruction of Nazism in the 1940s and that since 1945 had been battling against the USA and its capitalist allies was now itself dead.

The Invasion of Kuwait and Operation Desert Storm

The Soviet coup and the break-up of the USSR were to an extent overshadowed by the invasion of Kuwait and the military campaign that led to its liberation. The crisis began in August 1990 when thousands of Iraqi troops poured south over the border into Kuwait, a small oil-rich emirate in the northern Persian Gulf. Early attempts to set up a pro-Baghdad puppet government were soon abandoned, and orders were issued by Saddam Hussein that Kuwait should be formally annexed. By the end of the month, a presidential decree confirmed that Kuwait had become Iraq's nineteenth province.

Saddam Hussein had been the president of Iraq since 1979, having risen up through the ranks of the ruling Ba'ath Party that he had joined in the 1950s. During the 1980s, aid and technology from China, the Soviet Bloc and the West had been used to build Iraq's army into the fourth largest in the world although this was used to little effect in the eight-year war with Iran. The Ba'ath Party had been founded on the principle of pan-Arab nationalism and, as such, found it easy to reject the borders and constraints placed on the Arab world by the Ottoman, British and French empires. Saddam Hussein used this to lay claim to Kuwait, which had been a British protectorate until independence in 1961.

After the end of the Iran-Iraq War in 1988, Saddam Hussein had increased pressure on Kuwait by continually reiterating the claim that Kuwait was an Iraqi province lost during Ottoman colonial times. In reality, Saddam's claim had more to do with the billions of dollars that Kuwait had lent Iraq during the war with Iran and which in 1990 still remained unpaid. Some analysts have also suggested that in the months leading up to the invasion, Saddam Hussein was led to believe, especially by US diplomats working in the area, that an Iraqi invasion of its smaller southern neighbour would not be seriously challenged by the West.

However, the invasion was quickly condemned and efforts through the autumn were begun to build a coalition force capable of liberating Kuwait. The first priority that this coalition set itself was the protection of the northern border of Saudi Arabia, which was vulnerable to a second Iraqi offensive, and eventually troops drawn from twenty-eight countries joined the coalition operation in northern Saudi Arabia, code-named Desert Shield.

As the coalition was brought together through September and October 1990, a series of diplomatic initiatives were launched to try and bring about a non-military resolution to the crisis. In particular, King Hussein of Jordan worked hard to negotiate a face-saving compromise although his refusal to condemn Saddam Hussein was eventually to lose him much support in the West. Meanwhile, Saddam Hussein had taken hostage some 300 Western nationals in Baghdad who, it was feared, were to be used as human shields.

They were eventually released in early December after visits from such international luminaries as Edward Heath, the ex-British prime minister, and Jesse Jackson, the veteran civil rights campaigner and US presidential candidate. In addition to the highly publicised fate of these hostages, there was also the plight of the thousands of migrant workers, predominantly from the subcontinent and South East Asia, who had been working in Kuwait and Iraq during the invasion. They now found themselves stranded in the Gulf and were to spend many miserable months in refugee camps before their eventual repatriation.

During the diplomatic efforts to resolve the crisis through September and October 1990, Saddam Hussein continually tried to link the invasion of Kuwait with the Arab-Israeli conflict, and threatened to bring Israel into the crisis by launching Scud missile attacks on its cities. He hoped that this would split the countries ranged against him by forcing Arab members, including Saudi Arabia and Syria, to leave a coalition that included Israel. Under intense pressure from the USA to refrain from retaliation in the event of an attack and fortified by the US Patriot anti-missile defence system that was quickly installed on its borders, Israel was never provoked in the way Saddam Hussein had hoped and the coalition remained intact.

In the meantime, a number of UN Security Council resolutions were passed against Iraq, including one condemning the invasion and another authorising the immediate implementation of economic sanctions. But by November 1990, economic and political pressure had made little headway and this prompted the passing of UN Resolution 678. This authorised the use of force against Iraq if the withdrawal of its troops from Kuwait had not taken place before 15 January 1991.

Two reasons motivated President Bush, the leading figure behind the coalition, into moving so fast. The first concerned the huge cost of maintaining the coalition force in the Gulf. The second, and perhaps more important reason, concerned the health and well-being of those remaining in Kuwait. Reports since August had suggested the widespread use of torture and murder by the Iraqi army of occupation.

Final diplomatic efforts to resolve the crisis were made during the first few weeks of 1991, and these included an unsuccessful meeting in Geneva between James Baker, the US secretary of state, and Tariq Aziz, his Iraqi counterpart. These last-ditch efforts culminated in the three-day visit to Baghdad by the UN secretary general in the week before the 15 January deadline. By this time, a coalition strike force of over half a million troops had been amassed in the northern deserts of Saudi Arabia.

On 17 January 1991, the aerial bombardment of Iraq and Iraqi forces in Kuwait was launched as Operation Desert Shield was superceded by Operation Desert Storm. In the first few days of the conflict, this concentrated on Iraqi air force facilities and, after having guaranteed aerial supremacy with their destruction, selected targets in Iraq and occupied Kuwait were bombed incessantly for six weeks.

By the end of Desert Storm, coalition aircraft had successfully destroyed the military and industrial infrastructure of Iraq. But these attacks also killed tens of thousands of Iraqi civilians and forced many others to live without clean water, electricity and other basic amenities. In an attempt to split the coalition, Saddam Hussein ordered that Scud missile attacks be launched against Israel, and Tel Aviv in particular was to suffer. But the Israeli government resisted the urge to launch retaliatory strikes that Israeli and US leaders knew would strain the ability of some Arab members to stay in the coalition. The war in the air had lasted a month before Saddam Hussein was forced to compromise, announcing that Iraqi forces would leave Kuwait. However, the conditions that he set proved unacceptable to leaders of the coalition and the aerial bombardment continued.

On 24 February 1991, the land war was launched, with coalition troops moving into occupied Kuwait and southern Iraq. In response, Iraqi forces in Kuwait carried out their threat to set alight Kuwait's oilfields, creating one of the century's worst environmental disasters. The coalition advance was rapid and, despite public announcements from Baghdad that Iraqi ground forces were winning the 'Mother of all Battles', the remarkably quick assault soon became a rout. Within two days, Kuwaiti and Saudi Arabian forces were the first coalition troops to enter liberated Kuwait City, and soon after other coalition forces moved up to take the Iraqi port of Basra. By then, Iraqi forces in occupied Kuwait were in full and chaotic retreat along roads running northwards back into Iraq, with the continued aerial bombardment of this demoralised group widely criticised in the West. On 28 February 1991, President Bush ordered a ceasefire and four days later, Iraqi generals and General Norman Schwarzkopf, the commander of the coalition forces, met to sign the surrender documents that ended the war.

George Bush may in retrospect have regretted his decision to end the war with the liberation of Kuwait and not use the total military superiority of the coalition force to bring about the fall of the Iraqi dictator. Saddam Hussein remained in power long after Bush had been defeated by Bill Clinton in 1992 and, despite the presence of the UN, was ruthless against Shiite uprisings in the south and Kurdish uprisings in the north in the months that followed. Certainly, Bush may have later regretted not doing more to help these revolts, but the force that had liberated Kuwait was a very disparate coalition and it showed no inclination to go beyond the confines of the UN resolutions that demanded the liberation of Kuwait.

A month after the final ceasefire, Resolution 687, which demanded the destruction of all Iraqi weapons of mass destruction, was passed by the General Assembly of the UN. This applied to all chemical, biological and nuclear weaponry and the UN set up a special agency, UNSCOM, to monitor Iraqi compliance. However, Saddam Hussein had still not complied seven years later and in February 1998 Kofi Annan, the UN secretary general, travelled to Baghdad to negotiate a face-saving compromise for the Iraqi leader. Only this saved the Iraqi people from the threat of renewed air strikes. However, later in the year, Saddam Hussein had still not complied with UN demands, and in December 1998 a damning UNSCOM report on Iraq's intentions led to a US and British-led bombing campaign that lasted intermittently into the next century.

The most obvious result of Saddam Hussein not complying with the UN and with UNSCOM was the suffering of the Iraqi people who endured a decade of economic sanctions as a result of their leader's intransigence. Although a deal was struck that allowed Iraq to sell oil in return for food and medical supplies, this did little to alleviate the misery. Once again, sanctions proved of little use against a determined dictator and resulted in the deaths of thousands of Iraqis each year from malnutrition or lack of medical care. The sanctions, the suffering of the Iraqi people and the dictatorship of Saddam Hussein all continued into the new century.

An Increase of Tension in the Balkans and the Bosnian Civil War
The coalition victory in the war against Iraq had shown the UN at its best. It was not long, however, before civil war in Yugoslavia was to show it at its worst. As the other countries emerging from communism in the early 1990s worked to reform and modernise along Western democratic lines, Yugoslavia erupted into civil war in 1992. For three years, the world community, the European Community and the UN continued to posture and prevaricate while horrors not seen in Europe since the era of the Nazis were visited on the people of the region. It was only finally in 1995 that they summoned up enough diplomatic will to force the warring parties, and especially the Bosnian Serbs, to open negotiations to end the conflict.

Yugoslavia consisted of six distinct federated states that for over thirty-five years until 1980 had been ruled by the benevolent but strict communist regime of Marshal Tito. These states consisted of the rich northern state of Slovenia with its borders with Italy and Austria, the Roman Catholic-dominated Croatia, the mountainous and ethnically diverse republics of Montenegro and Bosnia-Herzegovina, the small but fiercely independent Macedonia and the Christian Orthodox-dominated Serbia, which was also Yugoslavia's biggest state.

With Tito dominating Yugoslavia as he did for most of the Cold War, all remained relatively quiet and calm. But his death in 1980 coincided with a downturn in the economy and the country spent the last decade under communist rule facing increasingly austere economic policies, growing inflation and a deteriorating standard of living. This was the background to the events that triggered the collapse of communism, the break-up of Yugoslavia itself and the gradual two-year slide into civil war and genocide.

The catalyst for this war was Serbia that since 1989 had been ruled by a populist, nationalist, right-wing government led by Slobodan Milošević. Under Milošević's rule, this had managed to increase ethnic tension throughout the country to dangerous levels. Milošević's ultimate ambition was to carve out a Greater Serbia from the six states that made up Yugoslavia, and drive out any non-Serbs from the lands he claimed. This was particularly the case in Kosovo, an autonomous region within Serbia where some 90% of the population, the Kosovars, were ethnically Albanian and Muslim. Their defeat and subjugation in the 1980s had been the first step in his overall long-term plan.

Increased pressure and harassment of the majority Kosovar population was ordered, and marches and demonstrations by protesters from the Kosovar community were viciously put down by the Serbian-dominated police and security forces. In March 1989, a new anti-Kosovar constitution that ended its autonomous status was forced on Kosovo. As a consequence, the Muslim Kosovar community lived there as second-class citizens until full-scale war broke out ten years later.

Open warfare eventually broke out in Yugoslavia in the summer of 1991. But this had been preceded by an increasingly serious split between Serbia, which was developing into a nationalistic totalitarian police state, and the more liberal Western-leaning regimes emerging in Croatia and Slovenia. This situation had deteriorated through 1990 and into 1991, with Milošević stepping up his rhetoric against the new, democratically elected governments in these two republics. With the old state of Yugoslavia fast becoming no more than a name on a map, Croatia and Slovenia became increasingly worried about this build-up of tension and, in order to shield themselves from Serb attack, both declared independence in June 1991. Both increasingly looked to the European Community, and to NATO, for protection and safety.

Milošević and his government in Belgrade were less concerned about Slovenia, whose border had historically been easier to define and which contained few ethnic Serbians. Croatia, however, where 10% of the population was ethnically Serb, was another matter entirely and it was in this population that support for the notion of a Greater Serbia found its focus. This sense of nationalism was matched in the Croatian community that gathered around the strong anti-Serbian government of Franjo Tudjman.

Once war did break out, Serb advances were swift and decisive and by the spring of 1992, when the UN special envoy Cyrus Vance brokered a deal that brought the war to an end, as much as a third of Croatia had been taken over by Serbia. At the same time, the appalling nature of the war was becoming clear, with reports of massacres and atrocities by both sides soon reaching the world's media.

However, no sooner had a negotiated settlement ended the war in Croatia than violence erupted in Bosnia-Herzegovina where both Croatia and Serbia held claims. Bosnia-Herzegovina was Yugoslavia's most ethnically diverse republic where just over 40% of the population was Muslim. They lived side-by-side with the Serb community that made up about a third of the population. The vast majority of the remainder were ethnically Croat.

Problems in Bosnia-Herzegovina were further exacerbated by the integration of the three communities throughout the republic, with members of each group living next to each other in the many villages that dotted the republic. The barbarity and cruelty of the atrocities perpetrated by neighbour on neighbour made the conflict in Bosnia-Herzegovina even more harrowing than the one that the world had just witnessed in Croatia.

The leader of the Bosnian Serbs, Radovan Karadžić, was to use the support of the Milošević government to foment trouble in Bosnia-Herzegovina. In the wake of the war in Croatia, he used disagreements over referendum proposals as a pretext for declaring full-scale war on his Croat and Muslim opponents, and quickly ordered the siege of Sarajevo. In the three-sided civil war that quickly developed, it was the Bosnian Serbs under Karadžić who soon took control.

In a war noted for its horror and barbarity, it was the Bosnian Serbs, perhaps because they were the most militarily successful of the three warring factions, who were soon being condemned by the world community for a string of atrocities in the villages and towns they came to dominate. As a result, the phrase 'ethnic cleansing' entered the world's lexicon as over two million Bosnian Muslims and ethnic Croats living in Bosnia-Herzegovina were either killed or forced from their homes by the Bosnian-Serb army led by General Ratko Mladić.

The world community stood almost paralysed as Sarajevo was bombed daily and the Vance-Owen peace plan, creating a patchwork of autonomous zones of control splitting the country, was rejected by all sides. Meanwhile, the Bosnian Serbs were secretly supplied with arms from Belgrade and Eastern Europe while an embargo on arms denied the other sides, and especially the Bosnian Muslims, the military hardware they needed to protect themselves.

When Karadžić declared the creation of the state of Republica Serbska in the spring of 1993, the horrors being perpetrated by his army had been widely reported for a year, and television pictures were reaching the world of Bosnian-Serb concentration camps. Another particular horror emerging from these pictures was the targeting of civilians in an attempt to create a sense of fear of extermination within whole communities. Terror was being used in its most brutal form to ethnically cleanse Republica Serbska of its undesirable non-Serb population. Houses standing side by side were destroyed or left alone according to whether the owner was Muslim, Croat or Serb. This plan to force the large-scale evacuation of non-Serbs largely worked.

Meanwhile, the leaders of the Western world and Russia set up a contact group to represent the world community in the conflict. This quickly arranged so-called safe havens within Bosnia-Herzegovina where refugees, especially from the Muslim community, might seek safety and security. In essence, these safe havens were set up to help stop the genocide of ethnic cleansing being carried out by Bosnian-Serb hit squads all across Bosnia-Herzegovina. In reality, they did little to protect those in need, with the soldiers manning them never given either the authority or the firepower to defend their positions properly.

This was particularly the case with the Dutch force protecting the UN safe haven at Srebenica. This was overrun by the army of Mladić himself in July 1995, with the Dutch unable to protect the 5,000 or so Bosnian Muslim men in their care. These men were marched out of the safe haven at Srebenica, with most being systematically executed in various warehouses, fields and forests nearby.

However, the Bosnian Serbs were not the only group guilty of programmes of ethnic cleansing. Since the defeat of Croatia in the civil war against Serbia in 1991, Tudjman had overseen the build-up of the Croatian military and in

1995 he ordered the launching of a counter-offensive into the area around Krajina. As a result, over 100,000 Serbs were driven from their homes. In retaliation, Bosnian-Serb forces retaliated in the safe havens around Srebrenica and Zepa, slaughtering thousands of Croat and Muslim civilians. With the will of the international community and the UN openly flouted, the number of dead continued to rise.

Eventually, the resolve of the world community stiffened after a Bosnian-Serb mortar attack on Sarajevo's main market in August 1995. As a result, the USA became increasingly active in the dispute and led NATO air attacks on Bosnian-Serb heavy artillery positions on the hills overlooking Sarajevo from where the attack had been launched. This air offensive was able to force a temporary Bosnian-Serb withdrawal.

In the aftermath of the market attack on Sarajevo, President Clinton organised a summit meeting between the presidents of Croatia, Bosnia-Herzegovina and Yugoslavia at Dayton, Ohio, and made it clear to all three that further NATO military action would be forthcoming if an agreement was not found. In essence, Clinton's plan was to drive a wedge between Karadžić and Milošević, forcing the latter, who had become president of a newly constituted Yugoslavia comprising Serbia and Montenegro in 1992, to agree a settlement with the men Karadžić had spent three years fighting.

A peace deal was eventually signed at Dayton after three weeks of bargaining. In general terms, Bosnia-Herzegovina was split in half, creating a loosely constructed Croat-Muslim federation and a Bosnian-Serb republic. The peace was to be policed by an international peacekeeping force called I-FOR and some attempt was made to make Sarajevo into an integrated capital. An international court was also set up at The Hague to deal with war crimes, with Karadžić and Mladić, in essence the Bosnian-Serb leadership, both indicted.

In practice, the Dayton agreement gave the lion's share of land to the Bosnian Serbs, the worst perpetrators of the violence and ethnic cleansing. The Bosnian Muslims who had suffered so much in the war that brought genocide back to Europe were to receive the least. Their leaders complained bitterly at Dayton that their rights were being ignored, but the war had killed half a million people and in the end they were as weary of the killing as anyone else.

In the aftermath of the Dayton agreement, a wary peace broke out in Bosnia-Herzegovina, with the three communities trying to bring some sort of normality back to their lives. A heavy presence of peacekeepers was maintained, but old rivalries and hatreds were never very far from the surface and many observers came to believe that war again would break out if it were not for the soldiers of I-FOR. It was not long before Milošević's aspirations for a Greater Serbia began to resurface, despite the peace agreement hammered out at Dayton, and before the end of the century the international community again became involved in a second conflict in the Balkans when Serb aggression in Kosovo resulted in another war.

The Rwandan Civil War of 1994

Old ethnic and racial divisions similar to those in Yugoslavia were also behind the terrible civil war that erupted in the small, central African state of Rwanda in April 1994. Rwanda was a mountainous country famous for its gorillas, and its population of some eight million had traditionally earned its subsistence living off the land. The Tutsi tribe had for hundreds of years been the country's ruling feudal class and made up about 10% of the population. But the Tutsi royal family had been overthrown in 1961, just before independence from Belgium, and Rwanda had since then been ruled by governments dominated by the majority Hutus. Many Tutsis, as a result, had been forced into exile where they had remained for a generation.

However, by the end of the 1980s the thirty-year monopoly on power enjoyed by the Hutus was being challenged by the Tutsi-dominated Rwandan Patriotic Front whose forces were concentrated in Uganda to the north. Sporadic attacks launched by the RPF during the early 1990s had led to inroads into northern Rwanda, and negotiations between the two sides had eventually led to a ceasefire in 1992. However, this proved to be short-lived, with violence again erupting in 1993. Sadly, this was only a precursor to the horror awaiting the Rwandan people the following year.

In April 1994, the aircraft carrying the presidents of both Rwanda and Burundi, returning from peace talks in Tanzania, crashed in suspicious circumstances while approaching the airport at Kigali, Rwanda's capital. It was never discovered who was behind this attack although extremists from both sides were suspected. After the blowing up of the presidential flight, the government was taken over by hard-line Hutus who immediately ordered the assassination of the acting prime minister who was killed, alongside ten Belgian UN peacekeepers who were mutilated trying to protect her, in a UN compound just outside the capital on the first morning of the conflict.

This was followed by a wave of violence against the moderate Hutu supporters of the dead president and then, more brutally, against the Tutsi minority. This initial outburst of genocide killed tens of thousands, with still more forced to seek safety in hastily assembled refugee camps in Zaire and

Tanzania. The UN force in Rwanda that had been sent to maintain the ceasefire in 1993 remained, but was powerless to stop the carnage, and diplomats were slow, as they had been in Yugoslavia, to formulate a forthright and practical strategy to protect the fleeing masses.

While diplomats vacillated at the UN in New York, the government of France decided to act unilaterally and sent in 2,500 soldiers to evacuate their own nationals and find and protect those Tutsis fleeing from the Hutu-dominated Rwandan Army suspected of carrying out most of the killings. However, the Tutsi RPF rebels were themselves on the move, sweeping south from bases in southern Uganda to take the capital, before moving westwards to chase the badly organised and ill-disciplined Rwandan Army into Zaire.

It was there that huge refugee camps had grown up around the towns of Goma and Bukavu. Thousands were to die in these camps from typhoid and cholera, with aid bound for them remaining stranded in Uganda and Kenya. This was because safety guarantees for the shipment of the supplies could not be agreed between the UN and the various warring factions. Meanwhile, aid workers in the refugee camps became increasingly concerned about the problem of ethnic violence in the camps themselves. As the Tutsi rebels took control of the country, a wave of retaliatory massacres of Hutus began, with many involved in the original genocide now being killed themselves.

However, in July 1994, only three months after the initial carnage had begun, a ceasefire was brokered that led to the formation of a Tutsi-dominated government. Soon the return of the displaced Tutsi population slowly began although it was a long time before the Hutu refugees were to follow. In fact, fear of further persecution meant that there still remained in 1996 a sizeable population from both tribal groups unwilling or unable to return to Rwanda, a situation that was to place a great deal of strain on Rwanda's relations with its neighbours, and in particular Zaire, in the years to come.

Indeed, the failure of the Zairian army to deal with the Rwandan refugee problem in the east of the country was a major factor in bringing about the coup that ended the corrupt thirty-year rule of President Mobutu Sese Seko. Mobutu was replaced by Laurent Kabila who immediately changed the name of the country from Zaire to the Democratic Republic of Congo. The ethnic violence and genocide that had killed so many in Rwanda was also to be experienced by the people of Kabila's DR Congo in the last years of the century. They joined the people of, among others, Somalia, Liberia, Sierra Leone and Angola who had also suffered from the effects of prolonged civil wars.

Meanwhile, Rwandans returning from refugee camps in Zaire, Uganda and

Tanzania found their country in chaos. The judicial system had broken down completely, and it was clear that the perpetrators of the genocide from both sides were never going to be held accountable for their actions in a fair and equitable way. As violence eased in Rwanda, tribal violence between Tutsis and Hutus broke out in Burundi to the south, with the tribal rivalry that has led to major confrontations cyclically over time repeated once again.

The Clinton Administration and the Middle East Peace Process

The wars in both Bosnia-Herzegovina and Rwanda took place during the first term in office of Bill Clinton whose victory in November 1992 brought an end to twelve years of Republican rule. His success came despite a series of allegations during the election campaign concerning marital infidelity and draft dodging during the Vietnam War. These had threatened to ruin his campaign before it had properly begun.

His election was perhaps even more surprising given the unprecedented success of the Bush presidency that had seen not only the end of the Cold War but also the highly successful military campaign against Iraq. However, a downturn in the economy, a continuing feud with the Senate over the budget deficit and a general feeling that a change at the top was needed after twelve years of Republican rule all conspired to allow Clinton to become his country's third-youngest president ever.

The early years of Clinton's presidency were littered with mistakes both at home and abroad, amid continued allegations concerning not only his private life but also his business affairs while serving as governor in Arkansas. These were matters that dogged Clinton throughout both terms of his presidency and indirectly led to his impeachment in 1999. The Democrats lost heavily in the mid-term elections in 1994, and few analysts at the time believed that Clinton would recover and run a successful re-election campaign in 1996. However, he was to prove his critics wrong when, again with Al Gore as his running mate, he beat the Republican challenge of Robert Dole.

Domestically, Clinton began his presidency committed to slashing the budget deficit, but also embarked on a series of welfare reforms and put his wife in charge of plans to get medical insurance more widely accessible. In foreign affairs, he often seemed unclear about the direction that he wanted to take his country in the new post-Cold War world, and was particularly criticised over US involvement in Haiti and in the Somalian civil war where US lives were lost. The USA was also rocked by the Oklahoma City Bombing in April 1995, the most deadly terrorist attack on American soil of the century. This killed 168 people, and was set off in reaction to the botched siege of the Davidian sect at Waco in Texas the previous year by federal government forces.

In his second term, he was again challenged abroad when a series of bombings of US embassies in Africa were linked to Islamic extremists. His response was to bomb suspected terrorist bases in Somalia and Afghanistan although the legitimacy, and indeed the political sense, of such actions was brought into question.

One region in which Clinton did find success was the Middle East where renewed US diplomacy reignited the peace process that had stalled after the 1982 Israeli invasion of Lebanon. Since that time, little had been done to bring the two sides together and a series of crises in the 1980s seemed to suggest that reconciliation was impossible. In particular, tension surrounded the building of more Jewish settlements in the Occupied Territories, which had led to the Arab *intifada,* or uprising, of 1997, and to the growth in support for Hezbollah and Hamas in southern Lebanon and the Gaza Strip respectively, militant Islamic groups dedicated to the destruction of Israel.

However, Clinton indicated soon after his election that the Middle East peace process was something to which he was deeply committed, and he let it be known that the USA was becoming impatient at the intransigence of both sides. Discussions had begun in Madrid in 1991, and increased diplomatic pressure in 1993 led to secret talks arranged by the Norwegian government that eventually led to the signing of the first of the Oslo Accords, a series of agreements between the two sides that were negotiated between 1993 and 1995. The first of these was ratified at a high-profile White House ceremony in September 1993 that culminated with the historic handshake between Yasser Arafat, the leader of the PLO, and Yitzhak Rabin, the Israeli prime minister. This was in front of a highly influential audience that included two former US presidents, Jimmy Carter and George Bush Snr.

In the accord, the Israeli government accepted the PLO's right to represent the Palestinian people while the PLO agreed to renounce terrorism and accept Israel's right to exist. The accord went on to timetable a three-stage peace process that was to begin with the withdrawal of Israeli forces from Jericho and the Gaza Strip. This was to be followed by free elections to elect Palestinian representatives there, and finally culminated in the negotiated withdrawal of Israeli forces from many other towns and settlements in the Occupied Territories.

Progress over these withdrawals during the years ahead was painfully slow, with the Palestinian Authority, the entity run by Arafat set up to rule the territory given back, accusing Israel of breaking promises made at Oslo. The Israelis countered with claims that they were only interested in maintaining Israel's security, and accused the Palestinian Authority of not properly dealing with Hamas and other groups active in areas under its control. In addition, Rabin faced pressure from within Israel to protect the rights of the roughly 140,000 Jewish settlers who had moved into the Occupied Territories since the war of 1967.

Relations were particularly frayed in the West Bank town of Hebron, a town of some 100,000 people, where the Israeli army maintained a sizeable presence in order to protect a community of only about 400 Jewish settlers. The town of Hebron was crucially important to both sides as it was where the tomb of the patriarch, Abraham, was located. Abraham, or Ibrahim as he is known in Islam, was seen as the founding father of both Judaism and Islam.

The political situation was also harmed by a series of massacres perpetrated by extremists from both sides who were opposed to the peace process. These saw the deaths of twenty-nine Muslim worshippers in 1994 at a mosque in Hebron, the murders of a group of Israeli school children at a tourist spot near the Jordanian border and the assassination of Rabin himself in November 1995. This was carried out by a young Jewish zealot who shot Rabin as he arrived to address a rally in Tel Aviv organised in support of the Oslo process.

Rabin was replaced by Shimon Peres, his foreign minister, but a general election the following year led to the election of the more conservative and hawkish government of Benjamin Netanyahu. From the start, Netanyahu took a far more hardline approach to negotiations with the Palestinians, and Arafat was forced back to the negotiating table time and time again. Although accepting the Oslo Accords in principal, Netanyahu made it clear that he was unwilling to move the peace process forward until fears over Israeli internal security had been properly addressed. This meant countless delays to the peace process and little progress was made until January 1997 when an agreement over the thorny issue of Hebron was finally agreed.

Hebron was the key to progress in talks over the future of the West Bank, and Netanyahu's commitment to withdraw was the first by a right-wing government concerning land traditionally considered to constitute ancient Israel. Some in his ruling Likud Party saw this as a sign of betrayal, but Netanyahu made it clear that the withdrawal of Israeli troops was contingent on Arafat guaranteeing, and delivering, security in the areas handed over. This gave Netanyahu an important political loophole that he used more than once during the next two years. But Netanyahu's agreement to withdraw Israeli troops from Hebron, the last Palestinian city still under military occupation, tied his Likud Party into the peace process for the first time.

These ties eventually led to the Wye Plantation Agreement that was signed in October 1998. The contents of the agreement were concluded in exhaustive talks between the Israelis and Palestinians, and were thrashed out with the help of Clinton and the cancer-ridden King Hussein of Jordan, with the final negotiating session lasting twenty-one hours. The agreement gave the Palestinian Authority control over 13% of the West Bank captured in 1967, while in return the Palestinian delegation agreed to amend its thirty-year-old charter that called for the destruction of Israel.

But the agreement was only possible after Netanyahu's late brinkmanship linked the agreement to the release of an American spy who had been convicted of passing on US secrets to Israel where he was considered a hero and where he had been granted citizenship. Despite the agreement at Wye, animosity between Netanyahu and Arafat clearly remained, and the agreement was only really possible through King Hussein's counsel, coupled with massive US pressure. This all seemed to show that future agreements in accordance with Oslo were going to be difficult, and problems surrounding the status of Jerusalem in particular were predicted.

However, financial scandals soon began to overshadow Netanyahu's government and an election defeat forced him from office in 1999. Netanyahu was replaced by Ehud Barak, Israel's most decorated soldier, and his Labour Party supporters hoped that the return to power of the party of Rabin would reinvigorate the peace process. But Barak soon made it clear that no further concessions would be agreed without firm guarantees about security. He also insisted that there would be no return to the borders of 1967, that Jerusalem would remain in Israeli hands and that full Palestinian independence would only be accepted after a full plebiscite of the Israeli people.

In July 1999, Barak made his first attempt to bump start the peace process, with land deals with the Palestinians and Syria at the heart of his early initiatives. However, exhaustive meetings in the USA over the return of the Golan Heights to Syria came to nothing, and the schism between the two sides widened after an escalation of violence in Israeli-occupied southern Lebanon at the end of the year. This centred on Israeli attacks on Hezbollah positions and culminated in international outcry following a pledge by the Israeli foreign minister to destroy Hezbollah completely. In this way, the Middle East peace process stumbled on into the new century with the divide between Israel and its Arab neighbours as wide as ever.

Russia under Boris Yeltsin and the War in Chechnya

The involvement of the USA in a series of overseas policy initiatives through the early years of the decade highlighted the decline in international importance of the former USSR. This had broken up in the aftermath of the abortive 1991 coup, with the fifteen republics each becoming independent nation states. The central figure in the defeat of the coup had been Boris Yeltsin, the president of the Russian Federation, and it was Yeltsin who was to dominate the politics of the largest of the former Soviet republics for the rest of the century.

Many in the West hoped that his charismatic style of leadership and his enthusiasm for capitalism would bring about the reforms needed to raise living standards. Sadly, these expectations were never fulfilled, with Russia and many other former Soviet republics remaining sadly inept at making the changes needed to transform ailing economic infrastructures. This inability, which contrasted so starkly with the successful changes that had taken place in communist China under Deng during the 1980s, left Russia poor and weak at the end of a decade that had started with such optimism.

Yeltsin's departure in 1999 ended sadly with ill health and constant diplomatic gaffes reducing him to something of a figure of international ridicule. But his arrival in office had started brightly enough with the Cold War at an end and the world looking on expectantly. He had the full support of the European Union and the USA, and both were keen to help in the massive task of restructuring the Russian economy. In 1993, Yeltsin used his international standing to suppress a rebellion by nationalists, and a referendum on the constitution in December strengthened the powers of the presidency. However, in their eagerness to replace the communist command economy, both Yeltsin and his Western backers allowed shortcuts to be made to vital reforms of both the economy and country's political structure.

The consequence of this was spiralling crime rates, the re-emergence of the communists as a force in Russian politics and a series of economic crises that eventually led to the total meltdown of 1998, with the rouble losing 75% of its value. During this collapse into economic chaos, Yeltsin's maverick grip on power remained as tight as ever as he appointed, and then dismissed, four prime ministers in quick succession in the last eighteen months of his presidency.

Russia's economic performance meant that Yeltsin could do little to influence negotiations concerning the eastwards expansion of NATO that took place during 1996. This expansion included many former Warsaw Pact countries that increasingly looked towards the West, NATO and the European Union. In March 1997, Yeltsin met with Clinton in Finland to try and find a settlement acceptable to Russia, and later in the year an accord was eventually signed that gave the impression that a compromise had been found. However, few were persuaded that the agreement was anything other than a sop to the Russian president. In the reality of a post-Cold War world dominated by the USA, there was little that Russia could do about the US-driven eastward expansion of the Western alliance.

Throughout the decade, Yeltsin faced criticism not only over the economy and his relationship with the West but also concerning his policy in breakaway Chechnya, a semi-autonomous Muslim republic in the Caucasus Mountains between the Caspian and Black Seas. Chechnya had first been attacked in December 1994 and in the twenty-one-month war that followed, 100,000 people had lost their lives. In Russia, the war was not popular and Yeltsin's handling of it led to electoral losses to both the nationalists and the communists.

The war eventually ended with an uneasy ceasefire that allowed Chechen fighters to leave the capital city, Grozny, before the badly mauled Russian army took charge. However, this did not come before the deaths of thousands of Russian conscripts in a number of unsuccessful attempts to take the city. But this brought little hope of a lasting peace, and war again broke out three years later. This was triggered by a series of bomb attacks in Moscow that killed over 300 Muscovites. These attacks were blamed on Muslim separatists from Chechnya and resulted in Russian troops massing once again on the Chechen border in September 1999.

After a brief air campaign, these troops were ordered over the border, precipitating a huge refugee problem that strained relations with the West. This was the situation in November 1999 when, at a meeting in Istanbul concerning peace and security in Europe, Clinton and Yeltsin met for the last time. It was the frostiest East-West meeting since the conclusion of the Cold War and ended with the theatrical departure of Yeltsin. In that regard, Yeltsin's behaviour in the late 1990s drew comparisons to Khrushchev's histrionics in the early 1960s.

For a month, the balance of the war in Chechnya ebbed and flowed before Russian commanders refocused their firepower on Grozny itself and, at the end of December, the all-out attack on the capital was launched. This had been preceded by an order for the complete evacuation of the Chechen capital, again provoking huge criticism in the West. Reports of torture, rape and intimidation circulated widely, and comparisons were soon made with the Serbian ethnic cleansing programmes in Bosnia and Kosovo.

A few days' grace was given by the Russian commanders to allow this evacuation during the Christmas period, and television pictures were beamed around the world of over 200,000 Chechens fleeing their homes in the capital. Faced with the same narrow streets that had cost so many conscript lives in the 1994 war, Russian commanders ordered a far more comprehensive campaign in the new year, with their forces slowly taking the city street by street during the first months of the new millennium. As the retreating rebels were forced back towards the Caucasus Mountains, the conflict continued on into the new century, with the Russian forces coming under increasing pressure to account for the stories of ethnic cleansing and summary executions that reports from the region seemed to suggest.

It was during a lull in the fighting in Chechnya that Yeltsin made his shock resignation announcement on the last New Year's Eve of the old century. He handed over power to his fourth prime minister in two years, Vladimir Putin. The charismatic leader who had presided over Russia's first decade free from communism left office six months early. Yeltsin's first term as president had not been too successful, but he remained popular and retained the support of the world community in his battle to modernise his country. However, his second term of government had lurched from one disaster to another, with the people of Russia becoming more and more disillusioned with his leadership.

This eventually culminated in the disasters of 1998 when Yeltsin sacked two governments of his own choosing during the collapse into economic chaos. A year later, he faced impeachment in the *Duma* on five charges that included murder, treason and even genocide. Although the impeachment charges were easily defeated, they illustrated the depth of feeling against him in certain sections of the country.

During his time at the Kremlin, Yeltsin was guilty of many mistakes. He increased the power of the presidency and used this to promote placemen and insiders who were replaced with bewildering rapidity. In his haste to overcome seventy years of Soviet stagnation, he allowed the economy to deteriorate into an out-of-control, black market style of capitalism that hurt a huge proportion of the Russian people. Yeltsin was increasingly seen as a maverick on the world stage, and his health and drinking led to important questions being asked both in the *Duma* and around the world about his competence to govern. He also allowed Russia to become an international centre for organised crime. But Yeltsin, like Gorbachev before him, will also be remembered for his successes, and most especially for his bravery and leadership against the coup leaders in 1991.

The Impeachment of President Clinton

President Yeltsin was not the only world leader to face the rigours of impeachment during the last years of the decade. The same fate befell President Clinton who became only the second-ever US president to be impeached and the first in the twentieth century. Clinton joined President Andrew Johnson who fell foul of legislators in the aftermath of the American Civil War and who was acquitted by the Senate by just one vote in 1868. Impeachment papers were also drawn up against Nixon in 1974 although his resignation came before proceedings were begun.

News of Clinton's problems first broke in February 1998 when the Starr Commission began looking into the role of the Clintons in a fraud case brought against Hillary Clinton's former law partners. The alleged crimes had taken place during Clinton's time as governor of Arkansas. Among other things, Starr's investigations had uncovered allegations made against the president by a government employee, Linda Tripp, who said she possessed tapes in which Monica Lewinsky, a former White House intern, talked about lying under oath about her intimate relationship with the president.

In reply to these revelations, which linked her husband to marital infidelity and accusations that he perverted the course of justice, Hillary Clinton reaffirmed her support for her spouse and alleged the existence of a massive right-wing conspiracy against her husband from within the Republican-dominated Congress. Clinton plainly stated on national television that he had never been involved sexually with Lewinsky, a claim that was to come back to haunt him in the months that followed.

As the president ordered a renewal of attacks against Iraq, the case against him hardened, with evidence about his relationship with Lewinsky becoming more and more concrete. This eventually culminated in a long report by Starr that gave very detailed accounts of the activities that the president had got up to with the intern in and around the Oval Office. As a result, the president again went on national television to confess his wrongdoings before asking for the forgiveness of Lewinsky, his family and the American people.

But this was not enough to save Clinton, and the long process that brought about his impeachment was soon set in motion. This started with an inquiry by the House Judiciary Committee, which was set up to decide if the president had committed the 'high crimes and misdemeanours' needed for the prosecution to proceed. Starr was himself interviewed about his report at the end of November 1998, and the following month the committee divided on party lines, voting twenty-one to fifteen in favour of impeaching the president.

The impeachment proceedings then took the form of two separate procedures. Firstly, the House of Representatives deliberated on whether the president had a case to answer. When it was decided that he did, proceedings moved on to the Senate where the president was put on trial, with proceedings presided over by the Chief Justice of the Supreme Court. It was at this stage in February 1999 that the Senate voted for acquittal, allowing the president to remain at the White House for the last two years of his tenure in office. By his side throughout stood Hillary Clinton who late in 1999 emerged from twenty-five years in his political shadow with the announcement that she intended to run for the Senate in the November 2000 election for the state of New York.

The Information Revolution and the Globalisation of Technology

Clinton's impeachment came at the end of a decade dominated by the USA, a situation that was made possible by the success of its economy. This was increasingly powered by the information revolution that transformed the world so extraordinarily during the decade. At the core of this change was the personal computer, the performance of companies such as Microsoft and Apple, and the huge growth in the use of the internet.

The internet used technology first developed in the space and arms programmes of the 1960s, with various advances through the 1970s and 1980s eventually leading to the launch of the World Wide Web in 1989. This allowed communication between computers through a series of servers, using hypertext transfer protocol, and it was the marriage between http., the language of computers, and the www., the network that they used, that was by the end of the decade to revolutionise the transfer of information in a way unimaginable even in 1990. Almost immediately after its public launch in January 1992, it became apparent that the internet was going to change the way the world worked as fundamentally as the car or the aeroplane had done in their day. As such, it immediately ranked as one the most important developments of the century.

The march of technology in the internet decade also had the most profound effect on the countries of South East Asia and the Pacific Rim. Growth in the area had begun with Japan, which within twenty years of Hiroshima and Nagasaki had transformed itself into the world's second-largest economy. The Japanese success was based on the car industry and Japanese cars soon flooded world markets. By the 1960s, Japan was also the world's major producer of electronic goods, and its electrical expertise was to put it at the forefront of the information revolution in the 1980s and 1990s. Japan's emergence was matched by, among others, Hong Kong, Taiwan, South Korea and Singapore, where industrial economies had developed by the 1960s.

These were joined by many other countries in the region over the next twenty years and by the early 1990s the Tiger economies of South East Asia were among the most productive in the world. This allowed the region to recover quickly from the crash of 1998 and re-emerge before the end of the century stronger and better equipped for the future. Importantly for the region, these countries were joined by China, which had transformed its economy in the 1980s under the leadership of Deng Xiaoping. Capitalist models of economic organisation were used in all these countries although, unlike in Russia in the 1990s, free-market economics did not generally mean any loosening of governmental control over society and politics.

The spread of technology also led to both India and Pakistan exploding the atom bomb in 1998, bringing scenes of national jubilation in both countries. The explosions broke twenty years of nuclear non-proliferation and brought punitive sanctions from the Western world. But with increased tension in Kashmir, both considered this a price worth paying. War eventually broke out in Kashmir in April 1999, with the Indian army fighting Pakistani-backed Kashmiri separatists who had managed to infiltrate beyond the Line of Control that separated the region. It was the fourth such war since the independence of the subcontinent in 1947, and tension rose when two Indian air force fighters were shot down.

Radicals in both countries urged their governments to escalate the war and, with the development of a nuclear capability by both sides, the increase in tension was viewed with great alarm across the world. The war rumbled on into July 1999 when Pakistani forces withdrew to the Line of Control that divided the disputed territory and a wary peace was brokered. However, this did not come before the war had claimed the lives of about 500 Indian soldiers and 1,000 separatists. In all, some 30,000 soldiers and civilians were killed in Kashmir in the 1990s alone.

The Governments of John Major and Tony Blair
In Europe, the 1980s had been a decade of strong economic growth. This had been followed by a slump in the early 1990s, but this did not stop the twelve members of the European Community signing up to the Maastricht Treaty in 1992. At its heart, the treaty confirmed a commitment to a single European currency although vigorous negotiations by Britain or Denmark secured far-

reaching concessions. It was also agreed at Maastricht to change the European Community into the European Union.

In the years that followed Maastricht, there were many in Europe who urged closer political as well as economic unity and these were led by the European Commissioner, Jacques Delors. This was not universally welcomed and in nations across the continent arguments broke out about just how much national sovereignty should be given up. Arguments also arose over accountability, especially after widespread corruption was uncovered in Brussels and Strasbourg later in the decade. This led to the resignation in March 1999 of Jacques Santer, who had succeeded Delors as president of the EU Commission in 1994, as well as, ultimately, all of the twenty commissioners who had served alongside him. However, their reluctance to resign highlighted still further problems to do with accountability and good governance, problems that seemed endemic in much of federal Europe.

Corruption in the EU was matched in Germany where Helmut Kohl's image as the chancellor who had masterminded the reunification of Germany was blemished when revelations surrounding secret accounts during his tenure in office were revealed at the end of 1999. However, despite the corruption allegations that tainted the image of the EU in the 1990s, the drive towards European integration remained one the most significant political, as well as economic, events of the second half of the century.

In Britain, the decade was dominated in many ways by the shadow of Mrs Thatcher who, increasingly opposed both from within the Conservative Party and from outside over the poll tax, Europe and the economy, had been forced to resign in November 1990. She was replaced as prime minister by John Major who arrived at Downing Street during a lean time for the Conservative Party. However, he surprised many by going on to win the election of April 1992, which guaranteed his party another five years in power. This meant that by 1997 the Conservatives had ruled at Westminster for seventeen years, the longest by a single party in the twentieth century.

Major had won the leadership contest following Thatcher's resignation because he was seen as the candidate most acceptable to both sides of his party that had faced civil war over the issue of Europe. However, his first priority was not over the issue of Europe that was to cause him so much grief later. Rather, Major's primary concern was a sluggish economy, which showed little sign of growth and which did not improve until halfway through the decade. Major also faced the huge challenge of bringing peace to Northern Ireland, and his government was part of the initiative that brought about a temporary ceasefire in 1995. Although this lasted for less than a year, it gave an impetus to the peace process that was carried on with such success under the next government.

Major had come to power as the candidate most likely to unite the Conservative Party over the issue of Europe. However, the constant criticism he received from both sides of his party eventually forced him to find a radical solution to his problems, and in 1995 he resigned, forcing an election for the party leadership. Basing his re-election campaign solely on a vote of confidence in his policies on Europe, he challenged his detractors to 'put up or shut up'.

This challenge was taken up by John Redwood, a leading Eurosceptic opponent from within the cabinet who Major beat convincingly in the subsequent election. But the extent to which Major was able to unite the party behind him as a result of his win remained questionable, and conflict over Europe was to continue to dog his party up to and beyond electoral defeat in 1997 when the party moved to a more Eurosceptic standpoint over European federalism and the single currency under a new leader, William Hague.

Major was also dogged by a series of sleaze accusations against various Conservative MPs and lost the election in May 1997 to a new and resurgent Labour Party. Under the leadership of Tony Blair, New Labour had ruthlessly transformed itself by the mid-1990s from the old-fashioned party of the previous decade that supported unilateral disarmament, was pledged to overturn the privatisation programme of the 1980s and had continued to support Clause Four of the party's constitution that argued for public ownership. These more left-leaning policies, which were so obviously vote losers with the British public, were culled ruthlessly from the Labour message, and by 1997 little of substance separated its policies from those of the ruling Conservative Party.

Claiming to represent the middle ground of political opinion, New Labour in essence had accepted many of the changes made by the Conservatives during their seventeen years in power although one major difference concerned their policy over devolution for Scotland and Wales. New Labour made devolution a central pledge in its election manifesto, and consequently voters in Scotland and Wales went to the polls to elect devolved parliaments in May 1999. In the Scottish case, this meant that a Scottish parliament sat at Edinburgh for the first time since the Act of Union in 1707.

One other major event in the late 1990s that affected the lives of millions not only in Britain but also around the world was the death of Diana, Princess of Wales. She died in a high-speed car accident in a Paris underpass in August 1997, setting off an extraordinary outburst of public grief. Thousands flocked to Kensington Palace, her residence in London after her divorce, in the week after her death, with literally tonnes of floral tributes left at her gates. Her funeral service brought London to a standstill.

Diana, whose death came exactly a week before that of Mother Teresa of Calcutta who Diana had met and worked with on a number of occasions, was finally laid to rest on an island sanctuary at her family's ancestral estate in Northamptonshire. Diana's appeal and popularity was unique, with her work for the underprivileged and her glamour combining to make her one of the most famous and photographed women of the century. Her death not only united the country in grief but also raised important constitutional questions about the role that the Royal Family would play going into the new century. This debate had begun earlier in the decade when a series of problems in 1992, which was described by the queen as her 'annus horribilis', had led to a very bad year for her and the Royal Family in particular and for the institution of the monarchy in general.

In its 1997 manifesto, New Labour had committed itself to building on the Northern Ireland peace process successes of the previous government. These included the 1995 ceasefire and the Mitchell Report of the following year, and matters progressed quickly, with politicians on both sides of the sectarian divide working hard for peace. As a result, an all-party agreement that offered hope to the province for the first time in a generation was concluded in April 1998.

This Good Friday Agreement had at its core three key elements. Firstly, the governments of Britain and Ireland agreed to settle their constitutional claims over Northern Ireland, which both accepted as part of the United Kingdom. The second concerned the setting up of a new Northern Ireland Assembly in Belfast, with ministerial posts in an Executive shared out through proportional representation, while the last concerned the decommissioning of paramilitary weapons. It was agreement over this third element that was to cause such strife in the years to come.

Referendums held separately in both Northern Ireland and the Republic in June 1998 resulted in the people of both overwhelmingly embracing the peace process, and in August 1998 the search for peace was reinvigorated by the reaction to the Omagh bombing that killed twenty-eight Saturday afternoon shoppers. Aimed at reopening the sectarian divide, the bomb was planted by the self-styled Real IRA, a splinter group that opposed the peace process. But, in fact, the bombing of Omagh produced the opposite effect, drawing together politicians on both sides of the political divide in search of peace.

Negotiations continued into 1999 with the early release of terrorist prisoners, the composition of the Northern Ireland Assembly and the decommissioning of paramilitary weapons dominating the political agenda. More than once, progress forward seemed impossible although the presence of Senator George Mitchell, the architect of the Good Friday Agreement upon which the peace was to be based, in the review process in the autumn allowed the peace process to remain on track.

At the core of the dispute through much of 1999 was the question of Provisional IRA decommissioning, with the Ulster Unionists, the province's largest single political party, insisting that their participation in the Northern Ireland Assembly was directly linked to the issue. Sinn Fein was the political wing of Provisional IRA, and matters were not helped when it was revealed that the British government had sanctioned the bugging of a car used by Gerry Adams and Martin McGuinness, the leaders of Sinn Fein, during the ongoing negotiations.

Crisis point was finally reached in November 1999 and Unionist fears over the Provisional IRA's refusal to decommission were only finally allayed by promises that Sinn Fein would be ejected from the political process if Provisional IRA decommissioning had not been started by February 2000. These promises were jointly made by the British and Irish governments. As a result, and only after the constitutional changes made by London and Dublin had come into force, the power-sharing Executive of the Assembly met for the first time in Belfast in December 1999.

Embracing all sections of Northern Irish society, it immediately faced problems over interpretations concerning decommissioning that led to its suspension early in the new year. In this way, the peace process precariously limped into the new century. Despite the peace process of the late 1990s, Northern Ireland remained, like Rwanda, Bosnia and Kosovo, deeply divided racially, ethnically and religiously. However, the guns and bombs were silent as the century closed and the politicians were still talking, which, after a generation of violence, allowed the people of the region some sense of hope.

The War in Kosovo

While Northern Ireland was enjoying the relative peace of the ceasefire, crisis erupted once again in the Balkans, with reports of Bosnian-style Serb programmes of ethnic cleansing reaching the West in October 1998. These reports were coming out of Kosovo where the Kosovar Albanian population had endured ten years of racial and ethnic persecution following the collapse of communist rule. Western diplomats and politicians were particularly worried about the role being played in these atrocities by the Yugoslav government. The tense situation in Kosovo was not helped by the fact that the region had been of crucial importance to the cultural and historical identities of both the Muslim Kosovar and Serb communities since the Middle Ages.

Through the 1990s, it was Serbian soldiers and special police units from the rump Yugoslavia that had come to dominate the province, and it was they who were accused of the worst violence. However, as the decade ended, they had been increasingly opposed by soldiers of the Kosovo Liberation Army and it was the growth in support for this force, the KLA, that had provoked these early programmes of ethnic cleansing.

As the crisis deepened, with 1998 giving way to 1999, delegates from all sides of the conflict convened at Rambouillet near Paris at a round-table conference organised by NATO. Eventually, a peace deal was thrashed out in March 1999 and this was signed by all parties, except Yugoslavia itself, which argued that it was being in essence forced to cede Kosovan independence. So as the Rambouillet Conference broke up and with the crisis deepening with no agreement from the Yugoslavian delegates, NATO threatened air strikes against Yugoslav positions in Kosovo if Serbian police and militia units were not removed. This came amid continuing allegations of ethnic cleansing from the thousands of Kosovar Albanians fleeing across the borders into Macedonia and Albania.

However, the threat of an air campaign in March 1999 proved to have little effect on either Milošević's plans or the resolve of the Serbs in Kosovo itself. Indeed, as a result of the threat, they stepped up their efforts and in March and early April 1999 organised the systematic ethnic cleansing of Albanian Kosovar settlements in the Drenica and Pagarusa valleys in central Kosovo. Eventually, up to a million Kosovars were forced from their homes amid the looting, burning, rape and murder.

During this time, Richard Holbrooke, President Clinton's special ambassador to the Balkans, worked tirelessly, but ultimately without success, to secure an agreement with Milošević that stopped these Serbian atrocities. Meanwhile, the killing and ethnic cleansing continued. As the numbers fleeing from Kosovo increased, the fate of the refugees was further complicated by the decision by Macedonia and Albania to close their borders, and the refugees were only let in after huge aid packages to help pay for their keep were pledged from the outside world.

In early April 1999, as NATO dignitaries were preparing to commemorate the fiftieth anniversary of their organisation, the first air strikes against Serbian targets in Yugoslavia and Kosovo were launched. Russia's initial reaction to the strikes was deeply critical, and Yeltsin immediately threw into doubt the agreement over NATO expansion eastwards that he had signed with Clinton in 1997. As the post-Cold War *rapprochement* between East and West deteriorated, tension was further increased when Yeltsin announced that, as a result of the conflict in the Balkans, Russian nuclear missiles had been repositioned once again to threaten NATO cities in the West.

In the middle of April, three US servicemen were captured while on patrol on the border between Macedonia and Kosovo and taken to Belgrade where they were displayed on Yugoslav state television. Their capture galvanised US public opinion against Yugoslavia and allowed Clinton to continue to make threats about launching a ground war if the killing did not stop. The three were eventually released a month later through the intervention of Jesse Jackson who had also been instrumental in securing the release of hostages during the Gulf War eight years earlier.

Throughout the month that the three servicemen spent in captivity, the air strikes had carried on incessantly while at the same time reports from refugees escaping Kosovo spoke of further massacres and the systematic ethnic cleansing of Kosovar villages by Serb militias. The air strikes had not, as NATO commanders and Western politicians had predicted, stopped the slaughter and the genocide in Kosovo. In fact, it seemed that NATO military action had intensified Belgrade's determination to ethnically cleanse the breakaway republic before any ground war could be launched.

The initial response to the war from the Russian government was extremely angry although Russian diplomats backed away from Yeltsin's initial declaration that the conflict could lead to World War Three, and by late April 1999 Russia was heavily involved in the diplomatic efforts to end the conflict. In the meantime, the bombing campaign on Belgrade and other Yugoslavian cities and towns intensified, with the Serbian television headquarters in Belgrade destroyed. This heightened the debate in the West about the legitimacy of strategic and civilian targets. By the end of April, a month after the launch of the campaign, 700 bombing sorties had been flown.

During the first week of May, it seemed that international co-operation might lead to a breakthrough and end the suffering in Kosovo. Russian efforts to mediate were improving the chances of peace, and diplomats in Belgrade reported that the Milošević government was edging towards compromise. The presence of UN peacekeepers in Kosovo was conceded, but Milošević still insisted that this force should not be drawn from NATO. However, any hopes for peace were set back by fresh reports of a new wave of purges by Serbian militias and special police forces in Kosovo.

The prospect of a diplomatic settlement was finally dashed on 8 May 1999 when the Chinese embassy in Belgrade was bombed in a NATO night raid that left, among others, three Chinese diplomats dead. The building had been wrongly identified as a Yugoslav government building connected with arms procurement. Huge demonstrations in Beijing at the British and US embassies brought thousands of Chinese students and protesters onto the streets, and Russian diplomats stayed away from peace talks held in London.

However, two days later Milošević ordered the partial withdrawal of troops and militias from Kosovo in what was seen by many as an attempt to bring about a compromise with NATO without conceding defeat completely. However, any overtures towards a face-saving compromise were ignored by NATO leaders who insisted that all the five points agreed by the G8 group of industrial nations would have to be met in full before they would call off NATO air strikes. Central to these was the total withdrawal of Serbian personnel from Kosovo. Milošević's predicament was further complicated at the end of May when he was indicted for war crimes at The Hague.

Eventually, the Yugoslav parliament voted in early June 1999 to accept the NATO demands and the total withdrawal of Serbian troops and police from Kosovo began under strict NATO control. Five days later, representatives from both sides signed the papers that ended the war. It had lasted for only just over three months, but it had created over a million refugees.

Almost immediately, the displaced Kosovar refugees began pouring back over the borders, returning to their homes and villages that had been set alight by the departing Serbs in a last act of defiance. The KLA, which itself stood accused of complicity in a number of atrocities, was in the forefront of moves back into the province before delicate talks with NATO peacekeepers resulted in their disarmament. Soon, the first casualties from landmines planted during the war were reported, with refugees eager to return home often ignoring NATO pleas to remain in the camps in Macedonia and Albania until the minefields had been cleared.

Within a week of the end of the war, hundreds of thousands of Kosovars had left these camps and were making their way back home. In cities such as Pristina, the Kosovan capital, and other ethnically cleansed cities and towns throughout Kosovo, NATO troops supervised the almost total evacuation of the Serb population while at the same time looking after the arrival of the returning Kosovars.

Any hope of some sort of ethnically diverse Kosovo, safe for all sides, seemed very unlikely in the days that followed. Indeed, it was not long before reprisals began against the many Serbs forced to flee Kosovo with the retreating Yugoslav army. The murder in July of fourteen Serb farmers tending their harvests in central Kosovo illustrated the difficulty facing K-FOR, the NATO force of peacekeepers left to maintain law and order in Kosovo. As in Bosnia, it seemed that these problems were likely to last long into the new century.

The Last New Year's Eve of the Twentieth Century

As the people of Northern Ireland, Kosovo, Bosnia and the many other places around the world where conflict was commonplace contemplated an uncertain future, the old century passed away and the new one began. Celebrated in cities and towns across the world with a series of spectacular firework displays that lasted throughout the hours it took for the whole world to pass into the new century and the new millennium, the world had been massively changed by the century that was left behind. Science and technological progress had sent a man to the moon and machines still further to the outer reaches of the solar system while transport, medical and information revolutions had changed the world forever.

But most of the world's huge population still lived lives of basic subsistence, with most people spending their days engaged in very much the same ways as their great-grandparents a hundred years before. For the vast majority across the developing world, where the greater part of those who lived through the twentieth century spent their lives, the everyday chores of collecting water and tending to flocks and fields dominated life in 1999 as they had in 1900, and for this mass of humanity, the progress of the century touched their lives only fleetingly. For these countless millions, malnutrition, natural catastrophes, conflict, social injustice and the daily grind of intensive and monotonous labour directed everyday existence at the end of the twentieth century just as they had done at its beginning, and for centuries and millennia before that.

However, there can be no question that the century brought about the most extraordinary changes and, in essence, it was a century of scientific and technological advancement, the greatest leap forward ever made by mankind in a single century. The scale and the breadth of these changes made it such a special time, with the social, economic and political ramifications, both good and bad, felt worldwide.

Developments in transport transformed the world, with car and aeroplane travel dominating the world at the end of the century in a way unimaginable a hundred years before. At the time of Queen Victoria's death, there were perhaps 20-25,000 cars in the whole world, a number that was to grow to a staggering half a billion a hundred years later. In 1900, it would have taken around seven or eight weeks to travel from Britain to Australia in the fastest steamship then available. In August 1989, it was possible, though not commercially viable, for this same journey from London to Sydney to be made non-stop by aeroplane for the first time in just twenty hours and nine minutes. Just as the railways had revolutionised the nineteenth century, so air travel and the car transformed the twentieth.

In medicine, research in the late nineteenth century had changed the principles on which medical theory had been based since the times of the ancient world, and these changes and advancements continued throughout the new century. Early breakthroughs led to a series of improvements in the treatment and management of disease, and between 1928 and 1941 a huge leap forward was made with the discovery and development of penicillin. Vaccination programmes went to war on killer diseases as the century progressed, and developments in sanitation and public health made cities all over the world much safer places to live. Improvements in surgical techniques and operating procedures also made their mark.

As a result of all these changes, life expectancy increased and mortality rates dropped across much of the world as life became cleaner and less precarious. However, despite these changes, large swathes of the world at the end of the century still remained the breeding ground for infectious diseases, with malaria, cholera, typhus and many other diseases, often spread by dirty water supplies, remaining major killers. AIDS also, especially in sub-Saharan Africa, remained a major problem.

In total, according to a Red Cross report commissioned by the UN, a total of thirteen million people died in 1999 from preventable infectious diseases. This equated to approximately 36,000 people every day. In October 1999, India's population joined China's in going past the one billion mark, and certainly the old century closed with worries increasing about the world's ability to feed and keep healthy a population, especially in the developing world, that was growing at a fantastic rate.

The telecommunications industry also changed life immeasurably through the century. The telephone was in its infancy in 1900 as was the science behind radio and television, but all were to make an enormous mark over the next hundred years. By the last years of the century, the personal computer and the Internet Revolution of the 1990s could be added to these, bringing about new possibilities and expectations for a new age of progress, and making instant and universal communication and information transfer an everyday norm.

To a great extent, the century belonged to the USA, with its economy dominating the world in 1999 as never before. A sleeping giant in 1900, it grew through World War One and the boom years of the 1920s, recovered and developed in the 1930s after the world slump that followed the Wall Street Crash before emerging from World War Two unscathed and awesomely powerful. This extraordinary dominance continued through the Cold War until the eventual implosion of the USSR and the communist world in the late 1980s and early 1990s.

But it was also very much a European century, with two world wars fought to decide how it should be governed, and with a Cold War that was often fought within its boundaries. But Europe at the century's end housed and accommodated only 7% of the world's population, and its disproportionate consumption of over 20% of the world's industrial and commercial product, a legacy of earlier imperial and economic domination, was perhaps a factor that was becoming less and less sustainable.

The success of the USA and the Western world was based on capitalism and liberal democracy and in these lay the foundations of much of the century's success and wealth. Both were severely challenged through the century, firstly by the radical right in the 1930s and 1940s and then by the USSR and the communist bloc throughout the Cold War. However, both fascism and communism were defeated, and around the world both the capitalist and liberal democratic creeds were to grow stronger as the century progressed. Indeed, one of the characteristics of the last two decades of the century was their spread, encouraged, as they were, by a resurgent and bullish USA. The growth of vibrant capitalist economies was particularly strong in South East Asia and the Pacific Rim, with China itself entering the new century and the new millennium as a sleeping giant.

But the century had also seen the most enormous destruction, with the international community coming no closer to ending war in 1999 than it had been in 1900. This was a situation not helped, as the century progressed, by a constant improvement in the technology used to fight these wars, with better guns, tanks, aircraft and warships only bringing added misery to the countless millions who suffered. Two immensely damaging world wars had taken up a whole decade of the century and, in all, some 240 major wars and conflicts had killed upwards of a hundred million people through the century. That computed into a death rate of about 2,740 for every day of the century. The

UN had many successes in its fifty-five-year history to 1999, but the re-emergence of genocide as an instrument of war in the 1990s was one of the most striking and horrifying problems it faced as the new millennium began.

At the beginning of the century, many had come to believe that the progress of nineteenth-century science was going to create a better, safer and more prosperous world. Soon a world war, a trade depression, the rise of the aggressor states and a Cold War had dampened these aspirations, but still the world continued to progress in the most extraordinary way. This meant that, as the new millennium began, many shared the same hopes and aspirations of their Victorian forefathers a hundred years before.

In the last year of the century, DNA from a frozen mammoth discovered in the tundra of Siberia was extracted, and scientists predicted that they would soon be able to recreate an animal that has been extinct for thousands of years. Looking further afield, similar scientific marvels were taking place in space and the thirtieth anniversary of the moon landing was used to give a female astronaut the command of a shuttle mission for the first time. Her task was to place in orbit the largest telescope ever made. Its job was to look out into outer space further than ever before. As the world continues to spin away from the twentieth century, what this will be able to tell us only time, and the next century, will tell.